STANDARD
LOAN

UNLESS RECALLED BY ANOTHER READER
THIS ITEM MAY BE BORROWED FOR
FOUR WEEKS

To renew, telephone:
01243 816089 (Bishop Otter)
01243 816099 (Bognor Regis)

This reader comprises a collection of papers published in connection with the Open University courses E326 *Managing Schools: Challenge and Response* and E629 *Managing Educational Change*. These examine the concepts of education management in the light of actual management situations and decision-making processes in educational institutions.

This reader is one part of an Open University integrated teaching system and the selection is therefore related to other material available to students. The editors have attempted nevertheless to make it of value to all those concerned with school management. Opinions expressed in it are not necessarily those of the course team or of the University.

It is not necessary to become an undergraduate of the Open University in order to take the course of which this reader is part. Further information about the course and about the Advanced Diploma in Educational Management, of which it can form a component, may be obtained by writing to: The Associate Student Central Office, The Open University, PO Box 76, Milton Keynes, MK7 6AN.

Acknowledgements

The editors wish to thank Sonia Bentley, Steven Drodge, Margaret Martin, Barbara Phillips, Caroline Fairbairn, Don Lee, Frances Boland, Linda Wingrove, Verity Tranter and George Richards, who helped in the developmental testing of the material relating to these courses.

MANAGING CHANGE IN EDUCATION:
Individual and Organizational Perspectives

Edited by
Nigel Bennett, Megan Crawford and
Colin Riches

at The Open University

Published in association with
The Open University

P·C·P
Paul Chapman
Publishing Ltd

Paul Chapman Publishing Ltd
144 Liverpool Road
London
N1 1LA

British Library Cataloguing in Publication Data

Managing Change in Education: Individual
and Organisational Perspectives
I. Bennett, Nigel

ISBN 1-85396-211-2

Typeset by Inforum, Rowlands Castle, Hants
Printed and bound by
Athenaeum Press, Newcastle-upon-Tyne

A B C D E F G H 9 8 7 6 5 4 3 2

CONTENTS

1. **Introduction:** Managing Educational Change:
   the Centrality of Values and Meanings
   Nigel Bennett, Megan Crawford and Colin Riches   1

PART 1: Making Sense of Management   17
2. MCI and Educational Management: 19
   the Calderdale/Qudos Project
   John Jagger
3. Developing Managerial Capabilities in Education   34
   Ernie Cave and Cyril Wilkinson
4. Total Quality Management in Education   46
   John West-Burnham

PART 2: Exploring Collegiality   59
5. Rethinking Collegiality: Teachers' Views   61
   Penny Campbell and Geoff Southworth
6. Contrived Collegiality: 80
   the Micropolitics of Teacher Collaboration
   Andrew Hargreaves
7. Management by Halves: 95
   Women Teachers and School Management
   Elisabeth Al-Khalifa

PART 3: Managing Sustained Change   107
8. Causes/Processes of Implementation and Continuation   109
   Michael Fullan

9. A Model for Managing an Excellent School   132
   Headley Beare, Brian J. Caldwell and Ross H. Millikan
10. Flexible Planning: 151
    a Key to the Management of Multiple Innovations
    Mike Wallace
11. Strategic Planning: 166
    Managing Colleges into the Next Century
    Ann Limb

PART 4: Working Together   179
12. How are Decisions Made in Departments and Schools?   181
    Peter Earley and Felicity Fletcher-Campbell
13. The Dynamics of Intense Work Groups: 202
    a Study of British String Quartets
    J. Keith Murnighan and Donald E. Conlon
14. Developing Communication Skills in Interviewing   219
    Colin R. Riches
15. Strategies for Management Development: 235
    Towards Coherence?
    Howard Green

PART 5: Self-Management and Development   253
16. Appraisal and Equal Opportunities   255
    Meryl Thompson
17. The Management of Time   269
    Cyril Wilkinson
18. Teachers' Coping Resources   284
    Jack Dunham

Index   299
Author Index   307

ACKNOWLEDGEMENTS

We thank those listed below for their permission to use the following copyrighted material:

Ch. 2, J. Jagger, MCI and Educational Management: the Calderdale/Qudos Project © 1992, The Open University.

Ch. 3, E. Cave and C. Wilkinson, Developing Managerial Capabilities in Education © 1991, E. Cave and C. Wilkinson.

Ch. 4, J. West-Burnham, Total Quality Management in Education, Copyright 1991, The Open University.

Ch. 5, P. Campbell and G. Southworth, Rethinking Collegiality: teachers' views (Edited version of a paper for the American Educational Research Association, April 1990).

Ch. 6, A. Hargreaves (1991) Contrived Collegiality: the micropolitics of teacher collaboration, in Blase J. (ed.) *The Politics of Life in Schools*, reprinted by permission of Sage Publications Inc.

Ch. 7, E. Al-Khalifa, Management by Halves: Women Teachers and School Management, in De Lyon, H. and Migniulo, F.W. (eds) (1989) *Women Teachers: Issues and Experiences*, Open University Press.

Ch. 8, M. Fullan, Causes/Processes of Implementation and Continuation, in *The Meaning of Educational Change* (1991) Cassell Education Ltd.

Ch. 9, H. Beare, B. J. Caldwell and R. H. Millikan (1989) A Model for Managing an Excellent School, in *Creating an Excellent School*, Routledge.

Ch. 10, M. Wallace (1991) Flexible Planning: a key to the management of multiple innovations (Edited version of a paper published in *Educational Management and Administration*, Vol. 19, No. 3, pp. 180–192).

Ch. 11, A. Limb (1990) Managing Colleges into the next century, Coombe Lodge Report, Vol. 22, no. 5, pp. 379–394.

Ch. 12, P. Earley and F. Fletcher-Campbell, How are Decisions Made in Departments and Schools? in *The Time to Manage* (1990) NFER/ Routledge.

Ch. 13, J. Keith Murnighan and Donald E. Conlon (1991) Reprinted from The Dynamics of Intense Work Groups: a Study of British String Quartets, published in *Administrative Science Quarterly*, Vol. 36, no. 2, pp. 165–186, by permission of *Administrative Science Quarterly*. Copyright 1991 by Cornell University.

Ch. 14, C. R. Riches (1992) Developing Communciation Skills in Interviewing. Copyright 1992 by C. R. Riches.

Ch. 15, H. Green (1991) Strategies for Management Development: Towards Coherence?, from D. B. Stevens (ed.) *Under New Management*, Longman Group UK.

Ch. 16, M. Thompson (1989) Appraisal and Equal Opportunities in A. Evans and J. Tomlinson *Teacher Appraisal: a nationwide approach*, Jessica Kingsley.

Ch. 17, C. Wilkinson (1990) The Management of Time, in E. Cave and C. Wilkinson, *Local Management of Schools*, Routledge.

Ch. 18, J. Dunham (1992) Teachers' Coping Resources, in J. Dunham, *Stress in Teaching*, Routledge.

1

INTRODUCTION:
Managing Educational Change:
the Centrality of Values and Meanings

Nigel Bennett, Megan Crawford and Colin Riches

Since the early 1980s school and college managements throughout the world have had to cope with a set of responsibilities and expectations which have been changing with increasing speed. The changes are not all in the same direction: in Australia and New Zealand, for example, they are largely about decentralization, whereas in the United Kingdom power is shifting from local authorities simultaneously to central government and individual institutions. Many of the changes are radical and their consequences unclear. Consequently, uncertainty is almost all that management can be certain of.

These changes are both *structural* alterations to the service and significant but less obvious changes in *culture* and *expectations*. Schools are gaining responsibility for their own financial decisions. Colleges are becoming centrally funded corporations outside local authority control. Since the imposition of new pay and conditions in England and Wales in 1987, almost all teachers have some responsibilities outside their classrooms. These changes are important, requiring new skills from those charged with managing their implementation within the institutions and creating a changed institutional environment within which to work. An important management responsibility is helping one's colleagues to cope with the changes created in their work.

Important though these developments are, however, there is also a wider debate taking place about the nature of education, its relation to training, and the role and responsibilities of teachers and lecturers. Are they less autonomous agents now than when they operated essentially as free agents within the constraints of the public examination syllabus? What is the relationship, for example, between teacher and parent over the child's work, or lecturer and employer over the nature of training? What is expected of them? Such changes are more difficult to identify, and therefore even harder to respond to and cope with, than the more specific structural developments created by government policy.

Thus a key theme of this collection of articles is that change is not just about the creation of new policies and procedures to implement external mandates. It is also about the development of personal strategies by individuals to respond to, and seek to influence the impact of, structural and cultural change: personal change as much as organizational change. It therefore combines papers which discuss aspects of organizational form and culture with others which look at individual and group responses to the pressures which they feel.

This collection is not an attempt to provide a litany of best practice: precepts which can guide your actions in the future, or quick fix solutions to Monday's problems. (We do hope, though, that reading this book will make Monday easier to deal with!) Rather, it is a debate on how educational managers can deal with a complex and difficult environment. Without this debate, the actions we take could too easily lack coherence and clarity, leading to a weakened educational service, less able to provide the service demanded of it.

Educational managers are not alone in facing major changes. The same kinds of pressures are also affecting business, industry and commerce. Sixteen years after the first Open University course on management in education was published, the applicability of management thinking to education is still widely questioned. But are the traditional canons and solutions of management literature still applicable to *general* management?

Management literature is now witnessing one of its periodic cultural shifts. Writers such as Peters (1989), Garratt (1987) and Pedler, Burgoyne and Boydell (1991) have challenged traditional ways of thinking about organizations and their relationship with the outside world. Theories such as Total Quality Management have challenged orthodox views of the relationship between management and workers in organizations, and even raised the question of whether such a relationship can be said to exist at all. A major dimension of such new thinking is that it is using a new language to express its ideas. For example, you cannot think in terms of Total Quality Management and include hierarchies in your frame of reference, because 'hierarchy' involves ideas like chains of command, limited spans of control for each person in the hierarchy, and ever-taller pyramids as the organization grows. Such ideas simply have no place in the way of thinking which is Total Quality Management.

Our thinking about educational management is also expressed through language which has particular meanings surrounding it. A discussion of educational change must consider how different groups see their work and view the implications of change. It must also examine how teachers' views of their work and their relations with their colleagues influence their potential responses to change. More widely, the language and metaphors employed in writing and thinking about management and education influence our views of what is right and good in those areas of our work. Thus much of this reader is about the meanings contained in and attributed to language, and the values which underpin them. What do we see management in education as involving? What do we see as necessary for schools and colleges to run successfully? Do others share this view? What are the implications of this for thinking about how to bring about and cope with change? Should we think about this from the point of view of the organization or the individual in it – or from that of the recipient? How does the perspective affect how we think about our individual and institutional development?

VALUES, MEANINGS AND ASSUMPTIONS

The language we use to express and describe what we do carries with it a set of expectations and assumptions which affect both what we can see and appreciate and how much of another person's view we can understand. This was apparent in the days of secondary school amalgamations, when teachers from grammar and secondary modern traditions had to come to terms with each others' frames of reference: what was 'acceptable' behaviour? An 'able' pupil? 'Suitable' dress for a teacher? 'Good' teaching? Such words carried assumptions and expectations which bore different meanings in the two traditions which were being asked to amalgamate. Successful comprehensive schools were those which were able in some way to create a new set of meanings for them. Similarly, many teachers resist the meanings implicit in the use of commercial and business language in relation to education. To speak of education existing in a market-place, and to use metaphors of production to describe the process of learning and teaching, is seen by some as turning education into a commodity, importing into the educational world an alien set of values.

It is important to ask where conflicting values and meanings come from. Some come from tradition, and are unique to an individual institution, or subunit within one, such as a House at a public school. Others will come from forms of professional acculturation: from norms of acceptable behaviour generated through work in a range of different schools and inculcated through the work of inspectors or from individuals' training. Individuals will have developed others from their professional or general reading, or from other external sources such as their political or religious beliefs. This combination of beliefs and values, derived from a variety of sources, will shape beliefs about what is proper behaviour for teachers in schools or colleges towards their students, towards parents or students' sponsors, and towards each other. It will establish, for example, whether it is deemed acceptable behaviour for a teacher to enter another teacher's classroom, or whether a teacher can acknowledge failure or difficulty.

This suggests that values come from experience, and to a very large extent that would be our position. However, 'experience' is a loose term, which suffers from being contrasted with 'theory' as the basis of our actions. 'Experience' is not a random collection of past events: it has been raked over, pondered and sorted into a set of expectations and predictions about likely happenings and proper responses. That *is* a 'theory': indeed, it is more wide-ranging than scientific theories because, as we have argued, the decision to stress certain events in our experience at the expense of others is influenced to a degree by our personal and professional values, and the meanings which we attach to events and actions as a result. Young (1981, 1983) has suggested that we should think of our values as part of an 'assumptive world', into which we fit together our cognitive understandings (facts), our affective understandings (feelings and values about the facts we perceive), our sense of how we relate to the world – where we fit in – which he calls our cathectic understanding, and the sense of a need to act in a given situation, which he calls our directive understanding. By fusing together these four elements, we make sense of the world and create a world picture of taken-for-granted assumptions which inform what might be regarded as our working values and norms – those feelings which inform our daily work.

Values and meanings, then, are a crucial part of considering the way in which individuals and organizations can manage educational change. We believe that 'theory' and experience go hand in hand in shaping values. The rest of this introduction will try to set up a framework to allow you to examine the meanings contained in the analyses and proposals contained in the articles chosen here, which will incorporate both management thinking and educational thinking. In our view, the best way of thinking about how to deal with change is by being eclectic: pragmatism informed by a clear sense of meanings and values, which recognizes the role of 'theory' in developing a sense of good practice.

We have framed this introduction in the same way as we have organized the articles which follow, and will refer to each article as we develop our argument. The articles in Part 1, apparently severely practical discussions of management development projects, also need examining in terms of the assumptions they offer about the nature of managerial work in general and in education in particular. Part 2 considers these meanings and assumptions in relation to educational organizations, focusing on a developing orthodoxy in thinking about schools and colleges – the collegial model. Part 3 relates these fundamental questions to what is seen as necessary for effective change to be introduced. Thereafter we focus increasingly on the individual, considering first in Part 4 the demands of working together, and concluding by returning via the Part 5 articles to the individual development considered in some of our Part 1 articles with an examination of themes around appraisal and self-management and development.

MEANINGS AND MANAGEMENT THEORY

Management activity is supposed to be about achieving particular goals or objectives with the minimum of delay and inconvenience. It is therefore about finding at least a satisfactory way of operating, and then trying to find ways of improving on it. In this sense it lays claim to be a *rational* activity. Ideally, it will find the *best* way of operating, but in practice it may have to reduce its ambitions to achieving the best which can be achieved *in the circumstances*. However, in view of the previous section you will not be surprised to find that we see 'rationality' as meaning quite different things in different circumstances, and this is visible in the articles in the first two parts of this reader. This is because they rest on quite different theories of management, and it will be helpful to your study of this book to show how the theoretical perspectives influence their authors' perceptions of what counts as good management behaviour, and how it can be assessed and improved.

Most management theory identifies four particular functions which need managing in any organization. Marketing management involves ensuring that any action intended in the organization is wanted by the people it is intended for. Financial management involves ensuring that the organization has the resources for what is intended to be the key task, and that those resources are used to maximum effect. Personnel management is concerned with ensuring that the necessary people are available to do the tasks needed by the organization, and the final function, 'production' management, is used as the omnibus term to describe whatever the organization does as its primary activity. Schools and colleges 'produce' education.

Before you decide whether to reject the production metaphor as irrelevant or culturally damaging to education, you should consider a number of meanings which spring out of this summary. One is the 'primacy of production': organizations exist for a purpose, and the management of demand, resources and staff is geared to providing the means to achieve that purpose. Thus, educational management is about facilitating teaching and learning, and managers who forget this basic fact, or who act in ways which interfere with teaching and learning, should not be deemed competent. We can also see an implicit expectation that the 'production' activity somehow increases the value of the resources employed. Thus, children leaving school should have benefitted from their time there. Thirdly, there is an assumption that the product is wanted: it is serving a perceived need. However, we can also identify here the assumption that the activity of the organization is working on something inert: taking raw materials and processing them in some way.

The classic orthodoxy of managerial organization, Taylorism or 'scientific management', extends these assumptions. Its key claim is that all production activities need to be broken down into their constituent elements, and workers trained to carry out each task. This is the principle of the production line: lots of specialists each carrying out one aspect of a job which has been organized as a linear process. The thinking is that by atomizing the task workers can be turned into human machines. However, the consequence is that their work needs to be monitored continually in case of breakdowns in the system. Consequently, the work of managers can be divided into five key tasks: planning the work of the organization, organizing the work-force so that it can be done in the best way, co-ordinating the work of those responsible for the different elements of the work process, giving commands to ensure that things are done properly, and controlling the work as it turns out. Because this is seen to be the one best way of organizing, a manager's work is about securing stability and continuity, avoiding breakdowns and sustaining production.

The metaphor which dominates this view of management is that of the organization as a machine, and the manager's task is to sustain mechanical procedures rather than take account of human concerns. Workers would be prepared to accept this because, in this view, humans were motivated by their wish to earn money. Its view of rational activity is an extreme one which seeks to remove human considerations entirely from managerial analysis. However, this narrow view was called into question as early as the 1920s. Writers such as Mayo (1933), Maslow (1954), Herzberg (Herzberg, Mausner and Snyderman, 1959) and Adair (1983) have stressed the importance of individual motivation and managers' need to attend to individual and group needs as well as the task. These analysts introduce a different set of meanings into their view of management responsibility: a mechanical view of people and organizations is replaced with a human meaning, and the idea of 'one best way' with that of the most appropriate way for the talents of the people involved and the nature of the task. This changes the entire focus and assumptions on which the organization will be structured, and the basis on which a manager's performance will be judged. However, it does not abandon rationality: rather, it modifies it. Neither does it abandon the atomistic approach: instead, it incorporates another dimension, that of giving due consideration to the work-force, into the work which has to be analysed.

Writers examining management from a feminist perspective, such as Al-Khalifa and Thompson in this volume, argue that the characteristics of managerial work outlined in traditional analyses are those traditionally associated with masculine behaviour: control, giving orders, demanding conformity, and playing down any sensitivity they might experience to others' feelings. They point out that women are greatly underrepresented in senior management positions in industry and commerce, and Al-Khalifa makes the point that since management training has become more widespread in education, the percentage of headteachers who are women has fallen. Their arguments suggest a further assumption in these traditional managerial perspectives, which would be consistent with social attitudes in the early twentieth century, when much of the seminal writing was done: that management is a male task.

Although the work of Mayo and others caused considerable softening of the original thinking of this perspective, it did not significantly challenge its assumptions. We can call this approach Model A, and identify three important aspects of it. First, it stresses management as a *control* function. Second, managers carry this out through a process of *segmentation* of the work of the organization. Third, the assumption it makes about the world within which managers operate is that it is, itself, rational: decisions are taken on the basis of complete information and good research, and not influenced by competing values, beliefs, or non-rational considerations.

In contrast to this perspective, with its emphasis on order and one best way of doing things, more recent writers have suggested that management is not about order but about coping with chaos, and that much of our behaviour is not rational at all. Mintzberg (1990a) argues that most managers' work is not about planning, organizing, and controlling, or making rational decisions on scientific bases, looking for the one best way of doing things. Instead, he says, management is typically about chaotic situations, 'firefighting' to deal with crises, and keeping the ship afloat amidst constantly threatening seas. The world of senior educational managers which Wallace describes in his chapter seems well described in Mintzberg's view of management.

In Mintzberg's view, managers' responsibility for their units or sub-units within an organization gives them the *authority* to lead and decide, but they gain the *ability* and *knowledge* to carry out those functions as a result of the informal network of information and understandings which they acquire from being in the organization. Thus their decisions are not guided by the data in sophisticated computerized information systems, but by information from a range of informal sources such as colleagues' gossip or chats with friends at the golf club or health club. They learn how to judge which sorts of information can be relied upon and which can be discounted. They also know which clients or colleagues are important and which ones are less significant. Thus they bring to bear on any situation a range of organized but essentially personal and non-scientific information, and act accordingly.

Mintzberg introduces a quite different set of assumptions into our thinking about management. Instead of scientific rationality, we have more intuitive *non-rationality* – not, be it noted, irrationality: that is something quite different! In a non-rational setting, there is no one best way, but many possibilities. The basis for deciding on a particular course of action is not the rational evaluation of data, but a combination of data, gossip, best-guessing and hunch. Mintzberg concluded his article, originally written in 1975, with a statement that we should identify the skills which are involved in coping with non-rational circumstances of chaos and uncertainty, and which are necessary for each of the ten roles he identified to be discharged effectively. They could then be taught through example and case study. In this, he adheres to the atomistic view of management, even as he dismissed the perspective which had spawned it. However, he emphasized that the ten roles he identified could not be separated one from another: they formed an integrated whole, a *gestalt*, and could not be seen in isolation. Subsequently, in a postscript to the reprint of his article (Mintzberg, 1990b), he questioned how far he should have pursued the idea of separating out the skills, arguing that as well as what he called cerebral skills there is also an insightful dimension to management, which rests on developing a whole picture of the way the organization works and relates to its environment. This emphasizes commitment rather than calculation, and uses the language of values and personal expectation rather than the language of numbers and rationality. This approach moves thinking about management firmly away from management as an activity aimed at bringing about the organization's completion of its key tasks in the one best way towards one based on a much greater acknowledgement of the importance of taking risks and having to back judgment. Certain of the tasks of the rational Model A still have to be carried out: planning is necessary, and organizing. But instead of a language of control and command, Mintzberg's later comments move us towards a set of meanings resting upon shared commitment, empowerment of the work-force, and delegation. We could characterize this view of management, with its limited rationality, as Model B. These models are summarized briefly in Table 1.1.

Table 1.1   Two models of management: a basis for studying the reader

	Model A	Model B
Relationship between manager and managed	Control	Empowerment
View of organizational activity	Segmentation	Holism
View of world	Totally rational: one best way	Limited rationality: multiple and perhaps competing rationalities

With this discussion in mind, we can consider briefly the three papers which examine this area. John Jagger reports on a competency-based approach to management development in Calderdale, using the analysis of management developed by the Management Charter Initiative (MCI). He reports favourably upon it, commenting that its practical applications were apparent at every stage. But it is noticeable that the project encountered difficulties, particularly from the rigid application of the hierarchical model of management which the MCI developed, and Jagger argues strongly for flexibility in its use. Cave and Wilkinson produce a less atomistic view of the key dimensions of good management performance, which places a greater emphasis on Mintzberg's insightful, holistic dimensions than perhaps Jagger's MCI-based scheme does. You should consider which set of meanings and assumptions about what counts as good management is more acceptable to your value system, and also to the needs of your organization and yourself as a manager.

West-Burnham's presentation of Total Quality Management is quite different in focus. Whereas the first two papers, along with much of this discussion, have focused on how assumptions have developed a view of the management process, West-Burnham is concerned to establish explicitly a new set of assumptions. You might consider, among other things, whether the Cave and Wilkinson or Jagger concepts of management development are likely to be more useful to organizations trying to develop along the lines advocated by West-Burnham.

MEANINGS AND THE NATURE OF EDUCATIONAL ORGANIZATIONS

The clash of meanings which we have identified as Models A and B can be identified in writings about organizations in general, and schools and colleges as organizations in particular.

Writings which stress control and segmentation can approach organizations from either the structural or the interpersonal perspective. Structural approaches would include the classic bureaucratic models derived from Weber

(1947), which stress *authority* as the basis of giving instructions. Authority derives from one's office or position, and flows from top to bottom within the organization. Responsibilities are clearly allocated between the various offices or positions. Goals are set and policies decided by senior staff, and carried out faithfully by subordinates. The division of the organization into sub-units is therefore carried out within a clear set of goals to which all members of the organization have allegiance.

The similarities between this model of organizations and that of the scientific management school are immediately apparent: separation of tasks into smaller units; authority vested in those senior to you, and passed to you only in sufficient quantity to allow you to do the job allotted to you; an emphasis on control. By comparison, the most obvious model of organizational functioning to look at division from an interpersonal perspective, the political or micro-political model, sees organizations not as structural unities but as arenas of struggle and contest. Individuals within the organization acquire *power*, not authority, by virtue of their professional expertise, their skills in drawing others into a dependency upon them, perhaps by providing advice or support in times of difficulty, or by creating temporary or permanent coalitions in order to achieve the particular policy decisions which they wish to see. Political models see all decisions as being actual or potential occasions for conflict, and therefore expect constant negotiation to take place routinely in order to achieve anything. Whereas in scientific or bureaucratic approaches the expectation is that people will act in accordance with instructions because there is one best way of doing things, in a political perspective everything rests upon the consent of those having to carry out the procedures or instructions, and this consent has continually to be regained.

The political perspective brings a major new development into our discussion. Whereas Model A takes the rational perspective to imply that those with authority in the organization can set the procedures, because their interests and those of the organization are identical, and synonymous with those of their workers, writers from a political perspective assume that the guiding principle of human behaviour is self-interest. Most writers who see human beings as operating from self-interest assume that we identify that self-interest through rational economic calculation (see, for example, Olson, 1971). This school of thought, known as public choice theory, usually accounts for our acceptance of collective activity such as taxation, which at first sight is not in our individual self-interest, on the grounds that we can identify activities which are best provided for collectively, such as defence or policing. However, this view is criticized by other writers (e.g. Kogan, 1986) for not paying sufficient attention to values such as altruism, or our political, moral, or religious beliefs, while yet others question how far individuals are prepared to go in acknowledging collective interests. Indeed, because general recognition of collective interests cannot be guaranteed, the danger of 'free rider' behaviour exists as individuals seek to maximize personal gain regardless of wider social consequences. Thus the political model has to stress how power must be exercised continually in order to keep the competing groups together. Otherwise, the centrifugal tendencies created by rational self-interest –

their pursuit of maximum personal economic well-being – will cause every organization and sub-unit within it, to fall apart.

This comparison is important when we examine the emerging orthodoxy of educational management: collegialism. It should be emphasized that much of the writing which advocates collegiality tends to be long on prescription and short on description. Indeed, the research projects summarized in the Campbell and Southworth reading are two of the few which explore schools where signs of collegiality are present.

Collegiality is seen as a means of creating unity by involving staff in the policy-making and decision-making process. Its central principle is that by owning the decision one is more likely to put it into practice and support it, since agreement creates a unity between individual and collective self-interest. Its language is the language of holism, consensus, co-operation, and interdependence. In the Campbell and Southworth paper the emphasis is on the creation of a culture of collaboration. It is a major challenge to the values and assumptions of other schools of thought, and stands at odds with many traditions within education. For example, it sits uneasily alongside the traditions of classroom autonomy, classroom privacy, and the denial of problems and difficulties which was widespread in education prior to the late 1980s and is still, we suspect, much more common in the secondary sector than is publicly acknowledged by many senior teachers.

Campbell and Southworth explore the characteristics of primary schools which were seen as moving towards collegial ways of working. They identify a number of cultural values which stress individual worth, interdependence, and security, but also stress the importance of leadership and the role of the head, and how it is exercised. The resonances with ideas of leadership and vision in West-Burnham's discussion of Total Quality Management are clear.

However, Hargreaves raises some crucial questions about the validity of this model, with its focus on consensus. From a political perspective, collegiality becomes a contrivance through which the leader can bring about what he or she wants. Hargreaves points up key analytical differences between 'real' and 'contrived' collegiality which suggest that fundamentally different meanings underpin the two ideas. From this perspective, contrived collegiality becomes a device for re-establishing the constructive view of rationality which a political view of organizational behaviour resting on individual economic self-interest may destroy. It becomes a management tool rather than, as Campbell and Southworth suggest, something organic. You might consider whether the language of Hargreaves's discussion is such that the consequence of moving the concept of collegiality from an organic development to a management tool is to invest it with meanings of dissatisfaction or deceit.

MEANINGS AND THE NATURE OF EDUCATIONAL CHANGE

We suggested earlier that change is about altering both practice and organization and individuals' perceptions of their roles and responsibilities. It will be clear from the foregoing that a movement by senior staff from a strongly hierarchical and directive mode of working to one stressing consensus and participation would involve major changes in the assumptions which every individual member of staff made about his or her role and relationships with one another, and what counted as legitimate and acceptable behaviour. Failure to address these basic issues would lead to failure of the innovation as the meanings attached to actions would remain set within the previous frame of reference and individuals' responses would be similarly constrained. For example, if staff meetings have always been occasions for passing on information and debate has always been stifled by the head, a lot of preparatory work will be needed before a new view of staff meetings can be seen as genuine and receive a genuine response.

Thus, as Fullan's chapter points out, change is a learning experience for all the adults involved. There is always a danger that implementation of change might become assimilation into existing practice, as in examples where TVEI became assimilated into the existing curriculum rather than providing a catalyst for wider change. For this reason, although it increases the danger of spectacular failure, there is, says Fullan, an argument for going for large-scale change so that those involved cannot assimilate new practices into old and so bury them in tradition. This increases the likelihood of resistance, and those involved in bringing the changes in must address the thinking behind the resistance. Fullan makes a strong case for the centrality of meanings in our analysis of change, and therefore in our development of approaches to its management. However, a key part of this educative process is ensuring that people try out the innovation and providing lots of support for them as they do it, so that actual practice forces a challenge to the meanings they bring to their working situation. This is a way of forcing the practice of change into the individual's assumptive world, which rests in the first instance on the exercise of authority rather than the operation of consent.

Change, then, is about both structure and process. The essence of our papers in this section of the reader is how far structure and process are amenable to rational analysis and planning. Beare *et al.* investigate a model of management in the light of key aspects of leadership and American research on the management of change. The model which they draw from the work of Caldwell and Spinks (1988) is one which establishes a clearly rational perspective on the relationship between purposes, values and actions, and argues for a collaborative approach to planning within clearly articulated annual goals: a kind of collegialized hierarchy. Wallace is sceptical, seeing that model as satisfactory in a stable setting and environment, but as unable to cope with multiple change and high levels of environmental turbulence. We hear again the echo of Mintzberg's attack on traditional management theory. But Wallace is concerned to explain how, in spite of the constant pressure to implement change, and frequent alteration to details of the requirements even as they are implemented, schools seem to retain considerable stability in practice and organization. His concept of flexible planning seems to be looking for a language which will fuse together rationality and holism. But it is noticeable that he sees this as essentially a responsibility for senior management: he seems drawn into a way of thinking about organizations which remains essentially hierarchical.

The management of educational change, it seems, is essentially a rational task, connecting the new into the old so that what is required is done but the vision of the organization and its task held by those who lead it is somehow sustained. Interestingly, radical management theorists such as Peters (1989), who see environmental turbulence as so great that a total transformation is needed of the meanings presented by the organization in every aspect of its structure and activity, regard such a process, of adding to and amending the established meanings of the organization, as inadequate: a whole new set of meanings has to be created. Limb's article on strategic planning in a college of further education shows how Peter's arguments can influence senior management towards more radical strategies, but it is interesting to consider how far her discussion of senior and middle management teams also draws her towards hierarchicalism.

The discussion of change in this reader rightly emphasizes the actions of managers in bringing about change, and we would not wish to understate this. However, we suggest that these articles show how, once again, the language we employ to think about and communicate what we want to do is crucial to the development of our thinking about what is involved, and how such thinking is rooted in our perception of what education, management and organization mean as terms. It is also crucial to how other people understand and respond to us.

MEANINGS AND WORKING TOGETHER

It is in our everyday dealings with colleagues that the tensions involved in the competing meanings surrounding terms like education, management and organization, their realization in practice, and visions of what they should involve and be like, are most immediately apparent. Campbell and Southworth demonstrate the existence in a number of primary schools of a culture of collaboration, which values individuality even as it values interdependence. However, they do not appear to address the question of how far an individual's individuality, or that of a sub-group, is sustainable against the wishes of the collegium. Nor is anything said about what happens to individuals who do not work comfortably in the collegium, or do not meet acceptable standards of performance.

The tension is further explored in Earley and Fletcher-Campbell, whose view of organizational culture emphasizes differentiation rather than integration (Meyerson and Martin, 1987). They see most departmental decision-making as essentially collegial, although examples of autocratic decision-making were also found. Departmental colleagues usually viewed these with dissatisfaction. However, alongside this enthusiasm for collegiality, which Earley and Fletcher-Campbell clearly associate with best practice, there was also a strong sense that following their extensive industrial action in the mid-1980s teachers were increasingly seeing departmental heads as paid to provide leadership, recommendations and suggestions, which could then be debated: more a consultative/participative mode of decision-making than a truly collegial one. In addition, even where collegiality was the order of the day, there was no expectation among members of the departments that their heads of depart-ment should operate in a similarly collegial way in school-wide settings: they were expected to fight the departmental corner. Since departmental cohesion and collegiality were enhanced by measures such as creating a departmental office as an alternative social base to the staff room, strong and collegial departments were actually dysfunctional to the wider cohesion of the school as a whole: instead, they were the bases of political activity.

Earley and Fletcher-Campbell demonstrate the implicit economic rationality of collegial models, and the way in which this creates potentially disruptive tension in the organization. These are explicitly addressed in the remarkable paper by Murnighan and Conlon, whose title appears to dismiss out of hand any relevance to education. Can any educational sub-unit – department, fac-ulty or team – be considered an 'intense work group' like a string quartet? In a string quartet, *all* of each individual's work is integrated into the performance of the group as a whole. Yet Murnighan and Conlon highlight central para-doxes about the role of different individuals when set against the needs of the quartet as a whole: leadership versus democracy, the role of the second violin, and confrontation versus compromise. They demonstrate that the successful quartets were those which faced and acknowledged the existence of these paradoxes, and incorporated their awareness of them into the way they oper-ated. The meanings which they attached not simply to their language but also to their roles within the group were crucial to their understanding of one another. The paradox of the role of the second violin, for example, has strong analogies to the problem of self-development as against institutional need: how do you resolve the conflict between an individual's personal need for career fulfilment through promotion and the need of the organization to keep an effective teacher and manager in a shortage area of the curriculum? Rational economic self-interest might coincide as long as the institution is able to offer additional salary to the person to stay, but this will not necessarily be enough. Many industrial and commercial companies will not release their employees for training which leads towards qualifications because they fear losing them to other employers once they are better qualified.

Green argues that organizations resolve this tension through succession plan-ning to facilitate the achievement of the development plan, suggesting that the demands this makes on resources can be met by using a combination of the school's in-service time and the individual's own time. This suggests that he does not see the tension in the previous paragraph as a key issue, but it is perhaps worth noting that at the time of writing the major clients of assessment centres such as Green's are local authorities rather than individual institutions.

Riches takes up another aspect of Murnighan and Conlon's discussion, focusing on the skills involved in achieving clear communication during interviews which will allow the negotiation and agreement of meanings.

Considerable skill in face-to-face contact, both formal and informal, is needed to resolve the kinds of paradoxes which it is argued can exist at all levels within educational organizations.

MEANINGS AND SELF-DEVELOPMENT

Rationality, then, can be destructive and create tensions between individuals within an organization and between the individual and the organization. This is perhaps most clearly visible in the issue of appraisal, where personal development and organizational improvement have to compete for primacy. Around the issue of appraisal circle major questions about the legitimacy and extent of managerial authority and the extent to which a person's manager can require changes in individual professional practice. These aspects of management return us to the questions in the first part of this introduction, when we considered the merits of atomistic and holistic views of management. The questions surrounding appraisal also raise, once again, the extent to which in emphasizing certain aspects of behaviour as 'good management practice' we disadvantage some groups at the expense of others, notably women and ethnic minorities, a significant point which is discussed by Thompson.

One theme of this introduction has been the tension between individual and organizational priorities. This tension is a major source of personal stress, just as the conflicting meanings in imposed changes help to raise people's concerns about the quality of their work, how it will be judged, and what will be expected of them. The reader closes with two papers which attempt to provide concrete assistance in resolving the tension. Dunham's work on stress management is well known, and his paper here distils key aspects of his advice on how to cope, while Wilkinson offers a range of techniques for making better use of our limited time. They are, in a sense, a final appeal for a kind of rationality which is not too extreme, which recognizes the competing tensions and tries to find ways of resolving them. Like the analysis of string quartets by Murnighan and Conlon, a major part of their advice is to recognize the problem and not run from it, and to recognize that the competing claims for our time and attention have to receive our attention in a way which reflects our own values and the meanings we attach to the requests and demands of others.

CONCLUDING COMMENT

Educational managers face many demands for change. They call into question traditional beliefs about the nature of the work of schools and colleges and their relationships with parents, children, students and employers. The emerging radical orthodoxy of management thinking places the customer at the centre of all action: customers determine the measure of quality, and serving them is the key purpose of all organizations. If the customer is completely satisfied, then profitability/survival is assured. This view challenges much conventional management thinking, forcing a re-examination of the meanings which we attribute to many of the words we use in describing organizations and the way they function. However, we also have to consider how we as individuals cope with the consequences of changing the rationality on which most of our organizations are established.

This discussion has developed two models through which to consider writing on management. It suggests that we create an assumptive world through which we make sense of the world around us and develop a basis on which we can act. The cognitive and affective understandings which contribute to our assumptive worlds are informed in large part by the meanings which we attach to words and ideas, often going far beyond their formal definitions. These extended meanings influence the value-based orientation to action which leads us to accept or reject the validity of the ideas and precepts we are faced with. It is through this grounding of our actions in our values that we can recognize the nature of the competing rationalities we face and find means of coping with them, whether as managers or as those being managed.

REFERENCES

Adair, J. (1983) *Effective Leadership*, Pan Books, London.

Caldwell, B. J. and Spinks, J. (1988) *The Self Managing School*, Falmer, Basingstoke.

Garratt, B. (1987) *The Learning Organization*, Fontana/Collins, London.

Herzberg, F., Mausner, B. and Snyderman, B.B. (1959) *The Motivation to Work*, Chapman & Hall, London.

Kogan, M. (1986) *Education Accountability: an Analytic Overview*, Hutchinson, London.

Maslow, A. (1954) *Motivation and Personality*, Harper, New York.

Mayo, E. (1933) *The Human Problems of an Industrial Civilisation*, Harvard Business School, Division of Research, Boston.

Meyerson, D. and Martin, J. (1987) Cultural change: an integration of three different views, *Journal of Management Studies*, Vol. 24, pp. 623–47.

Mintzberg, H. (1990a) The manager's job: folklore and fact, *Harvard Business Review*, March–April, pp. 163–76.

Mintzberg, H. (1990b) Retrospective commentary, Harvard Business Review, March–April, p. 170.

Olson, M. (1971) *The Logic of Collective Action: Public Goods and the Theory of Groups*, Harvard University Press, Cambridge, Mass.

Pedler, M., Burgoyne, J. and Boydell, T. (1991) *The Learning Company: a Strategy for Gaining the Competitive Advantage*, McGraw Hill, London.

Peters, T. (1989) *Thriving on Chaos*, Pan Books, London.

Weber, M. (1947) *The Theory of Social and Economic Organization*, Free Press, New York.

Young, K. (1981) Discretion as an implementation problem, in M. Adler and S. Asquith (eds.) *Discretion and Welfare*, Heinemann, London.

Young, K. (1983) Introduction, in K. Young (ed.) *National Interests and Local Government*, Heinemann, London.

PART 1:

Making Sense of Management

2

MCI AND EDUCATIONAL MANAGEMENT: the Calderdale/Qudos Project

John Jagger

ESTABLISHING THE PROJECT

The development within Calderdale LEA of a programme to further the professional development of educational managers came about through a series of
coincidences. The first was the decision to appoint a General Inspector for
Management Development. The second was the recognition by headteachers
of the implications of preparing for financial delegation. The third was the
development in Bradford of a firm of management consultants, Qudos (UK),
and, following heavy snow damage, their move to Halifax!

The common thread bringing these elements together was the then recently
published Management Charter Initiative (MCI). This was a commitment by
employers to further the development of their managers. It took the form of a
declaration of policy. However, in an attempt to produce a set of targets for
which individuals within the organization could aim, two sets of 'standards'
were created, supposedly representative of the abilities of fully competent first-
line and middle managers. Several firms were commissioned to pilot potential
means of exploiting these standards, among them Qudos (UK). The working
relationship was a common one: the LEA had a model of training it wished to
explore and inadequate funding to develop it; the schools had motivation and
personnel but no access to expertise or funding. Qudos had a contract to pilot
a new set of experimental management competency standards but no one to
pilot them with.

Each party had a different, but fortunately converging, set of criteria to
determine their involvement in any joint project. Schools needed to be satisfied
that the project developed people for the jobs they were doing and would be
required to do; would not be too time consuming; should be located where
possible in the school; would directly enhance the management practices of the

institution; would improve the confidence of educational managers in their ability to manage; and would support development as well as accreditation. The authority wanted a scheme which promoted a common language and management culture throughout the authority, not just in schools; stressed networking and the promotion of models of good practice; enhanced the self-esteem of managers within the service; could be developed cost-effectively across all departments of the council; caused minimum disruption to the work of schools; provided accurate analysis of training needs; recognized existing skills and was located if possible 'on the job'; and prepared managers for future roles. Qudos needed to build the project around the units of the MCI level-one management standards (first-line management); develop it towards delivering level-two standards (middle management); base the project around the accreditation of prior learning; and develop rather than simply deliver the programme since the role of Qudos was felt to be that of consultant rather than provider.

Following discussions between representatives of the LEA and the consultants a training model which seemed to meet the key needs of all parties was determined. This is shown diagramatically in Figure 2.1. A pilot group of twenty-four volunteers was identified consisting of members of staff from two 11–18 comprehensives, including heads of department, co-ordinators and deputy headteachers, some primary school heads and deputies, and four LEA officers. The officers soon left the programme, however, and have now joined a scheme for council staff.

Following the identification of the pilot group, a three-hour workshop serviced by Qudos introduced the philosophies behind the standards and their intended use. This was followed by an introductory workshop which sought to relate individuals' work practices to the standards. During this period, action learning 'sets' of eight were established, and group members were encouraged either to describe their jobs or to use their actual job descriptions to 'map' these fairly loosely against the full range of MCI 'units of competence' (described below) to establish any significant gaps which might require training. Advisers or mentors assisted the sets but did not attempt to lead them. Individual group members could ask for one-to-one contact with their mentor. On occasions, individuals, having sought reassurance from group members or their mentors, have approached their headteacher with the evidence of their lack of experience in that area as a part of their professional development.

Since the project began some changes have been made to the opening stages. The introduction is now two hours long and is followed by two sessions working as a large group. It was felt that more adviser/mentor support was required at this stage. During these two sessions the action learning sets are created.

Over a period of time, a comprehensive portfolio of evidence of competence cross-referenced to the standards is compiled and as this progresses the group member, the consultants and the mentor determine whether the assessment should be by interview. Where direct evidence has proved impossible to accumulate (not because of lack of competence but because of lack of

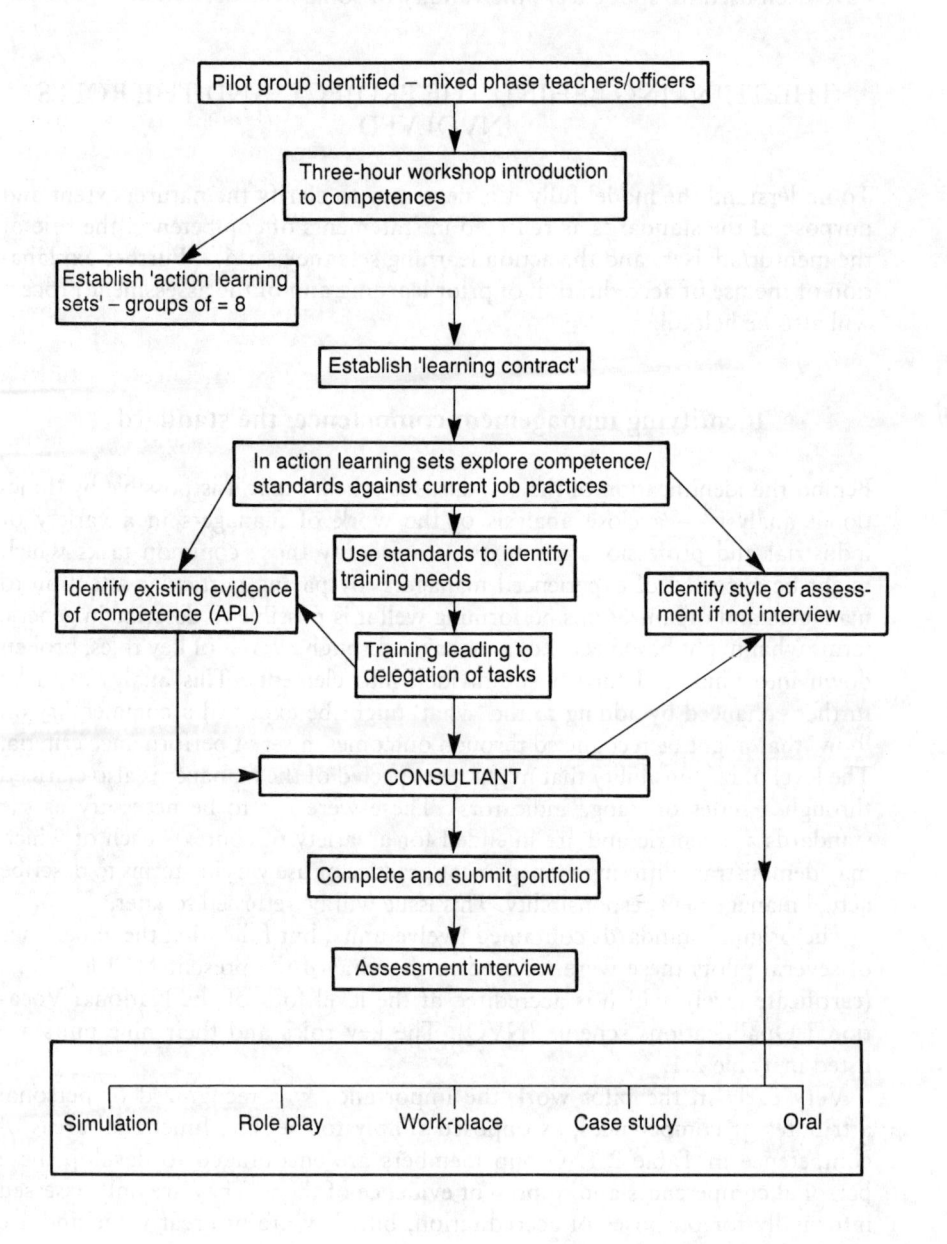

Figure 2.1 The original model for delivery

opportunity) then alternatives such as simulation or work-place observation have been used to 'spot check' the validity of some evidence.

THE THINKING BEHIND THE PROJECT, AND THE ROLES INVOLVED

To understand the model fully it is necessary to clarify the nature, extent and purpose of the standards as reflected in statements of competence, the role of the mentor/advisers and the action learning sets they service. Further explanation of the use of accreditation of prior learning and of the assessment process will also be helpful.

Identifying management competence: the standards

Behind the identification of the standards is a belief that it is possible by 'functional analysis' – a close analysis of the work of managers in a variety of industrial and professional contexts – to identify those common tasks which might be expected of experienced managers. By paying particular attention to managers and organizations performing well it is possible to describe in generic terms what might be expected of a manager through a series of key roles, broken down into units and further sub-divided into elements. This analysis can be further enhanced by adding to the 'what' might be expected a commentary on 'how' that might be recognized through outcomes: a set of performance criteria. The level of responsibility that might be expected of the manager is also clarified through a series of 'range indicators'. These were felt to be necessary as the standards are generic and are intended for a variety of contexts each of which may demonstrate differing management practice or use varying terms to describe actual management responsibility. This issue will be returned to later.

The original standards contained twelve units, but following the experience of several pilots these were reduced to the nine of the present MCI level one (certificate level), which is accredited at the level four of the National Vocational Qualifications scheme (NVQ). The key roles and their nine units are listed in Table 2.1.

Very early in the pilot work the importance was recognized of personal attributes or competences, as opposed simply to the nine functional areas of competence in Table 2.1. Group members are encouraged to develop these personal competences and to present evidence of them. They are only assessed informally for purposes of accreditation, but they are of great value and are emphasized for development purposes.

The standards can then be used:

(1) To provide a means of matching an individual job to a comprehensive analysis of what might be expected of a manager, and then to provide a training analysis for possible action;

Table 2.1 The Management Charter Initiative: key roles and their associated units of competence (key purpose: to achieve the organization's objectives and continue to improve performance). *Source:* MCI (1991), Section 3, p. II

Key role	Unit
Manage operations	1. Maintain and improve service and product operations
	2. Contribute to the implementation of change in services, product and systems
Manage finance	3. Recommend, monitor and control the use of resources
Manage people	4. Contribute to the recruitment and selection of personnel
	5. Develop teams, individuals and self to enhance performance
	6. Plan, allocate and evaluate work carried out by teams, individuals and self
	7. Create, maintain and enhance effective working relationships
Manage information	8. Seek, evaluate and organize information for action
	9. Exchange information to solve problems and make decisions

(2) To provide within action learning sets a basis for discussion about alternative strategies of evidence generation or personal development;

(3) To encourage groups or individuals to consider the motives behind described behaviours;

(4) To provide benchmarks as objective as possible against which to measure one's current performance and seek to improve it;

(5) To construct systems to ensure appropriate responses to recurring issues;

(6) To provide a common reference for the individual and their assessor.

Calderdale groups have also used them for the construction of job descriptions, providing a 'contract' to describe or a focus for appraisals, and writing descriptions or 'contracts' for desired training outcomes.

The action learning set

A key aspect of the process was the use of action learning sets. Their purpose was to exploit the support many people find from operating within a network of people they can grow to trust. Within such a group concerns can be raised and the quality of work assessed through discussion. Because of the need to recognize the demands of varying work contexts further meetings of pairs and trios from within each set were organized around participants' own timetables and work-loads. In the secondary schools these often happened on the premises, but where participants came from several work-places, homes and local hostelries became training bases. Rumour has it that one publican could be close to completing Unit 7!

The sets proved useful both for purposes of clarification and motivation and as occasions when strategies used or to use could be discussed and concerns shared. One particular strength was the opportunity they offered to discuss the very variable practices within what were at least nominally common roles. This was particularly true of primary school deputy heads. Sometimes they were full partners and headteachers actively planned their training, but others were class teachers who 'stood in' if the head was absent. The latter found that they now had a knowledge of what could be expected of them and with the confidence of the group to bolster them they sought to obtain wider experience by requesting appropriate delegation.

The full action learning set of eight met only four times between the initial meeting and assessment but the smaller groups met every two or three weeks. The four full meetings were to clarify issues causing concern, to discuss the nature or use of key pieces of evidence, to discuss alternative strategies for managing common situations identified in the standards but dealt with dif-ferently by various group members; and to set goals for future meetings. The smaller groups concentrated much more closely on the meanings and im-plications of individual standards and the way these were reflected in the working practices of individuals. There was much clarification of motives, sharing of strategies and exchanging of perceived good practice within these groups, and they played a major part in the developing of the participants' confidence.

The role of the mentor/adviser

In the pilot run the mentors/advisers were not educational managers. They had three main tasks:

(1) To ensure that the group was properly managed and supported;
(2) To ask those 'naive questions' which outsiders can raise, which enable participants to reflect on their own practice;
(3) To motivate and promote a desire to improve performance and establish a high group view of management expectations.

They were not judges of what might be acceptable for accreditation, although clearly their experience gave them some insight into this area. The role of assessor was, and remains, entirely separate from that of mentor. Assessment was in the hands of independent assessors approved by MCI and identified by the consultants.

In many lengthy processes there are key moments when breakdown is most likely to take place and the mentor/advisers play an important role in providing support in these difficult moments. Two of these occur very early in the process and individuals can lose heart if they are not adequately addressed.

The first one identified, that of relating the job people do to the standards, often meant persuading individuals to describe what they actually did and why. This involved the mentor helping candidates through the early confrontations with the language of the standards, and having someone at the first meetings who could prompt group members into relating their work practice, sometimes identified in their job descriptions but often less formally, to the broad descriptions of the MCI elements was most useful. Further, some managers, particularly those who were early in their management careers, rarely related their managerial role to the total needs of their school. Careful probing as to the importance of their role in ensuring the institution delivered 'products' or 'services' made group members more aware of the co-ordinating and managing roles they fulfilled.

The second area was the first attempts to provide evidence of competence in an element. This proved the area most difficult for individuals to come to terms with as most felt that 'evidence' referred only to evidence of outcome and tended to ignore evidence of facilitating the process. In many cases 'junior' members played little part in final outcomes but played major parts in areas such as audit, needs analysis, monitoring or evaluation. Often their links with outside agencies and clients were ignored and working notes that would have been valuable 'evidence' had been destroyed. Mentors were able to demonstrate that good recording actually enhanced individual and institutional accountability *and* provided rich evidence. As it was potential evidence such material was often carefully prepared.

Accreditation of prior learning

A more appropriate term would have been the accreditation of prior *experience* and learning, since what was being evaluated was how far previous learning, through courses or experience at work, had been internalized and was being reflected in individuals' management behaviour. Behind the concept was a recognition that time spent on teaching what is already known and demonstrated in behaviours is time wasted which could be more profitably spent developing additional required skills. Such behaviours had, of course, to be matched with the competences identified in the standards. However, they could be demonstrated by chance, or not be recognized as appropriate by the manager, so a key task of the assessor is not only to recognize the behaviours but also to establish the motives behind them and that the candidate has an awareness of these motives. The assessor also needs to establish whether the individuals' repertoire of management strategies demonstrates that awareness. If it does, it should result in support structures being developed to ensure reliable, prompt and appropriate responses should the circumstances be repeated.

The role of the assessor

Whilst almost all the candidates in the project entered for reasons of development rather than accreditation, working towards assessment certainly kept
many candidates 'to task'. The assessor is only met at the last action learning
set where he or she will, in conjunction with the candidate, determine the
nature of the assessment procedure to be adopted and the number of units to
be assessed. In the Calderdale Project this has usually been the entire set,
except for the personal competences which have been incorporated into the
model but are only assessed at the more senior diploma level.

Usually the assessment takes the form of a detailed interview (typically three
hours) where the assessor probes the candidate's motives and understanding
against the portfolio of evidence presented. On occasion this has been supplemented by direct observation through work-place visits. Theoretically, for it
has yet to be necessary, where the candidate's job description excludes an area
within the standards, simulation or role play might be considered. For example, where candidates are excluded from being involved in the recruitment
of personnel as part of their management role such simulations might involve
the creation of job specifications or advertisements.

There were initial concerns about whether a non-education assessor would
understand the context within which candidates operated. However, once the
candidates recognized that the elements themselves and the personal competences accompanying them expected managers to be able to explain that context, most candidates saw this as a challenge not a threat.

THE SECOND PHASE

Two key aspects of the extension of the project into its second phase were the
introduction of the diploma, which assesses a more senior level of management, and the further training of members of the first cohort as mentors/
advisers. The diploma model is substantially the same as that for the certificate,
with ten elements of competence instead of nine. In addition, there are three
further components of the programme.

The first is the inclusion of a management project on a priority topic identified within the development plan of the school or department. The nature of
these projects has varied considerably, including, for example,

• the reorganization of a split-site primary school;
• the organization of a residential field trip for primary age children;
• the relationship of a devolved budget to an emerging school development plan;
• the restructuring of the pastoral system in a large comprehensive school;
• curriculum development and change through the production of the school
  timetable.

The detail in all these projects is linked to relevant competences within the
standards, to strengthen the understanding that they are not the equivalent of

a set of still pictures but are, when met in practice, a moving picture. Presentational skills are also assessed by a presentation of around twenty minutes to a panel of educational and non-educational managers.

Since this project often involves other individuals within the organization, an extra unit relating to personal competences has also been added to the scheme for assessment.

The third addition is the keeping of critical incident diaries. This entails identifying important events that occur in candidates' work every day for six weeks, along with their response to them and, if necessary, the longer-term strategy adopted. These have two particular values. For the school, they have not only identified important events but, more importantly, those that recur. Unexpected or unique events have to be managed, but events that might be expected to happen again need a structural response so that dealing with them becomes more an administrative than a managerial task. The diary helps managers identify the sorts of support systems the school needs.

For the candidate the actions they took were mapped back to the standards to demonstrate their ability to analyse their own actions or possible actions in relation to the competences. This material should reveal either gaps that are not properly covered by the standards or alternatively areas in the standards not covered by the candidate's job experience. It also provides another source of evidence for interrogation by the assessor and a focus for discussion with action learning sets to establish both the rationale behind the management response and the reasons for discarding possible alternative actions. Carrying out this exercise seems to indicate that the standards do generally represent a comprehensive cover of the educational manager's job. There are peaks and these do not necessarily match exactly the mapping of other occupational diaries in the project. However, there is substantial common ground as to the frequency of interpersonal contacts – management is clearly about people. This raises the first of the issues which need discussion.

ISSUES IN IMPLEMENTING AND DEVELOPING THE PROJECT

The use of generic competences

Throughout the development of the project there was a national debate over the need to contextualize the standards for particular audiences. An early decision, and one still strongly supported, was not to do so.

Candidates certainly found the generic language difficult. However, coming to terms through discussion with the mentor about what an educational manager's product actually was, exploring the concept of client identification and of support systems or quality control meant that assumptions relating to existing management practice were immediately challenged. This challenge was reinforced by the mentors being practising managers but not from education.

Once individuals had come to terms with the language, many of the group members reported an increase in confidence as managers. This happened because they recognized that differences between themselves and other managers were differences more of language than of expectation or performance. It was described by one person as, 'for the first time feeling respectable amongst other managers from different contexts'. Despite considerable pressure to contextualize, then, the project has sought to protect the generic status, but as it has extended it has provided support material to seek to offer examples of source and forms of evidence that might be appropriate.

MCI constraints on evidence of competence

Candidates frequently felt that MCI, rather than the standards, imposed constraints on them which were not placed on industrial managers. This has been a particular concern with groups outside Calderdale that have included main grade teachers preparing for management but currently in posts not seen by MCI as managerial. The evidence of their skills in managing resources is welcomed, as is their management of professional and ancillary staff. Their evidence of their management of a product, say a curriculum, is sometimes accepted. However, the management of the process of its manufacture, the management of a learning environment, is not. Similarly the management of students is not acceptable, yet these may be young adults two years older than some employees.

It is important that teachers recognize that moving from teaching to managing often means identifying those curriculum and classroom management skills and transferring them to managing other things. The recognition by MCI of the generic nature of these skills would benefit all parties. It would make teachers less suspicious of 'management' and, most importantly, it would give main-scale teachers more easily identified access to the MCI standards themselves.

Matching the model and the context of management practice

The MCI model is built on a hierarchical model of organizational development. It assumes that certificate level candidates will be junior managers and so the range statements often use language such as 'being aware of' or 'supporting others in'. At diploma level the language becomes more about 'having responsibility for' or 'ensuring that'. Strategic decisions seem largely reserved for the as-yet unwritten level beyond the diploma. Such a hierarchy of responsibility does not reflect the working practices of many organizations which expect many of their staff to manage projects from the creation of an idea to the delivery of a product.

The main difficulty this creates is the potential underestimation of the capacities of some managers who might operate at diploma level in some units, certificate level in others, and beyond diploma level in others. The ultimate accountability might be with the senior manager, the headteacher, but the responsibility is with the 'middle manager'. Even within nominally hierarchical institutions the responsibility for management and leadership can be diffused through varying organizational levels. Within schools, particularly primary schools, very young, relatively inexperienced professionally trained teachers often have curriculum management and leadership roles that may result in them managing people, information, resources and change from very 'junior' positions.

Because of this the division envisaged by MCI between certificate, diploma and 'Masters' levels, between 'having responsibility for', 'initiating' and 'strategically planning', is inappropriate. The standards permit flexibility of interpretation, and a lack of imagination in their use should not restrict that flexibility.

The context within which managers work affects the balance of exposure to different units. There needs to be a match between the organization's structure, the nature of the work, and the assumptions of the model. All the managers in the second phase of the project felt that they operated within most of the units of competence fairly regularly over the six-week period of their critical incident diaries. It was found that senior managers in primary schools operated across a very broad spectrum of management competences. Although there were occasions where experience had not permitted an individual to demonstrate competence and reflect it in recorded evidence, particularly in grievance procedures or in recruitment, there was clear evidence that with appropriate delegation, preparation and support, most managers in primary schools would be able to present evidence of competence across all nine units.

By comparison, some secondary school managers had become very specialized and had difficulty in presenting evidence of competence in some units. Although they could present as evidence of competence material generated in a previous post, this was generally felt to be unhelpful. Indeed it was felt that current management roles were in danger of not adapting to the more flexible and broad development required to respond to changing management needs. Schools need to recognize and prepare for the fact that they may need to create opportunities within their structures and work practices for newly developed managers to use their new-found skills other than simply by the 'reward' of accreditation. Some of the frustrations that might result from schools not having the flexibility within their management structure, or even the available budget to reflect enhanced skills through increased pay, need to be anticipated. However, a greater problem seems to be the frustrations that can emerge from feeling more skilled, having more confidence, and being denied the opportunity to use these talents.

The need for a developmental focus

There was concern that whilst the model retained an emphasis on prior evidence there was little opportunity for any 'value-added' element through development either for the individual or their organization. Activity was being focused towards accreditation and not development. However, discussions within action learning sets had often been around the areas of initiating change, managing change and responding to recognized situations. This gently evolving debate around the functions of leadership, management administration and accountability led to the recognition that leadership was essentially about having a view of something better than that which is currently practised and that it is evidenced in skills relating to influencing and clarifying that view. The implication that leadership was therefore about the planned destabilization of an organization was raised and discussed in at least two sets, and it became understood that the group members themselves had the potential to destabilize existing practice in their institutions.

Although many of the candidates were at times seeking to carry out this leadership function most of the evidence presented against the standards came from their other functions. These included managing the organization towards a stable position or operating the administrative support systems created to service the annual cycle of delivering the curriculum. However, the move to delegated budgets and the work in most schools in producing school development plans has enabled many candidates to provide evidence of longer-term strategies relating to the development and maintenance of premises, the creation of new staffing structures and much more monitoring of consumption. The move to managing one's own finances has meant much more school-based decision-making. This may not always have been welcomed by school managers but it has brought about extensive development of management skills – and provided a godsend for those seeking evidence of competence!

Since discussion in the action learning sets centred around quality of response, several areas of development occurred rapidly. Headteachers foresaw through discussion with their middle managers opportunities for appropriate delegation and experience to prepare them for broader or more demanding management opportunities; the evidence of accountability of management processes and decisions was substantially enhanced; and candidates were able to demonstrate an awareness of the difference between a job done and a job done well.

Further, there has been evidence of immediate 'value added' to both individuals and institutions. The generation of evidence for assessment resting on the outcomes of tasks has enhanced systems of accountability. Initiating or improving support systems has allowed issues that had previously had to be individually managed to become matters to be dealt with by others through routine administrative systems, and the simplification of complex systems has allowed others to access and use them. Shared leadership and management through delegation have extended the management expertise available to the organization and, as a result, accepted practices have been increasingly questioned.

Workload and motivation

All parties involved were concerned about workload at first. Clearly work time spent on the project is in the broadest of terms an opportunity cost to the school or individual. The initial aim was to move towards accreditation over a year with an estimated workload of about an hour a week. In practice this averaged out at around one and a half hours per week over eight months. The actual times varied from one individual ready for assessment in all the units in four months to two candidates working as a pair, one of whom had a career change mid-project, taking twenty months to submit for assessment.

Motivation was substantial. Responses to external evaluators three to four months into the projects recorded numerous comments such as: 'It's the first time anyone's ever given me a pat on the back for a job clearly well done – even if it's only me giving it!'; 'I feel able to talk as an equal on management issues with other (industrial) managers'; 'My husband's firm would like to become involved.'

Indeed, there is some danger of the generation of the portfolio of evidence becoming more important than the quality of its content. There was an initial temptation for candidates to seek to prove their industry rather than identifying 'What am I doing or likely to do that would best demonstrate my competence?' The mentors played an important part in insisting on evidence of competence. At the first introductory session group members were asked to identify for the next meeting as much evidence as they could around one unit with which they felt most comfortable. The next meeting then concentrated on discussing what those pieces of evidence actually demonstrated, and looked at the ways different people sought to illustrate similar standards. However, in no case was there evidence of the process detrimentally affecting the ultimate product it was meant to enhance – the management of schools and the learning of students.

Accreditation and the assessment of competence

A different sort of motivational issue was observed in both the pilot and second phase groups. The pilot group had included people who were motivated by a search for a route to personal development and those seeking accreditation. Although the project provides for both, two major concerns were apparent among those seeking accreditation: firstly, were there easier routes, if more expensive, to obtaining it? This model involves sustained analysis and activity and considerable personal discipline. The full action learning sets met only four times in eight months and the sub-divided pairs, trios or foursomes, about every four weeks. Secondly, would the award have any currency? Since then the project has spun off similar initiatives in other LEAs and within industry. Within Calderdale LEA involvement in the project is now seen as a 'desirable' if not yet 'essential' criterion on job specifications. Even so, there is still debate on whether 'competence' can be assessed objectively.

The demonstration of competence comes from making it evident that the impact of management behaviours has been recognized by the candidate. Assessing this puts a much greater burden of interpretation on the assessor who must not only have specific experience but have generalized this through further experience and analysed it through applied knowledge to enable him or her to probe the motives behind the candidate's decision. The assessor must recognize the candidate's ability to identify a problem, determine an appropriate strategy and evaluate its possible and actual outcomes. Assessment therefore becomes a relatively subjective procedure although measured against a detailed criterion-referenced structure.

Who makes the best mentors?

In the pilot stage, the mentors/advisers to the action learning sets were drawn from industrial and commercial management. In the second phase some are educational managers. Each has its strengths and deficiencies. Non-educationalists were very good at challenging assumptions and by having sometimes a different management culture they often challenged motives and did not get over-involved with outcomes. There were, however, sometimes difficulties in the early stages of the relationship with the action learning sets because of the mentors' own lack of confidence in presenting. Educational managers proved very helpful in developing early confidence in the candidates but less successful at challenging assumptions. Further, they sometimes slipped into a teaching role. Mentors, both those from educational roots and others, have to recognize that they are managers of a self-supporting learning group. Their chief function is to enable those within the group to reflect on their own practice and that of others. They are not purveyors of best practice nor providers of training.

LOOKING AHEAD

The third phase of the project seeks to extend it as an entitlement to all primary school deputies, a group where the skills gap between headteacher and deputy could widen considerably because of local management of schools unless genuine shared leadership and management is encouraged. At the secondary level it will seek to explore a model of institutional readiness so as to avoid the frustrations already recorded when developed managers are unable to use their skills. The problem has already been addressed to some extent in one secondary school where the INSET co-ordinator has sought to develop a system of shadowing opportunities for those seeing development. This has involved in-house and industrial placements but has not been able to address the fundamental problem of people who now feel there is a lack of demand for their proven skills in their everyday role. One of the key areas of phase three will be to seek to prepare schools better for involvement in MCI and make a strategic management response to the potential problems. This should also address an area of some weakness in the standards themselves.

CONCLUSION

The debate around the use of competences and the so-called behaviourist view it is supposed to engender is but a new manifestation of an old argument. Some would like to find within management the objectivity of a pure science reflected in predictable and measurable inputs and outcomes, and some consider it to be an art form. Others, however, see it as a craft, and craftspeople work by an understanding of the limits and tolerances of the medium with which they work, be this clay, iron, or in the case of educational managers, people. Management is about judgement and judgement is difficult to communicate. A map of where we have travelled in our quest for judgement enables those who re-explore to operate within a better defined understanding of the issues they are likely to confront.

People using maps often get lost not because they do not know where they are going but because they have not established where they are. The MCI standards have proved to be of benefit for establishing that base position, and the training model we have developed has provided the support to progress from that initial position to a shared objective both with the sympathetic company of the action learning set and with the reassurance of an experienced guide.

REFERENCE

Management Charter Initiative (MCI) (1991) *The Management Standards Implementation Pack*, MCI, London.

3

DEVELOPING MANAGERIAL CAPABILITIES IN EDUCATION

Ernie Cave and Cyril Wilkinson

This material has been abridged

A two-phase research project undertaken by the Education Management Unit of the University of Ulster investigated two issues: What do education managers need to be good at? How can their capability be improved?

In the first phase the researchers sought to identify and distil essential capacities which the education manager requires in order to perform effectively in key areas of management. A management capability model emerged and is presented as a working tool which might be used in planning management development initiatives. The second phase explored how the model might be used to plan development programmes that are more specifically targeted in their intentions.

THE BACKGROUND

The major concern in the management literature in the 1980s has been the development of management competences. Since the purpose of the study of management is to improve performance, it is not surprising that attention should be focused on an analysis of what abilities managers need in order to be effective and various categorizations have emerged. The beginnings of the research for generic management competences can be traced back to the 1970s when the American Management Associations (AMA) launched a project based on observation and analysis of 1,800 management jobs.

In the AMA managerial competency model which emerged competence is defined as 'a generic knowledge, motive, trait, self-image, social role, or skill of a person that is causally linked to superior performance on the job' (Hayes,

1979). The model identifies, in addition to specific knowledge competence, four clusters of generic competences which they identify as intellectual, entrepreneurial, socio-emotional and interpersonal. In Britain academic study and research was given a marked stimulus by the Management Charter Initiative (MCI), a large-scale industry-led management development programme supported by central government which now involves over 200 UK leading private and public organizations. A price to be paid for government support, particularly in the British political scene, given the relatively short periods between elections, is that results have to be visible, immediate and measurable. Consequently there has been an inevitable tendency to produce checklists often containing an undifferentiated collection of personal characteristics, mechanistic skills, management processes and much more complex abilities.

In the field of education the growing recognition of the crucial importance of good management practices in school was dramatically strengthened by the impact of 'local management of schools' imposed by the 1988 Education Reform Act. Central government clearly regards management development as a key element in its declared strategy for ensuring improvement in the quality of education to meet the needs of industry and the economy. Fortunately the years that followed the Act have coincided with the period when serious doubts are being expressed about the basic idea of analysing a professional management task into itemized elements of competence. It is increasingly recognized that the overall ability to perform effectively is more than the sum of a set of subordinate abilities. Jacobs (1989) makes the point that while it is possible, by obtaining and carefully analysing performance data, to identify clusters of behaviour that can be reliably and logically classified as competences, what is obtained is only a partial and fragmented view of the complexity of management. Management performance involves other activity which is difficult to isolate and describe; it involves qualities and abilities which are not easy to observe or discover; it has outcomes which defy measurement.

The Management Task Force set up by the Secretary of State for Education to identify and explore some of the issues involved in management development in schools has largely rejected the prescription of training in an arbitrarily determined set of skills as the way forward. This has contributed to a growing conviction that those who manage are in the best position to identify what their needs may be. This approach is reinforced by a current general political philosophy that 'the customer knows best'. Thus the identification of need is a major concern among providers of management development and it is generally held that it is essential for schools to feel ownership of the programmes through being fully and directly involved in planning their content, style and procedures.

The idea that managers themselves are best able to determine their own development needs has a common sense appeal, and the needs of practitioners as they perceive them provides a reasonable starting point in attempting to determine what competences are required and how they might be developed. There are, however, a number of obvious difficulties. Even those strongly committed to full participation by schools in devising education management programmes admit that 'current concerns force an attitude of short-termism and coping with immediate practicalities rather than long-term planning' (Styan, 1991). Thus it is not surprising that solutions to pressing problems are a need more strongly felt than the search for underlying generic capabilities. Also, it cannot be assumed that practitioners, however willing, will be able to engage in the diagnostic and analytical process necessary to identify competences associated with effectiveness. The methods required to probe beyond and beneath the easily identifiable daily concerns and practices of managing are likely to be based on rigorous analysis, reflection and debate by practitioners and are as yet largely underdeveloped.

THE RESEARCH METHODOLOGY

In determining an appropriate method of enquiry the researchers were informed from three sources: The Peer Assisted Learning Project of the Far West Laboratory for Education Research and Development, San Francisco (The PAL Project), personal experience of peer group interaction, and focus groups as a form of qualitative research.

Effective peer group interaction, an integral part of the action research approach, is the cornerstone of the Master of Science programme at the University of Ulster. Groups are encouraged to engage in reflective enquiry which seeks to analyse and understand their own and others' practice leading to courses of action for sustained improvement. Creative thinking is also encouraged as a complementary activity by which is meant the ability to form novel associations from looking at the elements of managerial reality in an open and unconstrained way. This approach offered the possibility of uncovering, if they existed, elusive generic capabilities from complex realities.

The focus group as a form of qualitative research has many characteristics in common with features of the above approach: 'The hallmark of the focus group is the explicit use of the group interaction to produce data and insights that would be less accessible without the interaction found in a group' (Morgan, 1988). The style of approach is exploratory rather than hypothesis testing and based on interview and interaction. Surprisingly focus groups have not been widely used in research in the social sciences or education, but the method clearly offers a valuable vehicle for group members experienced in rigorous reflective analysis.

For this research six headteachers were chosen from the primary, secondary and further education sectors and two female members were included to allow for possible differences in style and practice. All are alumni of the MSc programme and had the advantage of three years of cognitive development in the group dynamics described above.

The researchers acted as moderators, adopting a detached style which allowed members to raise and explore issues they felt were significant but maintaining proximity to the focus of enquiry. Criteria were identified and applied which governed the quality of interaction, namely, coverage of a broad range of matters recognized on significant, precise and detailed accounts, and rigorous searching analysis. The group met on ten occasions during the period June 1988–November 1989. In each of these tape-recorded sessions members were encouraged to identify situations/incidents in their practice, to reflect on the intentions and outcomes of the action taken, and to attempt to distil from their discussions what they perceived to be the capacities necessary for success.

GROUP DELIBERATIONS

The constraints of a relatively brief paper prevent a detailed account of each of the ten sessions. As decision-making is the vital element in the managing task two contrasting decision issues are selected as examples. In the account which follows contributors are identified by sector (primary (PS), or secondary (SS), or further education (FE)); status (maintained (M), i.e. Catholic, or state (S)); and gender (male (m), or female (f)).

Example 1

During the opening session in Drumcree High School, whether or not to join Education for Mutual Understanding (EMU) was offered as an issue requiring a Yes/No decision within a short time-span. EMU is a major curriculum project in Northern Ireland and is heavily resourced and supported by the Department of Education and the present education minister. It seeks to encourage sympathetic and understanding relationships between Catholic and Protestant schools. However, it has been opposed by many local politicians, churches and community members who see it both as a first step towards integrated schooling and an imposed initiative from central government at Westminster. Everyone in the group regarded it as a critically important decision with clear political overtones as well as educational implications. In two schools in particular the political/community aspects dominated. One school is in a strongly nationalist area seeking to preserve its distinctive Irish culture and identity. Nevertheless the headteacher saw his task as persuading the governors to enter the project. The other school is in a staunch unionist area and the headteacher was well aware that her governors would oppose any political interference they perceived as emanating from Westminster. The EMU issue instigated a lengthy discussion about the tactics that might be used. There was some disagreement over the question of how much direction/information should be given to a board of governors. All concurred that they were able to influence their boards of governors and a vital tactic was the winning of support of key figures. All were able to recognize the key figures in their governing bodies and stressed the paramount importance of good relationships with the chairperson. They felt it was also important to know the interests, dispositions and beliefs of all members of the boards of governors.

It was also apparent in this opening session that many of the concepts and capacities identified and sharpened in later group meetings as constituting what managers need to be good at were freely used. Having recognized EMU as a potentially emotive political issue, they saw the capacity to read the situation as critically important: the board of governors, teacher attitudes, community perceptions, resource implications, reactions of the Department of Education and the area boards (LEAs) were consequential variables in the circumstances. Concepts like balanced judgement, political acumen, judicious caution, and skills like reconnaissance, persuading, negotiating and bargaining recurred in the discussion.

Example 2

Some of the literature on decision-making distinguishes between 'routine' decisions (structured, certain, simple, recurring, standardized) and 'non-routine' decisions (unstructured, uncertain, complex, non-recurring, novel). In one group session the danger of assuming that routine recurring decisions are necessarily simple and certain became apparent. The conclusion was reached that the capable manager is one who has the insight to recognize when apparently simple decisions may have complex undertones.

Discussion had centred on the broad issue of the expected consequence of the new legislation which has been introduced in Northern Ireland in parallel with the Education Reform Act, 1988. One of the group, almost as an aside, posed the question: 'What do we do if a teacher asks for leave of absence not provided for by the regulations?' On the face of it this is a routine issue where agreed procedures and required information are readily available. In the case of further education this indeed appears to be so. The FE principal pointed out that his staff have clear contracts and 'it should just be played by the book'. He added, 'Of course, in FE the principal can distance himself from such decisions'. In the primary and secondary sectors the situation is less clear cut. Although regulations governing leave of absence exist, the primary and secondary headteachers felt that strict adherence to such a tight delineation could easily lead to staff also playing by the book. They argued that flexibility was needed but that such flexibility could create its own potential difficulties and that the exercise of judgement, tact and sensitivity was essential.

The conversation broadened into a fuller discussion of the kinds of relationships between headteacher and teaching staff that characterize effective schools and colleges. Marked differences in attitude and opinion became apparent which partly reflected differences in context but, more markedly, differences in personality and perceptions. In particular the female members emphasized the importance of close, supportive relationships. One of them made the point: 'We have introduced counselling for pupils but we seem to neglect the important area of counselling for our staff.' (SS/s/f). Once again the issue of relationships with staff seemed to hinge on balanced judgement.

Differences between the views of the FE principal and the headteachers in the primary and secondary sectors were revealed: 'The powers of the principal are awesome in the new situation. You are part of the employer. You cannot have a close relationship. You will have to distance yourself from the informal relationships which exist in any college.' (FE/S/m). The opposing view was most strongly expressed by a female headteacher: 'You cannot step back. You will lose the spirit of the school and its main purposes. You must win the respect of the staff. You have to build bridges and establish relationships with key figures.' (SS/M/f).

When the attention of the group was directed to the focal issue of what the manager needs to be good at in establishing and maintaining co-operative relationships or, more broadly, in managing people, the usual interpersonal skills were offered – communicating, negotiating, bargaining, influencing, counselling. There were, however, many caveats expressed and there was a general consensus that more fundamental cerebral capacities distinguish the more effective manager from the less effective: thinking on your feet, balanced judgement, assessing the situation.

SUMMARY AND CONCLUSIONS

What emerged from the conversations was a more complex picture than presented in much of the literature on management competence. In the end the group identified three elements that constitute capability:

(1) Knowledge – relevant information relating to the school's context, functions and processes which the manager needs to possess or have ready access to.
(2) Skills – techniques that can be acquired through training and that can be improved through practice.
(3) Higher order capacities – generic cognitive abilities which determine appropriate action.

The proposition which emerges from the investigation is that while knowledge and skills are prerequisite tools in the process of managing a given situation the group strongly argues that it is the higher order capacities which are the vital elements in the process of using knowledge and skills in effective action.

There was common assent on the main areas of knowledge required by senior managers in schools: professional knowledge of educational principles and practices, knowledge of theories and models of management, and knowledge of the social, political and legal contexts. Equally the discrete skills required by managers were generally agreed: persuading, bargaining, explaining, listening, reporting, informing, counselling, appraising, chairing, interviewing, and team building are typical of a list which keeps being added to. Skills have been enumerated in key areas like curriculum, organization and resource management, and development programmes are often predicated on the assumption, often unexamined, that these can be effectively managed through the acquisition of skills that are teachable, learnable and transferable. Few analyses have been made of the nature of the enabling capacities needed to apply skills appropriately in the complex situations in which managers in schools find themselves daily. Since these higher order capacities were deemed by the group to be those which characterized the above average performers, they naturally became the main focus of continuing discussion. The researchers present here the attempt to capture and clarify the ideas which emerged from intense, prolonged discussion involving complex philosophical and psychological issues. The following key higher order capacities were finally identified from a distillation of complex interrelated concepts: reading the situation, balanced judgement, intuition and political acumen.

Reading the situation

This emerged as the overriding capacity and was voiced in a variety of ways: 'picking up the vibes around you'; 'keeping your antennae out'; 'being aware of other possibilities and options'; 'able to assess and weigh up all the factors in the situation'; 'being alert and receptive to what is going on'.

It was also seen to apply to a wide range of decision-making circumstances: long-term strategic planning, handling crisis situations and recurring, daily encounters. The FE principal in particular stressed that sensitive awareness and diagnosis are important in the light of the new legislation and the growing volume of boundary management. The views expressed seemed to recognize that 'reading the situation' involves more than mere diagnosis; it includes continuous response and deliberate action to influence evolving circumstances. The need for action was constantly stressed: 'You need to read the situation as accurately and quickly as possible and be seen to take appropriate action.' (SS/M/f). Reconnaissance, identification of areas requiring attention, analysis, reflection, synthesis and evaluation were seen as contributory elements, many of which occur in the other cognitive activities which are identified.

Balanced judgement

The ability to exercise balanced judgement was also seen as critical. Group members saw it as related to problem-solving in that, once a situation has arisen or a problem has been recognized, analysis follows and key factors are identified and evaluated in the process of choosing a course of action. It was clear that as the group distilled their thinking over a number of sessions they did not see it as an exercise in mechanical logic: 'It is not merely clinical analysis but a combination of that with intuition.' (FE/S/m). There was considerable agreement that the kind of judgement necessary is significantly different from judgement in the legal sense: 'You have to be prepared to base decisions on much softer evidence than would be accepted in a court of law. You very rarely have time to collect all the evidence you would like and you have to exercise judgement on a partial picture. Values also can't be left out of the picture.' (FE/S/m). The issue of values arose in a number of contexts but particularly in relation to the context created by the new legislation: 'You must be aware of the values you are perceived to embody and perceived to protect.' (FE/S/m). 'Can schools preach moral and ethical priorities and not live by them?' (PS/S/m). 'Does school reflect the world out there as it is – or should it project what the world out there might be?' (SS/M/f).

It is interesting that while many writers speak about making sound judgements the recurring theme in the discussion was about balanced judgement. The group saw the examining and weighing of the advantages and disadvantages of factors in often ambiguous and conflicting circumstances as important and the testing of decisions against the priorities and values of the school. Balanced judgement was seen as particularly important in time of crisis and dilemma.

Intuition

Intuition was seen as serving judgement, following a long debate about the relationships between experience, creative thinking, judgement and intuition. The group did not agree with a conception of intuition as devoid of thought. 'Intuition is more than mere hunch or guesswork. It may start as a gut feeling but is tested against the bank of your own experience.' (FE/S/m).

Two key elements recurred in the attempt to capture the essence of intuition: the part played by experience and the part played by a thinking process. The groups saw stored memory and ordered experience as important. It is interesting that they independently derived a conception close to that outlined by a number of recent writers (De Bono, 1982; Ishenberg, 1987; Mintzberg, 1987), who suggest that the basis of intuition lies in the ability spontaneously to tap the mind's compressed store of experience, knowledge and understanding. A top executive in industry expresses a view, reported in Vaughan (1979), which would clearly be accepted by members of the group: 'I don't think intuition is some magical thing. I think it is a subconscious drawing from innumerable experiences that are stored. You draw from this reserve without conscious thought.' Similarly, the group perceptions of the role of thinking in intuition are similar to aspects of the concept of creativity developed by a number of writers. Henry (1991) regards creativity as 'associated with imagination, insight, invention, motivation, ingenuity, inspiration and intuition'. The cerebral aspects of intuition were constantly stressed by the group.

Political acumen

While political skills have featured prominently in lists of what managers need to be good at, the group make an important distinction between possession of political skills, like bargaining, and political acumen: 'It's not enough to know how to bargain but when to bargain. Timing is all important.' (FE/M/m). Their notion of political acumen is closely tied in with thinking on one's feet, learning from experience, reading the situation and using intuition: 'It is about hearing what people are not saying. That's part of political awareness.' (PS/S/m). Thus political awareness has to do with sensitivity and with flexibility to take account of changing situations rather than relying simply on experience: 'You, others and circumstances will have changed.' (SS/S/f). In discussion of the new legislation the group stressed the importance of such tactics as controlling information, identifying and cultivating key parties, establishing effective networks, developing credibility and occupying public space.

REVIEW

In an early session one group member captured the initial feelings about effective headteachers: 'You know who they are but you don't know why they are.' (PS/S/m). In the final review session the group claimed to have come to a clearer understanding of the 'why'. They felt that while they had greater conceptual clarity it was still difficult to put the essence into words. They seem to confirm the assertion in Pye (1988) that managerial behaviour is 'something about which we can know more than we can tell'.

Equally, in the ten sessions there was much more told than can be reported in this brief account. For example, the group saw personal qualities like integrity, stamina, commitment and conviction as fundamental and greater emphasis was placed on the foundation role of value systems than appears in the account.

PHASE TWO

For the second phase of the investigation three headteachers from the original group were retained. Three new members were included who had also successfully completed the MSc in Education Management programme. There was a deliberate widening of group background to include a broader spectrum from education and the health service. In the account which follows contributions are identified as before by sector: primary (P), secondary (S), further education (FE), higher education (HE), area board (equivalent to LEA) (AB), nurse education (NE), and by gender: male (m), or female (f).

Throughout the five sessions held the three key elements of knowledge, skills and higher order capacities identified during the first phase were reconsidered and confirmed: that is, managerial capability is realized in effective action in which knowledge and skills are used appropriately through the exercise of higher order capacities.

The four higher order capacities of reading the situation, balanced judgement, intuition and political acumen were also confirmed throughout the sessions. Creativity was seen as making a vital contribution to the higher order capacities and managerial capability, particularly in times of complex, turbulent change in public and private sector management. Kindred terms like imagination, insight, originality and inventive thinking were seen as appropriate in such times of flux. The group believed that effective management integrated the more systematic analysis, reflection and synthesis implied by classical, rational approaches with creative perspectives which look for new, unanticipated, unexpected ways of seeing, thinking and doing. In this the group are reflecting the view emerging in recent management literature that rational enquiry and non-rational insight should be complementary. Wisdom also appeared as a central concept in the group discussions and there was some debate about what constituted the wise manager. One group member tended to equate wisdom with a degree of caution which inhibits action and creativity but others in the group argued that creativity and risk-taking should be seen as important elements of wise management.

The central concern for the second phase was the question: what are the implications for planning management development programmes? The group felt that much of the thinking on management development failed to distinguish clearly enough between management processes, key management areas and managerial capability. Group members argued for a three-dimensional model which recognized that managerial capability is exercised in key management areas through generic managing processes. There was agreement that in education, as in all organizations, generic management processes can be identified which include deciding, communicating, devising and influencing (Wilkinson and Cave, 1987). The key areas identified in educational institutions were resources, curriculum, organization and administration. With the changing emphasis on competition and accountability external and boundary management were seen as crucial areas. The group argued that management development programmes need to identify the underlying capacities required to be good at these processes in these areas.

The single overriding message that the group stressed is that management development initiatives should develop managerial capability and need to be clearly targeted in their intentions. The three elements of knowledge, skills and higher order capacities clearly interrelate as one group member stated: 'Knowledge, skills and higher order capacities are all interleaving in that knowledge and skills have their contributions to make to higher order capacities. They all influence each other in many ways.' (HE/m). The group emphasized the importance of targeting initiatives both in terms of what is appropriate and in recognition that at different times during a manager's career different balances and kinds of learning are likely to be necessary. Group members also presented the view that all teachers are managers and have significant contributions to make to the health of the organization, particularly in present and future times of large-scale change and turbulence. For education and the health service this implies a change of culture, both within the system and institutions, which rests on openness, trust, sharing and participation by all.

The transmission of required knowledge is relatively straightforward and may be offered in oral, written and visual forms or in combination. Equally, well-established procedures for the acquisition of management skills exist through approaches like workshops, social skills training programmes and those employing more sophisticated technology like interactive video. Although not underestimating the importance of acquiring specific and appropriate knowledge and receiving training in management skills, the new group reaffirmed and strongly supported the belief that higher order capacities are the determining factor in effective management action: 'Management is a cluster of skills involving things like influencing, good communication and so forth. It's that but it's much more than that. You can never be fully trained in it.' (FE/m). While they agreed that higher order capacities are needed at all stages in a teacher's career, they argued that they assume increasing importance with promotion. Several members gave examples of teachers who had found difficulty as they progressed.

Much group debate centred on how higher order capacities might be developed. They questioned the usefulness of 'second-hand' experience like simulation exercises in that 'solutions' are more easily arrived at freed from the constraints of a real context. They also felt that facile answers to simulated situations can be accepted when the problems presented are not owned by the participants and therefore concerns of accountability do not arise. They maintained that, while higher order capacities may develop *through experience* there are also ways in which *learning from experience* can be assisted: 'You probably have to learn it on the job but it's more than learning on the job. This is where the group is so important. The sense you make of your own experiences results from the group. This has to be related back into your continuing experience.' (P/m).

Thus the value of sharing and utilizing the breadth of experience and expertise through peer group interaction as has taken place in the focus group was recognized and the group came down heavily in favour of this approach. It developed precisely the kinds of self-analysis, awareness and critical reflection through which the higher order capacities might be developed: the research method becomes the developmental medium. The researchers certainly became aware that the members of the focus group developed both individually and as a group during the course of the research and there were qualitative differences in terms of the criteria of range, specificity and depth between initial and later sessions.

However, members emphasized that peer group conversation needs monitoring and guidance. They saw a real danger in sessions becoming anecdotal. The term 'mentor' was used to describe this advisory, guiding role and it was felt that this person should be 'itinerant', that is, outside the group, to avoid the possibility of claustrophobia and lack of breadth likely in a restricted setting. They regarded it as essential that the mentor should have high credibility as a practitioner and the consultant in the medical world was offered as a pertinent example. The importance of identifying accurately the essential needs of managers was stressed and it was argued that the mentor had a crucial role to play in diagnosing the underlying causes rather than the symptoms, and in recognizing the importance of the lasting and the long-term rather than the immediate and short-term which tend to distort management priorities. Managers with differing backgrounds and experience and in different positions in the organization will require relevant, and indeed individual, development programmes which are tailored to meet their needs. In the final session it was proposed that underpinning the thinking processes which are at the heart of effective management is the asking of right questions in an attempt to arrive at appropriate answers. Such questioning and ensuing reflection may be applied to past experience, to present circumstances and to anticipation of the future under the guidance of an experienced, skilled mentor.

It is interesting that the group arrived independently at a conception of management which is similar to that presented in recent literature on creative management (see Henry, 1991). The model that they present as a working tool for planning effective development programmes appears to be worth trying out.

ACKNOWLEDGEMENTS

The researchers record their indebtedness to the members of the focus groups for their vital contribution: Martin Bradley, Jim Billingsley, David Green, Raymond Harbinson, Jim Hunter, Sister Yvonne Jennings, Louis Knox, Penny McKeown, P.J. O'Grady and John Watson.

REFERENCES

De Bono, E. (1982) Letter as appendix in B. Heirs and B. Pherson, *The Mind of the Organisation*, Harper & Row, New York.

Hayes, J. (1979) A new look at managerial competence: the AMA model of worthy performance, *Management Review*, November.

Henry, J. (ed.) (1991) *Creative Management*, Sage, London.

Ishenberg, D. (1987) The tactics of strategic opportunism, *Harvard Business Review*, November/December.

Jacobs, R. (1989) Getting the measure of management competence, *Personnel Management*, June.

Mintzberg, H. (1987) Crafting strategy, *Harvard Business Review*, July/August.

Morgan, D. (1988) *Focus Groups as Quantitative Research*, Sage, London.

Pye, A. (1988) Management competence in the public sector, *Public Money and Management*, Winter.

Styan, D. (1991) Local management of schools: changing roles and relationships, in P. Holly (ed.) *Developing Managers in Education*, CRAC Publications, Hobsons Publishing PCC, Cambridge.

Vaughan, F.E. (1979) *Awakening Intuition*, Anchor Books, New York.

Wilkinson, C. and Cave, E. (1987) *Teaching and Managing: Inseparable Activities in Schools*, Croom Helm, London.

4

TOTAL QUALITY MANAGEMENT IN EDUCATION

John West-Burnham

The reforms of the education service in the 1980s provide the most fundamental challenges to the prevailing orthodoxies of the management of educational institutions. The changes are so profound that any attempt to respond to them using established principles and processes is likely to be dysfunctional. At the same time there is a critical need to establish a moral basis for educational management so that the demands of the reforms do not result in pragmatic and expedient responses. This chapter argues that Total Quality Management (TQM) offers a vehicle for schools and colleges to manage themselves effectively in a time of rapid change and retain a clear focus on the essential and dominant purposes of education.

The Education Reform Act 1988 and related legislation in Scotland and Northern Ireland has had the net effect of shifting responsibility, authority and accountability to the institutional level, eroding the traditional infrastructure of support and focusing on to individual institutions the previously diffuse patterns of management activity. In essence the changes are encapsulated in the concept of the 'self-governing' school or college. The specific requirements on schools in England and Wales to manage the national curriculum, LMS and appraisal in the context of parental choice and the impact of incorporation on post-compulsory institutions create demands which are of a different order of magnitude to anything previously encountered. The possibility of institutions *not* managing themselves has now been removed as an option. In the context of consumer choice failing institutions will be allowed the ultimate failure.

A further factor is the changing culture in which schools and colleges will have to operate. As the quality movement extends into the commercial and public sectors so expectations on all providers will change. Parents will increasingly be working in TQM companies, school-leavers and students will be seeking employment in organizations managed according to quality criteria.

There will inevitably be increasingly specific demands on schools and colleges as suppliers. Most readers will be familiar with the British Standard 'kitemark'; as well as being an indication of safety, there is a kitemark for quality management systems, BS 5750. Some further education colleges are having to seek BS 5750 accreditation in order to be able to deal with registered companies.

Sallis (1991) has identified four imperatives for change which he argues point towards a total quality approach. The professional imperative implies a commitment to client needs and the obligation to meet those needs by deploying knowledge and skills to best effect. The moral imperative is the need to find a basis for management action which is firmly rooted in the key purposes of educational institutions. Quality approaches are offered as a way of meeting long-standing concerns about the nature of management in schools and colleges. Sallis extends the applicability of TQM to education by arguing that there are two further imperatives operating, the competitive and survival. These are closely linked but in essence the emergence of a market economy in education requires the evolution of strategies which reconcile the first two imperatives with the need to ensure institutional viability.

There is a need for educational institutions to develop a sophisticated response to this new climate. On the one hand this has profound dangers in that schools and colleges might be seduced into adopting structures and procedures which convey a veneer of efficiency but which lose sight of the key purposes of educational institutions. There is the danger of the triumph of the 'men in grey suits' – a situation where administration becomes a substitute for managing and where power relationships replace professional relationships. Shipman characterizes the issue in the following terms:

> By concentrating school management on top-down procedures, training has missed both the opportunity to help teachers raise standards and to use their interest in helping children learn. . . . By the late 1980s, management literature outside education was stressing not only the importance of vision at the top, but of the need to encourage intitiative at all levels of the organization. Yet there is still no sign of any shift around management training in education. The stress is still on means confused with ends and on administration not management.

(Shipman, 1990, p. 149)

The combination of the need to respond to the 1988 Act and preserve the integrity of the learning process is further complicated by a third factor – the concern with quality. The issue of quality in education is a perennial one and the standard response has been in Platonic terms – to see it as an intellectual problem to be grappled with which, by definition, is probably not capable of solutions. Quality has been perceived as an ideal, an absolute like truth, justice and beauty which we can only ever aspire to. The definition of quality in education is for philosopher-kings and not for children, parents or teachers!

This approach is no longer acceptable, appropriate or desirable. Changing social expectations, the concept of 'rights' being expressed in practical terms, the emergence of a culture of expectation where customer needs are paramount, mean that institutions have to be in a dynamic interaction with those for whom they are created to provide a service. The shift is from quality as an ideal to be attained to quality as a relationship to be managed. For industry and commerce, and increasingly for the public sector, TQM represents a powerful means of meeting this challenge. It is not possible to list all the organizations involved in the quality movement; evidence of increasing activity is to be found in the number of companies seeking BS 5750 accreditation, the number of public bodies adopting TQM, the increasing levels of training provided and the volume of literature available. It will be for the reader to decide how far it is an appropriate response for schools and colleges. TQM has three crucial features which distinguish it from other theories of managing. Firstly, it is holistic, it permeates every aspect of an organization, every relationship and every process. It therefore offers an integrity and coherence which is lacking in most other models. Secondly, it is value driven: TQM places fundamental significance on values and purpose. It therefore introduces a moral imperative into management which would seem necessary in the context of the education of children and young people. Thirdly, it is about managing the interpersonal components of all organizations and equally acknowledges the interdependence between an organization and its environment.

THE NATURE OF TQM

The pedigree of TQM can be traced to the work of two Americans, Deming and Juran. Both approached the issue of quality from a background of statistics used in manufacturing processes in the engineering industry. Their work was first widely adopted in Japan, 'discovered' in the USA in the late 1970s and subsequently (as often is the case) in Britain in the early 1980s. Deming and Juran extended the original base of their work into all aspects of organizational management and their foundations have been built on by a number of practitioner–writers, notably Crosby (1979). The impact of their ideas can be found in the origins of manufactured goods in households and garages across Britain, for the dominance of imported consumer goods, notably Japanese in origin, can be largely explained in terms of quality.

There is not a single, homogeneous theory of TQM. The 'gurus' and their disciples have produced sets of precepts which are broadly in accord but differ in significant respects. Most importantly TQM has to evolve in response to the needs, context and values of a specific organization. There will therefore be significant differences between an engineering company and an airline, a retail organization and public sector activities in the way in which TQM is interpreted and applied. However, certain fundamental principles will remain constant and these can be identified by synthesizing the key imperatives of the originators of TQM:

(1) The definition of quality is that of the customer, not the supplier.

(2) Customers are defined as anyone who receives a product or service, i.e. they are internal and external to the organization and not just the 'person who pays'.
(3) Quality consists of meeting stated needs, requirements and standards.
(4) Quality is achieved by the prevention of work that does not meet standards; not by the detection of failure but by continuously improving the service or product.
(5) The move to quality is driven by senior management but is the responsibility of all those in the organization; quality has to be 'built in' to every process.
(6) Quality is measured by statistical processes, the cost of quality is the cost of non-conformance with stated requirements, the 'gap' between expectation and delivery.
(7) The most powerful vehicle for ensuring quality relationships is the effective team.
(8) Education and training are fundamental to the quality organization.

These components demonstrate the factors in understanding the relationship between TQM and quality control and quality assurance. Quality control is a well-established practice in most industrial concerns; it involves monitoring, checking and controlling, i.e. inspection. Control is a historic activity: it takes place after the event and is carried out by a third party, not the producer. Responsibility is therefore removed from the person who actually makes the product. Quality assurance by contrast is anticipatory: standards and procedures are clearly defined in advance and the worker is trained to be able to meet them. This approach is best exemplified in BS 5750 which defines the processes deemed necessary to operate quality systems and deliver products which conform to customer requirements. TQM builds on quality assurance by extending the principles to every aspect of organizational life and not just the manufacturing or service process. TQM recognizes and respects the potential of every individual to be more than the extension of an operating procedure. It also stresses the need for individual autonomy, the need to feel in personal control and not a victim. Workers know *what* they have to produce but are able to decide for themselves *how* to produce it. TQM organizations outperform their rivals because they are better at identifying and meeting customer requirements and because they recognize that employees are customers with requirements as much as the recipients of products and services.

THE COMPONENTS OF TQM

Managing for total quality requires the integration of a complex range of interacting factors. These are shown in Figure 4.1.

The customer

In the TQM organization the customer or client is defined as the person or group in receipt of a product or service. Thus the customer is not external to

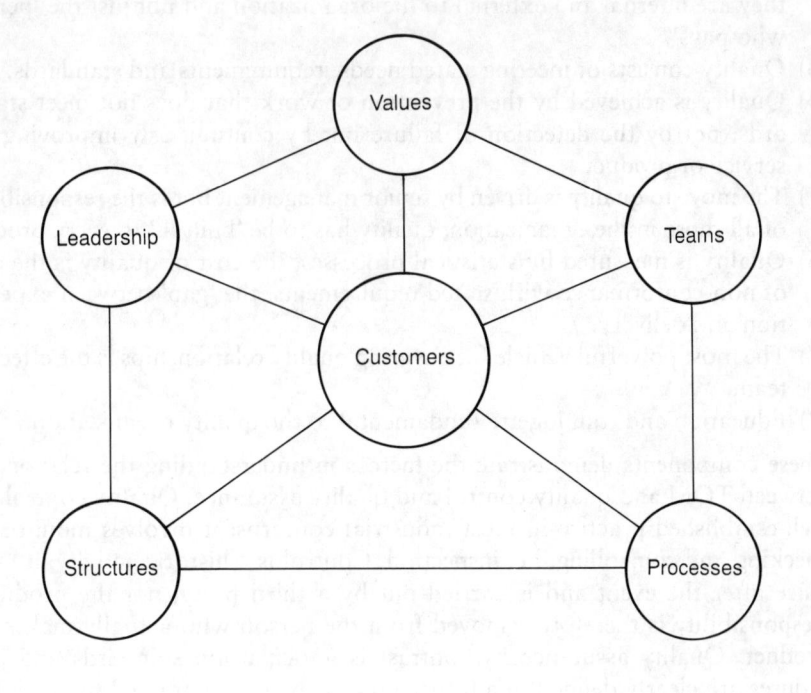

Figure 4.1 The components of TQM

the organization but exists at every stage required to complete the manufacture of a product or delivery of a service. The most potent image is that of the 'chain' of customers, linked together by the process. Each 'sub-unit' or link exists only in relationship to other links; interdependence is the hallmark of TQM organizations.

Managing for quality requires organizations to find out customer requirements by asking and listening. TQM requires listening organizations which ask the right questions of the right people and then act on the replies. A further crucial concept is that the organization only exists for its customers, it has no other purpose or justification. Many TQM companies have statements of philosophy which argue that quality comes before profit – the logic is simple: if customer needs are met then profitability is inevitable. TQM companies are obsessive about customer care and satisfaction because they have established a correlation between customer satisfaction, reducing costs and enhancing profitability.

In practical terms this means obtaining regular feedback to ensure that services are as required, for example that school prospectuses are written in appropriate language, teaching strategies are relevant and reports provide significant data. This implies regular monitoring and evaluation at each stage of the provision of a product or service.

Values

What distinguishes TQM organizations from others is the emphasis on, and significance attached to, the values of the organization and the way in which the vision is communicated and permeates working relationships. Research in the commercial and educational sectors confirms that the most successful organizations have explicit and shared values which are not moral abstractions but the basis for decision-making and action. Mission is central to total quality management in that it:

- provides a sense of direction and purpose,
- acts as a unifying factor,
- provides criteria for decision-making,
- articulates values,
- ensures consistency of purpose,
- defines customers,
- characterizes the organization to its community,
- provides challenge and motivation.

One of the most powerful features of TQM is its high ethical content and the way in which principle is the basis for practice. Schools and colleges almost always have aims and objectives, the issue is how far they are used as the basis for decision-making, notably in budget planning.

Leadership

If moral integrity is fundamental to TQM then leadership is the means by which it is expressed. Leadership is defined in the context of TQM as providing and driving the vision. TQM draws a sharp distinction between leading, managing and administering. Quality leadership has the following components.

(1) Vision: this is the clear view as to where the organization is going – the values, hopes and aspirations are actively communicated and used as the basis for action. Vision is not the monopoly of leadership but it is their primary responsibility to articulate it.

(2) Creativity: in order to make the vision live, leadership has to be creative; to find solutions to problems, to unravel complexity, to analyse rather than describe and to generate solutions that address the issue. Thinking is therefore a crucial leadership activity.

(3) Sensitivity: this is a problematic area but in essence quality leadership is about the quality of personal relationships, consistency of behaviour and providing a personal model which is expressed in very specific skills: active listening, giving feedback, negotiating, giving praise, managing conflict, networking and empathizing.

(4) Empowerment: a fundamental characteristic of leadership in the context of TQM is the need to release the potential of individuals, allowing them to

flourish and grow as people rather than as employees – to release their capacity for infinite improvement. Empowerment is given practical expression through delegation and training which allow the individual to develop personal responsibility and control. In essence the person is trusted through a belief in their capacity for growth.

(5) Managing change: the quality leader loves change, recognizes it as the abiding and dominant social dynamic and leads the organization so as to become changing rather than changed. This involves the creation of a learning organization which shifts from reaction to anticipation and which emphasizes appropriate behaviour as the basis for responding to the environment. The TQM organization integrates personal development into organizational development by enhancing personal capability. Leadership is not about preserving the status quo.

The leader of the TQM organization is, in essence, concerned about values and people, setting the direction and allowing people to achieve targets, being concerned with the macro and the micro. The issue for education is the extent to which leadership is differentiated from management and administration. Torrington and Weightman (1989) discuss the problem in terms of the secondary school deputy head who spends 40% of her time on administration – which is defined as work that can be done by an intelligent 16-year-old. Management, by contrast, is concerned with implementing the vision, with translating principles into practice through planning, delegating, monitoring, budgeting and developing.

Teams

A team is a quality group. All the literature on teams stresses the importance of clarity of purpose and effective interpersonal relationships as the basis for effective teamwork. Both in theory and practice teams are seen as fundamental to the management of quality in organizations. Effective teams display the following characteristics:

- Explicit and shared values; the team has a common vocabulary and sense of direction.
- Situational leadership; the team is sufficiently mature to base leadership on function and need rather than power and status, skills are more important than hierarchical factors.
- Commitment; there is pride in team membership.
- Clear task; the outcome that the team is created to achieve is clear, realistic and understood.
- Review; effective teams learn and develop by a process of continuous feedback and review.
- Openness; teams achieve a high level of candour in review and exchange.
- Collaboration; decisions are shared and have full commitment.
- Action; quality teams make things happen.

Effective teams balance task and process – they get the job done, improve personal relationships and enhance individual members.

Quality circles are one of the best-known manifestations of the TQM movement. In essence they are teams established as part of the work process to improve operating procedures. Too often teams in schools and colleges are historical accidents and little thought is given to their composition or development. There is often a substantial emphasis on task with little recognition of the importance of social issues.

Processes

A key feature of managing for quality is defining the components of work processes. This is where BS 5750 is particularly relevant. In essence, once customer requirements have been established then it is necessary to set up processes and procedures to ensure conformity to those requirements. In one sense it is necessary to minimize variation from the desired norm. BS 5750 identifies the following components of managing processes:

- Systems should be established to manage all processes with the emphasis on prevention.
- Documentation should be produced including a quality manual which outlines procedures in detail and establishes record-keeping systems.
- The system should incorporate a feedback mechanism to facilitate customer responses.
- Quality audits should take place to verify the implementation of the procedures.

In practical terms this means the specifying of 'correct procedures' (and the training necessary to implement them) so that conformance to requirements is an inevitable outcome rather than an aspiration. The way in which processes are managed centres on measurement. Measurement is used to ensure conformity to standards, to identify the cost of deviation and to monitor the efficiency of any improvements made to the process. Improving work processes is the means by which quality is delivered, processes are worked on to ensure that they produce goods and services which are closer to customer requirements and so add value. The cost of quality is not the cost of improving processes but the cost of not conforming to customer requirements. The management of this process is a useful exemplification of TQM in action, the most appropriate people to take the decisions about improving processes are those who are 'closest to the customer'. Thus the appropriate procedures are defined by those who have the responsibility to implement them but working to clear organizational guidelines. This principle is usefully illustrated by Handy (1990) who refers to the 'inverted do'nut'. The solid core of the do'nut is tightly specified and explicitly defines that which must be done. The outer ring is available for discretion, interpretation and local initiative. It is the outer ring which allows for individual and team autonomy whilst ensuring consistency and conformity to organizational goals and values.

The management of the quality process has to take into account three factors:

(1) The identification and communication of customer requirements.
(2) The identification and communication of demands on the supplier.
(3) The provision of skills, resources and procedures necessary to complete the process.

Unless the 'links in the chain' are clear the process cannot function. Education is very good at defining some key processes, notably the curriculum; management processes are not always as well established. The results of SATs and examinations can be used to modify teaching strategies as they can provide diagnostic data. If management processes are to be improved then there is a need to develop quantifiable outcomes which facilitate analysis of meetings, budgets, training, etc.

Structures

Organizations which attempt to introduce TQM without reviewing their structure are probably doomed to failure. Few organizations have structures which are customer focused, they tend to be based on formal hierarchies bound together by bureaucratic working practices.

The customer is often a 'nuisance', getting in the way of the machine running smoothly. The TQM organization aspires to meet the following criteria:

• The whole organization is 'close' to the customer, suppliers talk directly to clients.
• Effective work teams are used as the basis for the structure rather than as incidental to it.
• The structure facilitates real delegation, teams and individuals are allowed maximum control of their work.
• The structure is a practical manifestation of the values of the organization.

The theoretical structure of the quality organization resembles a coalition of autonomous teams able to interact directly with customers and with each other, all linked to senior management teams responsible for strategy. However, the centre holds only as much power as is necessary – authority and responsibility are delegated by senior management to teams commensurate with the task they have to do. There is no one model for the structure of a quality organization; what is important is that the structure should facilitate task and process.

Most large schools and colleges work on a hierarchical structure; it is difficult to identify the educational, professional or management rationale for such an approach. The curriculum is delivered by subject teams. Schools and colleges function, usually, by problem-solving coalitions that come together for a specific purpose. Quality organizations seek to reconcile form and function by having structures that reflect the reality of working relationships. The parallel structures for academic and pastoral systems in secondary schools are a classic example of form not matching function; most schools would argue that the academic and pastoral processes and structures are interdependent yet the actual organizational pattern denies this.

TQM IN THE CONTEXT OF EDUCATION

It is difficult to find a neat categorization of TQM in terms of theoretical models. Its origins are very much in an analysis of perceived success and the extrapolation of the factors contributing to that success. The model might therefore be conceived of as a pragmatic one, i.e. theory is derived from practice and does not require intellectual legitimation. Indeed writers on quality frequently warn against the dangers of an overly 'acadmic' response to the principles enunciated; there are frequent cautions against 'paralysis by analysis'. TQM is perceived as management in action and organizational effectiveness is the sole legitimation.

There is, as yet, very little empirical evidence available on the impact of quality approaches in schools and colleges. Samuels (1991) provides useful indicators of some areas of school management that lend themselves to a TQM approach:

- the experience of pupils when taken by a supply teacher,
- the impact of the homework policy,
- consistency in entry criteria for the sixth form,
- heads of department being responsible for their work areas,
- response times for repairs and maintenance.

However, in reviewing the applicability of TQM to the education service it is helpful to see how it relates to existing analytical models. In its stress upon organizational goals, the central importance of leadership and the importance of establishing systems to manage processes TQM coincides with the formal models of management outlined by Bush (1986). However, the applicability of the bureaucratic model is immediately challenged by the emphasis on teams, social processes and the empowering and developmental model of leadership. There is no doubt that the individual is subordinated to the organization in terms of values but the TQM organization then accepts the need to secure the commitment and personal involvement of the individual, i.e. there is no question of denying personal integrity. There is also a recognition that values are only given expression through individual action.

The emphasis on teams raises the issue of democratic and collegial models. The criteria for effective teams are highly reminiscent of the characteristics of collegiality as outlined by Bush (1986). The requirement for open decision-making, and the emphasis on individual responses to the organization all appear to locate TQM firmly in a human relations view of management. It may well be that TQM represents the next generation of thinking in management theory where the criteria are practical rather than ideological. TQM represents a form of conceptual pluralism, i.e. it does not derive all of its components from a single theoretical base but rather takes its premises from elements of models which meet the empirical requirements derived from quality organizations.

In this sense TQM is very attractive to most organizations because it is not culturally specific; it can evolve in response to the particular circumstances assuming that there is a supplier–customer relationship. Thus TQM is operating in Japan, the USA, Germany and Britain. It is operating successfully in giant car manufacturers, hospital accident and emergency units, charitable organizations, local government, etc. It would therefore seem possible that it might apply to schools and colleges. Although there are no detailed evaluations of TQM in education available there are some helpful parallels to draw on. Hopkins (1987) identifies a range of factors which characterize effective schools:

- curriculum-focused leadership,
- supportive climate,
- emphasis on learning,
- clear goals and high expectations,
- monitoring performance,
- continuous staff development,
- parental involvement,
- LEA support.

Fullan (1985) stresses the importance of process issues in developing effective schools, i.e. leadership as a process, consensual value systems, sophisticated social interactions and collaborative planning. The links between these approaches and the principles outlined in Figure 4.1 are clear and would seem to reinforce the view that the principles of TQM are already available to schools, however implicitly.

However, there are a number of possible objections to TQM in the education service, especially schools and colleges:

(1) Professional autonomy – 'no person is an island but teachers come pretty close'. Teaching is often perceived of as an essentially solitary activity which therefore creates a high degree of individual control. Such an approach is clearly alien to the co-operative ethos of TQM. However, serious questions have to be raised as to the validity of this approach. The twinned requirements of the self-governing school and the national curriculum argue against the validity of the individualistic approach. Schools are increasingly having to respond as organizations and the management of the national curriculum requires high levels of integration and collaboration whilst preserving team and personal discretion.

(2) Managerialism – 'management is about conformity, education is about preparing the individual to live in a democratic society'. This view argues that education and management are inimical. As has been argued above, TQM is a process which derives its content and values from the needs of its clients. Thus TQM in a company producing luxury cars will be driven by

consumerism – in a school it needs to be driven by educational values. Indeed it could well be argued that the respect for the individual central to TQM is preferable to the reactive, *ad hoc*, routinized administration that passes for management in some educational institutions.

(3) The customer – there has always been a problem in defining whom education is for, the child? the parent? the taxpayer? the State? The TQM response is to accept all claims to client status. It is the process that defines the customer and accountability and not a debate between alternative value systems. Thus the child is the customer in the classroom, the parent is the customer for reporting procedures, the LEA, DES and HMI are equally customers in context. One of the problematics in applying TQM to education is how potential tensions between these customers might be reconciled.

(4) Problematic outcomes – if education is viewed as a liberal, humanizing, long-term and heuristic process then an objective-driven approach such as TQM seems alien. However, it could be argued that the educated person is as tangible a concept as the satisfied customer or the healthy patient. Ends are elusive but it is possible to identify specific processes and activities that contribute to the outcome. It is these that are managed. Creating a love of literature may be problematic but specifying texts to be read, in what sequence, what learning methods are appropriate, how to assess progress, etc., can all be planned, measured and reviewed.

Total Quality Management is as yet relatively untried in the public sector in Britain; in the USA it is increasingly a norm. A great deal of empirical work is necessary to understand just how relevant the approach is to schools and colleges. However, it does offer a systematic, holistic and value-driven approach which has the potential to be developed. The most cogent argument for adopting TQM is the extent to which existing practices are felt to be appropriate and successful for schools and colleges in an era of increasing institutional autonomy.

REFERENCES

Bush, T. (1986) *Theories of Educational Management*, Paul Chapman Publishing, London.
Crosby, P. (1979) *Quality is Free,* Mcgraw Hill, New York.
Handy, C. (1990) *Inside Organizations*, BBC, London.
Hopkins, D. (1987) *Improving the Quality of Schooling,* Falmer Press, Lewes.
Sallis, E. (1991) Total Quality Management and further education. Paper presented at the BEMAS conference, 1991.
Samuels, G. (1991) The Q-word in action, *Education*, 22 November, p. 412.
Shipman, M. (1990) *In Search of Learning*, Basil Blackwell, Oxford.
Torrington, D. and Weightman, J. (1989) *The Reality of School Management*, Basil Blackwell, Oxford.

PART 2:

Exploring Collegiality

5

RETHINKING COLLEGIALITY:
Teachers' Views
Penny Campbell and Geoff Southworth

This material has been abridged

INTRODUCTION

The virtues of collegiality have been broadcast for some time in both England and North America. Research studies investigating [. . .] school effectiveness reveal teacher participation and collaboration as key process factors (e.g. Purkey and Smith, 1983, 1985; Rosenholtz, 1985; Reid, Hopkins and Holly, 1987; Mortimore *et al.*, 1988). The quest for school improvement has also tended to underwrite the promotion of collegiality. As Lieberman (1986) says, 'schools cannot be improved without people working together'. In England and Wales too, throughout the 1980s (and before) policy statements, surveys, inspection reports and enquiries from central government, HM Inspectors of Schools, and other committees (e.g. DES, 1978, 1980, 1982, 1984; Welsh Office, 1985; ILEA, 1985; House of Commons, 1986; DES, 1987; Schools Council, 1981, 1983) have implied a reasonably consistent model of 'good' management practice. In essence this model is seen as a process where all professional staff participate actively in negotiating an agreed curriculum and contribute jointly to planning, implementing and evaluating its delivery (Wallace, 1988). The advent of a National Curriculum, following the 1988 Education Reform Act, has created many changes in schools but it does not reduce the perceived need for school-based collaborative developments. Indeed, the National Curriculum places a heavy burden of curriculum implementation upon primary schools and points towards the need for a collegial approach to management (Campbell, 1989). In other words, in the past and in the foreseeable future collegiality has been and continues to be the preferred and 'official' way for staff to manage the curriculum and develop the school.

Although collegiality has been persistently promoted as a concept it raises a number of questions and concerns which in this paper we want to explore. In the first section we will critically review the concepts of collegiality. In the next two sections we will draw upon two recent research projects, the Primary School Staff Relationships Project and the Whole School Curriculum Development Project, to see if empirical work concerned with how teachers worked together can provide insights into the nature of teacher collaboration and the role of the headteacher. In the conclusion we will outline how these two projects illuminate the concept of collegiality.

COLLEGIALITY: SOME QUESTIONS AND CONCERNS

First, those who advocate collegiality do so on the basis of prescription rather than description. Whilst in North America work has been undertaken (e.g. Little, 1982, 1987, 1989; Little and Long, 1985; Lieberman, 1986, 1988a), in England the closest we have to descriptions of collegiality is a single study examining effective junior schools and departments. Twelve key process factors were identified, four of which relate to collegiality:

(1) Purposeful leadership of the staff by the headteacher;
(2) The involvement of the deputy head;
(3) The involvement of teachers;
(4) Consistency amongst teachers.

(Mortimore *et al.*, 1988, pp. 250–1)

Mortimore's study is important since it suggests that collegiality may not be simply an act of faith, but it does not take us much further in answering the question, what does collegiality look like? In England, despite the clear value position of those who promote it, we still await a response to this question and, whilst we wait we need, as Hargreaves (1982) warns, to be wary of exhortatory accounts.

Second, the lack of empirical work is compounded by weak definitions. The term collegiality is often used as if its meaning was commonly understood (e.g. Tomlinson, 1986; Richards, 1986; Thomas, 1987) yet when scrutinized such writers mean only that teachers should 'work together'. Campbell provides a more focused view when he says 'collegiality implies delegation of curriculum leadership to members of staff with designated curriculum responsibilities – curriculum co-ordinators – and distinctive subject expertise' (Campbell, 1989). But this is a coarse-grained definition and, as Campbell acknowledges, is open to interpretation. Collegiality could mean many different things in different schools and with different colleagues.

Third, there is a need for greater analysis of the concepts connected with collegiality. Wallace (1988), for example, touches upon democracy, consultation, leadership, hierarchy and collaboration but at no point does he examine

them. Amongst some of these notions tensions exist as Bush (1986) and Southworth (1987a) have shown. Democracy and hierarchy, participation and control, leadership and collaboration do not necessarily sit easily alongside one
another. In the absence of case studies showing how these matters are resolved
'on the ground', in schools, we await a comprehensive analysis.

Fourth, those who prescribe collegiality tend to accentuate the presumed
advantages rather than the likely in-school obstacles to its implementation.
Writers who question collegiality note two sets of obstacles: time, and roles
(Alexander, 1984; Campbell, 1985; Bush, 1986; Southworth, 1987a). Time is
a problem because teachers in primary schools are almost always full-time
class teachers with virtually no non-contact time. Moreover, in smaller schools
(i.e. schools with fewer than 100 children on roll) headteachers are required to
teach a class of children. This lack of 'slack' in a school's staffing establishment
(acknowledged by an all-party House of Commons Select Committee on
'Achievement in Primary Schools' (1986)) effectively means teachers cannot
meet during teaching periods nor easily observe one another at work. Thus
teachers with delegated across-school responsibilities (e.g. to develop science
activities; implement a record-keeping system) must do so after school when
the teaching and learning have ceased. Although valuable work does occur
then (e.g. teacher meetings, workshops) opportunities for teachers to influence
one another's practice are impeded (Campbell, 1985).

Roles are an issue for several reasons. One is that collegiality is likely to
reduce the autonomy of individual teachers and headteachers. Headteachers
express concerns about the possibility that collegiality decentralizes authority
in the school. Traditionally primary school headteachers have regarded the
school as 'theirs' (Coulson, 1976; Alexander, 1984; Southworth, 1987a,
1988a) in ways similar to Wolcott's notion of a principal's sense of proprietary
interest in 'his' school (Wolcott, 1973). These feelings of ownership, when
coupled with the head's legal responsibilities mean that primary heads have a
'formidable concentration of power' (Alexander, 1984) which recent legislation (Education Acts 1986, 1988; DES, 1989) may have altered but not necessarily diminished. In our experience many heads perceive collegiality as
decreasing their power, typically because they no longer hold either the power
of veto or the prerogative of having the last word on everything. Moreover, it
should be recognized that what is at stake for a head is not just power but
identity. Given a head's close association and 'geo-identification' (Coulson,
1976) with the school alterations to who determines what happens in the
school may well affect a head's sense of professional identity. Consequently,
heads are faced not merely with a change of style but may be facing a change of
occupational self. How this will take place is far from clear. Miller and Lieberman (1982) regard changes in a principal's role as taking time and needing
support. Latterly, Lieberman (1988a) has said such changes will not take place
easily and will stir up some deeply rooted beliefs about leadership and relationships. Further, as Nias (1987a) argues, changes in occupational identity
involve feelings of losing control, anxiety and conflict. The closer the identification of the self with work the more these increase.

Collegiality also runs counter to the notion that decison-making in schools is 'zoned' (Lortie, 1969; Coulson, 1978): the teacher decides what happens in his/her classroom, the head decides on matters of general school policy and administration. Just as heads, for their part, may experience a loss of identity in a collegial school so too may teachers. Nias (1989) argues that primary school teaching is individualistic, solitary and personal and, as an occupation, teaching makes heavy demands upon the self. Shifts from working in closed isolated settings to more open and communal ones may change not only the school's culture (Lieberman, 1988a) but also teachers' conception of their work, whom they see as reference groups (Nias, 1985) and what it feels like to be a teacher (Nias, 1989). Whilst there is some evidence for saying that breaking the isolation of classrooms enables teachers to give and receive help and be better equipped for classroom work (Little, 1987; Lieberman, 1988b), attaining this state [. . .] appears to be difficult (Little, 1985). It involves overcoming ambivalences and uncertainties about acting as a leader/consultant to colleagues (Campbell, 1985; Lieberman, 1988a; Holly and Southworth, 1989). Also, working with colleagues and being, from time to time, expected to give a lead expands the work of a teacher: teaching becomes a dual role (Packwood, 1984; Campbell, 1985). Although there are signs that this dual role is now an expectation placed upon the great majority of teachers (House of Commons, 1986), working with colleagues remains for some teachers a new departure for which they may be ill-prepared and/or disposed. Whilst a 'mutual aid' construction of collegiality (Little, 1989) is appealing, how teachers develop such a pattern is not stated and looks to be far from straightforward.

Our fifth concern centres around the capacity of teachers to work in groups. The persistence of privacy in teaching (Little, 1989), and of heads feeling relatively independent in 'their' schools, is hardly the basis for developing group work. Collegiality not only asks teachers and heads to be less independent and more interdependent, it also implies that in becoming more interdependent teachers accept and learn to work together in collaborative groups. While at a general level the last twenty years have seen an increase in the numbers of staff meetings which now occur in schools this is not to say the capacity of staff to work productively in groups has necessarily altered dramatically. Experience from in-service courses we organize suggests that many staff meetings are passive information-giving events presided over by the headteacher. Interaction, a condition of groups (Chell, 1985), may be limited and the two zones of authority only nominally brought together within a group. Moreover, working together implies some measure of cohesion otherwise the 'group' will be an aggregate of individuals. How do independent teachers develop into cohesive groups? What 'glues' the group together? Are cohesive groups so homogeneous that they are cosy, self-referencing clubs? How might teachers learn from one another's differences?

This latter question has been posed by Nias (1987a). She believes groups can be powerful arenas for exposing people to different viewpoints, but to be fully effective as change agents they need to have certain characteristics. The group should be big enough to provide a diversity of views but small enough for everyone to be heard. Members must be mutually supportive but ready to challenge and disagree. They must be willing to accept responsibility for their own ideas. Their relationship must be as egalitarian as possible though the group is likely to have a leader who is willing to protect and encourage the free expression of views. The group will be long enough in existence and meet sufficiently often for challenge and change to take place. Nias goes on to say: 'Unfortunately neither teaching as an occupation nor schools as institutions favour the development of such groups', not least because potential conflict in primary school staff rooms tends to be treated as a pathological symptom rather than as a naturally occurring phenomenon the resolution of which can lead to personal and collective growth (Nias, 1987a; see also Pollard, 1985; Yeomans, 1985).

The belief that staff can always reach agreement over institutional purposes and policies lies at the heart of all participatory approaches (Bush, 1986). [. . .] Handy (1981, pp. 160–1) argues that groups develop in four successive stages: (1) forming; (2) storming; (3) norming; (4) performing. Although a group can perform at all stages of development it is only at stage four that Handy believes a group is sufficiently mature to be fully productive. Nias, too, has suggested that since group cohesion develops slowly it follows that collegiality too will take time to develop. Moreover, the length of time is likely to increase the more frequently the staff group's membership alters (e.g. staff turnover).

These five concerns outline our reservations about collegiality, particularly in terms of its general applicability for all schools. A sixth concern is that collegiality is recommended principally by those outside schools: researchers, advisers, consultants, HM Inspectors. Teachers' views on collegiality are not widely known. The absence of such evidence and of case studies of collegial schools raises several questions. What conditions in a school facilitate collegiality? Is it 'force-fed' or can it occur 'naturally'? What do teachers and headteachers think about collegiality? We need responses to such questions otherwise collegiality may become something which is imposed upon teachers: are teachers being worked on in order to work together?

This brief review suggests that collegiality is a hazy and imprecise notion. Even so, the idea continues to have currency and remains attractive (Campbell, 1989). The problem is that at present collegiality as advocated is more a matter of style than substance: behold the wood, the trees come later!

Against this background of questions and concerns two research projects were devised and based at the Cambridge Institute of Education: the Primary School Staff Relationships Project (PSSR) funded by the Economic and Social Research Council (ESRC) and the Cambridge Institute 1985–7; and the Whole School Curriculum Development Project (WSCD) funded wholly by the ESRC, 1988–90. We turn now to these to see how they help illuminate our understanding of collegiality.

PRIMARY SCHOOL STAFF RELATIONSHIPS PROJECT

At the outset of this project (PSSR), the research team (Jennifer Nias (director), Geoff Southworth, Robin Yeomans) were conscious that advocates of collegiality had not shown what this phenomenon looked like in practice. They therefore took a limited view and set out to provide first-hand accounts of how headteachers, teachers and other staff behaved when they 'worked together'. In the absence of any other fine-grained analysis of staff relationships, and the structures which shape and support them it was decided to limit the team's enquiries to schools where, in very loose terms, 'things were going well'. Further questions of definition were left unresolved. For one thing the team did not know and wanted to discover what staff themselves meant by 'working together'. The project did not set out to explore or report on classroom practice believing that the time and personnel that were available would be best employed in attempting to understand schools as settings in which adults work.

The enquiry was limited to five schools with between five and twelve teaching staff (including the headteacher) a secretary and at least one ancillary worker. Details of the research methodology are reported elsewhere (see Nias, 1987b; Southworth, 1987b; Yeomans, 1987). The enquiry was ethnographic with team members acting as participant observers. The team worked as part-time teachers, nominally for one day a week, in their host schools over the course of a school year (September 1985–July 1986). Towards the end of the year in school, all staff were interviewed, some more than once. At the close of the year's fieldwork, case studies were constructed based upon extensive field notes and interviews, the aim being to produce analytical studies rich in first-hand accounts. These studies were cleared with the schools' staff and then used for subsequent analysis and the identification of themes. The project findings have been published (see Nias, Southworth and Yeomans, 1989); what now follows is a brief summary with illustrations, of some of the findings relevant to this paper's topic.

The main concept to emerge from the five studies is that of 'organizational culture' where culture is loosely defined as 'the way we do it here', that is, as a set of norms about ways of behaving, perceiving and understanding. A culture is, however, underpinned by jointly held beliefs and values and symbolized for members of the culture by objects, rituals and ceremonies. Each of the five project schools had its own culture which embodied strongly held beliefs about the social and moral purposes of education and about the nature of effective educational practice. These beliefs originated with the headteachers. In three of the schools the head had worked for a long time in each school over ten years to develop and sustain an organizational culture the project team describe as a 'culture of collaboration'. This, it was felt, enabled the teaching and ancillary staff to work closely together in a natural, taken-for-granted way. In the other two schools the heads were endeavouring to develop a culture of collaboration but were impeded by conflicting values held by long-established staff members. Over the course of the year's fieldwork some key individuals (e.g. deputy headteacher, curriculum leaders) left each of these schools and this enabled the new and developing culture to become more firmly established, not least because in both schools it already existed in sub-groups.

A culture of collaboration

The culture of collaboration was built on four interacting beliefs: individuals should be valued but, because they are inseparable from the group of which they are part, groups too should be fostered and valued; the most effective ways of promoting these values are through a sense of mutual security and consequent openness. We will briefly look at each.

Valuing individuals as people

In the schools where a culture of collaboration existed, even the most mundane and apparently insignificant details of staff behaviour were consistent with its values. Respect for individuals occurred in many guises. There were few status distinctions, all staff used the staff room and joined in conversations and humour. Newcomers felt free to speak and valued, as one novitiate teacher said: 'They [the staff] treat me as an individual, here to do a job, not to be looked down upon or anything like that. I'm like anybody really.' Everyone who came to the schools was made welcome: '*Teacher (recently appointed)*: They [the staff] make everybody very welcome. It's marvellous and I like the way they've got time for parents and involve the parents a lot in the school . . . they care and that's what came across to me.' [. . .]

Valuing individuals for their contribution to others

In addition to respecting and nurturing others as individuals in their own right, heads, teachers and ancillaries in the collaborative schools perceived the differences between them as a mutually enriching source of collective strength: '*Teacher*: Working in a team doesn't mean that everybody's the same and everybody's so busy saying yes, yes, yes to one another that nothing happens. That deadens it. You've got to have different personalities and different ideas to spark other people off, but it can be done without aggression.' [. . .]

Everyone's contribution to the school was valued. Gratitude and appreciation were regularly and openly expressed. 'It's never taken for granted and it's never left to just one teacher – all staff make the point of expressing their appreciation to whoever they are thanking.' [. . .]

Valuing interdependence – belonging to a group

Individual staff members at three of the schools valued one another as people, each with his/her own identity, personality, interests, skills, experiences and potential. Yet they also appreciated the diversity which this brought to the school. Likewise, interdependence has two aspects. Together the members of each staff made a group which was valued because it provided a sense of belonging. At the same time they accepted a collective responsibility for the work of the school so creating a sense of team in which staff helped, encouraged and substituted for one another: [. . .] '*Teacher*: There's a great deal of warmth between us and it's almost like a family that closes ranks against outsiders when it's being attacked by a piece of gossip or an occasion of vandalism.'

Valuing interdependence – working as a team

Whilst group membership was effectively satisfying it was not the whole story since in the three collaborative schools staff also felt a sense of collective responsibility for their work and saw themselves as a team. One head wrote in a school document: 'We feel that the consideration and closeness which characterizes relationships between adult members pervades the school as a whole. Thus issues like infant–junior department liaison are less important than the sense of the school as a whole' (Curriculum Award Folder).

Being a 'team' meant to recognize and value the unique contribution of each member to a joint enterprise. It did not necessarily mean doing the same job nor working in the same teaching space but it did mean working to the same ends.

The sense of collective responsibility showed itself in many ways. Most noticeable was the habitual way in which everyone advised, supported and helped one another.

Teacher: If you say 'I'm doing such and such, I haven't got any good ideas', there will be six or seven different ideas thrown at you instantly. Or if you get halfway through doing something and you happen to say 'Oh, it's not working', or 'It's going wrong', there's always someone who is willing to help in any sort of situation. And in dealing with the children you never feel, if you have a problem, that you're cut off, there's always somebody else who is willing to help you. It's often the case [in other schools that] there is someone around who is capable of helping, but not always that they will help, but in this school that doesn't seem to be so. Everyone seems very ready to help.

Teamwork meant sharing success as well as concerns. The staff were as ready to show and tell one another what they were proud of as they were to seek help, as prepared to accept praise as they were to give it [. . .]

[. . .] on competitive lines, in a way. People work individually, they resolve problems in the classroom individually and the tensions that arise by controlling children . . . . I think that people here do work not to be like that . . . there is an awareness that you don't need to be like that in a school. I can think of a lot of instances where people haven't been concerned about their status and their position in that sort of way . . . . People here consciously try not to be like that.
Leader of visiting German party to Isabel (the head): In Germany we have competitions in schools to see who has the most beautiful classroom. Could you do that in your school?
Isabel: No, it wouldn't work here. We work as a team and try to support each other.

(Fieldnote: June)

A sense of shared endeavour could even override the traditional and treasured relationship between teachers and their classes:

> Mention was made at one point of a child and I said to Jane, 'Is that your Sarah? I nearly said "our" meaning to identify myself with her because I'd just spent a week in her classroom.' She said, 'No, do say "our", I never think of a child as mine.'

(Fieldnote: March)

Individuals adjusted their plans in response to the needs of others. Flexibility was common: '*Ancillary*: If anybody sees that something needs doing, they will do it. It's not generally one person that does it. We all do it, if we see that something needs doing, whoever sees it will do it.' Staff also accepted collective responsibility for communications. [. . .]

Valuing security

This belief and the next are linked. Security is a condition for the growth of openness and openness is the best way of simultaneously fostering the individual and the group. They are connected by a notion of interdependence which meant mutual constraint as well as enrichment. To accept as all the staff did that one is dependent on anyone else is to admit that there are limits to one's autonomy. Limits operated in various ways, spoken and unspoken, but, whatever their nature or extent, acceptance of them was mandatory:

> *Teacher*: To work here you'd have to be prepared to work as part of this team. If you persisted in not being part of a team you could exist here but you wouldn't be happy. You could make it but not in any satisfying sense . . . . If you're not prepared to submit, in the Biblical sense, you're not going to be an effective team member. But once you can see it's in the best interests of the children, it's easy.

Though to submit is to accept another's power over oneself, when all members of a team do so their power over each other is evenly balanced and becomes influence instead. So within a situation of agreed interdependence: '*Teacher*: We're all influencing each other, I'm quite convinced of that.' However, an exception to this was the headteacher since staff in the collaborative schools deferred to their heads. In part this can be explained by the fact that the beliefs underlying that 'culture of collaboration' emanated from and were exemplified by the heads of the three schools. Since all staff agreed with these beliefs the heads enjoyed a degree of personal authority which transcended that of other staff. Also, staff generally accepted the role of head and were willing to defer to their head's positional power. Third, primary heads and teachers are members not just of their schools but also of an occupation which traditionally sets store by its members' ability to control pupils and which is in addition hierarchically structured: teachers exercise authority over others but are often themselves authority dependent (Abercrombie, 1981; Nias, 1987a). In other words, the 'culture of collaboration' coexisted in the project schools within a wider occupational culture which seemed to limit the extent to which teachers expected to be able to influence their heads and which sustained the heads' expectation to be the first amongst equals.

The fact that the heads' responsibility for the main policies in their schools was virtually unchallenged and that staff exercised a good deal of mutual influence over one another made the collaborative schools very secure places in which to work.

Valuing openness

Many of the day-to-day attitudes and actions of the staff demonstrated the value they attached to openness. Heads, teachers and ancillaries were ready to admit publicly to a sense of failure:

> *Teacher*: In the other schools I've taught in you *didn't* fail. If you did you kept it very quiet. It took me a good four months when I came here to realize that . . . when you had problems you didn't hide them away, you voiced them and you got them sorted out instantly instead of taking them home and worrying about them.

Staff were also ready to display other negative emotions, such as guilt, anxiety and anger. And it was regarded as normal for individuals to voice irritation or dissent directly to one another. Disagreements were accepted as part of life: '*Teacher*: Differences of opinion do emerge but we're all very open, straightforward. If we don't agree with someone we do say so. You know, you just state that you didn't agree and that you thought such and such . . . it doesn't need to be argument.' [. . .]

Headteachers

An important aspect of organizational culture was the work of the headteachers. We note earlier how staff in the collaborative schools accepted their head's authority. Staff also acknowledged and conceded the heads' proprietary interest in the schools: '*Teacher*: I would say he (the head) is the school.' And staff understood that their respective heads had a sense of mission: '*Teacher*: Graham (the head) has these beliefs that have filtered through the whole school, the whole staff.' As a result the heads were founders of the schools' culture (see also Schein, 1985; Sergiovanni, 1984).

The heads developed and sustained the culture via their own sense of example (e.g. teaching, taking assemblies, dealings with staff), positive reinforcement and careful selection of staff when opportunities to recruit arose. The heads were also keenly aware of what was happening daily in 'their' schools and demonstrated a 'dedicated obsessiveness' (Coulson, 1976) with all aspects of the school's life and work. Moreover, because they were frequently touring the school and present in the staff room, talking, listening, joining in with the teaching and planning, they were members of the staff group. They could simultaneously occupy two positions, leader and member, and this prevented them from being aloof and isolated from the staff. [. . .]

Although there was an asymmetrical distribution of power between the head and staff, just as with teachers and pupils in classrooms, to be less powerful is not to be powerless. Heads and staff negotiated a 'working consensus' (Pollard, 1985) which involved some degree of accommodation to each other's interests. Thus, it was no surprise that the heads negotiated – both explicitly and implicitly – and sought compromises. However, the heads were only prepared to compromise on some things. They would not, for instance, alter their most deeply and strongly held beliefs. This would, presumably, have been too injurious to the head's professional identity. Therefore, negotiation occurred within the parameters of each head's professional convictions. Similarly, compromises were reached in order to preserve the self-image of individual staff. Negotiations were often subtle, coded, and tacit and 'truces' were sometimes struck. The heads also had to be skilled in keeping negotiations 'open' so that fresh compromises could be later reached as and when circumstances allowed.

On the basis of the evidence from PSSR the following points can be made about collegiality. Where teachers worked well together they did so within an organizational culture which was founded on shared beliefs and values. These originated with the headteachers and determined the nature of the social relationships within the schools. Because of this the heads neither lost their personal sense of identity nor was their authority diminished. It seemed clear that the close social relationships which were characteristic of schools where such an organization culture existed were highly valued by teachers and were seen by them as an important component of working together. However, it seemed that, in some schools, good working relationships existed amongst teachers with different aims whilst, in others, teachers worked productively to implement shared curricular goals and agreed policies. Similarly social cohesion appeared to lead in some schools, but not in others, to curricular growth. There was no unambiguous connection between positive staff relationships and whole school curricular planning or development. It was clear from this that there was a need to explore, firstly, the ways in which teachers worked together to agree and implement policy and, secondly, the nature and importance of social cohesion and leadership to curriculum development. It was out of these concerns that the Whole School Curriculum Development and Staff Relations in Primary Schools Project evolved.

WHOLE SCHOOL CURRICULUM DEVELOPMENT PROJECT

This research set out to identify and study the formal and informal ways in which curricular decisions were made and implemented, and the location and nature of curricular and social leadership. In addition we intended to examine whether agreement to implement specific curricular policies had any effect upon pupil's learning experiences. We hoped this would enable us to provide further analysis of the concept of collegiality.

The research team (Jennifer Nias, Geoff Southworth, Penelope Campbell) worked as part-time teachers in five schools during the academic year 1988–9 and used the same research methodology as that of the Primary School Staff Relationships Project already described. [. . .] By this time we were aware that teachers rarely used the word 'collegiality' amongst themselves, but we wanted to gain some more insight into what they understood by the concept so at the end of most interviews we posed two related questions. They were: What do you think a 'whole school' is? Is this school a 'whole school'? We hoped these would give the teachers the opportunity to talk about the ideals and realities of working together without predetermining the content of their responses. The term 'whole school' was deliberately chosen. Though not coterminous with 'collegiality', it was felt to be a term to which the teachers were likely to ascribe a related meaning. Their responses to the questions might therefore be expected to throw light on their understanding of what it means to work collegially. This analysis draws substantially upon the teachers' replies to these two questions in an early attempt to fulfil the third of the intentions cited above, namely, to provide a further analysis of the concept of collegiality.

It seems that there are seven interrelated components to teachers' understanding of the notion of 'whole school'. Each of them relates in some way to the developing notion of collegiality. The categories are: purposing the same, working together, having a sense of community, getting on with one another, acknowledging individuality, knowing what's going on in the school generally, having an effective leader. The categories are listed according to the number of times they were mentioned by teachers. This should not be taken necessarily to imply that the category of 'purposing the same' is of greatest and the category of effective leadership of least importance in the minds of teachers.

Purposing the same

This category encompasses the beliefs, intentions and actions of all the teachers within the school. References to each of these were often impossible to separate from one another and they clearly related to shared curricular goals.

Teachers felt that it was important that they should have compatible ideals, agree the same aims and share the same purpose. '*Teacher*: To me a "whole school" is one when every single person shares . . . compatible ideals and moves towards them.' '*Teacher*: If you are aiming for a "whole school" . . . then everybody has got to agree about aims and purpose.' [. . .] The outworking of this in a 'whole school' could be found, the teachers seemed to be saying, in common policies and consistent approaches. '*Teacher*: I suppose everybody is thinking basically the same so that there is a "whole school" approach to things like general aims, a "whole school" approach to parents, a "whole school" approach to . . . multi-cultural issues . . . behaviour . . . special needs, those sort of things that run throughout the curriculum.' [. . .]

Working together

Although the teachers in our study commonly used the phrase 'working to-gether' to describe what they felt to be a major characteristic of a 'whole school' it was clear that they did not necessarily share the same meaning. 'Working together' could mean as little, in practice, as coping in a crisis. '*Teacher*: I know there is friction with the staff, but I think if there is a time when we all have to pull together we do.' Or it could mean the ideal of shared responsibility and commitment. '*Teacher*: It's the goal of everybody . . . giving as much and everybody as much in charge as everybody else.'

More commonly it was used to describe involvement in decision-making, participation in the formulation and implementation of policy and a willing-ness to place the common good before personal interests.

> *Teacher*: Everyone within that environment is contributing to decision, to practice, to policy. . . . Everybody concerned with [the school], with the children, owns the practice . . . because they have contributed, and are continuing to contribute, to it in terms of decision-making and in terms of managing, in terms of operating. . . . It's a very high level of participation.

> *Teacher*: It's working together as a team, being able to share ideas in order to help each other, which will give . . . [a school] . . . its strength because you can't develop anything in isolation. [. . .]

The headteacher played what was apparently a crucial role in establishing and sustaining the nature of these working relationships.

> *Teacher*: The whole school ethos about being together as a group and sharing things was very strong and extremely important. . . . There must be something about the way Ella has wanted to work and what she values. . . . She's wanted the staff . . . working more on an informal level together to create some sort of sharing which she's consciously sought . . . and that's brought some sort of whole school being together . . . and . . . the informality encouraged parents to feel part of the school so that the children were in an atmosphere where they saw parents and teachers working together as partners.

Having a sense of community

Many of the teachers had a sense of the school as a community. Some of them sought to identify the members of this community. None limited their conception to the teaching staff even when they understood the phrase 'whole school' to refer to those with formal responsibility. At the least they included non-teaching staff, most commonly included parents as well and sometimes governors and children. '*Teacher*: It's all children, all staff and all the parents and governors, and when I say all the staff I mean the caretaker, the cleaners, the kitchen staff, everybody.' Some also included the community of which the school was a part. '*Teacher*: It should really be the community as well, shouldn't it? Because we've had people come in and contribute. We go out and give things to them.' [. . .] All this promoted feelings of identification, ownership and pride among the members of the community. '*Teacher*: Everyone who's involved with the school feeling that it's their school . . . that they can identify with the school.' [. . .]

Getting on with one another

Though this category is clearly related to the previous one, it is subtly different. It is not to do with who belongs to the community but with how well the members of the community get on with one another. Though teachers spoke primarily of the personal and professional relationships existing between themselves, these ideally extended to all the members of the community. '*Teacher*: It's how we react with one another . . . . It's . . . relationships, personal as well as profession-al.' The central importance of getting on with one another was related to the effective functioning of the school. '*Teacher*: The schools function best where the relationships are good – that really is the crux of it.' [. . .]

Acknowledging individuality

Whenever teachers made comments about the importance of valuing the individuals within a school it was within the context of the contribution each made to the corporate work of the school. '*Teacher*: Whole school? It's a collection of individuals using their skills, expertise and enthusiasms in whatever way they can to benefit the community.'

The teachers seemed to think that individuals should have the opportunities to voice their opinions, to participate in decision-making processes, to make their own contribution to the work of the school by fulfilling a unique role, to develop their own expertise and to exercise a degree of autonomy over their own classroom practice. [. . .]

One headteacher felt that the exercising of personal autonomy within the classroom might be associated with successful 'whole school' development.

> *Teacher*: I wonder whether successful whole school development doesn't actually require a degree of autonomy for it to be successful . . . . I think they've got to feel probably that they are able to make a worthwhile and recognized contribution in the eyes of other people with whom they are working . . . and at the same time they've got to feel that they're able to achieve an individual status for themselves in the day-to-day classroom practice. The two go together. I'm certain they do.

Knowing what's going on

Teachers felt that part of being a 'whole school' was having a knowledge of the school that transcended the individual's own classroom boundaries and encompassed the practice of colleagues. [. . .]

This required two things of them as individuals – a willingness to learn what was happening elsewhere in the school and a willingness to be open about their own practice. [. . .]

The consequence of this was that they shared ideas and offered suggestions. '*Teacher*: Sitting in the staff room people talk about what they're going to do and people do come up with suggestions.' [. . .]

Having an effective leader

The picture of a 'good' headteacher which emerged from the teachers' comments on a 'whole school' was of a person to whom they could talk and with whom they could discuss, who did not dictate, who was effectively a part of the staff group and whose philosophy was clear and shared by colleagues. '*Teacher*: Have a good leader that you can talk to and discuss things with.' '*Teacher*: I know schools where the head's turned round and said, "You've got to do this". That isn't the feeling here.' [. . .]

What emerges from this analysis is that collegiality, in the eyes of these English primary school teachers, ideally has to do with both working and feeling together. It supports the findings of the PSSR project that there is an effective component of working together which teachers value and find satisfying. They express the warm feelings they experience in family or community terms. The WSCD project found that these feelings of satisfaction were often related not only to shared beliefs about the ways in which people should behave towards one another, but also to shared beliefs about educational goals. Teachers expressed this in terms of sharing the same aims and moving in the same direction.

CONCLUSION

At the end of the previous two sections we have made links with each project's findings and some of our initial questions and concerns. In this section we want to outline how the two projects illuminate the notion of collegiality. The PSSR and WSCD projects show a group of schools scattered along a continuum which stretches from independence to interdependence. The idea of a continuum comes from Little (1989) who offered it in a provisional sense to illustrate her thinking at the time. We too want to adopt it in a provisional way. The continuum helps to show that in schools where staff are trying to work collaboratively there is a movement away from independent to interdependent activity (although the latter does not exclude scope for independence). However, we believe that movement along the continuum does not occur on a single strand. Rather, we conceive the continuum as being composed of several strands. We say this because the projects suggest four component strands to collaboration. There may be others but our evidence suggests:

- personal relationships (e.g. social interaction and cohesion);
- professional relationships (e.g. paired teaching, working parties, curricular leaders);
- social and moral intentions (e.g. beliefs about behaviour, pupil discipline);
- curriculum intentions (e.g. curriculum policy statements).

These four, as WSCD shows, interweave and interrelate. We find it helpful to think in terms of strands because knowledge of the ten schools in the two projects suggests that each school was at a different point on each strand. For example, one school might be well along the personal relationships and social and moral intention strands but not so far along the other two.

However, 'movement' on the continuum will not necessarily mean progress from one pole towards its opposite. Our work in the schools also leads us to say that movement will involve some backwards and forwards motions as staff collectively and individually make accommodation for changes in attitude, disposition and personnel. 'Progress' on the continuum is dynamic and involves a sense of tension because schools are not static places (Nias, Southworth and Yeomans, 1989).

To say that the strands interrelate is not to say we know how each affects the other. At the end of PSSR we were unclear as to how the culture of collaboration influenced classroom practice though we hope analysis of WSCD will offer some insights. Nor do we know if there is any 'sequence' to adopt: is it, for example, efficacious to emphasize professional relations before or after personal ones? Also, it is not possible to predict what classroom practice is affected by relationships and intentions.

Our use of the term intentions is deliberate insofar as we wanted to show that underpinning moves to collaboration are beliefs. Collaboration relies not only on the ability of staff to meet together and share equipment and information, it also rests upon staff sharing common beliefs. Whilst for some teachers working together meant as little as acting together in a crisis, for others it meant sharing beliefs (e.g. purposing the same). Since beliefs are usually strongly held convictions a sense of depth is implied. Collegiality is both broad and deep.

If it is possible that collegiality is 'broad' and 'deep' then it is also likely that it takes time to develop. It is not insignificant that the heads in the three collaborative PSSR schools had been in post for over ten years. Moreover, developing shared beliefs is far from straightforward or speedy. Indeed we heard in all project schools accounts that suggest collaboration sometimes accelerated only when certain staff left and there were opportunities to recruit staff who 'fitted in' (for example, see Nias, Southworth and Yeomans, 1989, pp. 136–41).

In turn this suggests that where cohesion exists so too might likemindedness. As yet we cannot say whether cohesion amongst staff provides the conditions for creative activity or insularity and inertia though PSSR suggests neither automatically follows.

Selection of staff is a key task of the headteacher and at a number of points the importance of the headteacher has been indicated. The heads were founders of their schools' culture, were seen to hold a proprietary interest in the school, led through example, influenced by colleagues, and negotiated a working consensus. The heads of the collaborative schools did not appear to suffer a loss of identity. Indeed, since they were both leaders and members of a staff group which subscribed to their beliefs the heads enjoyed considerable authority. It would be simplistic to say the heads in the collaborative schools controlled what happened there but they certainly exerted a great deal of influence and occasionally used their power directly. Since this influence was transacted through one-to-one contacts, formal and informal meetings, and negotiations, the heads more noticeably than others revealed a micro-political dimension to the notion of collegiality. Obvious as this may seem, given recent work and the idea that schools are arenas of struggle where notions of hierarchy and equality, democracy and coercion coexist in close proximity (Bell, 1987, pp. 15 and 19), the micro-political aspects need emphasizing since those who promote collegiality appear to be unaware of their existence.

At this point we are not able to offer a definition of collegiality. What we can suggest is that it involves staff working together in a school where the culture is cohesive and educational and social beliefs are shared. The school is led by a headteacher who, having founded the culture, sustains the beliefs and is a member of the staff group.

We began this paper by saying collegiality has been advocated on a national scale. However, since only some and not all of our project schools exhibited these collegial characteristics (cohesion, shared beliefs) it is necessary to say that whilst collegiality is nationally prescribed it is unlikely to occur to the same extent. In which case one wonders about the appropriateness of such wholesale advocacy of a simple style, or is there really only one way to run an effective school?

REFERENCES

Abercrombie, J. (1981) Changing basic assumptions about teaching and learning, in D. Boud (ed.) *Developing Student Autonomy in Learning*, Kogan Page, London.

Alexander, R. (1984) *Primary Teaching*, Holt, Rinehart & Winston, London.

Ball, S. (1987) *The Micro-Politics of the School*, Methuen, London.

Bush, T. (1986) *Theories of Educational Management*, Paul Chapman Publishing, London.

Campbell, R.J. (1985) *Developing the Primary School Curriculum*, Holt, Rinehart & Winston, London.

Campbell, R.J. (1989) The Education Reform Act 1988: some implications for curriculum decision-making in primary schools, in M. Preedy (ed.) *Approaches to Curriculum Management*, Open University Press, Milton Keynes.

Chell, E. (1985) *Participation and Organization: A Social Psychological Approach*, Macmillan, London.

Coulson, A.A. (1978) Power and decision-making in the primary school, in C. Richards (ed.) *Power and the Curriculum: Issues in Curriculum Studies*, Nafferton Books, Driffield, pp. 64–74.

DES (1978) *Primary Education in England*, HMSO, London.

DES (1980) *A View of the Curriculum: HMI Series: Matters for Discussion*, HMSO, London.

DES (1982) *Education 5 to 9: An Illustrative Survey of 80 First Schools in England,* HMSO, London.

DES (1984) *Education Observed,* DES, London (see also numbers 2 (1984) and 3 (1985) of this series).

DES (1987) *Primary Schools: Some Aspects of Good Practice,* HMSO, London.

DES (1989) *School Teachers' Pay and Conditions Document 1989,* HMSO, London.

Handy, C. (1981) *Understanding Organizations* (2nd edn), Penguin Books, London.

Hargreaves, A. (1982) The rhetoric of school-centred innovation, *Journal of Curriculum Studies,* Vol. 14, no. 3, pp. 251–66.

Holly, P. and Southworth, G. (1989) *The Developing School,* Falmer Press, London.

House of Commons Select Committee (1986) *Achievement in Primary Schools,* Vol. 1, HMSO, London.

ILEA (1985) *Improving Primary School, Report of the Committee of Enquiry,* Inner London Education Authority.

Lieberman, A. (1986) Collaborative work, *Educational Leadership,* Vol. 43, no. 5, pp. 4–8.

Lieberman, A. (1988a) Expanding the leadership team, *Educational Leadership,* Vol. 45, no. 5, pp. 4–8.

Lieberman, A. (1988b) Teachers and principals: turf, tensions and new tasks, *Phi Delta Kappa,* Vol. 69, no. 9, pp. 648–53.

Little, J.W. (1982) Norms of collegiality and experimentation: workplace conditions of school success, *American Educational Research Journal,* Vol. 19, pp. 325–40.

Little, J.W. (1985) Teachers as teacher advisers: the delicacy of collegial leadership, *Educational Leadership,* Vol. 43, no. 3, pp. 34–6.

Little, J.W. (1987) Teachers as colleagues, in V. Richardson-Koehler (ed.) *Educators' Handbook: A Research Perspective,* Longman, New York, pp. 491–518.

Little, J.W. (1989) The persistence of privacy: autonomy and initiative in teachers' professional relations. Paper presented at AERA, San Francisco.

Little, J.W. and Long, C. (1985) Portraits of school-based collegial teams, Far West Laboratory, San Francisco (mimeo).

Lortie, (1969) The balance of control and autonomy in elementary school teaching, in A. Etzioni (ed.) *The Semi-Professionals and their Organization,* Free Press, New York.

Miller, L. and Lieberman, A. (1982) School leadership between the cracks, *Educational Leadership,* Vol. 39, no. 5, pp. 362–7.

Mortimore, P., Sammons, P., Stoll, L., Lewis, D. and Ecob, R. (1988) *School Matters,* Open Books, Wells.

Nias, D.J. (1985) Reference groups in primary teaching: talking, listening and identity, in S.J. Ball and I.F. Goodson (eds) *Issues in Education and Training Series 3: Teachers' Lives and Careers,* Falmer Press, Lewes.

Nias, D.J. (1987a) Learning from difference: a collegial approach to change, in W.J. Smyth (ed.) *Educating Teachers: Changing the Nature of Pedagogical Knowledge,* Falmer Press, Lewes.

Nias, D.J. (1987b) The Primary School Staff Relationships Project: origins, aims and methods, *Cambridge Journal of Education,* Vol. 17, no. 2, pp. 83–5.

Nias, D.J. (1989) *Primary Teachers Talking: a Study of Teaching as Work,* Routledge, London.

Nias, D.J., Southworth, G.W. and Yeomans, R. (1989) *Staff Relationships in the Primary School,* Cassell, London.

Packwood, T. (1984) The introduction of staff responsibility for subject development in a junior school, in S. Goulding, J. Bell, T. Bush, A. Fox and J. Goodey (eds) *Case Studies in Educational Management,* Harper & Row, London, pp. 85–94.

Pollard, A. (1985) *The Social World of the Primary School,* Cassell, London.

Purkey, S.C. and Smith, M.S. (1983) Effective schools: a review, *Elementary School Journal,* Vol. 83, no. 4, pp. 427–52.

Purkey, S.C. and Smith, M.S. (1985) School reform: The district policy implications of the effective schools literature, *The Elementary School Journal*, Vol. 85, no. 3.

Reid, K., Hopkins, D. and Holly, P. (1987) *Towards the Effective School*, Blackwell, London.

Richards, C. (1986) The Curriculum from 5–16, *Education 3–13*, Vol. 14, no. 1, pp. 3–8.

Rosenholtz, S. (1985) Effective Schools: interpreting the evidence, *American Journal of Education*, Vol. 93, no. 3, pp. 352–86.

Schein, E.H. (1985) *Organizational Culture and Leadership*, Jossey-Bass, San Francisco.

Schools Council (1981) *The Practical Curriculum*, Methuen, London.

Schools Council (1983) *Primary Practice*, Methuen, London.

Sergiovanni, T.J. (1984) Leadership and excellence in schooling, *Educational Leadership*, Vol. 41, no. 5, pp. 4–13.

Southworth, G. (1987a) Primary school headteachers and collegiality, in G. Southworth (ed.) *Readings in Primary School Management*, Falmer Press, Lewes, pp. 61–75.

Southworth, G. (1987b) The experience of fieldwork; or insider dealings, who profits?, *Cambridge Journal of Education*, Vol. 17, no. 2, pp. 86–8.

Southworth, G. (1988a) Looking at leadership: English primary school headteachers at work, *Education 3–13*, Vol. 16, no. 2, pp. 53–6.

Southworth, G. (1988b) The glue of schools, *Times Educational Supplement*, 20 May, p. B27.

Thomas, N. (1987) Team spirit, *Child Education*, January, pp. 10–11.

Tomlinson, J. (1986) Primary education: the way ahead, *Primary Education Review* (National Union of Teachers), Autumn, no. 2–3.

Wallace, M. (1988) Towards a collegiate approach to curriculum management in primary and middle schools, *School Organization*, Vol. 8, pp. 25–34.

Welsh Office (1985) *Leadership in Primary Schools*, Welsh Office, Cardiff.

Wolcott, (1973) The man in the principal's office: an ethnography, Waveland Press, Prospect Heights, (1984 reissue).

Yeomans, R. (1985) Are primary teachers primarily people?, in G. Southworth (ed.) (1987) *Readings in Primary School Management*, Falmer Press, Lewes, pp. 80–9.

Yeomans, R. (1987) Checking and adjusting the lens; case study clearance, *Cambridge Journal of Education*, Vol. 17, no. 2, pp. 89–90.

6

CONTRIVED COLLEGIALITY:
the Micropolitics of Teacher Collaboration

Andrew Hargreaves

This material has been abridged

Collegiality is rapidly becoming one of the new orthodoxies of educational change and school improvement. Advocates of collegiality have shown little modesty in proclaiming its virtue. Collegiality among teachers and between teachers and their principals has been advanced as one of the most fruitful strategies for fostering teacher development. Collegiality, it is argued, takes teacher development beyond personal, idiosyncratic reflection, and beyond dependence on outside "experts", to a point where teachers can learn from each other, sharing and developing their expertise together (Lieberman & Miller, 1984). There are also claims, as well as some research evidence, that suggest that the confidence that comes with collegial sharing and support leads to greater readiness to experiment and take risks, and with it a commitment to continuous improvement among teachers as a recognized part of their professional obligation. In this sense, collegiality is seen as forming a vital bridge between school improvement and teacher development (Bird & Little, 1986; Rosenholtz, 1989). Certainly, aspects of collegiality in terms of shared decision making and staff consultation are among those process factors that are repeatedly identified as correlating with positive school outcomes in studies of school effectiveness (Mortimore, Sammons, Stoll, Lewis, & Ecob, 1988; Purkey & Smith, 1983; Reynolds, 1985; Rutter, Maughan, Mortimore, Ousten, & Smith, 1979).

If collegiality is seen as promoting professional growth and internally generated school improvement, it is also widely viewed as a way of securing effective implementation of externally introduced changes (Fullan, 1991; Huberman & Miles, 1984). The contribution made by collegiality to the implementation of centralized curriculum reform is a key factor here. Where curriculum reform is more school based in nature, the case for and contribution of collegiality is relatively straightforward. The creation of productive and supportive collegial relationships among teachers has long been seen as a prerequisite for effective school-based curriculum development (Campbell, 1985; Skilbeck, 1984). In many respects, collegiality brings teacher development and curriculum development together (Rudduck, 1991; Stenhouse, 1980). Indeed, the failure of many school-based curriculum development initiatives is attributable, at least in part, to the failure to build and sustain the collegial working relationships essential to their success (Hargreaves, 1989).

Many writers have argued that the effective implementation of more centralized curricular reforms also depends on the development of collegial relationships and joint planning among each school's teaching staff; allowing central guidelines to be interpreted and adapted to the context of each particular school; and building commitment and understanding among the teachers responsible for implementing the newly devised curricula (Campbell, 1989). With trends in many systems towards school-based management or local management of schools, the collective responsibility of teachers to implement centrally defined curriculum mandates places even greater reliance on the development of collegiality at school level.

Although not quite a cure-all, the alleged benefits of collegiality for organizational health and effectiveness therefore appear to be both numerous and widespread. Shulman (1989) brings together some of the key arguments when he says:

> Teacher collegiality and collaboration are not merely important for the improvement of morale and teacher satisfaction . . . but are absolutely necessary if we wish teaching to be of the highest order. . . . Collegiality and collaboration are also needed to ensure that teachers benefit from their experiences and continue to grow during their careers. (p. 2) [. . .]

Collegiality, then, forms a significant plank of policies to restructure schools from without and to reform them from within. Much of the burden of educational reform has been placed upon its fragile shoulders. School improvement, curriculum reform, teacher development, and leadership development are all seen as being dependent, to some extent, on the building of positive collegial relationships for their success. Consequently, while collegiality is not itself the subject of any national, state, or provincial mandates, its successful development is viewed as essential to the effective delivery of reforms that are mandated at national or local levels. Among many reformers and administrators, collegiality has become the key to change.

CRITIQUES OF COLLEGIALITY

Collegiality may have become an important focal point for a growing administrative and intellectual consensus about desirable directions for change and improvement. But collegiality has not been without its critics, either.

Most critiques of collegiality have focused on difficulties of implementation, particularly issues of time for teachers to work together (Bird & Little, 1986; Bullough, 1988; Campbell, 1985; Gitlin, 1987; Little, 1984) and issues concerning the unfamiliarity that many teachers have with the collegial role (Campbell, 1985; Campbell & Southworth, 1990; Nias, 1987). These criticisms are of a relatively specific, technical, managerial nature.

A second set of critiques of collegiality concern its meaning, which is often discussed as if it were widely understood. In practice, though, what passes for collegiality takes many different forms. In terms of specific initiatives alone, collegiality can take the form of team teaching, collaborative planning, peer coaching, mentor relationships, professional dialogue, and collaborative action research, to name but a few. More informally, it can be expressed through staff room talk, conversation outside the classroom, help and advice regarding resources, and scores of other small but significant actions. In the sense that all these things involve teachers working together, they are all versions of collegiality. But beyond that simple commonality, these activities are quite different. They have quite different implications for teacher autonomy and teacher empowerment.

What matters here is not that there are many different kinds of collegiality. What matters, rather, is that the characteristics and virtues of some kinds of collegiality are often falsely attributed to other kinds as well, or perhaps to collegiality in general. Teacher empowerment, critical reflection, commitment to continuous improvement – these are claims that are commonly made for collegiality in general but that in practice apply only to particular versions of it.

Because there are so many faces of collegiality, its professed attractions as a whole should be treated with caution. There is no such thing as 'real' or 'true' collaboration or collegiality. There are only different forms of collegiality that have different consequences and serve different purposes. Moreover, those forms that are most compatible with the widely declared benefits of teacher empowerment and reflective practice are also the forms that are the least common (Little, 1984). In our headlong rush to manage collegiality, it therefore seems important that we first take time to understand its meaning.

These questions about the meaning of collegiality lead, inexorably, to questions about who guides and controls collegiality; about its micropolitics. These questions form a third set of criticisms about teacher collegiality. As Cooper (1988) puts it in a biting critique of popular conceptions of collegiality:

> Whose culture is it anyway? If teachers are told what to be professional about, how, where and with whom to collaborate, and what blueprint of professional conduct to follow, then the culture that evolves will be foreign to the setting. They will once again have "received" a culture. (p. 47)

Discussions about and advocacy of collaboration and collegiality have largely taken place within a particular perspective on human relationships: the cultural perspective. In the main, this cultural perspective has been grounded in traditions of sociological functionalism, social anthropology, and corporate management.

It is a perspective that emphasizes what is shared and held in common in human relationships: values, habits, norms, beliefs, and "the way we do things around here" (Deal & Kennedy, 1982; Schein, 1984). This perspective is pervasive in literature on staff cultures in schools and school systems (e.g., Leithwood & Jantzi, 1990; Musella & Davis, in press; Rosenholtz, 1989).

There are two problems with this perspective. First, the existence of shared culture is presumed no matter how complex and differentiated the organization being studied. The possibility that some highly complex organizations may have no shared culture of any substance is not acknowledged.

Second, the theoretical and methodological emphasis on what is shared in the organization may exaggerate the consensus-based aspects of human relationships, according them an importance in research studies that outweighs their significance in practice. In some organizations, the differences and disagreements among participants are more significant than what they happen to share (Woods, 1990). This is often true of secondary schools with their balkanized relations between departments, for instance (Hargreaves, 1992).

A second perspective on human relationships, one that is less well represented in literature and research on educational administration, is the micropolitical perspective. According to Blase (1988, p. 113), this perspective deals with 'the use of power to achieve preferred outcomes in educational settings'. In the micropolitical perspective, the differences between groups in an organization are more highlighted than the similarities (Hoyle, 1986). The ways that some individuals and groups can realize their values at the expense of others, or have the power and influence to shape others' values in the image of their own, is a key concern. In the cultural perspective, leadership is a matter of management and legitimacy. In the micropolitical perspective it is more a question of power and control (Ball, 1987).

These two perspectives present us with a very different outlook concerning our understandings of collaboration and collegiality. In the more dominant cultural perspective, collaborative cultures express and emerge from a process of consensus building that is facilitated by a largely benevolent and skilled educational management. In the micropolitical perspective, collegiality results from the exercise of organizational power by control-conscious administrators. In these cases, collegiality is either an unwanted managerial imposition from the point of view of teachers subjected to it, or more usually, a way of co-opting teachers to fulfilling administrative purposes and the implementation of external mandates. From the micropolitical perspective, collegiality is often bound up with either direct administrative constraint or the indirect management of consent. [. . .]

The dominance of the first perspective in research on school culture has given undue emphasis to more consensus-driven interpretations of and prescriptions regarding staff collegiality. I want to draw attention to the less well-understood and less frequently acknowledged dimensions of school culture and teacher collegiality – those of a more micropolitical nature.

Once the micropolitical perspective is adopted, it has important implications for our understanding of collegiality and the questions we ask about it. It casts doubt, for instance, on the widely advocated virtues of team teaching, of collegiality at the classroom level, where there are substantial differences of values and beliefs among the teachers involved. As Huberman (1990) has expressed it, sculptors may often want to see each other sculpt, to talk about sculpting with fellow artists, and to go to exhibitions of their work, but they would never sculpt with a colleague on the same piece of marble. Because of frequent differences in beliefs and approach, Huberman says, teachers may be no different from sculptors in this respect.

Second, the micropolitical perspective raises questions about the rights of the individual and the protection of individuality in the face of group pressure. Norms of collegiality are sometimes treated as if they were administrative laws of collegiality. Teachers who prefer to continue working alone all, or some of the time, can be unfairly ostracized. Some teachers plan better in solitude than they do with their colleagues. And the protection of their individuality and discretion of judgment is also a protection of their right to disagree and reflect critically on the value and worth of that on which they are being asked to collaborate. The micropolitical perspective raises questions about the implications of collegiality for individuality and solitude. [. . .]

Third, the micropolitical perspective inquires into the circumstances where collaboration becomes cooptation – as in collaboration with the enemy. It asks where collaboration becomes a commitment not to developing and realizing purposes of one's own but to implementing purposes devised by others. Hartley (1986), for instance, has criticized the tendency toward shorter, school-based, experiential forms of in-service education for teachers on the grounds that they are cooptative in precisely this sense – that they cultivate emotional commitment to externally mandated changes at the expense of rational deliberation and critique about their worth and applicability (see also Hargreaves & Reynolds, 1989).

Fourth, the micropolitical perspective encourages us to discriminate between the different forms that collaboration takes, to examine who constitutes those different forms and to ask whose interests they serve in each case. In the parallel case of many working class pupils, for instance, their culture has been found to be highly cooperative, embodying powerful forms of solidarity and mutual support, but this takes a form that has a spontaneity, unpredictability, and cultural dynamic that teachers and administrators find uncomfortable and difficult to control (Quicke, 1986). As a result, the cooperative skills that are part of the students' own culture are either not recognized as such, or are actively dismissed as illegitimate "cheating" (Rudduck, 1991). In their place, alternative forms of collaboration are created through bureaucratically contrived and administratively controlled forms of cooperation, such as active learning and cooperative learning. [. . .]

The micropolitical perspective sensitizes us to the possible existence of similar processes in the construction of collegiality among teachers: the substitution of more evolutionary, spontaneous, and unpredictable forms of teacher collaboration by administratively controlled forms of collegiality. It is this kind of administratively constructed or contrived collegiality that I want to explore in the remainder of this chapter.

CONTRIVED COLLEGIALITY

Collaborative working arrangements and relationships between teachers and their colleagues can be divided into two broad types, depending on the kind of administrative control and intervention that is exercised in each case.

In collaborative cultures (Hargreaves, in press; Nias, Southworth, & Yeomans, 1989), collaborative working relationships between teachers and their colleagues are

- *spontaneous.* They emerge primarily from the teachers themselves as a social group. They may be administratively supported and facilitated by helpful scheduling arrangements, by principals offering to cover classes, or by example in the behaviour of educational leaders; ultimately, however, collaborative working relationships evolve from and are sustained through the teaching community itself.
- *voluntary.* Collaborative work relations arise not from administrative constraint or compulsion but from their perceived value among teachers that derives from experience, inclination, or noncoercive persuasion that working together is both enjoyable and productive.
- *development oriented.* In collaborative cultures, teachers work together primarily to develop initiatives of their own, or to work on externally supported or mandated initiatives to which they themselves have a commitment. In collaborative cultures, teachers most often establish the tasks and purposes for working together, rather than meet to implement the purposes of others. Teachers here are people who initiate change as much as, or more than, they react to it. When they have to respond to external mandates, they do so selectively, drawing on their professional confidence and discretionary judgment as a community (Fullan, 1991).
- *pervasive across time and space.* In collaborative cultures, working together is not often a scheduled activity (like a regular planning session) that can be administratively fixed as taking place at a designated time in a designated place. Scheduled meetings and planning sessions may form part of collaborative cultures, but they do not dominate the arrangements for working together. In collaborative cultures, much of the way teachers work together is in almost unnoticed, brief yet frequent, informal encounters. This may take the form of such actions as passing words and glances, praises and thanks, offers to exchange classes in tough times, suggestions about new ideas, informal discussions about new units, sharing problems, or meeting parents together. Collaborative cultures are, in this sense, not clearly or closely regulated. They are constitutive of the very way that the teacher's working life operates in the school.
- *unpredictable.* Because, in collaborative cultures, teachers have discretion and control over what will be developed, the outcomes of collaboration are often uncertain and not easily predicted. In implementation-oriented systems where most decisions about purpose and program are centralized at the school board or provincial/state/national level, this unpredictability can

be administratively perplexing. In general, therefore, collaborative cultures are incompatible with school systems in which decisions about curriculum and evaluation are highly centralized. The difficulty for administrators seeking to help develop collaborative cultures may therefore be a difficulty not so much of human relations but of political control.

The comparative, combined features of contrived collegiality are as follows:

- *administratively regulated.* Contrived collegiality does not evolve spontaneously from the initiative of teachers, but is an administrative imposition that requires teachers to meet and work together.
- *compulsory.* Contrived collegiality makes working together a matter of compulsion, as in mandatory peer coaching, team teaching, and collaborative planning arrangements. In contrived collegiality, there is little discretion afforded to individuality or solitude (Hargreaves, in press). Compulsion may be direct, or it may be indirect in terms of associated promises of promotion and veiled threats of withdrawal of support for teachers' other favored projects, for example.
- *implementation-oriented.* Under conditions of contrived collegiality, teachers are required or 'persuaded' to work together to implement the mandates of others – most directly those of the principal, or indirectly those of the school board, the state, or the nation. Such mandates may take the form of a national curriculum, accelerated learning programs, or cooperative learning strategies, for example. Here, collegial cooperation is closely tied with administrative cooptation.
- *fixed in time and space.* Contrived collegiality takes place in particular places at particular times. This is part of its administrative regulation. When, for example, peer coaching sessions, collaborative planning meetings in preparation time, and mentor meetings alone constitute teachers' joint working relationships, they amount to trying to secure cooperation by contrivance.
- *predictable.* Contrived collegiality is designed to have relatively high predictability in its outcomes. This cannot, of course, be guaranteed, and, as we shall see, the outcomes of contrived collegiality are sometimes perverse. But control over its purposes and regulation of its time and placement are designed to increase the predictability of teacher collegiality and its outcomes.

The study

I now want to explore some practical, school-based realizations of contrived collegiality, drawing on a recently completed study of how elementary teachers use scheduled preparation time in the school day of approximately 120 minutes per week and how this use of preparation relates to teachers' other working commitments inside and outside the school day. This study was both qualitative and exploratory in nature. Its purpose was not to investigate the meanings that teachers and principals attached to preparation time and other noncontact time and the interpretations they put on its use. The study did not examine only specific issues concerning preparation time itself, but also wider patterns of working as a teacher, and the ways that those patterns related to teachers' lives more generally. [. . .]

The study was conducted in a range of school sites across two school boards in southern Ontario, Canada. The data discussed here were drawn from one of the boards: a board that had a specific commitment to developing collaborative planning in a group of its schools. This provided an opportunity to examine a limiting case for teacher individualism, a place where it would be least likely to be found. Six elementary schools were studied in this board, as in the second board. The chosen family of schools was part of the collaboration planning initiative, although the schools also varied in size, program type, and urban/rural location.

Interviews took place with 6 principals and 14 teachers in the 6 study schools discussed here. No principal or teacher refused to participate or declined to be taped.

It should be stressed that this chapter is not an evaluation of the collaborative planning initiative overall. Nor is it an attempt to estimate in quantitative terms the strength of contrived collegiality within that initiative. Rather, it is designed to draw attention from a micropolitical perspective to aspects of collegiality emerging from the data that have received little or no emphasis thus far in more general, positively inclined discussions of teacher collaboration.

I will focus here on [two] specific realizations of contrived collegiality that emerged from the study and that illustrate both the properties and the consequences of this pattern of teacher collaboration. These realizations of contrived collegiality are mandated preparation time use [and] consultation with special education resource teachers.

1. Mandated preparation time use

In debates surrounding the introduction of preparation time in many Ontario school boards, one of the arguments used in its support was that it would provide teachers with the opportunity to meet and consult with their colleagues during the school day. For most teachers we interviewed, preparation time, or "planning time" as it was sometimes called, was not at all the best time to plan, however. Preparation time periods were usually fairly short: 40 minutes or less. Many minutes were often lost looking after classes until the next teacher arrived, taking children to the gym for their physical education class with another teacher and supervising them getting changed before that, walking across to the staff room or library if the teacher's own classroom was in use, and other activities. [. . .]

Teachers commonly regarded preparation time as too short for sustained planning, be it collective or individual. Indeed, so scarce was the time, that teachers frequently commented they needed to do their planning before prep time – at home perhaps – so they knew exactly how the prep time was going to be used and what jobs they were going to do at that time. Teachers here preferred to plan at other times – at lunch, before school, and after school, for instance. Preparation time, rather, was used more to 'clear the decks' of the innumerable small tasks, like photocopying and telephoning, that could be dispatched less efficiently at other times like lunch, when the rest of the school's teachers would be clamoring for the same resources. This pattern of work in preparation time was highly useful for many teachers and freed up time for them to plan in a more sustained way at other points in the school day. [. . .]

Marking, doing stencils, photocopying, cutting and pasting, doing bulletin boards – these were the usual stuff of preparation time for most teachers.

Larger preparation time periods (doubles) were more suited to extended planning, either alone or with colleagues. A number of teachers preferred some of their time to be 'chunked' in this way to facilitate planning. But when these extended preparation time periods were designed specifically for collaborating with colleagues, teachers were still concerned to have scheduled time to prepare for their own classes.

For other teachers, however, preparation time was ideal for planning with colleagues. Responsibilities for coaching and refereeing sports teams, for instance, gave some teachers little opportunity to meet with colleagues at other times. For a number of women teachers, in particular a single parent with a child who often had to be taken to psychiatric appointments immediately after school, pressing domestic responsibilities made it difficult for them to stay long with colleagues after school. Much of their planning took place at home, often late at night. For them, preparation time was a good time to work with colleagues.

Teachers' work and life circumstances vary. The teacher's work is highly contexted. It is not and cannot be standardized in the way that administrators sometimes want it to be. Preparation time (and its uses) therefore has an inevitably complicated and highly contexted relationship to these variable work and life circumstances. There is no unambiguous administrative formula for dealing with this. It would be of little value to calculate how many teachers in one school would support and benefit from scheduled collaborative planning time and how many would not, and then decide, on some percentage basis, whether mandating such uses for preparation time would be worthwhile. The important administrative principle here, rather, would appear to be one of administrative flexibility and discretion in delegating decisions about how preparation time periods are to be used to teachers themselves.

That flexibility is important for at least three reasons: to place preparation time usage in the realistic context of teachers' wider life and work circumstances; to allow preparation time use to be responsive to the day-by-day, week-by-week variations in required tasks and priorities; and, not least, to acknowledge the professionalism of teachers as defined by Schon (1983) in terms of their rights and opportunities to exercise discretionary judgment in the best interests of those students for whom they care and hold responsibility.

Some interview responses from teachers indicated that while they would normally use preparation periods for the collaborative purposes designated by the principal, in a proportion of those periods, they would retreat to their own room or other space in order to work alone for their own classes, clearing away the plethora of little tasks for which preparation time is seen as so important. Yet in doing so, they would feel guilty, aware that they were going against the wishes of their principal. [. . .]

One principal related how he discovered that teachers he had personally covered so they could be released to plan together were, on the occasion he checked up on them, not planning together at all, but working, preparing, and marking alone:

> I used to take the kids myself and do different things with them. . . . I thought the teachers were getting together – planning . . . and I thought, 'Oh well, I'll ask somebody to watch the kids while I go and see what's going on in the planning.' I walked down the hall and three teachers were all in different rooms, marking. So I said, 'Whoa!! There's something wrong here.' But you know, they always have a rationalization – 'Well, we got to the point where we needed to do this! Trust us! We will get together on our own time to do the planning.'

Infuriating as it might seem to administrators, especially when they have given up their precious time to facilitate collaborative planning, it is important, for the reasons reviewed earlier, to allow discretion and flexibility for teachers in their use of preparation time at any particular moment. It is, of course, helpful to use scheduling in order to release teachers together, as a contrivance to facilitate collaboration and collegiality, not to control it. Difficult as it may sometimes be for them, it is important for principals to continue giving their time to covering for teachers so they can be released, even though teachers may not always use that released time to work together, as expected. I am not suggesting here that administrators abrogate their responsibility for fulfilling the school's purposes and priorities. It is, however, important for reasons of sheer practicality and of respect for teachers' professionalism that teachers are awarded high discretion and flexibility in how those priorities are met. With regard to collaborative planning, one implication of this study is that principals might do better to set expectations for the *task* (preferably through discussion and development with teachers) rather than expectations for the *time*. What teachers would then be held accountable for would be commitment to and completion of the task not obedience in their use of the time.

2. Consultation with special education resource teachers

A second manifestation of contrived collegiality can be seen in the arrangements for consultation between special education teachers and classroom teachers. [. . .] With the integration of more special education students into regular classes, the special education teacher's role has been undergoing a shift from a restorative role, where identified children would be withdrawn from classes, 'treated' by the special education teacher, and then 'restored' to regular class work at a later stage, to an integrative role, where the special education

resource teacher supports the regular teacher in adapting instruction for identified children within normal classroom work (Wilson, 1983). One implication
of this development has been a need for closer consultation between special
education teachers and regular classroom teachers to monitor and program for
identified children in regular classes.

In schools within the collaboratively inclined board in this study, preparation time was often used or scheduled to facilitate this process of consultation
with special education resource teachers (SERTS).

In many cases, these required consultations were not just expected or administratively facilitated, but directly mandated to occur in particular places at
particular times. These consultations between classroom teachers and special
education resource teachers raised issues that were similar to those entailed in
required consultations between grade partners in preparation time. Flexibility
in use of time was again deemed important by teachers. Teachers perceived
special education support from the resource teacher as necessary, important,
and valuable, although the intensity of that need and the depth of support
needed varied with the program, the changing nature of students' difficulties
and needs, and other factors. Yet setting aside time each week when the
teacher was required to meet with resource staff was seen by many as un-
helpfully inflexible, as unresponsive to the changing needs of the students, the
program, the teacher, and the classroom. Many teachers emphasized the importance of meeting with special education staff when there was a need to meet
– when there was a purpose for the meeting (which might be and often was
outside preparation time just as much as within it). Sometimes, however, they
would find that on meeting the resource teacher, there was no business to
discuss that week, and once again they would tacitly agree to go their own
ways and work alone, without informing the principal. [. . .]

Judging from their accounts of how they consulted with special education
teachers, regular teachers, as a group, seem a rather perverse lot. Teachers who
have scheduled time to meet with their SERTS may prefer to do so at other
times. Other teachers may initiate consultation arrangements of their own in
prep time. And one teacher regretted that special education teachers were not
available for consultation during prep time in her school, so that she had to
meet with them in short snatches 'on the fly' instead. This apparent perversity
does not necessarily reveal inconsistency or any proclivity to oppose whatever
arrangements are available. Rather, these comments point once more to the
heavily contexted nature of teachers' work, and the difficulty that standardized
administrative procedures for developing collegiality have in accommodating
these particular and shifting circumstances of teaching.

Two issues of *expertise* compounded this relationship between classroom
teachers, special education resource staff, and the use of preparation time. Expertise is an important criterion for collaboration among teachers. Sharing as
such is not itself usually enough (Hargreaves & Wignall, 1989). This general
principle also applies to relationships between classroom teachers and special
education resource staff in particular. Acknowledgement of complementary expertise on the part of the special education resource staff is important. Where

classroom teachers have previous special education expertise, or where, as is increasingly common among Ontario elementary teachers, they possess special education qualifications as advanced as the resource personnel themselves, then meetings with resource staff can seem unnecessary. To teachers in this position, regular scheduled consultations with the special education resource teacher can sometimes appear to contribute little to their existing expertise and understanding. Because of this, teachers and resource staff again sometimes tacitly agreed not to meet on a regular basis, but only as required. [. . .]

What implications might be drawn here? [. . .] This principle of acknowledging existing expertise among one's colleagues might also apply to those who find themselves in positions of teacher leadership more generally. [. . .] This sharing is not sharing among the skilled and less skilled, the expert and the novice, but among communities of professional equals, committed to continuous improvement (Rosenholtz, 1989). [. . .]

CONCLUSIONS AND IMPLICATIONS

One of the benefits and the pleasures of qualitative research is the surprises it yields, surprises that are primarily driven by the data. The study reported here began with an elegantly formulated research question that asked whether newly provided preparation time would bring about the development of collegiality among teachers, or whether the use of such time would be absorbed into the existing culture of teacher individualism. Yet, the study generated findings more complex and perhaps more interesting than the possibilities posed by either of those alternatives. [. . .] Where collegiality was present, more important than its occurrence, as such, was its meaning.

One of the realizations of teacher collaboration was what I have called contrived collegiality. This reconstituted the cooperative principles of human association among teachers in administratively regulated and predictable forms. In contrived collegiality, collaboration among teachers was compulsory, not voluntary; was bounded and fixed in time and space; was implementation oriented rather than development oriented; and was meant to be predictable rather than unpredictable in its outcomes.

The realizations and implications of contrived collegiality were explored in [two] areas of teacher collaboration: mandated collaboration and joint planning in preparation time, [and] required consultation with special education resource teachers at scheduled times. [. . .] In micropolitical and more broadly sociopolitical terms, contrived collegiality is not merely an example of personal insensitivity among particular administrators. Rather, it is constitutive of sociopolitical and administrative systems that are less than fully serious about their rhetorical commitment to teacher empowerment. They are systems prepared to delegate to teachers and indeed hold them accountable for the collective, shared responsibility for implmentation, while allocating to themselves increasingly centralized responsibility for the development and imposition of educational purposes through curriculum and assessment mandates. They are systems of state regulation and control in which the business of conception and planning is increasingly separated from that of technical execution (Apple, 1982). In many respects, and in many instances, humanistic rhetorics of collegiality and empowerment disguise that fundamental and deepening division.

Two of the major consequences of contrived collegiality, it was found, are inflexibility and inefficiency – in terms of teachers not meeting when they should [and] of meeting when there is no business to discuss. [. . .] This inflexibility of mandated collegiality makes it difficult for programs to be adjusted to the purposes and practicalities of particular school and classroom settings. It also overrides teachers' professionalism in their exercise of discretionary judgment in the circumstances and with the children they know best.

Understood in micropolitical and sociopolitical terms, contrived collegiality and its consequences are more than problems of individual insensitivity, then. More sensitivity and flexibility among school principals in the management of collegiality can certainly help alleviate some of its unwanted effects, of course. But the issue underlying contrived collegiality is ultimately one that must be addressed by school systems at the highest level. It is an issue of willingness to give to schools and their teachers, substantial responsibility for development as well as implementation, for curriculum as well as instruction. It is an issue of commitment to unwriting the details of board- or state-driven curriculum guidelines, to giving communities of teachers the necessary flexibility to work with each other in developing programs of their own. Ultimately, it is an issue of serious and wide-ranging rather than merely cosmetic empowerment of our teachers and our schools. What remains to be seen is whether principals, school system administrators, and politicians are prepared to bite that particular bullet.

REFERENCES

Apple, M. (1982) *Education and power*. London: Methuen.
Ball, S. (1987) *The micropolitics of the school*. London: Methuen.
Bird, T., & Little, J.W. (1986) How schools organize the teaching occupation. *The Elementary School Journal*, 86(4), 493–512.
Blase, J. (1988) The teachers' political orientation vis-à-vis the principal: The micropolitics of the school. *Politics of Education Association Yearbook*, 3(5), 113–126.
Bullough, R., Jr. (1988) Accommodation and tension: Teachers, teacher role, and the culture of teaching. In L.E. Beyer & M. Apple (Eds.), *The curriculum: Problems, politics and possibilities*. Albany: State University of New York Press.
Campbell, P.J. (1985) *Developing the primary curriculum*. London: Holt, Rinehart & Winston.
Campbell, R.J. (1989) The Education Reform Act 1988: Some implications for curriculum decision making in primary schools. In M. Preedy (Ed.), *Approaches to curriculum management*. Milton Keynes, England: Open University Press.
Campbell, R.J. & Southworth, G. (1990, April). *Rethinking collegiality: Teachers' views*. Paper presented to the annual meeting of the American Educational Research Association, Boston.
Cooper, M. (1988) Whose culture is it anyway? In A. Lieberman (Ed.), *Building a professional culture in schools* (pp. 45–54). New York: Teachers College Press.

Deal, T.E., & Kennedy, A. (1982) *Corporate cultures.* Reading, MA: Addison-Wesley.

Fullan, M. (1991) *The new meaning of educational change* (rev. ed.). Toronto: OISE.

Gitlin, A. (1987) Common school structures and teacher behaviour. In L.E. Beyer & M. Apple (Eds.), *The curriculum: Problems, politics and possibilities.* Albany: State University of New York Press.

Hargreaves, A. (1989) *Curriculum and assessment reform.* Toronto: OISE.

Hargreaves, A. (1992) Cultures of teaching. In A. Hargreaves & M. Fullan (Eds.), *Understanding teacher development.* New York: Teacher College Press.

Hargreaves, A., & Reynolds, D. (1989) *Educational policies: Controversies and critiques.* Lewes, UK: Falmer.

Hargreaves, A., & Wignall, R. (1989) *Time for the teacher: A study of collegial relations and preparation time use among elementary school teachers.* Transfer Grant Project 51/1070. Toronto: Ontario Institute for Studies in Education.

Hartley, D. (1986) Structural isomorphism and the management of consent in education. *Journal of Education Policy,* 1, 229–237.

Hoyle, E. (1986) *The politics of school management.* London: Hodder & Stoughton.

Huberman, M. (1990, April) *The social context of instruction in schools.* Paper presented at the annual meeting of the American Educational Research Association, Boston.

Huberman, M. & Miles, M. (1984) *Innovation up close: How school improvement works.* New York: Plenum.

Leithwood, K., & Jantzi, D. (1990, April) *Transformational leadership: How principals can help reform school cultures.* Paper presented at the annual meeting of the American Educational Research Association, Boston.

Lieberman, A., & Miller, L. (1984) *Teachers, their world and their work: Implications for school improvement.* Alexandria, VA: ASCD.

Little, J.W. (1984) Seductive images and organization realities in professional development. *Teachers' College Record,* 86(1), 84–102.

Mortimore, P., Sammons, P., Stoll, L., Lewis, D., & Ecob, R. (1988) *School matters.* Berkeley: University of California Press.

Musella, D., & Davis, J. (in press) Assessing organizational culture: Implications for leaders of organizational change. In K. Leithwood & D. Musella (Eds.), *Understanding school system administration.* New York & Philadelphia: Falmer.

Nias, J. (1987) Learning from difference: A collegial approach to change. In W.J. Smyth (Ed.), *Educating teachers: Changing the nature of pedagogical knowledge* (pp. 98–120). Lewes, UK: Falmer.

Nias, J., Southworth, G., & Yeomans, R. (1989) *Staff relationships in the primary school.* London: Cassells.

Purkey, S.C., & Smith, M. (1983) Effective schools: A review. *Elementary School Journal,* 83, 4, 427–452.

Quicke, J. (1986) Personal and social education: A triangulated evaluation of an innovation. *Educational Review,* 38(3), 217–228.

Reynolds, D. (Ed.). (1985) *Studying school effectiveness.* Lewes, UK: Falmer.

Rosenholtz, S. (1989) *Teachers' workplace.* New York: Longman.

Rudduck, J. (1991) *Innovation, involvement and understanding.* Milton Keynes, England: Open University Press.

Rutter, M., Maughan, B., Mortimore, P., Ousten, J., & Smith, A. (1979) *Fifteen thousand hours.* London: Open Books.

Schein, E.H. (1984, Winter) Coming to a new awareness of organizational culture. *Sloan Management Review,* 3–16.

Schon, D. (1983) *The reflective practitioner: How professionals think in action.* New York: Basic Books.

Shulman, L. (1989) *Teaching alone, learning together: Needed agendas for the new reforms.* Paper prepared for the conference on Restructuring Schooling for Quality Education, Trinity University, San Antonio, TX.

Skilbeck, M. (1984) *School-based curriculum development*. London: Paul Chapman Publishing.

Stenhouse, L. (1980) *Curriculum research and development in action*. London: Heinemann.

Wilson, A. (1983) *A consumer's guide to Bill 82: Special education in Ontario*. Toronto: OISE.

Woods, P. (1990) *Teacher skills and strategies*. New York & Philadelphia: Falmer.

7

MANAGEMENT BY HALVES:
Women Teachers and School Management

Elisabeth Al-Khalifa

If the process of promotion and development were working properly about 44% of senior management would be women. (Bryan Nicholson, Chairman of the Manpower Services Commission 1986).

Nicholson's comments on the representation of women in management in general have equal force and validity if applied to the situation of women in teaching (although his figure would have to be revised upwards to 60 per cent in order to reflect the representation of women in teaching). Recent studies of teachers' careers have shown some of the ways in which promotion and development are not 'working properly'. See for example National Union of Teachers and Equal Opportunities Commission (1980); National Union of Teachers (1984); Inner London Education Authority (1984; 1987); Grant (1986); Kant (1985); Addison and Al-Khalifa (in preparation). The problem which Nicholson was addressing – the neglect of what he referred to as 'womanpower' – is also one which is manifest in teaching. Women have not always been so neglected a group in promotion and educational leadership in schools, as Eileen Byrne shows in her discussion of trends in teacher promotion (Byrne 1978: 214–19). However, the promotion position of women has deteriorated in the last twenty years with women clustering in greater proportions on Scales 1 and 2 and with few signs of a reverse in this decline. In a period of considerable reorganization, first through comprehensive reorganization, then through closures and amalgamations owing to falling rolls, women seem to have been disadvantaged in promotion processes. In particular, where single-sex schools have been closed and replaced by mixed comprehensives, and infant schools amalgamated with junior schools, there has been a pattern of preference for male headteachers over female ones.

Research into teachers' careers has suggested a range of factors which contribute to the disparities in promotional status between men and women teachers. Studies such as those cited above have noted the negative effects of sex-stereotyping and sex discrimination on promotion procedures and on women's opportunities for development. Other factors are also at work which can affect women's opportunities and choices in career development, and these include the understandings that women themselves may have about their own development and career needs. Some of these perceptions may result in decisions which exclude promotion moves into senior posts because of a belief in the greater value and satisfaction to be derived from class teaching. There is also evidence to suggest that women can be scrupulous in self-evaluation and therefore more critical and selective about career moves than many men teachers (Inner London Education Authority 1984). Personal priorities and responsibilities outside work roles can also be seen to vie with professional commitments.

For many women with dependants, the balancing of different roles and responsibilities is a considerable organizational achievement, but is also experienced as a source of pressure. A move into management then comes to be seen as compounding this problem; for some, such a move brings the likelihood of unwelcome additional stress. In the attempt to maintain a balance in their lives, women may hesitate to seek promotion into management posts, deterred by anticipated difficulties in preserving such a balance. The scope which class teaching and curriculum-linked posts offer for organizing their lives in ways which accommodate competing demands on their time, while preserving professional growth, contrasts with the expectation of greater inflexibility and restrictiveness associated with management work.

Promotion into management posts is perceived by some women as a move in which there would be a gap between the teacher's view of her own competence and skills, and those demanded by the job itself. This is a view which appears to be shared by many men too, and by selectors (although usually from a different perspective, based on negative stereotyping of women's abilities and career commitment). School leadership is so often linked to stereotypically defined masculine traits and behaviours, especially 'strength' and detachment. For example, one woman teacher, a deputy headteacher, was told by an LEA officer after failing to be appointed to a headship:

> It's a tough situation, awkward governors, a lot to be done. Needs a man; he won't get so involved.
>
> (Grant 1986)

The work of headteachers can and does vary, according to the individual incumbent, and the size and type of school. The reduction of behaviours, skills and knowledge seen as critical to effective headship to a small range of personal characteristics is part of a wider mythology about the nature of leadership, and belies the variety and complexity of the job. It is, nevertheless, a mythology which has a 'masculine' bias, with a powerful hold in teacher culture, both in how some teachers adhere to such views and work with them, and how others, especially women, distance themselves from the myth and the values it appears to reflect and represent about leadership and teacher work.

Hoyle (1986) has drawn attention to the role and importance of symbols in the study of school management, and he reminds us of the emphasis some organizational theorists have placed on the symbolic aspects of leadership and management. He points out that 'schools are particularly rich in symbolization'. It is certainly the case that 'the symbolic order of the school' is one which includes messages about the relationship of men and women, and schools as organizations restate and rework social understandings of male dominance and female dependence, and of gender roles, in everyday language and interaction (Addison and Al-Khalifa, in preparation). Hoyle does not explore this particular issue in his treatment of symbolism but he describes major strategies which may have symbolic interest in school management and leadership, including the patterns of association among staff and head, the spatial relationships between staff, the nature of meetings, roles, and documentation. These aspects of the symbolic dimension of schools that Hoyle outlines can easily be translated into experiences familiar to most teachers which denote the masculine character of school leadership. The association of masculinity, male authority and school leadership is pervasive in the life of the school. It can be seen, for example, in the behaviour of the head who loosens his tie and throws off his jacket as he joins a male-only group of colleagues in the mixed staffroom and equally so in the male teacher with his standard suit and clipboard in hand, the embodiment of male authority.

The building up of school management and headship as masculine is part of the history of the individual school's life as well as of educational culture as a whole, but this process has been intensified by the emergence of the concept of 'management' itself. Twenty years ago it would not have been possible to have written a chapter about management and women teachers, because the term itself is a recent arrival in the school order and the language of teachers. Basic textbooks and research on school management now proliferate, and the study of headship is central to this. A shift has occurred in how headship is understood, best summarized by Hughes' accounts of headship (1975; 1983). He draws attention to the movement away from the 'headteacher tradition', emphasizing personal relations linked with professional leadership, towards a dual-role concept described by Hughes as 'leading professional' and 'chief executive', a typology which introduces the managerial role of headship.

The description of school leadership and headship within a framework of management and organization theory has been assisted by contributions from those working outside the school system, and exemplified by the work of Everard (1982), Handy (1984), Gray (1982), among others. At the same time, the increasing involvement of the MSC in schools has also given currency to concepts, approaches, and values drawn from management practice in other employment sectors. Such changes in thinking about school headship can be understood to reflect the reality of greater complexity in school administration and organization, and of the changing relationships between school, government and society, and the tasks schools face. As part of a debate on school accountability and effectiveness, the 1970s and 1980s have seen a growth in research into educational management and attempts to describe managerial work in schools and effective management.

However, this growing emphasis on 'management' and on the centrality of the management function to organizational effectiveness is not restricted to education, but a feature of most fields of employment. The 'new managerialism' represents a search for rationality and certainty which commentators set against a dramatic backdrop of turbulence and change. During this period, there has been a decline of women in management positions, parallel to the kind of decline we have seen in schools.

The kinds of ideas that have prevailed about school headships mentioned earlier have drawn new strength from current concepts of management and from general descriptions of management behaviour. The development of management theory applied to schools has increased the likelihood of association between organizational leadership and masculinity, and indeed between leadership and hierarchy.

Hoyle discusses how the term 'management' in itself symbolizes

> a rationalistic approach to the coordination of schools. Notwithstanding the fact that the majority of schools are primary schools and structurally relatively simple organisations, there has been a widespread adoption of the term for the running of schools.
>
> (Hoyle 1986: 157)

He suggests that the adoption of the term may convey to the world the complexity of running a school and serve to encourage the self-image of the teachers as pursuing a 'masculine task'. If this analysis is correct, then it is logical to expect that the role of manager will be seen as incompatible with femininity, and should not be filled by women. The exception to this is where the work engaged in is already perceived as feminine, as in the case of those sectors of education which are seen as expressive in function rather than instrumental, such as nursery and infant work.

The 'headteacher tradition' of headship referred to earlier tended to focus on the headteacher's personality, personal authority and teaching experience. The managerial model is essentially a technicist model, which stresses school organizational problems as technical problems (Davies 1986) amenable to rational problem-solving techniques. Such a perspective emphasizes characteristics which are commonly depicted as 'masculine': analytical detachment, strong task direction, 'hard-nosed' toughness. As Marshall (1984: 19) suggests, 'leadership characteristics and the masculine sex role correspond so closely that they are simply different labels for the same concept'. In the case of schools, this correspondence is reinforced by an emphasis on physical strength and size as a desirable attribute indicative of a capacity to control.

Interestingly the association of masculinity with management spills over into perceptions about the 'managed'. Management tasks relating to the curriculum, staff development, and evaluation are conceptualized as if gender neutral, or with masculinity as the salient yardstick in measuring staff and pupil needs. Knowledge and experience of gender-linked issues are not normally required preparation for management, and demonstrable skills in relating to women staff and girl pupils are not sought out as necessary qualities for the performance of staff and pupil management. It is one of the anomalies of the literature on management and its practice, that headteachers can be considered 'effective' while disregarding the needs of girl pupils and demonstrating ineptitude in their relationships with women colleagues.

Masculine images of management thus overlay and strengthen existing prejudices about women in leadership positions and serve to rationalize the exclusive male character of educational management, reaffirming its naturalness and appropriateness irrespective of the nature of the tasks involved.

There is evidence that this convergence of masculinity and management roles is in some ways accepted at face value by women teachers as well as by men. The reluctance of women teachers to take up management courses (Inner London Education Authority 1984) is in part explained by a belief that there is a mismatch between their own skills, experience and personal qualities and those required in management. Additionally, the term management serves to confuse and obscure the nature of the work performed by headteachers, and a degree of mystification and pseudo-scientism reinforces other reservations women may have about school management.

Much of the uncertainty women may feel about management posts is undoubtedly based on concrete features of women's experience. Women teachers constantly receive strong messages from managers and other colleagues which are likely deterrents in themselves from pursuing promotion opportunities into senior management, and foster doubts about the appropriateness of management work as a career option for women:

> You are not encouraged to think about promotion – none of the female members of staff were. The head encouraged the men – they were approached by the head to go on management courses. None of the female members of staff were encouraged or even asked to consider it.
>
> (Woman primary teacher)

My own experience of working with women teachers and headteachers in recent years on career development and management development has offered opportunities to observe how women themselves perceive and experience management work in schools. This development work strongly suggests that insufficient attention is paid to the significance of women's own responses and ideas about management in determining training needs and in shaping our ideas about the management of schools.

Much of what women describe and discuss in the context of career development work reveals self-doubt about their level of suitability and preparedness for management. One group of women managers acknowledged that a major benefit of working together was having the opportunity to define management, and to recognize the work they did as management. They has resisted applying the label of 'manager' to themselves and saw this as a tendency among women.

Such a reluctance to identify with the role is not limited to women. As has been discussed above, management is a relatively new concept in schools and many teachers are still learning to interpret and understand the significance of this for their work. Feelings of unease about management among women in the development groups did not only originate from uncertainty about the meaning of management, however. The women concerned also demonstrated clear reasons drawn from their own experience for ambivalence about management and a resistance to identifying closely with management roles as these are currently understood. Such resistance and distancing is grounded in a positive valuation of their own 'femininity' and alternative perspectives on valued and effective behaviours in school management.

For many women, the image of management projected by practitioners and selectors is not compelling. It is not just a lack of knowledge or training which serves to create barriers for women but their rejection of those elements of the role which they see as masculine. In particular, women managers pinpoint aspects of management practice which they find repugnant or dysfunctional – namely aggressive competitive behaviours, an emphasis on control rather than negotiation and collaboration, and the pursuit of competition rather than shared problem-solving – a point of view shared by one male commentator (Gray 1987) writing about the experience of training male heads. As one group of women heads and deputies put it:

> We want a change in school management – feminine characteristics are currently devalued, we want account to be taken of qualities which women particularly can bring to school management and ways of working which women appear to value and prefer, but which differ from the norms and values of school management generally.

As they saw it, the management style in a school connects with the nature of the total school curriculum, and can limit the learning experiences which pupils have: 'We want schools to be different – management needs to reflect this.'

The resistance among these women to identifying themselves as 'managers' is not a simple consequence of a lack of training in management, or a lack of confidence, but a positive statement about self-worth and espoused values. For many of these women, their experience and skills as educationalists and as heads were felt to be positive and valuable by them but denied or not legitimized by current ideas and practices within the school context.

For women considering a career move into management, the discrepancy between their aspirations and ideas about management and the options actually modelled by colleagues, signal that there are considerable risks attached to promotion, and for some, the cost is too high:

> I've been working with a group of men on a management course as part of my MEd and it's decided me – I'm not going to take my applications for deputy posts further – I can't face working with men like that.
>
> (Woman secondary teacher)

Moreover, the caution with which some women approach management posts and promotion reflects an appreciation of the difficulties they may have to face which men are not exposed to. In particular, women see that their future work environment will be male dominated and both senior staff and those they supervise anticipate male leadership:

> I think most senior posts are taken by men and men prefer to work with men. If a woman is to compete at this level she has to be absolutely first rate . . . very confident and assertive. Men do not like working for women. (Woman secondary teacher)
>
> (Inner London Education Authority 1987)

When a woman takes a management post in what was previously a male domain, whether in primary or secondary schools, this perceived intrusion leaves her exposed and vulnerable. Inevitably she faces challenges to her working styles and leadership based on sex stereotypes and unease about women in leadership positions. The man teacher who said: 'It grates to have a woman in any position of authority over me' (Clwyd County Council/Equal Opportunities Commission 1983) in so bluntly expressing his rejection of women's leadership, was not an eccentric, but was stating a standpoint shared by many men, and only too familiar to women teachers. Women are well aware of the forms which challenges from male colleagues may take, whether through patronizing behaviours, avoidance, or openly aggressive responses and harassment, and recognize the impact of this on their work and the stress this can engender.

Such challenges take on specific as well as general patterns and for black women in management the experience of racism and sexism converges. Black women teachers taking part in training, and talking and writing about their work, acknowledge an experience of sexism shared with white women teachers. However, it is not assumed here that black women teachers necessarily start from perspectives or assumptions about women's experience and sexism which are the same as those of many white women teachers. As black women teachers indicate, access to management posts and working as managers present them with formidable additional difficulties because of the operation of racism.

Black teachers are targets of race stereotyping which negates their professional status and competence. Black women, however, encounter further harassment and excluding strategies which make the maintenance of their authority and credibility more precarious. The inability of many white teachers to accept that black women can be in positions of authority is reflected in a flow of dismissive treatment and condescension. Black women comment especially on recurrent harassment they face in schools arising from the particular race stereotypes about black women. They report the preoccupation of white men teachers with their dress and appearance, and an underlying view of black women's sexuality:

> I think men have this stereotype of you as a black woman – perhaps you will be grateful to them for their attentions, that they can proposition you, or they can call you by the ridiculous names men dream of. Nudge, nudge – I know your type of people . . . what I'm saying is that black women are in a particularly vulnerable position because of this racist

stereotype about them, as sexual beings and sexual creatures. It's the hysterical stereotype of black women being licentious and very sexually active, very emotional and passionate, in the worst sense. I think this can be a very serious thing to handle, given that they might be the only black member of staff, which is very often the case.

(Afro-Caribbean teacher, women managers group)

A woman to them is a lower creature, but an Asian woman is even lower. It's totally a sexual object – you know – 'a bit of black' sort of thing.

(Sikh woman teacher, talking about men teachers in her school)

Irrespective of the capacity of black women to deal with such challenges, this kind of interaction diverts attention from black women's professional role, denies their experience, competence and authority as managers and teachers, and is a persistent source of stress.

The high visibility of black women in management positions further intensifies the possibility of isolation and exposure to pressures coming from white colleagues who view black managers in an over-critical and often hostile way. At the same time, even more than is the case for white women, it is inevitable that this small group of black women managers work with high expectations of themselves in seeking to support other black teachers and pupils, but in doing so, creating further pressures for themselves.

Management work is therefore made more difficult for women generally, because of isolation and the need to negotiate their way through challenges to their right to manage. Such challenges come not only from staff but also from outsiders such as advisers, parents and governors. The stresses of such a situation and the effort to maintain values and aims which have integrity for an individual woman is a problem she usually has to deal with unsupported. These same features of women's experience in management are those which other women looking for models and encouragement note and have to consider in their career plans.

In a study of primary teachers and headteachers, Nias (1986) has argued that 'the subjective reality of teaching is living with paradox', that is, in her view, the contradictory character of teaching, which embodies conflict between controlling and liberating roles. She identifies a key feature of teacher identity in primary schools as the pursuit of 'wholeness',

blurring the boundaries between their personal and professional lives . . . . Both as teachers and as staff members . . . their metaphors and their body language emphasised supporting, holding, enfolding, belonging.

(Nias 1986: 13)

This analysis has some resonance not only with the experience of women generally, but also for those in management, who seek to bridge the personal and professional aspects of their lives and to reduce the gap between public and private roles. However, discrete role engagement and the divorce of the public and the private are very much features of masculine and management role behaviour. The dominant images of management and modes of working are antagonistic to such role reconciliation although the evidence from work with women would suggest that this integration is central to women's work.

It would appear that if women's perspectives on themselves as managers are to be realized, some reconsideration and re-evaluation of management is needed, and as Gray has suggested, this is a necessary step towards improving school management. At the moment, with women encountering increased rather than diminished obstacles to a central role in work organizations the outlook is not promising. As Mangham (1979) has commented, those who have power in an organization are able to structure the environment and the meanings so that

> the vocabulary available to the individual members and the nature of the concepts given currency in the organization selectively operate to emphasize certain realities and make other parts of reality invisible.
>
> (Mangham 1979: 82)

Until recently, the organizational meanings promoted in educational institutions have been those which de-emphasize women's contributions, and their actual and potential role as leaders and managers. The present scenario of turbulence and change depicted in much current general management literature has resulted in an enthusiasm for 'changing the culture' of organizations, and an advocacy of different management behaviour which is closer in character to behaviours typically associated with 'feminine' behaviours, notably collaborative and co-operative behaviours and humanistic values.

This trend would seem to indicate greater opportunities for women in management if 'feminine' styles of work were to be valued and sought after. In reality, little of this has been translated into practical action and the possible contribution of women in building this new culture is ignored. While the language of collaboration is appropriated by male managers, change remains at the level of rhetoric, and certainly has not been to the benefit of women in terms of pay, status and power in work organizations.

Observers of school management such as Gray (1982; 1987) or Handy (1984) have given indications of models of management which would enhance the life of schools and these are closer to the ideas expressed by the women managers and teachers reported here. Hoyle's comments on management and Nias's work on primary teachers also indicate serious weaknesses in the ways in which school management is at present conceptualized and again evidence from personal and career development work with women teachers suggests that there is some convergence in these debates.

One consequence, therefore, of focusing on women's concerns and women's role in management, is to highlight the inadequacies of current practice and thinking about school management and to indicate pointers for change in theory and practice which would improve management practice and ensure a gender perspective on this. At the same time, action for change needs to incorporate training initiatives which draw on the experience of work done in women's training and women-only management training. This area which is very much determined and led by women has described some enabling strategies for women and possibilities for change.

First, single-sex training for women, whether for career and personal development or for those specifically in management positions, has tremendous potential for empowering women and encouraging women to be confident about the validity of their experience and ideas about their own needs and their approaches to management. Second, the experience of working in women-only groups provides an opportunity for support, renewal and a stimulus for development. Indeed, it can come as a welcome relief from the often all-male environment or isolation of their normal working situation:

> What a contrast between the situation established in our group and the workplace – working in the group has allowed us to expose problems – is this possible for men?
>
> (Group of women heads and deputies)

Third, where black women managers or teachers are able to work together an opportunity is available for similar processes but with the additional benefit of the women being able to deal with the acute isolation often experienced and the pressures they are exposed to as a result of racism among white colleagues. It is also important for white women working in mixed black/white groups to recognize, accept and act on their role and responsibilities in supporting black colleagues and working with them against racist practices.

Fourth, the learning styles and content on such courses frequently draw on strategies of experiential learning, group problem-solving and co-counselling around participants' concerns which are especially effective in enabling managers to define and act on management issues facing them. In particular, development work which sets out to address women's position in teaching is more able to integrate management and other professional issues with the specific features of women's experience which bear on their work experience. For many women this contrasts favourably with the content and approaches of many general school management courses.

Fifth, single-sex training provides opportunities for networking which is supportive to participants on re-entry to work and which can help to maintain the impetus of training activities.

Women's training is a form of positive action which assists women in their development but it is not an adequate solution to the problems and barriers impeding women's access to management. Many of these barriers derive from organizational features of the education service and the effects of sexism in schools. Any training initiatives for women have to be matched with policy which recognizes sex inequality, and training for all managers in this area.

At present, a major obstacle to change in management development lies in the way in which control of decision-making about management training and the allocation of resources for this rests with men. Most policy-making and research is determined and provided by men, whether in higher education establishments, local government, the DES, or through management consultancy.

Until now, the impetus for change has come from women individually or through their collective action but almost invariably from positions of limited institutional power. Some changes are possible through organizational channels such as the National Development Centre for School Management Training at Bristol University, through teachers' associations and the EOC, all of whom are capable of exerting some influence in the shaping and resourcing of management training and women teachers' access to this. The changes in funding arrangements for in-service training (GRIST) have also created new opportunities in some areas for shifts in provision with more appropriate opportunities for women, and for tackling the problem of men's attitudes.

However, women teachers will continue to have avenues for training and development closed, while LEAs fail to use their considerable power to effect change through the allocation of funds, and through policy initiatives which impinge directly on the practice of advisers and school management teams.

Moreover, management training has to change to take account of the perspectives which gender issues raise. At present not only do training and related research adhere to traditional masculine models of management, but also lecturers and trainers can display a level of ignorance and prejudice which ensures that women are patronized and undermined. It is not surprising that women on management courses should view management training and management itself with a jaundiced eye, having been told that they should 'stick to the shopping', exposed to films such as *The Right Man for the Job* or undergoing a course of advanced study on management which makes no reference to gender issues.

Women's training controlled by women is a counter to such signal marginalization but no major change is possible without a significant reorientation in training and management practice which affects men's attitudes and behaviours as well. Course providers and school managers need to reconsider whether in their work they actually acknowledge and act on the development needs of the women teachers who make up 60 per cent of the teacher population, and for whom they have managerial responsibility. At present this is not the case.

Without changes in management practice which respond to these issues, school management is inevitably inadequate and ineffective. It fails to utilize the skills, experience and knowledge that women offer, and also fails to offer an education service for all.

REFERENCES

Addison, B. and Al-Khalifa, E. (in preparation) *Politics and Gender in Professional Work*.

Byrne, E. (1978) *Women and Education*, London, Tavistock.

Clwyd County Council/Equal Opportunities Commission (1983) *Equal Opportunities and the Secondary Curriculum*, Cardiff, EOC/Clwyd County Council.

Davies, L. (1986) 'Women, educational management and the Third World: a comparative framework for analysis', *International Journal of Educational Development*, Oxford, 6(1), 61–75.

Everard, K.B. (1982) *Management in Comprehensive Schools*, York, Centre for the Study of Comprehensive Schools.

Grant, R. (1986) 'A career in teaching: a survey of teachers' perceptions with particular reference to the careers of women teachers', paper presented to the British Educational Research Association Annual Conference, Bristol.

Gray, H.L. (ed.) (1982) *The Management of Educational Institutions*, Basingstoke, Falmer Press.

Gray, H.L. (1987) 'Problems in helping head teachers to learn about management', *Educational Management and Administration*, Harlow, 15(1), 35–42.

Handy, C. (1984) *Taken for Granted? Understanding Schools as Organizations*, York, Longman.

Hoyle, E. (1986) *The Politics of School Management*, London, Hodder & Stoughton.

Hughes, M.G. (1975) 'The professional-as-administrator: the case of the secondary school head', in R.S. Peters (ed.) *The Role of the Head*, London, Routledge & Kegan Paul.

Hughes, M.G. (1983) 'The role and tasks of heads of schools in England and Wales: research studies and professional development provision', in S. Hegarty (ed.) *Training for Management in Schools*, London, NFER/Nelson.

Inner London Education Authority (1984) *Women's Careers in Teaching: A Survey of Teachers' Views*, London, ILEA Research and Statistics.

Inner London Education Authority (1987) *Women's Careers in Secondary and Primary Teaching: The Birmingham Study*, by R. Martini, London, ILEA Research and Statistics.

Kant, L. (1985) 'A question of judgement', in J. Whyte *et al.*, *Girl Friendly Schooling*, London, Methuen.

Mangham, I. (1979) *The Politics of Organisational Change*, London, Associated Business Press.

Marshall, J. (1984) *Women Managers: Travellers in a Male World*, Chichester, Wiley.

National Union of Teachers (1984) *Primary Teachers in Coventry*, Coventry NUT Equal Opportunities Subcommittee.

National Union of Teachers and Equal Opportunities Commission (1980) *Promotion and Woman Teacher*, London, NUT/EOC.

Nias, J. (1986) 'What is it to 'feel like a teacher'?: the subjective reality of primary teaching', paper presented at the British Educational Research Association Annual Conference, Bristol.

PART 3:

Managing Sustained Change

PART 3

Managing System Change

8

CAUSES/PROCESSES OF IMPLEMENTATION AND CONTINUATION

Michael Fullan

This material has been abridged

> Well, the hard work is done. We have the policy passed; now all you have
> to do is implement it.
>
> – Outgoing deputy minister of education to colleague

Educational change is technically simple and socially complex. While the
simplicity of the technical aspect is no doubt overstated, anyone who has been
involved in a major change effort will intuitively grasp the meaning of and
concur with the complexity of the social dimension. A large part of the problem of educational change may be less a question of dogmatic resistance and
bad intentions (although there is certainly some of both) and more a question
of the difficulties related to planning and coordinating a multilevel social process involving thousands of people. [. . .]

In this chapter I identify those factors that affect whether or not an initiated
or decided-upon change happens in practice. The processes beyond adoption
are more intricate, because they involve more people, and real change (as
distinct from verbal or 'on-paper' decisions) is at stake. [. . .]

The persistence of people-related problems in educational change has forged
greater knowledge about what makes for success. If we constantly remind
ourselves that educational change is a *learning experience for the adults involved* (teachers, administrators, parents, etc.) as well as for children, we will
be going a long way in understanding the dynamics of the factors of change
described in this chapter. [. . .]

The logic of the change process [. . .] is essentially straightforward: However
changes get initiated, they proceed or not to some form of implementation and
continuation, resulting in some intended and/or unintended outcomes. In this

chapter we are interested in the factors and processes that affect implementation and continuation. Our goal is to identify the critical factors that commonly influence change in practice, and to obtain insights into how the implementation process works.

FACTORS AFFECTING IMPLEMENTATION

The idea of implementation and of the factors affecting actual use seems simple enough, but the concept has proven to be exceedingly elusive. Examples of successful improvement described in the research of the last 20 years seem to make common sense. More and more, the evidence points to a small number of key variables. It is obvious that they work, yet how they work is not necessarily clear. Intrinsic dilemmas in the change process, coupled with the intractability of some factors and the uniqueness of individual settings, make successful change a highly complex and subtle social process. Effective approaches to managing change call for

> combining and balancing factors that do not apparently go together – simultaneous simplicity-complexity, looseness-tightness, strong leadership-participation (or simultaneous bottom up-top downness), fidelity-adaptivity, and evaluation-nonevaluation. More than anything else, effective strategies for improvement require an understanding of the process, a way of thinking that cannot be captured in any list of steps or phases to be followed. (Fullan, 1985, p. 399)

While there is convergence on many of the findings, the sheer complexity of the change process has led researchers to search for different ways to best characterize implementation [. . .]. One method involves identifying a list of key factors associated with implementation success, such as the nature of the innovation, the roles of the principal, the district role, and so on. Another way is to attempt to depict the main themes, such as vision, empowerment, and the like. Both make important contributions: the former has the advantage of isolating and explaining specific roles; the latter is more likely to capture the dynamics of the change process.

We are going to use both methods in this chapter, labelled, respectively, key factors and key themes. In either case, one overriding qualification should be kept in mind. Describing educational change as a general phenomenon hides variations in large-scale change as compared with small-scale change, differences in units of analysis (e.g., individual classrooms vs. schools, districts, or whole countries), and so on. To understand the basic flow of change, we need not be concerned with these specifications at this time. But if we were interested in a particular change, we would have to make the necessary adjustments, depending on the unit of our interest. [. . .]

We should keep in mind that we are interested in factors or themes to the extent that they causally influence implementation (or more specifically the extent to which teachers and students change their practices, beliefs, use of

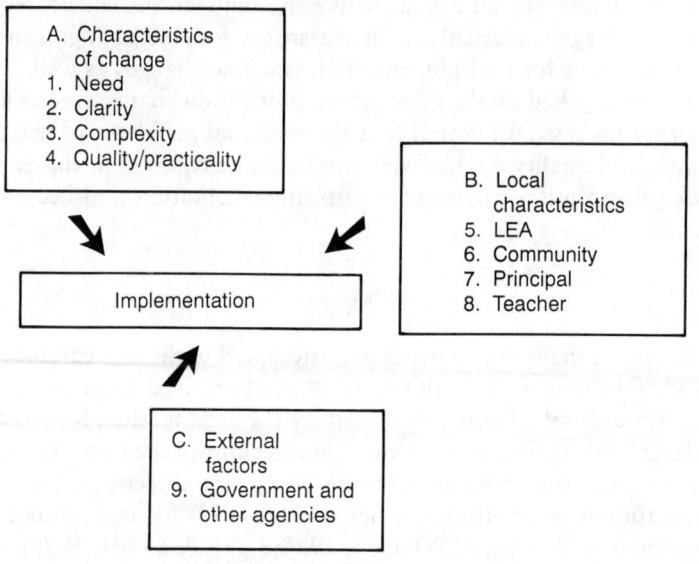

Figure 8.1 Interactive factors affecting implementation

new materials, etc.) in the direction of some sought after change. If any one or more factors or themes are working against implementation, the process will be less effective. Put positively, the more factors supporting implementation, the more change in practice will be accomplished. Finally, we should avoid thinking of sets of factors or themes in isolation from each other. They form a *system of variables* that interact to determine success or failure. Above all, educational change is a dynamic process involving interacting variables over time, regardless of whether the mode of analysis is factors or themes.

KEY FACTORS IN THE IMPLEMENTATION PROCESS

Figure 8.1 lists 9 critical factors organized into 3 main categories relating to (A) the characteristics of the innovation or change project, (B) local roles, and (C) external factors. In describing the roles I have tried to emphasize aspects that can be altered rather than those that are fixed or givens. The list is necessarily oversimplified. [. . .] At this time the goal is to obtain an overview and feel for the roles in the change process.

Factors related to characteristics of the change

Earlier research on the initiation and implementation process stressed the impact of the nature of the change itself on potential users, i.e., teachers in their classrooms. The characteristics of the change, its size, complexity, prescriptiveness, and practicality for teachers were considered in the light of the teachers'

111

t often in hindsight. While the innovations considered in such
'argely curriculum- or classroom-focused changes, the lessons
rue for multidimensional, systemic changes as well.
.ouched on the relevance of innovation characteristics as part of
.ation process. We found that the potential problems of need, clarity,
~omplexity, and quality neither were nor could be resolved at this early stage.
This lack of resolution carries over into implementation and becomes much
more visible.

Need

As noted earlier, many innovations are attempted without a careful examination of whether or not they address what are perceived to be priority needs.
Teachers, for example, frequently do not see the need for an advocated change.
Several large-scale studies in the United States confirm the importance of relating need to decisions about innovations or change directions. [. . .] Further,
implementation is more effective when it is relatively focused or specific needs
are identified (e.g., Emrick & Peterson, 1978; Louis & Sieber, 1979). Complex
or multifaceted reforms, such as those addressed in restructuring initiatives can
also be focused, but they require a great deal of effort to clarify the nature of
the needs being addressed (see David, 1989; Murphy, 1992).

While the importance of perceived or felt need is obvious, its role is not all
that straightforward. There are at least three complications. First, schools are
faced with overloaded improvement agendas. Therefore, it is a question of not
only whether a given need is important, but also how important it is relative to
other needs. Needless to say, this prioritizing among sets of desirables is not
easy, as people are reluctant to neglect any goals, even though it may be
unrealistic to address them all. [. . .] Second, precise needs are often not clear
at the beginning, especially with complex changes. People often become clearer
about their needs only when they start doing things, that is, during implementation itself. Third, need interacts with the other eight factors to produce
different patterns. Depending on the pattern, need can become further clarified
or obfuscated during the implementation process.

In summary, the 'fit' between a new program and district and/or school
needs is essential, but it may not become entirely clear until implementation is
underway. Huberman and Miles (1984) also remind us that by this early
implementation stage, people involved must perceive both that the needs being
addressed are significant *and* that they are making at least some progress
toward meeting them. Early rewards and some tangible success are critical
incentives during implementation.

Clarity

Clarity (about goals and means) is a perennial problem in the change process.
Even when there is agreement that some kind of change is needed, as when
teachers want to improve some area of the curriculum or improve the school as

a whole, the adopted change may not be at all clear about what teachers should do differently. [. . .] Lack of clarity – diffuse goals and unspecified means of implementation – represents a major problem at the implementation stage [. . .].

Legislation and many other new policies and programs are sometimes deliberately stated at a general level in order to avoid conflict and promote acceptance and adoption. Such policies often do not indicate how implementation is to be addressed. Curriculum guidelines have also suffered from vagueness of goals and especially of means of implementation.

There is little doubt that clarity is essential, but its meaning is subtle; too often we are left with *false clarity* instead. False clarity occurs when change is interpreted in an oversimplified way; that is, the proposed change has more to it than people perceive or realize. For example, [. . .] new or revised curriculum guidelines may be dismissed by some teachers on the grounds that 'we are already doing that'; but this is another illustration of false clarity if the teachers' perception is based only on the more superficial goal and content aspects of the guidelines to the neglect of beliefs and teaching strategies. Similarly, many of the latest curriculum guidelines [. . .] contain greater specificity of objectives and content than previous guidelines, with the result that teachers and others welcome them as 'finally providing direction'; however, these guidelines may be used in a literal way without the realization that certain teaching strategies and underlying beliefs are essential to implementing the guidelines effectively.

On the other hand, I have cited evidence above that not everyone experiences the comfort of false clarity. Unclear and unspecified changes can cause great anxiety and frustration to those sincerely trying to implement them. Clarity, of course, cannot be delivered on a platter. It is accomplished or not depending on the *process*. Nor is greater clarity an end in itself: Very simple and insignificant changes can be very clear, while more difficult and worthwhile ones may not be amenable to easy clarification. This brings me directly to the third related factor – complexity.

Complexity

Complexity refers to the difficulty and extent of change required of the individuals responsible for implementation. The [. . .] main idea is that any change can be examined with regard to difficulty, skill required, and extent of alterations in beliefs, teaching strategies, and use of materials. Many changes [. . .] require a sophisticated array of activities, structures, diagnoses, teaching strategies, and philosophical understanding if effective implementation is to be achieved.

While complexity creates problems for implementation, it may result in greater change because more is being attempted. Berman and McLaughlin (1977) found that 'ambitious projects were less successful in absolute terms of the percent of the project goals achieved, but they typically stimulated more teacher change than projects attempting less' (p. 88). Those changes that did occur were more thorough as a result of the extra effort that the project required or inspired. As Berman (1980) stated elsewhere, 'little ventured, nothing gained'. [. . .]

We face here a dilemma in the change process. On the one hand, we have evidence to suggest that the 'larger the scope and personal "demandingness" of a change, the greater the chance for success' (Crandall, et al., 1986, p. 25). On the other hand, attempting too much can result in massive failure. Huberman and Miles (1984) found that schools often attempt to implement innovations that are beyond their ability to carry out, a phenomenon they call 'over-reaching' and one we have seen since the 1960s.

In summary, simple changes may be easier to carry out, but they may not make much of a difference. Complex changes promise to accomplish more, which is good news given the kinds of changes in progress in the 1980s and 1990s, but they also demand more effort, and failure takes a greater toll. The answer seems to be to break complex changes into components and implement them in a divisible and/or incremental manner.

Yin, Herald, and Vogel (1977, p. 61), for example, studied 140 technological innovations across the criminal, justice, fire, health, education, transportation, and planning sectors. They classified the innovations according to whether they could be used/tested on a limited basis. Those cases where divisibility existed were associated with a higher frequency of success (improvement plus eventual incorporation). [. . .] Huberman and Miles (1984) also describe how ambitious change projects were implemented incrementally, but they caution, as I have in this chapter, that success depends on the presence of other conditions as well, such as sustained assistance (see the subsequent section on key themes).

Quality and practicality of program

The last factor associated directly with the nature of change concerns the quality and practicality of the change project – whether it is a new curriculum, a new policy, a restructured school, or whatever. The history of the quality of attempted changes relative to the other three variables (need, clarity, complexity) is revealing. To say that the importance of the quality of the change is self-evident is to underestimate how initiation decisions are made. Inadequate quality and even the simple unavailability of materials and other resources can result when adoption decisions are made on grounds of political necessity, or even on grounds of perceived need without time for development. [. . .] Ambitious projects are nearly always politically driven. As a result the time line between the initiation decision and startup is typically too short to attend to matters of quality. [. . .] The shorter the latter time line, the more problems there [are] (Huberman & Miles, 1984). The more complex the change, the more work there is to do on quality.

Changes in schools must also pass the test of the 'practicality ethic' of teachers (Doyle & Ponder, 1977–78). Practical changes are those that address salient needs, that fit well with the teachers' situation, that are focused, and that include concrete how-to-do-it possibilities (Mortimore et al., 1988). Practical does not necessarily mean easy, but it does mean the presence of next steps. Again we can see a dilemma in the change process. Changes that are practical, even though of good quality, may be trivial or offensive, while changes that are complex may not be practically worked out.

It is possible, indeed necessary, to combine ambitious change and quality. I have maintained that it is what people develop in their minds and actions that counts. People do not learn or accomplish complex changes by being told or shown what to do. Deeper meaning and solid change must be born over time. With particular changes, especially complex ones, one must struggle through ambivalence before one is sure that the new vision is workable and right (or unworkable and wrong). Good change is hard work; on the other hand, engaging in a bad change or avoiding needed changes may be even harder on us.

Local factors

This section analyzes the social conditions of change; the organization or setting in which people work; and the planned and unplanned events and activities that influence whether or not given change attempts will be productive. The local education authority* represents one major set of situational constraints or opportunities for effective change. [. . .]

The research on the role of organizations in change indicates that 'planned change has become a matter of both motivating from without and orchestrating from within' (Firestone & Corbett, 1987, p. 321). The individual school may be the unit of change, but frequently change is the result of system initiatives that live or die based on the strategies and supports offered by the larger organization. This is especially true of multilevel, complex system-oriented innovations where what is being changed is the organizational culture itself.

The LEA

[. . .] Most attempts at collective change in education seem to fail, and failure means frustration, wasted time, feelings of incompetence and lack of support, and disillusionment. Since introducing innovations is a way of life in most [LEAs, they] build up track records in managing change. Whatever the track record at a given point in time, it represents a significant precondition relative to the next new initiative. The importance of the [authority's] history of innovation attempts can be stated in the form of a proposition: The more that teachers or others have had negative experiences with previous implementation attempts in the [authority] or elsewhere, the more cynical or apathetic

---

* *Editor's footnote:* The original text of this chapter refers to 'school districts' and 'school boards' in the North American context, rather than LEAs and governing bodies. The factors discussed concerning school districts are broadly applicable to the UK context.

they will be about the next change presented regardless of the merit of the new idea or program. [LEAs . . .] and countries can develop an incapacity for change as well as a capacity for it. [. . .]

On the other hand, nothing is more gratifying psychologically than attempting a change that works and benefits students. Success can beget more success. If the subjective meaning of change is so central, it is worth stressing that people carry meanings from one experience to the next. This psychological history of change is a major determinant of how seriously people try to implement new programs. [. . .]

Individual teachers and single schools can bring about change without the support of central administrators, but [LEA]-wide change will not happen. [. . .] All of the research cited in this chapter shows that the support of central administrators is critical for change in [LEA] practice. It also shows that general support or endorsement of a new program has very little influence on change in practice (for example, verbal support without implementation follow-through). Teachers and others know enough now, if they didn't 20 years ago, not to take change seriously unless central administrators *demonstrate through actions* that they should. [. . .]

Key central administrators set the conditions for implementation to the extent that they show specific forms of support and active knowledge and understanding of the realities of attempting to put a change into practice. To state it most forcefully, [LEA] administrators affect the quality of implementation to the extent that they understand and help to manage the set of factors and the processes described in this chapter.

Community characteristics

It is very difficult to generalize about the role of communities [. . .] vis-à-vis implementation. Corwin (1973) found that community support of the school was correlated positively with innovativeness. Smith and Keith (1971) and Gold and Miles (1981) tell the painful sagas of what happens when middle-class communities do not like the innovations they see in their schools. [. . .]

The role of communities is quite variable ranging from apathy to active involvement – with the latter varying from conflictful to cooperative modes depending on the conditions [. . .].*

The principal

[. . .] All major research on innovation and school effectiveness shows that the principal strongly influences the likelihood of change, but it also indicates that most principals do not play [curriculum] or change leadership roles. Berman and McLaughlin (1977) found that 'projects having the *active* support of the

* *Editor's footnote:* The discussion here relates entirely to research on North American organizational structures, and does not apply to the UK context. It has therefore been omitted.

principal were the most likely to fare well' (p. 124, their emphasis). Principals' actions serve to legitimate whether a change is to be taken seriously (and not all changes are) and to support teachers both psychologically and with resources. [. . .] If we recall the earlier dimensions of change (beliefs, teaching behaviour, curriculum materials), we might speculate that unless the principal gains some understanding of these dimensions (not necessarily as an expert or [a curriculum] leader) he or she will not be able to understand teachers' concerns – that is, will not be able to provide support for implementation. Such understanding requires interaction.

There is an abundance of other evidence [. . .] that describes how and why the principal is necessary for effective implementation. The principal is the person most likely to be in a position to shape the organizational conditions necessary for success, such as the development of shared goals, collaborative work structures and climates, and procedures for monitoring results. [. . .] The subjective world of principals is such that many of them suffer from the same problem in 'implementing a new role as facilitator of change' as do teachers in implementing new teaching roles: What the principal should do *specifically* to manage change at the school level is a complex affair for which the principal has little preparation. The psychological and sociological problems of change that confront the principal are at least as great as those that confront teachers. Without this sociological sympathy, many principals will feel exactly as teachers do: Other people simply do not seem to understand the problems they face.

The role of teachers

Both individual teacher characteristics and collective or collegial factors play roles in determining implementation. [. . .] Some teachers, depending on their personality and influenced by their previous experiences and stage of career, are more self-actualized and have a greater sense of efficacy, which leads them to take action and persist in the effort required to bring about successful implementation.

[. . .] Several researchers have found that some schools have a much higher proportion of change-oriented teachers than others (Little, 1982; Rosenholtz, 1989). Some of this is no doubt through selection, but it also seems to be the case that the culture or climate of the school can shape an individual's psychological state for better or for worse.

In the final analysis it is the actions of the individual that count. Since interaction with others influences what one does, relationships with other teachers is a critical variable. The theory of change that we have been evolving clearly points to the importance of peer relationships in the school. Change involves learning to do something new, and interaction is the primary basis for social learning. [. . .] Collegiality, open communication, trust, support and help, learning on the job, getting results, and job satisfaction and morale are closely interrelated. There is a vast difference between the 'learning-impoverished' schools and the 'learning-enriched' schools described by Rosenholtz (1989). Only 13 of the 78 schools in Rosenholtz' sample were classified as 'learning enriched,' but they provide powerful models of work environments that stimulate continuous improvements.

No words could sum up this discussion of school-level factors more accurately than those of Judith Little (1981), based on her study of work practice in six urban schools.

> School improvement is most surely and thoroughly achieved when:
> Teachers engage in frequent, continuous and increasingly concrete and precise *talk* about teaching practice (as distinct from teacher characteristics and failings, the social lives of teachers, the foibles and failures of students and their families, and the unfortunate demands of society on the school). By such talk, teachers build up a shared language adequate to the complexity of teaching, capable of distinguishing one practice and its virtue from another.
>
> Teachers and administrators frequently *observe* each other teaching, and provide each other with useful (if potentially frightening) evaluations of their teaching. Only such observation and feedback can provide shared *referents* for the shared language of teaching, and both demand and provide the precision and concreteness which makes the talk about teaching useful.
>
> Teachers and administrators *plan, design, research, evaluate and prepare teaching materials together*. The most prescient observations remain academic ('just theory') without the machinery to act on them. By joint work on materials, teachers and administrators share the considerable burden of development required by long-term improvement, confirm their emerging understanding of their approach, and make rising standards for their work attainable by them and by their students.
>
> Teachers and administrators *teach each other* the practice of teaching. (pp. 12–13, her emphasis)

Only two of the six schools in Little's study evidenced a very high percentage of these practices, but no more convincing picture of the conditions for developing *meaning* on the part of individual teachers and administrators could be portrayed than in the passage just quoted.

External factors

The last set of factors that influence implementation places the school or [LEA] in the context of the broader society. This means primarily the offices of the department of education, [. . .] faculties of education, and regional institutions. [. . .] The relationship of the school to these various outside agencies is quite complicated, but necessary to analyse in order to understand the forces that impinge on school personnel. [. . .]

[Regional] and national priorities for education are set according to the political forces and lobbying of interest groups, government bureaucracies, and elected representatives. Legislation, new policies, and new program initiatives arise from public concerns that the educational system is not doing an adequate job of teaching basics, developing career-relevant skills for the economic system, producing effective citizens, meeting the needs of at-risk children – recent immigrants or handicapped children or cultural minorities – and so on. [. . .] We have no reason whatsoever to imagine that these actions in their own right are related to implementation. Whether or not implementation occurs will depend on the congruence between the reforms and local needs, and how the changes are introduced and followed through.

Government agencies have been preoccupied with policy and program initiation, and until recently they vastly underestimated the problems and processes of implementation. We have a classic case of two entirely different worlds – the policy-maker on the one hand, and the local practitioner on the other hand. ('Divergent worlds' as Cowden & Cohen, 1979, call them.) [. . .] The most straightforward way of stating the problem is to say that local school systems and external authority agencies have not learned how to establish a *processual* relationship with each other. The relationship is more in the form of episodic events than processes: submission of requests for money, intermittent progress reports on what is being done, external evaluations – paper work, not people work. [. . .] Lack of role clarity, ambiguity about expectations, absence of regular interpersonal forums of communication, ambivalence between authority and support roles of external agencies, and solutions that are worse than the original problems combine to erode the likelihood of implementation.

The difficulties in the relationship between external and internal groups are central to the problem and process of meaning. Not only is meaning hard to come by when two different worlds have limited interaction, but misinterpretation, attribution of motives, feelings of being misunderstood, and disillusionment on both sides are almost guaranteed.

Government agencies have become increasingly aware of the importance and difficulty of implementation and are allocating resources to establishing implementation units, to assessing the quality of potential changes, to supporting staff development, to monitoring implementation of policies, and to addressing other factors discussed in this chapter. Whether they will be successful is a relative matter, related partly to the resources required to address problems and partly to the capacity of local school systems to use these resources effectively. [. . .]

Technical assistance for implementation (materials, consultancy, staff development, etc.) is frequently available in federal- or state-sponsored innovative programs. We have learned a great deal in the past few years about the conditions under which external help is needed and effective (Louis & Rosenblum, 1981; Crandall et al., 1982). The simplest observation at this juncture is that outside assistance or stimulation can influence implementation greatly, provided that it is integrated with the factors at the local level described above.

To conclude the discussion of external factors, the multiplicity of postadoption decisions after educational legislation or new policies involves several layers of agencies. That success is achieved in many instances is a reflection that some people 'out there' know what they are doing. Sharing and developing this know-how should be a major goal of those interested in educational change.

KEY THEMES IN THE IMPLEMENTATION PROCESS

Innovations have become increasingly more holistic in scope as reformers have realized that introducing single curriculum changes amounts to tinkering. As these changes have become more organic and multilevel, it has been necessary to rethink the change process. Discussing individual roles and lists of factors, while helpful to a point, seems no longer adequate. Researchers and initiators of change have reconceptualized and studied change projects by identifying key themes in successful improvement efforts. This has resulted in a much more dynamic and vivid picture of the change process. [. . .]

There are a number of recent studies that provide clear descriptions of the main themes in successful change at the school level (Louis & Miles, 1990; Marsh, 1988; Wilson & Corcoran, 1988). The message is consistent in this research that a small number of powerful themes in combination make a difference.

The most fully developed conceptualization of this new approach is contained in Louis and Miles' (1990) study of how urban high schools improve. They identify five major themes: vision-building, evolutionary planning and development, initiative-taking and empowerment, resource and assistance mobilization, and problem-coping. I used Louis and Miles' scheme as the starting point for developing Figure 8.2. I see six themes as paramount. Five are contained in Louis and Miles' study (I have relabelled resource and assistance mobilization as staff development and resource assistance, and problem-coping as monitoring/problem-coping). I have added a sixth theme, namely, restructuring, because it is clear that altering the organizational arrangements and roles in schools is essential to reform.

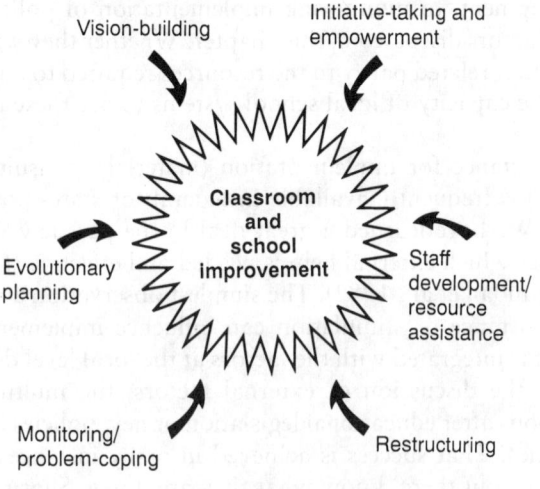

Figure 8.2   Key themes in improvement

Vision-building

Vision-building feeds into and is fed by all other themes in this section. It permeates the organization with values, purpose, and integrity for both the what and how of improvement. It is not an easy concept to work with, largely because its formation, implementation, shaping, and reshaping in specific organizations is a constant process.

Bennis and Nanus (1985) make it clear that vision formation is a dynamic interactive process. [. . .] Miles (1987) stresses that vision involves two dimensions: 'The first is a sharable, and shared vision of what the *school* could look like; it provides direction and driving power for change, and criteria for steering and choosing. . . . The second type is a shared vision of the *change process* . . . what will be the general game plan or strategy for getting there?' (p. 12) (their emphasis). Note the emphasis on *shared* sense of purpose concerning both the content and the process of change.

As reforms become more complex and directed to transforming the educational system, strategies for building a shared vision have to reflect a broader agenda. Anderson and Cox (1987, pp. 8, 9) suggest the following: be open to different views and perspectives, maintain a core of well-regarded and capable people to keep synthesizing and articulating the evolving view of the system, as much as possible allow for direct experiences with elements of the change (don't let people become passive observers), broaden the number of people aware of and committed to the change through communicating about it, build credibility through the use of symbols and public dialogue, legitimate emerging viewpoints in support of a new vision, be aware of shifts in the change process having an effect on the organization, implement partial solutions when necessary to act as building blocks for the larger effort, broaden political support, and, finally, find ways to dampen the opposition.

While virtually everyone agrees that vision is crucial, the practice of vision-building is not well understood. [. . .] See Rosenholtz, 1989, and Wilson and Corcoran, 1988, for good descriptions of successful vision-building in elementary and secondary schools, respectively.

Evolutionary planning

Once implementation was underway toward a desirable direction, the most successful schools in Louis and Miles' (1990) study adapted their plans as they went along to improve the fit between the change and conditions in the school to take advantage of unexpected developments and opportunities. Blending top-down initiative and bottom-up participation is often a characteristic of successful multilevel reforms that use what amounts to evolutionary planning approaches (Marsh, 1988). [. . .] Have a plan, but learn by doing is the message, one strongly echoed in the business literature (Kanter, 1989). As Tom Peters (1987) advises: 'Invest in applications-oriented small starts,' 'pursue team development of innovations,' 'encourage pilots of everything,' 'practice "creative supplying",' 'practice purposeful impatience,' 'support fast failures.' All of these are designed to foster an atmosphere of calculated risk-taking and constant multifaceted evolutionary development. [. . .]

Initiative-taking and empowerment

Since implementation is doing, getting and supporting people who are acting and interacting in purposeful directions is a major route to change. Louis and Miles (1990) found that initiative can come from different sources, but when it comes to implementation 'power sharing' is crucial. In their study, leaders in successful schools supported and stimulated initiative-taking by others; set up cross-hierarchical steering groups consisting of teachers, administrators, and sometimes parents and students; and delegated authority and resources to the steering groups, while maintaining active involvement in or liaison with the groups. Louis and Miles note that the leadership skills relative to this theme are difficult – such as giving up power without losing control, taking active initiative without shutting out others, and supporting others' initiative without becoming patronizing (see also Barth, 1990). Extending involvement and influence to clients (students and parents) is very much part of this theme [. . .].

Developing collaborative work cultures is also clearly central to this theme. It helps reduce the professional isolation of teachers, allowing the codification and sharing of successful practices and the provision of support [. . .]. Working together has the potential of raising morale and enthusiasm, opening the door to experimentation and increased sense of efficacy (Cohen, 1988; Rosenholtz, 1989). Constant communication and joint work provide the continuous pressure and support necessary for getting things done. [. . .] Implementation is very much a social process.

Staff development and resource assistance

The essence of educational change consists in learning new ways of thinking and doing, new skills, knowledge, attitudes, etc. It follows that staff development is a central theme related to change in practice. But, as with all the variables I am considering, the use of staff development can be grossly misapplied unless it is understood in relation to the meaning of change and the change process taken as a whole (Fullan, 1990). One of the great problems in educational reform is that there is too much well-intentioned 'ad hoc-ism' – the use of single, segmented solutions unconnected or unintegrated with their systemic realities. The result is more participation here, more materials production there, more in-service training everywhere – more, more, more. Well, when it comes to implementation, more is sometimes less.

The amount of staff training is not necessarily related to the quality of implementation, but it can be if it combines pre-implementation training with assistance during implementation, and uses a variety of trainers (see Huberman &

Miles, 1984; Louis & Rosenblum, 1981). [. . .] Most forms of in-service training are not designed to provide the ongoing, interactive, cumulative learning necessary to develop new conceptions, skills, and behaviour. Failure to realize that there is a need for in-service work *during implementation* is a common problem. No matter how much advance staff development occurs, it is when people actually try to implement new approaches and reforms that they have the most specific concerns and doubts. It is thus extremely important that people obtain some support at the early stages of attempted implementation. Getting over this initial critical hump represents a major breakthrough for working toward more thorough change (Huberman, 1981). [. . .]

Implementation, whether it is voluntary or imposed, is nothing other than a process of *learning something new*. One foundation of new learning is *interaction*. [. . .] Once this is said, examples of successful training approaches to implementation make sense (Huberman & Miles, 1984; Joyce & Showers, 1988; Louis & Miles, 1990; Marsh, 1988; Stallings, 1989). They are effective when they combine concrete, teacher-specific training activities, ongoing continuous assistance and support during the process of implementation, and regular meetings with peers and others. Research on implementation has demonstrated beyond a shadow of a doubt that these processes of sustained *interaction and staff development* are crucial regardless of what the change is concerned with. The more complex the change, the more interaction is required *during* implementation. People can and do change, but it requires social energy. School districts and schools can help generate extra energy by developing or otherwise supporting continuous staff development opportunities for teachers, administrators, and others.

Monitoring/problem-coping

The monitoring theme is not evaluation in the narrow sense of the term. It includes information systems, resources, and acting on the results through problem-coping and solving. Monitoring the *process* of change is just as important as measuring outcomes. [. . .]

Monitoring serves two functions. First, by making information on innovative practices available it provides access to good ideas. Many good practices go unreported because of the isolation of teachers, schools, and districts from each other. Second, it exposes new ideas to scrutiny, helping to weed out mistakes and further develop promising practices. According to Peters (1987), the best 'systems' to ensure correct choices are

(1) A clear vision,
(2) Sharing stories that illustrate how others, at all levels, have reacted to novel situations consistent with the vision, and
(3) Recognition for jobs well done. (p. 486)

The result, claims Peters, is 'a *control system* in the truest sense of that term' (p. 486, his emphasis).

Formal monitoring procedures by themselves do not produce better results. The 'intensification' of educational reform, [. . .] fails because it either does not measure what is most important or its findings are not linked to a process of improvement that incorporates and interrelates the six themes described in this section.

Monitoring the results and the process of change is especially important at the school level. All research on effective schools shows that paying constant attention to students' academic, personal, and social development is essential for success (Mortimore et al., 1988; Odden & Marsh, 1988).

Gathering data on implementation issues is also crucial. The success of implementation is highly dependent on the establishment of effective ways of getting information on how well or poorly a change is going in the classroom and school. The crux of the matter is getting the right people talking together on a regular basis with the right information at their disposal. [. . .] Louis and Miles (1990) stress that 'all serious improvement programs have problems' (p. 268). In their research unsuccessful sites used shallow coping strategies such as avoidance, denial, procrastination, and people-shuffling, while successful sites engaged in deep problem solving such as redesign, creating new roles, providing additional assistance and time, and the like.

Evaluation and monitoring progress is probably one of the most difficult and complex strategies for change 'to get right.' It is frequently misused or not used (Wise, 1988). It is usually the last component of a change initiative that gets effectively, if at all, put in place (Fullan, Anderson, & Newton, 1986). In the early stages of attempts at change, people are usually wary of gathering information. On the other hand, it is revealing to note that once an improvement process of the type described in this section is underway, teachers and others close to implementation are those most insistent on gathering and examining the results of their efforts. Good change processes develop trust, relevance, and the desire to get better results. Accountability and improvement can be effectively interwoven, but it requires great sophistication (see also McLaughlin & Pfeiffer, 1988).

Restructuring

I will not take on here the big question of restructuring school, district, and state systems (David, 1989; Elmore, 1989; Harvey & Crandall, 1988; Murphy, 1992). I refer more directly to how the school as a workplace is organized. I use structure in the sociological sense to include organizational arrangements, roles, finance and governance, and formal policies that explicitly build in working conditions that, so to speak, support and press for improvement. Time for individual and team planning, joint teaching arrangements, staff development policies, new roles such as mentors and coaches, and school improvement procedures are examples of structural change at the school level that are conducive to improvement. There is a strong conceptual rationale for the importance of restructuring schools, but there is not much empirical evidence of its positive effects. We are still at the early stages of restructuring experiments, which should serve to help clarify the concept and debug how it might best be implemented. I include restructuring as a theme for implementation because of its obvious importance and potential, and because much of the action in the 1990s will center on attempts to restructure schools and the relationships of schools to external forces.

In summary, these six themes – leadership and vision, evolutionary planning, initiative-taking and empowerment, staff development and assistance, monitoring/problem-coping, and restructuring – provide a dynamic and powerful image of the complexity and excitement of the implementation process. They feed into and on each other. All six themes in concert are required for substantial change to occur.

FACTORS AFFECTING CONTINUATION

Implementation is the big hurdle at the level of practice, but the question of the continuation of initiated reforms should be considered in its own right. In a sense continuation represents another adoption decision, which may be negative, and even if positive may not itself get implemented. Berman and Mc-Laughlin (1978, pp. 166–83) found that projects that were not implemented effectively were discontinued (as would be expected), but they also found that only a minority of those that were well implemented were continued beyond the period of federal funding. The reasons for lack of continuation were in the main the same ones that influenced implementation, except that their role became more sharply defined. Lack of interest or inability to fund 'special projects' out of district funds, and lack of money for staff development and staff support for both continuing and new teachers, signaled the end of many implemented programs. Lack of interest and support at the central district office (e.g., on the part of those who had taken on the project for opportunistic reason) was another reason for noncontinuation. Similarly, at the school level

> The principal was the key to both implementation and continuation. . . . After the end of the federal funding, the principal influenced continuation in . . . direct ways. Often because of turnover in the original cadre of project teachers, projects would have decayed without active efforts by principal to bring on new staff. . . . It was extremely difficult for teachers to go on using project methods or materials without the principal's explicit support. (Berman & McLaughlin, 1977, p. 188)

Berman and McLaughlin identified a small number of cases in which continuation was sustained. In addition to the specific factors just cited (active leadership, staff development, etc.), the authors noted

> District officials paid early attention to mobilizing broad-based support for the innovation. And after federal funding ended, mobilization efforts were increased to pave the way for the project's transition from its special status to its incorporation into key areas of district operations: the

budget, personnel assignment, curriculum support activities, and the instruction program. In short, the groundwork and planning for sustaining a change agent project had the early, active, and continued attention of school district managers. (Berman & McLaughlin, 1978, p. 20)

As a cautionary note, Berman and McLaughlin (1977, pp. 185–86) emphasize that the 'meaning of continuation' can be misleading. For example, a district may officially decide to continue a project, but teachers may not implement it (i.e., in terms of the dimensions of implementation). Or a district may decide to discontinue the program, but many of the teachers may have already assimilated it. In other words, the program may leave its mark on the district in ways that may be overlooked. Direct assistance from external authorities may be helpful for initial implementation; but when it comes to institutionalization, the larger the external resource support, the *less likely* the effort will be continued after external funds terminate, because the district will not be able to afford to incorporate the costs into its regular budget (Yin et al., 1977, p. 16).

The problem of continuation is endemic to all new programs irrespective of whether they arise from external initiative or are internally developed. Huberman and Miles (1984) stress that continuation or institutionalization of innovations depends on whether or not the change gets embedded or built into the structure (through policy, budget, timetable, etc.), has (by the time of the institutionalization phase) generated a critical mass of administrators and teachers who are skilled in and commited to the change, and has established procedures for continuing assistance (such as a trained cadre of assisters), especially relative to supporting new teachers and administrators. Corbett and associates (1984) also found that availability of support and incorporation of the change into policy or guidelines varied and was related to the likelihood of continuation. They did not find that the availability of evaluation data from effectiveness instruments was much of a factor in the decision to continue (mainly because few schools in their sample had collected such data).

We talk about continuation as the third phase in a planned change process, but it should be clear that the process is not simply linear and that all phases must be thought about from the beginning and continually thereafter. For example, one of the most powerful factors known to take its toll on continuation is staff and administrative turnover (Berman & McLaughlin, 1977; Huberman & Miles, 1984). Very few programs plan for the orientation and in-service support for new members who arrive after the program gets started. And arrive they do, chipping away, however unintentionally, at what is already a fragile process.

One final distinction is critical. How might we best think of the relationship between continuation of a specific project and 'future improvements' that go beyond the innovation or reform being attempted? This question can be profitably examined by considering both the case of single innovations and that of more ambitious reform projects at the school level.

With respect to single innovations, Crandall and associates (1986), drawing on the work of Hall and Loucks (1977), help us to understand that institutionalizing a given innovation is not an end in itself. The process 'begins with the individual user not even interested in attending to the innovation, but ends with the user so proficient that he or she is riding new winds, modifying the original innovation so that it in fact works better, or even looking for a practice that represents an improvement over the one just mastered' (Crandall et al., 1986, p. 44). Improvement of practice is thus a continuous process of renewal.

Similarly, schools that engage in major effectiveness or restructuring efforts are presumably interested in going beyond the original projects. Put more powerfully, school effectiveness projects are in the business of institutionalizing the long-term capacity for continuous improvement. We need to make this goal more explicit because one can succeed in the short run in establishing an exciting, innovative, effective school, only to find that it doesn't last (Little, 1988). Deeper changes in the very culture of the school and its relationship to outside agencies are at stake if we are to develop this generic capacity for improvement.

PERSPECTIVES ON THE CHANGE PROCESS

As we have seen, the implementation process is complex and dilemma ridden, but we have accumulated considerable knowledge and insight into the process of change over the past decade. Some of these lessons were not self-evident at the outset, although they make common sense once discovered. The main revelations in this journey include a combination of elements that we usually think of as mutually exclusive or as not operating in the manner that they do. There are four main insights that were not predictable, but have turned out to be important.

(1) Active initiation and participation,
(2) Pressure and support,
(3) Changes in behaviour and beliefs, and
(4) The overriding problem of ownership.

The first issue is how can reform get started when there are large numbers of people involved. There is no single answer, but it is increasingly clear that changes require some impetus to get started. There is no evidence that widespread involvement at the initiation stage is either feasible or effective. It is more likely the case that small groups of people begin and, if successful, build momentum. Active initiation, starting small and thinking big, bias for action, and learning by doing are all aspects of making change more manageable, by getting the process underway in a desirable direction. Participation, initiative-taking, and empowerment are key factors from the beginning, but sometimes do not get activated until a change process has begun.

Second, it is increasingly clear that both pressure and support are necessary for success. We usually think of pressure as a bad thing, and support as good. But there is a positive role for pressure in change. There are many forces maintaining the status quo. When change occurs it is because some pressure has built up that leads to action. During the change process interaction among implementers serves to integrate both pressure and support. One of the reasons that peer coaching works so effectively is that it combines pressure and support in a kind of seamless way. Successful change projects always include elements of both pressure and support. Pressure without support leads to resistance and alienation; support without pressure leads to drift or waste of resources.

Third, the relationship between changes in behaviour on the one hand, and changes in beliefs or understanding on the other hand requires careful consideration. Returning to the theme of meaning, it seems that most people do not discover new understandings until they have delved into something. In many cases, changes in behaviour precede rather than follow changes in belief (Fullan, 1985). Moreover, when people try something new they often suffer what I call 'the implementation dip'. Things get worse before they get better and clearer as people grapple with the meaning and skills of change (Joyce & Showers, 1988). We see then that the relationship between behavioral and belief change is reciprocal and ongoing, with change in doing or behavior a necessary experience on the way to breakthroughs in meaning and understanding.

The role of ownership is the fourth subtlety in the change process. Clearly, deep ownership of something new on the part of large numbers of people is tantamount to real change, but the fact is that ownership is not acquired that easily. And when people are apparently in favor of a particular change, they may not 'own it' in the sense of understanding it and being skilled at it, that is, they may not know what they are doing. Ownership in the sense of clarity, skill, and commitment is a progressive process. True ownership is not something that occurs magically at the beginning, but rather is something that comes out the other end of a successful change process.

In summary, the broad implications of the implementation process have several interrelated components. The first is that the crux of change involves the development of meaning in relation to a new idea, program, reform, or set of activities. But it is *individuals* who have to develop new meaning, and these individuals are insignificant parts of a gigantic, loosely organized, complex, messy social system that contains myriad different subjective worlds.

The causes of change also become more easily identifiable and understood once we possess an underlying conception of what constitutes change as a process over time. [. . .] Effective implementation depends on the *combination* of all the factors and themes described in this chapter. The characteristics of the nature of the change, the make-up of the [LEA], the character of individual schools and teachers, and the existence and form of external relationships interact to produce conditions for change or nonchange. The six critical themes co-exist or work at cross-purposes. It takes a fortunate combination of the right factors – a critical mass – to support and guide the process of re-learning, which respects the maintenance needs of individuals and groups and at the same time facilitates, stimulates, and prods people to change through a process of incremental and decremental fits and starts on the way to institutionalizing (or, if appropriate, rejecting) the change in question.

Moreover (as if we could stand more quandaries), there is frequently no definitive 'change in question' at the beginning of the process of implementation, especially for complex reforms. Situations vary, and we never fully know what implementation is or should look like until people in particular situations attempt to spell it out through use. Implementation *makes* further policy; it does not simply put predefined policy into practice (see Farrar, DeSanctis, & Cohen, 1979; Majone & Wildavsky, 1978; Berman, 1980). [. . .]

The odds against successful planned educational change are not small. [. . .] To bring about more effective change, we need to be able to explain not only what causes it but how to influence those causes. To implement programs successfully, we need better implementation plans; to get better implementation plans, we need to know how to change our planning process; to know how to change our planning process, we need to know how to produce better planners and implementers and on and on. Is it any wonder that the planning, doing, and coping with educational change is the 'science of muddling through' (Lindblom, 1959)? But it is a *science*. [. . .]

REFERENCES

Anderson, B., & Cox, P. (1987) *Configuring the education system for a shared future: Collaborative vision, action, reflection.* Andover, MA: Regional Laboratory for Educational Improvement of the Northeast and the Islands.

Barth, R. (1990) *Improving schools from within: Teachers, parents and principals can make the difference.* San Francisco: Jossey-Bass.

Bennis, W., & Nanus, B. (1985) *Leaders.* New York: Harper & Row.

Berman, P. (1980) Thinking about programmed and adaptive implementation: Matching strategies to situations. In H. Ingram & D. Mann (Eds.), *Why policies succeed or fail* (pp. 205–27). Beverly Hills, CA: Sage.

Berman, P., & McLaughlin, M. (1977) *Federal programs supporting educational change: Vol. VII. Factors affecting implementation and continuation.* Santa Monica, CA: Rand Corporation.

Berman, P., & McLaughlin, M. (1978) *Federal programs supporting educational change: Vol. VIII. Implementing and sustaining innovations.* Santa Monica, CA: Rand Corporation.

Cohen, M. (1988) Designing state assessment systems. *Phi Delta Kappan,* 70(8), 583–88.

Corbett, H.D., Dawson, J., & Firestone, W. (1984) *School context and school change.* New York: Teachers College Press.

Corwin, R. (1973) *Reform and organizational survival – The teacher corps as an instrument of educational change.* New York: Wiley.

Cowden, P., & Cohen, D. (1979) *Divergent worlds of practice.* Cambridge, MA: Huron Institute.

Crandall, D., and associates. (1982) *People, policies and practice: Examining the chain of school improvement* (Vols. 1–10). Andover, MA: The Network.

Crandall, D., Eiseman, J., & Louis, K. (1986) Strategic planning issues that bear on the success of school improvement efforts. *Educational Administration Quarterly,* 22(3), 21–53.

David, J.L. (1989) *Restructuring in progress: Lessons from pioneering districts.* Washington, DC: National Governors' Association.

Doyle, W., & Ponder, G. (1977–78) The practicality ethic in teacher decision making. *Interchange,* 8(3), 1–12.

Elmore, R.F. (1989) *Models of restructured schools.* Paper presented at American Educational Research Association annual meeting.

Emrick, J., & Peterson, S. (1978) *A synthesis of findings across five recent studies in educational dissemination and change.* San Francisco: Far West Laboratory for Educational Research and Development.

Farrar, E., DeSanctis, J., & Cohen, D. (1979) *Views from below: Implementation research in education.* Cambridge, MA: Huron Institute.

Firestone, W., & Corbett, H.D. (1987) Planned organizational change. In N. Boyand (Ed.), *Handbook of research on educational administration* (pp. 321–40). New York: Longman.

Fullan, M. (1985) Change process and strategies at the local level. *The Elementary School Journal, 84*(3), 391–420.

Fullan, M., Anderson, S., & Newton, E. (1986) *Support systems for implementing curriculum in school boards.* Toronto: OISE Press and Ontario Government Bookstore.

Gold, B., & Miles, M. (1981) *Whose school is it anyway? Parent-teacher conflict over an innovative school.* New York: Praeger.

Hall, G.E., & Loucks, S. (1977) A developmental model for determining whether the treatment is actually implemented. *American Educational Research Journal, 14*(3), 263–76.

Harvey, G., & Crandall, D.P. (1988) *A beginning look at the what and how of restructuring.* Andover, MA: The Network, and Regional Laboratory for Educational Improvement of the Northeast and the Islands.

Huberman, M. (1981) *Exemplary center for reading instruction (ECRI), Masepa, North Plains: A case study.* Andover, MA: The Network.

Huberman, M. (1983) Recipes for busy kitchens. *Knowledge: Creation, Diffusion, Utilization, 4,* 478–510.

Huberman, M., & Miles, M. (1984) *Innovation up close.* New York: Plenum.

Joyce, B., & Showers, B. (1988) *Student achievement through staff development.* New York: Longman.

Kanter, R.M. (1989) *When giants learn to dance.* New York: Simon & Schuster.

LaRocque, L., & Coleman, P. (1989) Quality control: School accountability and district ethos. In M. Holmes, K. Leithwood, & D. Musella (Eds.), *Educational policy for effective schools* (pp. 168–191). Toronto: OISE Press.

Lindblom, C. (1959) The science of muddling through, *Public Administration Review, 19,* 155–69.

Little, J.W. (1981) The power of organizational setting (Paper adapted from final report, *School success and staff development*). Washington, DC: National Institute of Education.

Little, J.W. (1982) Norms of collegiality and experimentation: Workplace conditions of school success. *American Educational Research Journal, 19,* 325–40.

Little, J.W. (1988) *Conditions of professional development in secondary schools.* Stanford, CA: Center for Research on the Context of Secondary Teaching.

Louis, K. & Miles, M.B. (1990) *Improving the urban high school: What works and why.* New York: Teachers College Press.

Louis, K., & Rosenblum, S. (1981) *Linking R & D with schools: A program and its implications for dissemination.* Washington, DC: National Institute of Education.

Louis, K., & Sieber, S. (1979) *Bureaucracy and the dispersed organization.* Norwood, NJ: Ablex.

Majone, G., & Wildavsky, A. (1978) Implementation as evolution. In H. Freeman (Ed.), *Policy studies annual review, Vol. II.* Beverly Hills, CA: Sage.

Marsh, D. (1988) *Key factors associated with the effective implementation and impact of California's educational reform.* Paper presented at the American Educational Research Association annual meeting.

McLaughlin, M., & Pfeiffer, R.S. (1988) *Teacher evaluation: Improvement, accountability, and effective learning.* New York: Teachers College Press.

Miles, M. (1987) *Practical guidelines for school administrators: How to get there.* Paper presented at American Educational Research Association annual meeting.

Mortimore, P., Sammons, P., Stoll, L., Lewis, D., & Ecob, R. (1988) *School matters: The junior years.* Somerset, United Kingdom: Open Books.

Murphy, J. (1992) *Restructuring schools: Capturing the phenomena.* New York: Teachers College Press.

Odden, A., & Marsh, D. (1988) How comprehensive reform legislation can improve secondary schools. *Phi Delta Kappan, 69*(8), 593–98.

Peters, T. (1987) *Thriving on chaos: Handbook for a management revolution.* New York: A. Knopf.

Rosenholtz, S. (1989) *Teachers' workplace: The social organization of schools.* New York: Longman.

Smith, L., & Keith, P. (1971) *Anatomy of educational innovation: An organizational analysis of an elementary school.* New York: Wiley.

Stallings, J.A. (1989) *School achievement effects and staff development: What are some critical factors?* Paper presented at American Educational Research Association annual meeting.

Wilson, B., & Corcoran, T. (1988) *Successful secondary schools: Visions of excellence in American public education.* Philadelphia: Falmer Press.

Wise, A. (1988) The two conflicting trends in school reform: Legislative learning revisited. *Phi Delta Kappan, 69*(5), 328–33.

Yin, R., Herald, K., & Vogel, M. (1977) *Tinkering with the system.* Lexington, MA: D.C. Heath.

9

A MODEL FOR MANAGING AN EXCELLENT SCHOOL

Headley Beare, Brian J. Caldwell and Ross H. Millikan

This material has been abridged

The vision for a school, however determined, must be brought to reality. The view of excellence which is envisaged should be reflected in statements about the philosophy and goals of the school. The educational needs of children and instructional programmes for the school will be determined in the light of these statements which will also give substance to important management processes wherein policies are formulated, priorities are set, plans are made, resources are allocated and teaching and learning proceeds, with regular, systematic appraisal of the programme. [. . .] The vision will be articulated in a manner which secures the commitment of all in the school community, with opportunities for leadership widely dispersed in the school. This commitment will be enhanced, as will the quality of decisions, with appropriate involvement of others in the decision-making process.

This chapter contains guidelines and illustrations for helping to bring vision to reality. We recommend a model for school management which provides a framework for accomplishing the following aspects of leadership [. . .]:

- *Purposing.* '. . . that continuous stream of actions by an organisation's formal leadership which have the effect of inducing clarity, consensus, and commitment regarding the organisation's basic purposes' (Vaill, 1986: 91)
- *Values.* 'Organisations are built on the unification of people around values' (Greenfield, 1986: 166)
- *School-site management and collaborative decision-making.* 'The staff of each school is given a considerable amount of responsibility and authority in determining the exact means by which they address the problem of increasing academic performance. This includes giving staffs more

authority over curricular and instructional decisions and allocation of building resources' (Purkey and Smith, 1985: 358)

- *Leadership density.* '. . . the extent to which leadership roles are shared and the extent to which leadership is broadly exercised' (Sergiovanni, 1987: 122)
- *Institutionalizing the vision.* 'The leader implants the vision in the structures and processes of the organisation, so that people experience the vision in the various patterned activities of the organisation' (Starratt, 1986).

Since bringing vision to reality may frequently involve changing the existing way of doing things, a model for school management must also contain strategies for the successful management of change. It is necessary, then, to review briefly what is now known about such strategies before describing and illustrating the model we recommend.

MANAGEMENT OF CHANGE

[. . .] One might ask: 'Are there generalizations about successful change which can be offered with [a high] degree of confidence?' We believe there are, and the purpose of this section of the chapter is to summarize the findings from one of the most recent and credible pieces of research about the management of change.

What follows is a summary of the findings of the *Project on Improving Urban High Schools* (Miles, 1987) which has been in progress for some time in the United States. We have chosen to share these findings for the following reasons:

- the project involved field-based research in schools which have been highly successful in implementing change
- the changes which had been successfully implemented fell into categories generally described as school improvement or school effectiveness or teacher effectiveness, and are thus relevant to the issue of excellence
- the findings are consistent with guidelines for the management of change which have been generally regarded as widely transferable
- the leader of the project, Matthew B. Miles, Center for Policy Research in New York, is one of the outstanding researchers and writers about organizational change, especially in education
- as noted by Miles (1987: 17), though the studies were carried out in urban high schools, there is no apparent reason why the findings should not be relevant to any kind of school in any setting (although we, with the reader, will put this observation to critical test).

The findings summarized on page 136 were derived from survey data from a national sample of 170 schools which had achieved varying degrees of success in implementation and from detailed case studies of 5 schools having a high degree of success with change of the kind described above.

Table 9.1 Relationships between factors in successful implementation of change (based on Miles, 1987)†

Factor	Is influenced by	Has influence on
Leadership	Precondition	Staff cohesiveness Good programme/fit Power sharing Rewards for staff Vision, Coping External networks Institutionalization
School autonomy	Precondition	Good programme/fit Control over resources
Staff cohesiveness	Precondition (Leadership)	Vision
Good programme/fit	Precondition Leadership School autonomy Evolutionary programme development	Power sharing Rewards for staff
Power sharing	Leadership Good programme/fit	Staff willingness/ initiative (Institutionalization)
Rewards for staff	Leadership Good programme/fit	Staff willingness/ initiative
Vision	Leadership Staff cohesiveness Control over staffing	Evolutionary programme development Staff willingness/ initiative
Control over staffing	School autonomy	Vision Staff willingness/ initiative
Control over resources	School autonomy	Evolutionary programme development

Factor	Is influenced by	Has influence on
Staff willingness/ initiative	Power sharing Rewards for staff Vision Control over staffing External networks	Evolutionary programme development 'Good implementation'
External networks	Leadership	Evolutionary programme development Staff willingness/ initiative Coping
Coping	Leadership External networks	Evolutionary programme development 'Good implementation' (Institutionalization)
Evolutionary programme development	Vision Control over resources External networks Staff willingness/ initiative Coping	Good programme/fit Organizational change 'Good implementation'
'Good implementation'	Evolutionary programme development Staff willingness/ initiative Coping	Institutionalization
Institutional- ization	Leadership (Power sharing) (Coping) 'Good implementation' Organizational change	
Organizational change	Evolutionary programme development	Institutionalization

† All relationships were observed causal relationships, except those in brackets which were hypothesized.

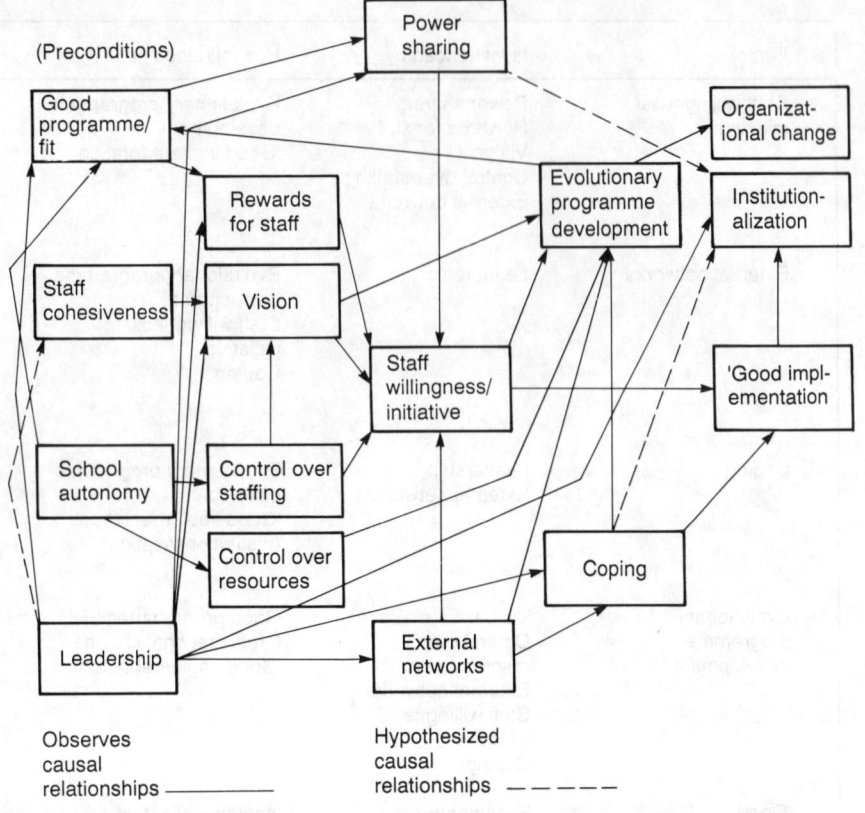

Figure 9.1 Illustration of relationships in successful implementation of change (Miles, 1987: 6)

Factors leading to successful implementation

Miles and his colleagues identified sixteen factors which seemed to account for successful implementation. Most are within the control of the principal and most call for particular patterns of working with and through staff. These factors are as follows, with the first four in the list being preconditions:

- Leadership   *(precondition)*
- School autonomy   *(precondition)*
- Staff cohesiveness   *(precondition)*
- Good programme/fit   *(precondition)*
- Power-sharing
- Rewards for staff
- Vision
- Control over staffing
- Control over resources
- Staff willingness/initiative
- Evolutionary programme development

- External networks
- Coping
- 'Good implementation'
- Institutionalization
- Organizational change

The first four factors were described as 'preconditions' because they can only be partly influenced by people at the school level. [. . .] The extent of school autonomy is often determined by policies formulated at the system level. Another precondition, staff cohesiveness, can be shaped to some extent by the principal and members of staff but is also influenced by the manner in which staff are appointed. The fourth precondition, a good programme/fit, refers to the extent to which the programme to be implemented is suited to schools in general and the particular community or culture. Miles and his colleagues found that major decisions related to programmes were generally made by people at the system level or by the principal.

A number of causal relationships were observed or hypothesized as summarised in Table 9.1 and illustrated in Figure 9.1. The following findings are noteworthy:

- Power sharing tended to occur after the major decisions about programmes were made but was critical to securing staff willingness/initiative which, in turn, was crucial to stabilizing the change after implementation (institutionalization)
- School autonomy extended to at least some control over staffing and other resources
- Programme development was evolutionary – 'a strong bias toward steady adaptation' (Miles, 1987: 13) – rather than implementation which was planned in detail at the outset
- The shared vision included a vision of the process of change as well as of a preferred and possible future for the school
- Empowerment of staff was important, with 'a critical mass of actively engaged people, usually up to a dozen or so' (*ibid:* 14), with expansion over time; bottom-up, departmentally based, planning groups and school councils were cited as examples of such empowered groups
- Internal and external assistance tailored to the special needs of the school was sought and sustained when success was achieved; assistance tended to be uniform in nature and limited to the 'front end' of the change process in less successful attempts at implementation
- Coping with problems was important if implementation was to be successful; successful schools used 'deep coping' strategies such as restaffing, securing greater control over resources, empowering, team building, and redesigning roles or the organization itself; unsuccessful schools tended to use 'shallow coping' strategies such as avoiding, denying, procrastinating or people-shuffling.

These findings [suggest the importance of various leadership factors] especially in regard to a shared vision, power-sharing ('leadership density'), and institu-

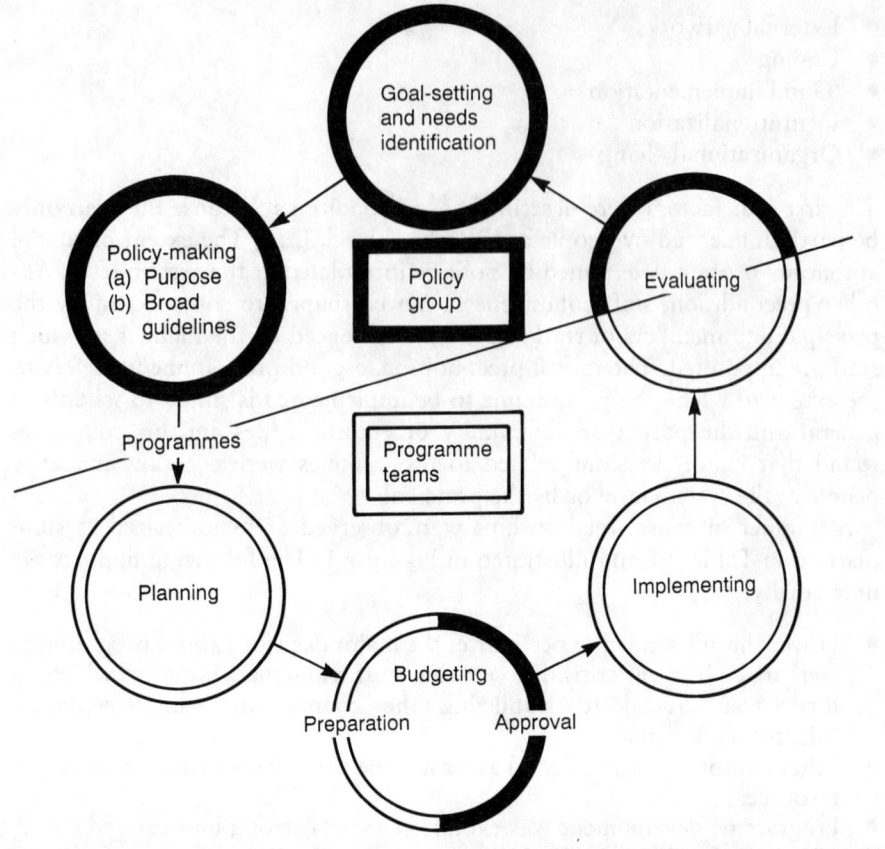

Figure 9.2 The Collaborative School Management Cycle (Caldwell and Spinks, 1988)

tionalizing the vision. They also identify other factors which can be influenced by leaders if change is to be successful, namely, staff cohesiveness, ensuring a good programme which 'fits' the school setting, rewards for staff, coping, and the formation and utilization of external networks. We believe the model for school management described and illustrated in the pages which follow incorporates the generalizations on leadership and strategies for the successful management of change which are suggested by the findings of the Miles study.

THE RECOMMENDED MODEL

We recommend the *Collaborative School Management Cycle* of Caldwell and Spinks (1988) as a model for school management which incorporates the generalizations and strategies related to leadership and change. An outline of the model is provided here along with a brief account of the research and development effort which led to its identification. The model is described as the Collaborative School Management Cycle and is illustrated in Figure 9.2. The cycle has six phases:

- Goal-setting and needs identification
- Policy-making, with policies consisting of statements of purpose and broad guidelines
- Planning of programmes
- Preparation and approval of programme budgets
- Implementing
- Evaluating.

Three special characteristics of the model are:

- the clear and unambiguous specification of those phases which are the concern of the group responsible for policy-making ('policy group') and of other phases which are the concern of the groups responsible for implementing policy ('programme teams'),
- a definition of policy which goes beyond a statement of general aims or purposes but is not so detailed as to specify action – it provides a brief statement of purpose and a set of broad guidelines, and
- the organizing of planning activities around programmes which correspond to the preferred patterns of work in the school.

The distinction between 'policy group' and 'programme teams' provides the framework for an approach to school management which is consistent with the generalizations about leadership and the strategies for the successful management of change. The people who constitute the policy group will vary from setting to setting. In Britain, under the provisions of the 1986 Education Act and the intentions of the national government as far as budgets in publicly funded schools are concerned, the policy group is the governing body. In government schools in Victoria, Australia, the policy group is a school council. In other places, the policy group may be the principal alone, principal and senior staff, or principal and senior staff with advice from teachers and other members of the school community. There may, in some instances, be different policy groups in the school, each addressing different sets of issues.

The activities of the school associated with learning and teaching and the support of learning and teaching are divided into programmes. The policies and priorities set by the policy group shape the planning of these programmes by members of programme teams who will be teachers in most instances, with a leader who may be designated as a head of department or programme coordinator, depending on local terminology and practice. It is this feature of the model which provides for power-sharing, with a 'critical mass' of actively engaged people (a finding of Miles and his colleagues on successful change) and 'leadership density' (generalization about leadership). Programme teams are responsible for preparing a plan for the implementation of policies related to their programmes and for identifying the resources required to support that plan. A programme plan and the proposed pattern for resource allocation together constitute a programme budget. The model thus affords a framework wherein a school can exercise control over the allocation of resources (a factor identified in the study reported by Miles), subject to the limits of school autonomy.

While programme budgets are prepared by programme teams, they must be approved by the policy group; they must reflect the policies and priorities established earlier by that group. This aspect of the model is consistent with the finding in the study reported by Miles that power-sharing in schools which successfully managed change tended to follow the making of 'major' decisions. Following implementation by programme teams, the evaluating phase is again a shared responsibility, with programme teams gathering information for programme evaluation and the policy group gathering further information as appropriate to make judgments on the effectiveness of policies and programmes.

In general, the policy group has responsibility for those phases which are emphasized in black in Figure 9.2 – largely those above the diagonal line – while programme teams work within a framework of policy to take responsibility for the remaining phases – largely those below the diagonal line. While a clear distinction is made between the responsibilities of the policy group and programme teams, there will in reality be a high degree of overlap as far as personnel are concerned and a continuing high level of formal and informal communication. [. . .]

GUIDELINES AND ILLUSTRATIONS

In this section of the chapter we use for illustrative purposes a vision for excellence that was offered [earlier in the book from which this chapter is taken] to illustrate vision in leadership. Included in the vision of the principal was the statement: 'Ruth (the principal) expects that curriculum and instruction should reflect the needs and interests of all children but that high expectations can be set and pursued with consistency and enthusiasm.' We shall provide illustrations for a primary school on this occasion.

[. . .] The principal may use a variety of strategies which result in general acceptance among staff and others that this vision should shape the programme of the school. This acceptance may take time, especially if some staff do not initially believe that it is possible to set high expectations for all students. However, these attitudes will change, especially as a result of sustained leadership of a symbolic nature including the use of rewards, choice of language and careful attention to the design of activities such as school ceremonies. Accomplishing this change of attitude is the essence of transforming leadership and a hallmark of excellence.

In time, then, this vision may be embodied in a statement of philosophy of the school. A school's philosophy is a statement of assumptions, values and beliefs about the nature and purpose of schooling, of learning and teaching processes, and processes which support learning and teaching. Included in a school's philosophy might be the following which reflects the aforementioned statement of vision.

We believe that it is desirable and possible to develop an educational programme at the school which will meet the needs and interests of every child in our community. Moreover, we believe that every child can achieve success in every learning experience in those parts of the school programme which have been selected as appropriate to the needs and interests of the child. We hold it important that every member of staff provide such learning opportunities for each child and that all parents and others in the school community be encouraged to give their strong support to the achievement of these expectations.

The goals, policies, plans, priorities, budgets and everyday activities in the school should all be consistent with the school's philosophy. That philosophy is the most fundamental benchmark for identifying needs and for programme evaluation.

Goal-setting

A goal is a statement of broad direction, general purpose or intent; it is general and timeless and is not concerned with a particular outcome at a particular point in time. Goals are usually formulated to reflect desired learning experiences and outcomes for the student. Some goals may also be concerned with the support of learning and the process of management.

The following are sample goals which reflect those parts of a statement of vision and school philosophy concerned with the setting of high expectations for all students:

- To ensure that each student enjoys learning and other experiences offered by the school
- To ensure that each student can attain a high level of reading ability, taking account of age and any special personal circumstances.

It is desirable that all in the school community be committed to goals as well as to the vision and philosophy of the school. Similar strategies for building commitment should therefore be followed, with formal adoption of goals being the outcome of a decision-making process designed to achieve consensus.

Another aspect of the first phase of the Collaborative School Management Cycle is identification of needs. Though we will qualify this definition, a need is considered to exist if 'what is' falls short of 'what should be'. Consider, for example one of the goals illustrated above: 'To ensure that each student can attain a high level of reading ability, taking account of age and any special personal circumstances.' For a particular primary school, the mean score on a standardized reading test given in Grade 3 was at the thirtieth percentile among mean scores for all primary schools in the state, that is, in only thirty per cent of primary schools was the mean score lower. This is a statement of 'what is' as far as levels of reading skill are concerned. Does a need for change exist? The answer depends on a judgement as to 'what ought to be' for such a school. Suppose a further comparison revealed that the mean score for the school in question exceeded the mean score for ninety per cent of all schools located in similar communities as far as student social and family background characteristics were concerned. The policy group might decide that investment of additional resources is unlikely to bring the school to the very top when such comparisons are made and that discrepancies between 'what is' and 'what ought to be' as far as other goals are concerned are such that other needs are greater or of higher priority. The group is likely to make a different judgement, however, if the second comparison reveals that mean reading scores exceed those of only fifty per cent of similar kinds of schools.

In general, the policy group must ask a number of questions before a need for change can be specified. A goal is just the starting point. The group must decide in practical terms 'what should be'. It must gather information about 'what is'. A judgement must then be made as to whether a gap is large enough for action to be taken. Will some harm be done if the gap is not closed? Can the gap be closed given a reasonable investment of resources? How important is this need compared with others?

Policy-making

Caldwell and Spinks (1988) describe a school policy as a statement of purpose and one or more guidelines as to how that purpose is to be achieved which, taken together, provide a framework for the operation of the school or programme. A school will have a number of policies, depending on its size and programme. Most policies will provide a framework for decisions related to the curriculum in areas such as mathematics, science and language. Other policies will affect all areas of the curriculum; for example, homework, assessment and reporting. Other categories of policy will concern the management of students (for example, discipline, field trips) and management processes in general (for example, a policy on decision-making or community involvement).

A primary school may have a policy on the development of reading skills which reflects that element of the statement of vision concerned with the setting of high expectations for all students and a goal or aim such as 'to ensure that each student can attain a high level of reading ability, taking account of age and any special personal circumstances'. [. . .]

Caldwell and Spinks recommend a model for the formulation of policy according to whether the issue at hand is contentious or non-contentious. A non-contentious issue is one for which there is general satisfaction with current practice in the school. A contentious issue is one for which there is disagreement on current practice among staff or others in the school community, or disagreement about the approach which should be taken if the issue is not currently addressed in the school. For non-contentious issues, Caldwell and Spinks recommend the simple documentation of existing practice in the agreed format for a policy statement. They suggest that a statement of policy should not exceed one page; any longer and it will be rarely read or changed. They also stress the importance of keeping the statement free of jargon so that it can be read and understood by all members of the school community.

For policy-making on contentious issues, Caldwell and Spinks recommend the appointment of a working party to prepare options for consideration by the policy group. The working party should be representative of those with expertise and a stake in the issue and it should obtain information from a variety of sources in preparing policy options. The desired outcome is consensus on a policy which is both desirable and feasible. The recommended approach provides a mechanism for empowering staff and others in preparing policy which provides a framework for action in bringing vision to reality.

Planning

Different levels of planning are possible in the recommended model for school management. These include corporate planning, strategic planning, programme planning, curriculum planning and instructional planning.

The most comprehensive approach is contained in the notion of corporate planning, defined by Caldwell and Spinks (1988) as:

> a continuous process in administration which links goal-setting, policy-making, short-term and long-term planning, budgeting and evaluation in a manner which spans all levels of the organization, secures appropriate involvement of people according to their responsibility for implementing plans as well as of people with an interest or stake in the outcomes of those plans, and provides a framework for the annual planning, budgeting and evaluation cycle.

A school may establish a corporate plan for, say, three years which will provide the framework for annual planning. Consider, for example, a school which has adopted the goal 'to ensure that each student can attain a high level of reading ability, taking account of age and any special personal circumstances'. Where evaluation has revealed that outcomes in the current reading programme fall well short of expectations, the school may plan to address the need over three years. Part of the corporate plan will refer to current levels of achievement in reading, desired outcomes at the end of three years, strategies for change to achieve the desired outcomes and the priority which is to be assigned to this initiative.

While distinctions between corporate planning and strategic planning are often unclear, we suggest that strategic planning is that aspect of corporate planning which involves the assessment of needs, the identification of desired outcomes, the determination of strategies to achieve desired outcomes and the assignment of priorities to various programmes and initiatives.

Schools throughout the western world are now faced with the need for ongoing curriculum change, especially at the secondary level. In Britain, for example, all publicly funded schools must now respond to the expectations embodied in a national curriculum. Government schools in most states of Australia now have a centrally determined curriculum framework. Adoption over three to five years is a normal expectation, an aspect of state or national 'strategic plans' which allows for an evolutionary approach to programme development at the school level. Such an approach was a characteristic of these schools which have successfully managed the process of change in studies conducted in the United States by Miles and his colleagues. The preparation of school-level corporate plans is thus consistent with what is known about successful management of change and with government expectations in a number of countries.

Distinctions can now be made between programme planning, curriculum planning and instructional planning. Programme planning is determining in general terms how a programme is to be implemented, specifying such things as the manner in which students will be grouped vertically (among class or year levels) and horizontally (within a class or year level); the number and nature of teachers and support staff associated with the programme; the supplies, equipment and services required; and initiatives (additions or deletions) which are noteworthy. Curriculum planning provides a relatively detailed specification of intended learning experiences, with details, for example, of what will be learned, how it will be learned and when it will be learned. Instructional planning is considered here to be the planning undertaken by individual teachers when implementing a curriculum plan in their own classrooms.

In the Collaborative School Management Cycle recommended by Caldwell and Spinks, a programme is an area of learning and teaching, or an area which supports learning and teaching, corresponding to the preferred patterns of work in a school. For example, since mathematics is taught in a secondary school, it is appropriate to refer to 'the Mathematics Programme'. Since a number of people will be involved in administration – a collection of activities which support learning and teaching – it is also appropriate to refer to 'the Administration Programme'. The programmes found in a school will or should reflect the philosophy and goals in that school which will, in turn, reflect the vision for the school. Rarely will two schools have the same set of programmes, even where schools must reflect state or national as well as local expectations.

In the Collaborative School Management Cycle, teachers and others involved in the implementation of a programme form a 'programme team' to prepare a programme plan which is consistent with the policies and priorities of the school as determined by the policy group. Each team will have a leader who usually, but not necessarily, has a position of formal responsibility in the staffing arrangements of the school. With many programmes in a school, there will be many programme teams and many programme leaders, thus providing further opportunity for empowerment and 'leadership density'.

Budgeting

A school budget may be viewed as a financial translation of an educational plan for the school. Budgeting is thus one aspect of planning but is shown as a separate phase of the management cycle in Figure 9.2. A programme budget is simply a financial translation of a programme plan. In the approach recommended by Caldwell and Spinks, programme teams will prepare a programme budget as part of the programme planning process.

Figure 9.3 contains an illustration of a programme plan and budget for an Individualized Learning Assistance Programme in a primary school which has adopted the vision and one of the goals which are the subject of illustration in this section of the chapter: 'Ruth (the principal) expects that curriculum and instruction should reflect the needs and interests of all children but that high expectations can be set and pursued with consistency and enthusiasm' (element of vision) and 'to ensure that each student can attain a high level of reading ability, taking account of age and any special personal circumstances' (goal). It is likely that these expectations will be addressed in several programmes, one of which might make provision for offering highly individualized assistance to children who may encounter major difficulty in a particular area of learning such as reading. There may, for example, be one or more teachers who have special responsibility for a programme designated as the Individualized Learning Assistance Programme.

In preparing a programme plan and budget, members of the programme team in the Individualized Learning Assistance Programme must take account of policies and priorities adopted by the policy group, the formulation of which would have seen their involvement. The plan and budget illustrated in Figure 9.3 contains:

- A statement of purpose and broad guidelines for the programme, being a summary of school policy on Individualized Learning Assistance
- A plan for implementing the programme in the forthcoming year, with elements in the plan arranged in order of priority and the plan being consistent with the aforementioned policy and priorities for the school
- A listing of resources required: a specification of staff, supplies, equipment and services to implement the plan, with 4.1–4.5 being the resources and estimated costs for 3.1 to 3.5, respectively, in the plan for implementation
- A plan for evaluating the programme, with the general approach following guidelines for programme evaluation.

An important feature of Figure 9.3 is that no programme plan and budget should exceed two pages. The aim is to minimize paperwork. Another feature is the costing for staff, even though the illustration might be for a school which does not directly 'pay' for staff. In this instance, the time allocation (40 units or periods) has been converted to a monetary equivalent on the basis that the average cost of instruction in offering a unit or period per week over the year is $700. Many schools may wish simply to list the number of units or periods per week.

Plans and budgets will be prepared for all programmes in the school. These will be consolidated in a collection of two-page proposals. A process of 'reconciliation' must then occur, with estimates of expenditure adjusted in the light of estimates of revenue. This reconciliation is best carried out by a small body of people appointed by the policy group. The consolidation of plans and budgets, with estimates of revenue and expenditure reconciled, is then forwarded to the policy group with a recommendation for adoption. The policy group is involved again at this point to ensure that plans and budgets are

Figure 9.3 Programme plan and budget for Individualized Learning Assistance Programme

---

1. Purpose

We intend to help all children attain the highest level of achievement of which they are capable. While learning activities in each classroom will be designed to meet the needs and interests of every child, we recognize that some will require extended periods of individual assistance in areas of basic learning such as reading, writing, spelling, and mathematics. We have established an Individualized Learning Assistance Programme to meet these needs.

2. Broad Guidelines

2.1   Achievement levels in areas of basic learning will be determined regularly through tests given to all children.

2.2   While every teacher will provide assistance to all children on an individual basis, the Individualized Learning Assistance Programme will be provided for those who fall below benchmarks established for their age/grade group.

2.3   Benchmarks will be established each year by the policy group after receiving recommendations from members of programme teams in areas of basic learning.

2.4   Teachers in the Individualized Learning Assistance Programme will work with students whose need for assistance has been identified. This assistance will be given either in the regular classroom or, in exceptional circumstances, in learning areas away from the classroom.

3. Plan for implementation

3.1   A review of achievement tests last year suggests the need for the equivalent of two full-time teachers to work in the programme.

3.2   Supervision of the programme will be provided by a member of senior staff.

3.3   A part-time teacher aide will be provided to assist in the preparation of learning materials.

3.4   Additional supplies and equipment will be required in the two rooms which will be devoted to the programme. These include reading and mathematics materials and the purchase of a large-print typewriter.

3.5   All teachers in areas of basic learning seek the assistance of a consultant in determining benchmarks for tests of achievement.

4. Resources required

Element	Teaching staff	Support staff	Supplies	Equipment	Services
4.1 Teachers: 50 units @ $700/unit	35000				
4.2 Supervision 2 units @ $900/unit	1800				
4.3 Teacher aide 5hrs/week 40 week's @ $10/hour		2000			
4.4 Supplies, reading and mathematics materials; typewriter			500	750	
4.5 Consultative assistance: 3hr seminar with travel costs @ $50 /hour					200
	36800	2000	500	750	200

Programme total   = $40250

5. Plan for evaluation (minor)

Teachers will review results of achievement tests in the areas of reading, spelling and mathematics in the light of benchmarks recommended last year and adopted by the policy group. This review and a general appraisal shall form the basis of recommendations for this programme next year.

consistent with policies and priorities established earlier in the Collaborative School Management Cycle. With refinements, the programme plan and budget can be adopted before the commencement of the school year. Essentially then, the educational plan will reflect the vision, philosophy, goals, needs, priorities and policies of the school.

Implementing the plan

With the adoption of the educational plan by the policy group, programme teams have the authorization to proceed with implementation in the year which follows. The major aspect of implementation is, of course, learning and teaching which is the life-blood for the school. As far as resources are concerned, there is no need for further reference to the policy group unless a need for major change emerges. Revenue and expenditure are monitored, with programme teams and the policy group receiving regular financial statements.

Evaluating

Evaluation is the gathering of information for the purpose of making a judgement. In the Collaborative School Management Cycle, evaluation is not a discrete activity carried out in isolation from other phases of management. The judgements which are made are important factors in decisions on the formulation of goals, the identification of needs, the setting of policies and priorities, the preparation of plans and budgets, and in the ongoing implementation of school programmes.

Caldwell and Spinks distinguish between minor evaluations carried out annually and major evaluations carried out less frequently on, say, a three- or five-year cycle. They suggest that all programmes be placed on such a cycle. The emphasis is on a manageable and usable approach to programme evaluation, in contrast to the frequently exhausting approach to school review and evaluation which is often encountered when an attempt has been made to evaluate all programmes in a single year. It is recommended that the report of a minor evaluation be a maximum of one page and that a report of a major evaluation be a maximum of two pages. Minor evaluations may be conducted informally and subjectively by members of the programme team who report on simple indicators of success, areas of concern and recommendations for change. A major evaluation in the same programme would be carried out more comprehensively and objectively by a team which is broadly representative of the school community, including members of the policy group. [. . .]

The model in operation

This approach has now been successfully adopted in hundreds of schools, notably in Victoria, Australia. The schedule of activities in schools which have now fully adopted the model is generally along the following lines. In Term 1, the policy group reviews reports of programme evaluations from the previous year to identify areas for action. Policies are then amended as appropriate, new needs identified and priorities established for the school year which follows, that is, which commences twelve months hence.

In Term 2, programme teams prepare programme plans and budgets for the following year. They work within the framework of policies and priorities set by the policy group, together with estimates of all of the resources to be available in the following year. Toward the end of Term 2, programme plans and budgets in proposal form are consolidated and reconciled against estimates of resources. The programme plan and budget is adopted in Term 3. Refinements will be made at the start of the next school year once final enrolments and revenue are known. Programme evaluation will be completed in Term 3 for consideration by the policy group in Term 1 to follow, thus ensuring the continuation of the cycle.

Schools need to set aside three to five years to adopt a model for management such as that outlined above. This time span is consistent with guidelines for the management of change in schools, including those which emerge from studies such as those by Miles and his colleagues reported earlier in the chapter.

SUMMARY

The purpose of this chapter was to outline a model for school management which would help bring a vision of excellence to reality. Such a model should be consistent with what is known about outstanding leadership [. . .], especially those aspects concerned with ensuring clarity, consensus and commitment to the purposes of the school (Vaill's concept of 'purposing'); the unification of people around values (an important role for leaders described by Greenfield); responsibility and authority at the school level (the characteristic of school-site management and collaborative decision-making contained in Purkey and Smith's model for creating an effective school); the sharing of leadership roles (Sergiovanni's concept of 'leadership density'); and implanting the vision for a school in policies, plans, budgets and processes so that day-to-day activities are shaped by the vision (Starratt's view that the leader must 'institutionalize' the vision).

Any model for management must be consistent with what is known about successful approaches to the management of change. The findings of recent studies by Miles and his colleagues in the USA were chosen to identify additional requirements for such a model. In addition to leadership [. . .], these requirements included a large measure of school autonomy, including some control over staffing and resources; staff cohesiveness; a school programme which was a good 'fit' with the school setting and needs in the community; power sharing among staff; rewards for staff; staff willingness and initiative and evolutionary programme development.

The Collaborative School Management Cycle described by Caldwell and Spinks was offered as a model for school management which is consistent with these requirements. This model integrates the processes of goal setting and needs identification, policy-making, planning, budgeting, implementing and evaluating in a continuous cycle. The vision for a school as it may be expressed in a statement of school philosophy becomes the driving force in school management, thus shaping day-to-day activities in the school. Power-sharing is evident in policy groups but, especially, in programme teams of people who have the responsibility for implementing policy. Leadership is widely dispersed. The approach provides a framework for evolutionary programme development. Some guidelines and illustration were offered for operation of the model which has now been successfully implemented in hundreds of schools and seems broadly transferable and adaptable.

This model for management provides a framework for day-to-day activities in the school, especially those described as the 'life-blood' of the school: learning and teaching. [. . .]

REFERENCES

Caldwell, B.J. and Spinks, J.M. (1988) *The Self-Managing School*, Falmer Press, London.

Greenfield, T.B. (1986) Leaders and Schools, in T.J. Sergiovanni and J.E. Corbally (eds), *Leadership and Organisational Culture, New Perspectives on Administrative Theory and Practice*, University of Chicago Press, Urbana, Ill.

Miles, M.B. (1987) Practical guidelines for school administrators: how to get there. Paper read at a symposium of Effective Schools Programs and the Urban High School, Washington D.C. Annual Meeting of the American Educational Research Association.

Purkey, S.C. and Smith, M.S. (1985) School reform: the district policy implications of the effective schools literature, *The Elementary School Journal*, Vol. 85.

Sergiovanni, T.J. (1987) The theoretical basis for cultural leadership, in L.T. Sheive and M.B. Schoenheit (eds), *1987 Yearbook of the Association for Supervision and Curriculum Development*, ASCA, Alexandria, VA.

Starratt, R.J. (1986) Excellence in education and quality of leadership. *Occasional Paper No. 1*, Southern Tasmanian Council for Educational Administration.

Vaill, P.B. (1986) The purposing of high performing systems, in Sergiovanni and Corbally, op. cit.

10

FLEXIBLE PLANNING:
a Key to the Management of Multiple Innovations

Mike Wallace

My purpose is to put forward a model of strategic planning that is consistent with the somewhat chaotic situation in which many British schools currently have to operate. The model to be offered here was developed in the light of recent exploratory research into the strategies that staff in schools adopt for coping with multiple changes. A full account of the findings of this study is given in Wallace (1991). While much more evidence is needed about planning strategies that are effective in particular contexts, informal discussions with senior school staff in several local education authorities (LEAs) suggest that the experiences leading to the approach to strategic development planning adopted in the research schools may be commonplace.

There is no shortage of external advice or, for many schools, external direction about how to undertake strategic planning. However, the findings imply that compulsory annual development plans for schools that many LEAs are currently introducing with the support of central government (see DES, 1989), and much advice from academics and practitioners such as Caldwell and Spinks (1988), may rest in part upon false assumptions. It may be significant that Spinks's 'collaborative planning cycle' was developed incrementally over seven years in an isolated school in Tasmania which enjoyed a relatively stable environment. The way in which various external innovations are being introduced into British schools may limit the form which school-level strategic planning can take if it is effectively to guide action to cope with the changes.

Some years ago Burns and Stalker (1961) suggested that different systems of management in commercial organizations were effective in different situations. This assertion was broadly confirmed by the studies of Derr and Gabarro (1972) in American school districts. The more effective of two districts facing a similar change had a management structure that better facilitated joint decision-making and conflict resolution, and had more elaborate procedures for achieving co-ordinated effort. In similar vein it is argued here that the effectiveness of particular planning processes in schools may be contingent upon their context. While planning procedures based on an annual cycle may be effective for schools in a stable environment, they may work less well in one which is more turbulent and unpredictable. Indeed, they may be more of a hindrance than a help if schools are required to follow procedures which are designed for a different context. Therefore it seems important to develop a planning model for a relatively unstable environment.

AN INCREASINGLY TURBULENT ENVIRONMENT

Some planning is necessary to maintain the yearly round of existing practice in schools. In addition, planning is required to implement any innovations that are adopted. For most schools in this country the balance between planning for maintenance and development has shifted dramatically in favour of development over the last few years. So pervasive of existing practice is innovation that plans for maintenance and development are likely to be closely interrelated.

There is a long tradition of innovations in educational and management practice that are initiated by teachers and headteachers. The role of new secondary heads as agents of change is particularly well documented (Weindling and Earley, 1987). Internal innovations have been complemented by LEA initiatives or projects, participation in most of which has been optional for schools. Recently certain LEA innovations, such as the promotion of equal opportunities for pupils and staff, have been made compulsory for schools in particular LEAs.

However, in the latter part of the last decade secondary schools have increasingly been encouraged to join the Technical and Vocational Education Initiative (TVEI) and its extension, an optional but highly resourced central government initiative. Many schools in both sectors have been involved in LEA initiatives stimulated by central government Education Support Grants, which enabled LEAs to bid for extra resources.

All mainstream state schools are now compelled to implement a controversial programme of central government reforms, many of which are embodied in the 1986 and 1988 Education Acts. On top of these education reforms, schools are also affected by other central government innovations. For example, a policy that has affected many schools is compulsory competitive tendering for local services such as the maintenance of school buildings and grounds resulting from the 1988 Local Government Act.

Many schools face a massive planning task because of the sheer scale of national innovations – whether directly or indirectly linked to education – and the pace of their introduction, primarily through LEAs which are themselves being restructured. The task is compounded by changes in the information available to schools on the form, scope and timing of the introduction of particular innovations as central government and LEA policies evolve.

In sum, alongside their ongoing work schools variably face an unprecedented number of major innovations originating with various central government departments, together with those originating with LEAs and with the schools themselves. The nature of many external innovations is liable to change unpredictably. It is in this rather frenetic context, which includes much ambiguity, that planning for maintenance and development must take place.

LIMITED RESEARCH EVIDENCE

The research described and analysed here was carried out in the autumn of 1989 and the spring term 1990. Focused, interpretive case studies (Merriam, 1988) were conducted in four schools in an LEA which had recently introduced a compulsory annual development plan. The schools were recommended by LEA staff as being effective in dealing with multiple changes. The LEA, a county authority, was undergoing radical change following the appointment of senior LEA staff who took initiatives informed by their previous experience in other LEAs and in response to pressure from central government reforms. The study schools were a primary school in a wealthy suburb, a junior school on a housing estate, a comprehensive school in the rural commuter belt surrounding a city, and an urban comprehensive school. All headteachers had been appointed in the last six years. While management practice in the schools differed at the level of detail, there was broad similarity between their experiences and their strategies for coping with innovations in the context of ongoing work.

The majority of influences upon planning in the schools were of the kind that any school may experience from time to time or were linked to central government policy. Acute disruption was caused on occasion through unpredictable crises such as staff illness. Chronic issues included a shortage of supply teachers for two schools. Certain issues arose from central government's education policies, such as plans to build a city technology college close to one secondary school. Others followed from policies unconnected with the education reforms, including a sharp drop in cleaning and grounds maintenance standards in another school as a result of competitive tendering imposed upon the local authority. The schools' plans were constrained by the uncertainty or surprise caused on occasion by information on external, mostly compulsory innovations, which was either inadequate, was in contradiction with earlier information or was provided at short notice. Most of these experiences could not have been foreseen by school staff. Examples included:

- unexpected delay for the primary sector schools in planning for English Key Stage Two while awaiting documents from the National Curriculum Council which did not arrive when anticipated;
- loss of momentum with the LEA's records of achievement initiative in the secondary schools when a central government minister announced that the compulsory component of pupils' records would be restricted to national curriculum attainment targets;
- frequent problems in planning the spending of the formula-funded LMS budget due to revision by the LEA's LMS support team of provisional

transition arrangements, arithmetical errors, and the discovery of unfore-
seen areas of expenditure;
- failure by senior staff in one secondary school to persuade LEA staff to
  accept, in place of the LEA's development plan, the submission of its own
  version which was already being implemented on the headteacher's
  initiative.

While some plans were carried through as predicted, the substance of schools'
development plans became less representative of changing priorities, targets
and detailed plans as the year progressed and did not in practice guide ongoing
development planning. Moreover, detailed plans and action to implement certain developments scheduled for the period beyond the existing development
plan were made long before LEA staff required the following year's development plan to be completed.

Incremental development planning of a less formal and rigid kind took place
in the four schools. It was led by the headteachers who, according to their
different styles, worked towards achieving their relatively stable vision of good
practice, with the support of the majority of staff and governors. Compara-
tively few major innovations were reported to have been initiated by staff other
than heads, who encouraged staff to express new ideas and responded suppor-
tively as long as these ideas accorded with their beliefs and values.

Recently the balance of innovations had swung towards externally initiated
changes, many of which were compulsory. The headteachers repeatedly sought
room to manoeuvre to realize their vision. Compulsory external innovations
were used opportunistically as a lever insofar as these innovations could be
assimilated or adapted to further the heads' broad goals. For example, both
primary sector heads capitalized upon the advent of the national curriculum to
encourage staff to make changes in line with their vision. Innovations that they
found less acceptable were modified or postponed: the primary sector heads
delayed completing an annual curriculum return imposed by the DES which
required a detailed breakdown of the time spent by pupils within each subject.
This demand conflicted with the thematic approach employed in both schools.
Increasingly, heads withheld from making changes to what they regarded as
existing good practice until final decisions about external innovations had been
made at central government and LEA levels. Their major concerns were to
defend staff against what they regarded as the undesirable consequences of
external innovations, including a heavy workload, associated stress and low
morale, and to protect pupils from perceived external threats to the quality of
their education.

The core of development planning was a process of more or less continual
creation, monitoring and adjustment of plans for the short and medium term,
consistent with the heads' long-term vision and such information as was available about the introduction of external innovations in the next few years. This
process required many strategic and detailed decisions to be made. Local networks of school and LEA contacts, together with the media, were used by
heads and their staff to seek out the latest information on LEA and central

government intentions and plans. Some decisions were likely to be revised whenever new action appeared to be needed to deal with spasmodic changes in information about external innovations, internal factors like the limited capacity of staff to shoulder an additional load or the imminent loss of expertise when individual staff gained promotion to another school, and other periodic crises and longer-term issues. Within this flexible approach cyclic planning for the academic and financial years was carried out through occasional consultative and strategic decision-making exercises coupled with considerable day-to-day monitoring and adjustment. The schools were thus able to cope both with the different stages reached at a given time in the academic and the financial year cycles and with alterations to annual plans following from changes, for example, in projected pupil numbers or the LMS budget.

The evidence for viewing the general approach to planning adopted in the research schools as at least reasonably effective was, first, the positive informed opinion of LEA staff about the ability of these schools to cope with multiple changes; second, the finding that many innovations were being implemented; and third, the implausibility of the proposition that schools could rely solely upon annual plans to guide action in a situation which might shift at any point during the year.

KEY FACTORS AFFECTING PLANNING

Several interrelated factors may be identified which influenced the form of planning processes in the schools to a varying extent, including:

- the multiplicity of goals, some of which came and went, that competed for attention at any time;
- unpredictable crises and issues affecting innovations and other work, alongside the predictability of most routine activity in school;
- the inability to predict some shifts in central government and LEA policies while being able to predict the possibility, if not the timing, of others;
- the combination of relative uncertainty about some external innovations or the arrangements for their introduction and clarity about others;
- the inconsistency between academic and financial year planning cycles – planning for one cycle covered only part of the other;
- the moderately high degree of control retained by headteachers over internal workings of the school coupled with a lack of control over the flow of external innovations, constraining their room to manoeuvre;
- the number and scope of the externally imposed innovations dictating the major focus for development and the heavy workload for staff and governors;
- routine planning for maintenance of the yearly round of existing practice being strongly influenced by the external innovations, which had implications for much ongoing work;

- difficulty in securing certain resources (especially time and expertise) needed to implement the range of innovations, exacerbated by the fact that some resourcing arrangements were themselves innovatory;
- the time-consuming effort required to co-ordinate action to achieve goals, especially in the secondary schools whose large staffs included subject-based groups with different interests and priorities;
- limited evaluation of progress with and outcomes of innovations due to lack of time and expertise and because of the diffuse nature of some innovations.

It is important to note that the context for development planning was neither wholly chaotic nor entirely stable. Rather, it was a complex mixture of routine work and change, with relative certainty and predictability in some areas and ambiguity and unpredictability in others, which varied over time.

The articulation by the headteachers of a long-term vision and the ways in which they gathered support for it are consistent with the notion of establishing a mission for a school. A sense of mission or common purpose is a factor which is widely associated with effective schools (see Renihan and Renihan, 1984; Hoyle, 1986). Procedures for establishing and gaining or renewing commitment to a mission have formed the basis of North American models of strategic planning (e.g. McCune, 1986; Steiner, 1979) which are echoed in the DES advice for schools on development planning. However, these models tend to imply that an occasional major review and planning exercise is the main activity through which a sense of mission is established and maintained. They do not capture the process of working towards a vision in an environment where spasmodically shifting and often unpredictable goals and means of achieving them may be externally imposed upon the school.

LINKS WITH MODELS OF DECISION-MAKING

Planning for development and maintenance encompasses strategic tasks, concerned with overall policy, and more detailed planning of each initiative. Decision-making lies at the heart of both policy-making and detailed planning and is frequently associated with other sub-processes such as consultation, negotiation, and giving information about decisions taken. Since any approach to planning will include decision-making it is worth clarifying how the research findings relate to different decision-making models.

Three widely known models are based upon very different assumptions. At one extreme, a highly rationalistic approach is advocated in classical management theory. (Accounts are provided in the critiques of March and Simon, 1958; Lindblom, 1959.) The model consists of sequential steps: agreeing upon fundamental values, clarifying goals to express these values, identifying a range of possible means to achieve them, analysing all important relevant factors, and determining the best means by predicting the outcome of employing each one. It is assumed that goals are clear and consistent, all relevant factors are

known, and means may be considered separately from goals. Implicitly, implementation of the best means may be effected once the decision is taken.

Many annual development plans for schools, including that introduced by the LEA in my research, and advice from the development plans project supported by the Department of Education and Science (DES), lean some way towards this model. An annual comprehensive review or audit leads to selection of priorites for development which are turned into specific targets as the basis for action plans. These plans are then implemented during the year, at the end of which progress is evaluated prior to drawing up detailed action plans for the following year within the next development plan. Thus a major periodic decision-making exercise enables goals (targets within priorities for development) to be identified and means (action plans) to be chosen, which are subsequently implemented. Insofar as the factors identified above point to some measure of agreement with headteachers upon values, clarity about goals, the availability of means, and a high degree of control at school level over its own development, a rationalistic approach to decision-making of this kind is plausible. However, the approach fails to take into account the many goals which had to be addressed at any time and the many revised and new decisions that occurred in the schools between annual decision-making exercises.

At the other extreme, an anarchic 'garbage can' model is described by March and Olsen (1976) and their collaborators in which the rationality of decision-making is denied. Their research was carried out in various educational institutions. Certain features of many organizations lead to ambiguity for their members: the poorly defined and inconsistent goals held by different individuals, their limited understanding about how various aspects of the organization work, and their variable participation in decision-making. Far from following from a logical sequence of analysis of goals and means, decisions are conceived as the outcome of idiosyncratic interaction in a 'garbage can' between four variables or 'streams' that flow into it: *problems*, whether part of official business or connected with personal concerns; *solutions*, consisting of individuals' ideas and preferences which they seek opportunities to realize – in other words solutions looking for a problem; *participants*, whose involvement in decision-making depends upon its priority relative to other demands upon their time; and *choice opportunities*, viewed as occasions when decisions are expected to be made. Despite the irrational nature of decision-making such organizations are sustained over time. Weiner (1976) has dubbed them 'organized anarchies'.

While decision-making in the study schools was hardly anarchic, this model does highlight some of the sources of ambiguity that constrained coherent development planning. At any point certain goals of the range being addressed were unclear and others conflicted, as a consequence of the evolution of the external innovations and the way they were introduced. The necessity of coping with fluctuating concurrent and consecutive goals led to frequent occasions for decision-making, which on occasion was perceived as short-term crisis management. The model also points to the influence of personal as well as

official interests that were undoubtedly present when some decisions were made. However, since the model rules out the possibility of rational processes leading from identification of problems to agreed solutions – let alone their implementation – it contradicts the degree to which coherence was maintained, principally by the headteachers, in a context of some ambiguity.

A dominant feature of planning in the schools was the need to respond to a decision made at LEA or central government level which was likely to have been perceived as rational by those who made it but appeared irrational or misguided to staff in school. Much ambiguity for schools followed from the disjunction between rational decisions taken at different levels in the education system. One primary school, for instance, was asked by LEA staff to seek governors' approval for its development plan, yet dates for all governors' meetings for the year had already been arranged in response to a previous LEA directive. No governors' meeting was planned for the period between the introduction of the plan and the deadline for its submission to the LEA. Following Boudon's (1986) emphasis upon the role of chance in social change, Smith and Crane (1990) show that many actions by one individual or group may impact on those of another without the intention or foresight of the people involved, especially when each party is insulated from others by boundaries that prevent participants anticipating the impact. The schools were frequently beset by ambiguity arising between organizational levels rather than from within.

Hoyle, writing as the current wave of education reform was mounting, argued that the cognitive limits to rationality in decision-making have become more severe in recent years as external pressures on schools have increased:

> Schools have become more interdependent with other forms of organization – commercial, industrial, welfare, legal, community, political, etc. – and the once-strong boundary around the school has become more permeable. The school has become a more open system and has to take into account more, and frequently competing, factors in its decision-making. Thus the cognitive limits to rationality become more acute as the school seeks to take into account the expectations of various sets of stakeholders.
>
> (Hoyle, 1986, p. 63)

A third model which acknowledges the cognitive limits to rationality without abandoning the notion altogether most closely matches the decision-making process in the schools. The rationalistic approach of classical management theory was criticized for its implausibility in real-life situations. March and Simon noted that it is seldom feasible to 'optimize' by selecting the best alternative after analysis of all possible alternatives. Most decision-making proceeds by more pragmatic 'satisficing', concerned solely with finding a satisfactory alternative which will improve the current state of affairs.

Lindblom (1959) developed this critique in putting forward an approach to decision-making proceeding by 'successive limited comparisons', concerned with the marginal differences between relatively few alternatives. He claimed that for complex social problems comprehensive analysis is impossible. More-

over, fundamental values, goals and means cannot be analysed and selected separately. Rather than begin by agreeing upon values prior to identifying goals then means, leading to evaluation of these means, one or more policy alternatives are selected for consideration where values are implicit in the choice of goals and means within each alternative. The analysis is more or less severely limited, the aim being to make a marginal improvement in the present situation. Therefore many possible radical alternatives are ruled out and some possible, often unpredictable, consequences of the alternatives under consideration are ignored. Decision-making is iterative, proceeding by trials, errors and revised trials. Subsequently Lindblom (1979) refined the model, implying that analysis may be more or less systematic. The approach already described, which he labelled as 'disjointed incrementalism', is common in practice. He advocated 'systematic analysis' in which successive limited comparisons are made rigorously in a deliberate attempt to be as systematic as possible without aspiring to a comprehensive analysis.

The process of developing annual development plans has much in common with systematic analysis, yet the yearly gap between strategic decision-making events is far too infrequent. The vision of good practice held by the head-teachers in the research schools, which was shared by many staff and governors, could potentially have constituted a radical shift in practice, rather than an incremental change. However, the ways in which they tended to work towards this vision were incremental. Successive limited comparisons were made whenever significant changes occurred connected with external innovations and other crises and issues that arose from time to time, whether linked to innovations or existing practice. Further, decision-making proceeded generally along the lines of disjointed incrementalism, being mainly informal, often in response to unexpected external pressure, and was confined to considering how to deal with one new factor in the context of existing decisions about changes and other ongoing work.

Certain externally imposed innovations, such as LMS and national curriculum assessment at Key Stages One to Three, represented quite a radical departure from existing school practice. However, an incremental approach to policy-making for the implementation of these innovations was adopted in the schools in line with the LEA or central government strategies for phasing in these innovations. The four schools experienced a period of partial delegation of the LMS budget and assessment was being introduced in stages following the central government timetable. The staff focused upon the implementation of each succeeding shift in existing practice as the relevant details were made clear by the LEA or central government agencies.

None of these models reflects fully the complexity of decision-making in the research schools, which fluctuated between the rationalistic, the ambiguous and the incremental. Louis and Miles (1990) have recently put forward the more promising notion of 'evolutionary planning' informed by their research into inner city high schools in the United States. Evolutionary planning is a compromise between the long-established models of decision-making and strategic planning centred upon shared commitment to a mission. Since no specific plan can last very long in an environment which is often chaotic, it is suggested that the effective response for a school is to 'cycle back and forth between efforts to gain normative consensus about what it may become, to plan strategies for getting there, and to carry out decentralized, incremental experimentation that harnesses the creativity of all members to the change effort'. Strategic planning or experimental activity may precede the other: often planning to build coherence follows from action to implement innovations. Equally, a sense of mission may emerge from less comprehensive 'themes' which encompass a range of innovations, rather than a mission specifying the innovatory activity. Where a shared mission is created, they argue that:

> strategies for achieving the mission are frequently reviewed and refined based on internal scanning for opportunities and successes. Strategy is viewed as a flexible tool, rather than as a semi-permanent extension of the mission: if rational planning is like blueprinting, evolutionary planning is more like taking a journey. There is a general destination, but many twists and turns as unexpected events occur along the way.
> (Louis and Miles, 1990, p. 193)

However, the model may have limited application in the British educational context. The pervasiveness of external intervention in schooling imposes elements of a mission upon schools while leaving some leeway for local interpretation. Spasmodic shifts in information about external innovations, allied with a diversity of unpredictable crises and issues, militate against a simple linkage between an enduring mission or set of themes and incremental activity connected with innovations.

Moreover, as the model is centrally concerned with change, it does not encompass the planning entailed in maintaining existing practice while implementing multiple innovations. Thus this model stops short of providing a conception of how various factors may affect the evolution of incremental activities connected with innovations, a mission, and any link between them. The model of flexible planning put forward below is an attempt to offer a more comprehensive conceptualization which reflects the context in this country.

FLEXIBILITY AND PLANNING: A DIALECTICAL RELATIONSHIP

'Flexible planning' is, perhaps, an oxymoron. Flexibility implies the ability to respond rapidly to changing circumstances while the notion of planning suggests the formulation of a design which will lead to a sequence of prespecified changes over time. A model of strategic planning which will guide action in schools in the current context, where some aspects may be turbulent while others remain stable, must therefore address a tension between two contradictory influences.

Flexibility is to be gained from incremental planning. Modifications to existing plans may be made rapidly as circumstances evolve without having to replan from scratch, alongside attempts to anticipate likely changes and to

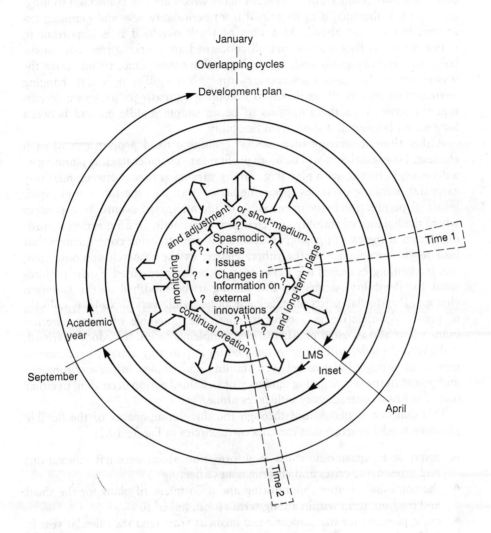

Figure 10.1 Flexible planning in the UK context

consider contingency plans without going into great detail. However, loss of coherence may result from short-term plans which are not connected to long-term aims. Coherence is to be gained from periodic review and planning exercises, looking far ahead. At a time of work overload it is important to maximize effort by ensuring that all concerned are working towards consistent, high-priority goals and, by pacing activity over time, to minimize the wasted effort that causes unnecessary stress. Yet rigidity in a fast-changing environment may result in decisions becoming increasingly irrelevant to current concerns. Thus there appears to be no simple middle ground between long-term planning and short-term flexibility.

Rather than conceiving of a model containing fixed proportions of each element, I suggest that it will be more profitable to consider flexible planning as a dialectical process, with planning activity varying at times between relatively extensive planning exercises specifying action well into the future and rapid, informal planning activity in response to unanticipated events. In a context where the balance of stability and change is continually in flux, action according to one of the two opposing influences will tend to bring consequences that lead to the ascendence of the other. Hence, as the research demonstrated, major planning exercises are likely soon to be supplemented by the requirement for flexibility, strategic plans having to be modified as the situation changes. Day-to-day crisis management alone, while very flexible, is unlikely to prove cost-effective in a context where the timetable of many external innovations allows some phasing of their implementation to reduce overload. A dialectical model will allow for vacillation in planning activity over time to match the shifting balance between stability and change in the environment and points to the self-negating tendency of sustained action according to either one of the two contradictory influences alone.

This dialectic is played out through the three components of the flexible planning model portrayed in the concentric circles in Figure 10.1:

- response to spasmodic shifts in information about external innovations and other acute crises and chronic issues affecting
- the continual creation, monitoring and adjustment of plans for the short and medium term within a long-term vision, linked to
- cyclic planning for the academic and financial years (and the calendar year in LEAs which have adopted this cycle for compulsory school development plans).

ROLLING PLANS

The basis of planning is the multiplicity of decisions about the future which may be roughly divided into three levels, although in reality they lie along a continuum (see the middle circle in Figure 10.1). First, there are 'broad sweep' plans for the long term within a vision of a desirable future, which may be shared through the articulation of a mission. Long-term plans may cover a period from, say, one to five years hence. Second, there are slightly more specific medium-term plans, spanning perhaps a month to a year ahead. Third, there are short-term, detailed plans covering the immediate future, spanning perhaps the present to one month away. These three levels of plan nest together, short-term and medium-term plans lying within more general long-term plans. As time passes these planning levels roll forward: what were long-term plans being developed into medium- and short-term plans, short-term plans being enacted and new long-term plans being created. The timetable of periodic events and activities within the overlapping cycles is addressed through these rolling plans. Procedures are required for regular consultation, decision-making, and disseminating information about decisions, which may include major periodic exercises such as whole school reviews and a structure of meetings for groups in various teaching, pastoral and managerial roles.

The basis of flexibility is a process of more or less continual creation, monitoring and adjustment of the rolling plans. Monitoring encompasses primarily informal means of gathering information internally about ongoing work and development, coupled with the active search for relevant information from outside – whether from the local community, neighbouring schools, the LEA or central government and its agencies. In this way it is possible to become fully informed and to respond to the many spasmodic, often unpredictable, internal short-term crises and longer-term issues that arise, along with changing information about external innovations (as depicted in the inner circle in Figure 10.1).

Procedures are required for continual monitoring, frequent adjustment of existing plans and occasional creation of new ones. Monitoring entails establishing relevant individual roles and tasks connected with seeking appropriate internal and external information. The need for communication of findings and adjustment and creation of plans implies a structure of regular meetings, together with a procedure for arranging *ad hoc* meetings to make decisions in response to unanticipated changes. Adjustment and creation of plans is not necessarily confined to definite proposals. Potential flexibility is maintained by contingency planning, but it is important to consider the extra effort required to devise such plans alongside the value of being prepared for possible changes. Through a modicum of contingency planning it is possible to reduce uncertainty to some extent. Some contingencies are more predictable than others. With some relatively predictable contingencies the uncertainty lies mainly in predicting exactly when, say, staff illness will occur or the Secretary of State will modify a demonstrably unworkable policy. A common decision in the study schools was to refrain from altering existing practice with certain external innovations on the assumption that the contingency of a change in policy was likely to arise sooner or later.

While the various overlapping cycles (illustrated in the outer circle of Figure 10.1) give rise to a regular sequence of planning events, all either constitute or are affected by external innovations. Therefore they too are subject to change as relevant policies evolve. Moreover, the inconsistency between the timing of the cycles means that it is difficult to dovetail together the plans for each. (It is notable that central government policies have brought about some inconsistencies. For example, the national curriculum is being phased in according to the academic year yet the national curriculum development plan covers staff development for the financial year.) Both these factors imply that an element of flexibility in planning is needed to cope with the annual cycles in addition to regular planning events for each one.

Thus the flexibile planning model appears to encompass the combination of linked continual, cyclic and spasmodic factors that my research suggests strategic planning in schools must address. Any particular time is represented by a narrow segment (for example Time 1 in Figure 10.1). It is possible to trace the progress of short-, medium- and long-term plans, their connection with the relevant point in each cycle, and the influence of spasmodic factors (say, from Time 1 to Time 2).

CONCLUSION

Evidently, further research is needed, both to elaborate in greater detail how flexible planning operates in a range of organizations, whether within or outside the education service, and in environments whose degree of turbulence varies. Whether the validity of the model is contingent upon a turbulent environment may be tested by research into strategic planning in organizations that operate in highly stable or extremely volatile situations.

If this model does turn out to be apposite for institutions in a turbulent context, there are significant practical implications. In surveying management development and training for schools at the time of the Education Reform Act (Wallace and Hall, 1989), my main concern over the LEA development plans for schools was that many were devoted exclusively to the reforms rather than to wider needs for management development support. It is possible that such development plans have not fulfilled their promise as a key to managing the reforms. On the strength of my limited research, an urgent priority seems now to provide management development and training support in the kind of flexible planning that is more likely to provide a key to managing the multiple innovations that the reforms represent.

ACKNOWLEDGEMENTS

The research on which this article is based was funded by the Economic and Social Research Council, whose support is gratefully acknowledged. I wish to thank the heads and staff of the study schools and the LEA staff who supported the project under difficult circumstances.

REFERENCES

Boudon, R. (1986) *Theories of Social Change*, Polity Press, Cambridge.
Burns, T. and Stalker, G.M. (1961) *The Management of Innovation*, Tavistock, London.

Caldwell, B. and Spinks, J. (1988) *The Self-Managing School,* Falmer Press, London.

Department of Education and Science (1989) *Planning for School Improvement: Advice to Governors, Headteachers and Teachers,* DES, London.

Derr, B. and Gabarro, J. (1972) An organizational contingency theory for education, *Educational Administration Quarterly,* Vol. 8, no. 2, pp. 26–43.

Hoyle, E. (1986) *The Politics of School Management,* Hodder and Stoughton, London.

Lindblom, C.E. (1959) The science of muddling through, *Public Administration Review,* Vol. 19, no. 2, pp. 79–88.

Lindblom, C.E. (1979) Still muddling, not yet through, *Public Administration Review,* Vol. 39, pp. 517–526.

Louis, S.K. and Miles, M.B. (1990) *Improving the Urban High School,* Teachers College Press, New York.

McCune, S.D. (1986) *Guide to Strategic Planning for Educators,* Association for Supervision and Curriculum Development, Alexandria, Virginia.

March, J. and Olsen, J. (eds) (1976) *Ambiguity and Choice in Organizations,* Universitetforlaget, Bergen.

March, J. and Simon, H. (1958) *Organizations,* John Wiley, New York.

Merriam, S. (1988) *Case Study Research in Education,* Jossey-Bass, London.

Renihan, F.I. and Renihan, P.J. (1984) Effective schools, effective administration and effective leadership, *The Canadian Administrator,* Vol. 24, no. 3, pp. 1–6.

Smith, M. and Crane, B. (1990) Managing chance: management challenges when integrating special needs teaching in the primary school, *Educational Management and Administration,* Vol. 18, no. 1, pp. 46–53.

Steiner, G. (1979) *Strategic Planning: What Every Manager Must Know,* The Free Press, New York.

Wallace, M. and Hall, V. (1989) Management development and training for schools in England and Wales: an overview, *Educational Management and Administration,* Vol. 17, no. 4, pp. 163–75.

Wallace, M. (1991) Coping with multiple innovations: an exploratory study, *School Organization,* Vol. 11, no. 2, pp. 187–209.

Weindling, D. and Earley, P. (1987) *Secondary Headship: The First Years,* NFER-Nelson, Windsor.

Weiner, S. (1976) Participation, deadlines and choice, in J. March and J. Olsen (eds.) op. cit.

11

STRATEGIC PLANNING:
Managing Colleges into the Next Century

Ann Limb

This chapter is written by the director of a further education college. She begins with a brief description of the college and its context.

INTRODUCTION

College details – Milton Keynes College

Milton Keynes College is a medium sized further education college with approximately 1100 full-time and over 5000 part-time students enrolled on a broad range of academic and vocational courses. It offers a comprehensive post-16 tertiary curriculum with learning programmes which embrace GCSE, AS and A level work as well as specific vocational training courses related to the needs of industry, commerce and the professions. Most of our full-time students are aged between 16 and 19 years and live in the Milton Keynes and North Buckinghamshire area, which is one of the fastest growing urban areas in the United Kingdom. The majority of our part-time learners are adults. In addition to studying at college, they may be engaged in a variety of other activities ranging from full- and part-time employment to unpaid work in and outside the home. Milton Keynes is an international and multi-racial city with access to 30 million people within two and a half hours drive, the city offers more business prospects than London. The Milton Keynes College mission aims to reflect and promote this environment through its emphasis on personal development and achievement, equality of opportunity and the effective use of human resources.

Strategic planning – building on an investment in human resources

One of the effects of the Education Reform Act has been the increased use of the term 'strategic planning' and the formalization of practices which had perhaps become understated features of the further education service. This paper aims to present a perspective on this issue which redresses the balance and asserts the value of investment in human resources. It is not concerned specifically with those aspects of strategic planning which relate, at a technical level, to a local education authority to the Department for Education or to the Department of Employment. While acknowledging that these are important, observations and comments here are confined to that part of the process concerned with planning inside a college. In making them I draw upon my own experiences at Milton Keynes College and on the writings of Tom Peters. It is Tom Peters' view in *Thriving on Chaos: a Handbook for Management Revolution* that:

> As we move into these turbulent, ambiguous nineties and beyond, strategy making should not involve the old forms of strategic analysis that we did in the seventies. The essence of strategy is the creation of organisational capabilities that will allow us to react opportunistically to whatever happens. In the fully developed organisation, the front line person should be capable of being involved in strategy making. (Peters 1988)

Research in the higher education sector in the United States confirms, in an educational context, Tom Peters' view. Planning approaches used by institutions there in the 1970s were generally based on bureaucratic notions about organizational functions. By the late 1970s, the problems of trying to use rational planning models in colleges were becoming increasingly recognized and the focus shifted to the notion of strategic planning based on a college's ability to adapt to the external environment. It is currently being acknowledged that the values of the academic culture may be inconsistent with strategic planning's emphasis on sensing, serving and satisfying markets. Alternative responses, particularly in times of rapid change, are therefore currently being considered.

The aim of the approach to strategic planning and management at Milton Keynes College was to build upon and enhance organizational capabilities which were developed as a result of a college restructuring undertaken in 1988. In consequence, the reorganization was predicated upon the assumption that the most valuable and costly resource of the college, the staff, should be involved in, and should derive maximum benefit from, the changes which occur. To this end, significant numbers of teaching and support staff gained promotion and increased status, salary and working conditions in the reorganized college. Subsequently, they have been supported through the change by participation in a senior and middle management development programme organized and delivered by an external consultant. This management development programme has been matched by a major programme of staff and curriculum development costing in the region of £100,000 per

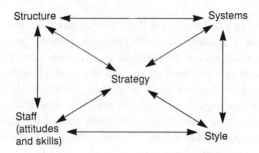

Figure 11.1   Strategic management

annum which aims to encourage all staff to play an active part in the college's continuing development. In this way, the college reorganization has attempted to recognize the importance of investing in people, and developing their skills.

In so doing, I found it helpful to look at strategic management and change in relation to other elements of organizational capability and to recognize the need to integrate these dimensions in order to ensure college development. These relationships are shown in Figure 11.1.

The requirement for the college to plan strategically presented an opportunity to acknowledge and test the value of this investment in its human resources. The approach which has been developed therefore aims to involve the staff of the college in the planning process and uses our line management structure as the mechanism for their participation. The majority of the full-time staff of Milton Keynes College are trained teachers with some industrial and commercial experience; planning skills form a part of their portfolio of competences. I believe it is both professionally honest and managerially sensible to value, develop and promote the use of those abilities in determining the college's strategic plan. The processes used and the methods described in this paper derive from, and reflect the skills, experience, interests and levels of commitment of Milton Keynes College staff. The college's reorganization, its current management structure, mission, value system, and ethos have determined this approach and have encouraged participation in the planning process from all the other major stakeholders in the college, namely the support staff, governors and students.

The starting point for our strategic planning and management is the college's mission. Our mission defines purpose and embodies our educational philosophy and values. It is a reference point by which we make decisions, determine implementation strategies and policy, judge behaviour and evaluate our performance. It informs and guides our strategic direction.

The active participation of over one-third of the full-time staff of the college in the determination of a mission statement is a key factor. This was achieved through the joint senior and middle management development programme.

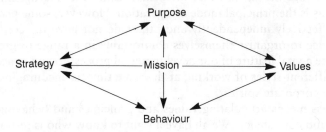

Figure 11.2   Relationship between strategy and mission

The relationships between strategy and mission are shown in Figure 11.2 which aims to illustrate the four main elements which combine to make an organization's mission effective.

The purpose of Milton Keynes College is clarified through a short statement of mission which currently reads as follows:

- We create opportunities for people to achieve their personal, educational and employment goals.
- We aim to provide a quality service, in an environment which enables all those involved to learn to their full potential.
- Our way of working demonstrates a commitment to personal growth. We seek to encourage all those who have contact with the college to value this approach.

The formulation of this mission statement is based on a set of articulated and shared values which encourage particular forms of interaction and behaviour. These were determined by the middle and senior management teams as part of the management development programme referred to above. They are as follows.

- The contribution made by each and every member of college staff is of equal value to the effective and efficient running of the organization. Our organizational structures and management style value teaching and support staff accordingly and both have access to the same facilities and opportunities.
- A commitment to the personal and professional development of the individual, for all employees of the college and for all students, leads to effective and creative work and fosters a high degree of professionalism.
- Learning about ourselves and each other means acknowledging that we all make mistakes sometimes. Viewing such experiences responsibly and positively ultimately leads to more effective forms of interaction between people.
- Individuals with information cannot avoid assuming responsibility.
- Learning is sometimes a difficult process, but it should aim to incorporate an appropriate sense of pleasure in achievement.

- Working together in informal or formal teams and sharing information and ideas is the principal mode of operation. However, some people work more effectively independently and others do not have the confidence or experience to organize themselves comfortably in a range of groups. It is therefore a vital feature of our developmental process to aim at accommodating different styles of working at the same time as encouraging a strong sense of corporate spirit.
- Openness means articulating values and principles and behaving with integrity and consistency. We all have a right to know who is responsible for making decisions and how they have been reached.

The increased emphasis on strategic planning which resulted from the Education Reform Act, encouraged us to look more closely at the strategy element of planning.

I needed to develop a planning mechanism at Milton Keynes College which aimed to value staff and involve them actively in the process. I focused on the newly organized line management structure as I believed it would help us to develop a whole college approach to planning and quality improvement. In so doing we have begun to link the establishment of institutional planning, development and review with the process of individual action planning, target setting and appraisal.

This link is supported by a management structure which is set within the context, purpose, values and behaviour outlined above. It is based on three layers of operation in relation to the student. It can be represented in simple diagrammatic form as shown in Figure 11.3.

We currently have over 6000 full- and part-time students. They are supported, in different ways, by approximately 260 full-time and part-time teaching and support staff who are based at one of three college centres. There are

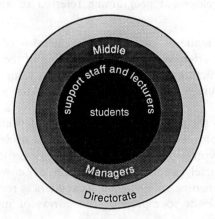

Figure 11.3   Levels of operations

approximately 100 staff at each centre although about a third at each centre move, on a day-to-day basis, from centre to centre. Each member of staff is associated with one centre and one team for the purposes of line supervision and managerial support. This is provided by a member of the middle management team which comprises 30 teaching and support staff.

The directorate consists of four members – three Assistant Directors and the Director. I have line management responsibility for each of the Assistant Directors. For purposes of day-to-day organization, whilst maintaining total accountability, I delegate the responsibility and authority for all operational activities of the college to the three Assistant Directors as follows:

- curriculum and learning strategies,
- finances and resources,
- marketing and development.

I moved from the post of Deputy Director to that of Director in the restructured college [. . .]. The need to develop mechanisms for effective strategic planning was imperative and the appropriateness of the organizational structure as a focus seemed logical. However, I determined that the staff would need both a framework and a timetable within which to operate. This had to be both meaningful and flexible and aim to combine what I called 'the requirement of management to manage' with the desire to encourage participation and autonomy from staff. It was also vital to have a simple, clearly understood, usable college-wide planning document. The framework, timescale and planning document we used are given in Appendix 1.

[. . .] Therefore, bearing in mind the range of external factors which could influence developments in Milton Keynes College (Appendix 2), I outlined 10 broad strategic priorities to the Assistant Directors. These were used as a basis for discussion within the directorate. They were set within the framework of the college mission statement. The directorate had an opportunity to discuss the priorities with a visiting HMI and subsequently with the Senior Education Officer (FE) for Buckinghamshire County Council. The priorities were generally agreed but in no rank order and they are listed in Appendix 3.

[. . .] I [then] held open meetings at each Centre of the college, to which all teaching and support staff were invited. I explained the 10 priorities and outlined the principles underlying the strategic planning process. I invited staff to become involved in the task and gave a schedule and format for implementation.

Part of this response involved staff, within delivery teams, in setting collective targets through discussion and negotiation with their personal middle manager. Where possible, this was also linked to agreement about an individual staff member's staff development needs, personal action plan, and yearly targets.

The middle managers were asked to produce both a three year development plan and a one year programme for their area of operation. In compiling these plans, it was expected they would take into account the objectives and capabilities of their teams and demonstrate consultation with them. This activity was supported and monitored by one of the three Assistant Directors.

In the same way that each middle manager discussed and negotiated a set of objectives and targets with their staff, so the Assistant Directors determined both a personal action plan and an annual programme in consultation with each individual middle manager. These two documents are used as the basis for regular managerial support and review. The personal action plan is a matter of concern for the Assistant Director and manager only. It is an entirely confidential contract between the two colleagues who agree on its use and purpose. It may be linked to appraisal of individual performance if both partners agree. The individual section annual programme however, contributes to the directorate three year plan and college annual programme and as such is an open document, available to all staff in the college, the academic board and the governing body. In reality, its detail is unlikely to be of great interest to an individual student, governor or staff member unless they have specific concerns, for example in the art, design and hairdressing curriculum or the examinations and statistics procedures. However, it is the task of the Director and the three Assistant Directors to consider the individual plans of each middle manager in order to synthesize their key points. In this way the directorate devised a yearly annual programme and a rolling three year development plan for the college. The Director and governors gave an indication of the overall pace of change in the light of available resources and whole college organizational capabilities.

Our timescale in the first year of operation was extremely short. It is shown in a schedule given in Appendix 1. It [. . .] resulted, however, in the production of three key documents for Milton Keynes College [. . .] – [two] annual programmes [. . .] and the development plan for [the next 4 years]. I believe that, as a result of our work, we were in a strong position to respond to the demands of the local education authority planning and budget cycles following the implementation of the planning and delegation scheme.

'Strategic planning' for Milton Keynes College has been an opportunity and a challenge. We undertook the process at a demanding time for the college and with little collective experience of such wholesale and detailed college-wide planning.

As our individual and collective skills have developed [. . .], we have had an opportunity to repeat the exercise and [. . .] extend the timescale shown in the schedule in Appendix 1. This has enabled us to set our strategic direction more clearly and succinctly and to organize our annual programmes to emphasize four priorities, namely:

- growth,
- quality,
- improved environment, and
- student-centred learning.

We have continued to follow the framework and processes outlined in this paper and to concentrate more, now we have the experience and time, on the detail and quality of the implementation strategies. We are continuing to evaluate our experience and to make revisions and modifications.

As we manage our colleges into the 21st century, I believe we have an opportunity to abandon the former 'manpower planning' models of development and put into practice a cost-effective and efficient approach to strategic planning based on 'investment in human capital'.

NOTE

1. This was begun in June 1988 and continues to date. The programme, devised and implemented in conjunction with external consultants, is based on the Director's commitment to a model of management based on openness and total quality and a belief in striving for continuous improvement.

APPENDIX 1

Strategic planning at Milton Keynes College – Schedule for first year of implementation

Timescale	Directorate strategic planning priorities	Middle managers and staff specific objectives
March	Directorate held open meetings for all staff at each of the three centres of the college to explain the planning process and invite staff to participate.	
10–25 April	Directorate to discuss and determine main priorities ←——→ 1 and 3 year Directorate to devise draft planning documents.	Middle managers and staff to engage in informal, unstructured discussion; look at mission statement in relation to their own areas of work.
25 April	Strategic priorities agreed. Planning documents produced. Presentation to middle managers.	Middle managers go through 10 strategic priorities with staff and relate to their own areas of work.
27 April–12 May		Middle managers to determine specific objectives for each curriculum/development/ resource area, following format suggested by directorate. Discussion and consultation with staff.
12 May–14 June	Directorate produce plans for academic board and governing body	Individual annual programme produced by each middle manager.
14 June	Directorate presentation to academic board	
15 November	Directorate presentation to governing body*	

* As a new governing body has been formed, we decided to present our [current] annual programme, investing in people, development skills and our ... development plan to them, even though, in reality, we were already in the process of implementation.

Framework for implementation

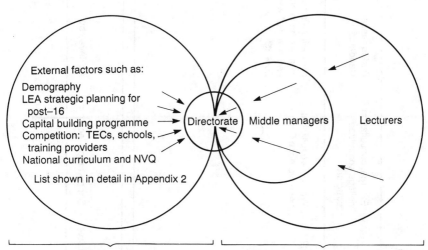

External factors such as:

Demography
LEA strategic planning for
  post–16
Capital building programme
Competition: TECs, schools,
  training providers
National curriculum and NVQ

List shown in detail in Appendix 2

Directorate

Middle managers

Lecturers

External

Internal

Directorate attempt to survey
external scene and determine college
strategic priorities in the light of this

Staff and middle managers invited to
participate by determining specific
objectives for their operational areas,
taking into account college strategic
priorities determined by directorate

Draft college-wide planning programme

Mission statement: Strategic priorities related to mission statement

Specific objectives	Key indicators including timescale and resource implications	Internal staff responsibility	External consultation & college committee structure	Performance standards
List of action to be taken	List of what we will have done, i.e. outcomes and how much it is likely to cost	Who does what?	Who do we tell what we have done?	How will we prove what we have done and how well we have done it?
Curriculum development including list of all courses/ learning programmes to be run	In the case of learning programmes current, actual and target student numbers should be given			
Staff development				
Institutional development, i.e. marketing				

Agreed college-wide planning document

Specific objectives	Process	Person responsible	Support required from	Achieved by

APPENDIX 2

External factors affecting strategic planning at Milton Keynes College

National legislation through Department of Education and Science, i.e. Education Reform Act and requirement for Buckinghamshire County Council to produce a strategic plan for post-16 education.

Other national bodies, e.g. Department of Employment, Training Agency, through TVEI, Youth Training, Employment Training and work-related further education development activities.

CBI targets in *Towards a Skills Revolution*.

TUC's *Skills 2000*.

Kenneth Baker's ACFHE speech February 1989 'FE, a New Strategy', and John McGregor's subsequent pronouncements on a 'core curriculum' post-16.

The activities of the Secondary Examinations and Assessment Council and the National Council for Vocational Qualifications.

Training Enterprise Councils (TECs), particularly the Milton Keynes and North Buckinghamshire TEC.

Strategic planning information from the Economic Development Units of Buckinghamshire County Council, Milton Keynes Borough Council and Milton Keynes Development Corporation.

Chief Education Officer's report to Buckinghamshire County Council's Education Committee on Staffing and Organization of Education Department in Buckinghamshire.

Milton Keynes College present three-site operation and Buckinghamshire County Council's submission to the Department of Education and Science for a major capital building at the Chaffron Way Centre.

Buckinghamshire County Council's discussions on the age of admission and transfer and the extension of selective education in Milton Keynes.

'The legacy of neglect' in the physical environment, equipment and resources of Milton Keynes College during the seventies and eighties.

The HMI paper *Core Skills*.

The effects of the local financial management of colleges as determined by the Buckinghamshire County Council's planning and delegation scheme.

Proposals on vocational education and training from British Petroleum.

The single European market in 1992.

The White Paper *Employment in the 1990s*.

APPENDIX 3

Milton Keynes College 10 strategic priorities

(1) Manage growth and expansion due to demographic trends and increased participation in FE.

(2) Expand flexible curriculum delivery and student-centred learning.
(3) Provide high quality education and training for all.
(4) Earn market value and establish credibility.
(5) Investigate new provision in response to local and national demand.
(6) Formulate and implement a range of internal policies.
(7) Correlate our strategic planning with the strategic planning of relevant external agencies.
(8) Monitor and evaluate effects of the Education Reform Act and other government legislation.
(9) Monitor and evaluate efficiency of provision related to effectiveness.
(10) Promote and nurture human resource development for all.

REFERENCES

Confederation of British Industry (1989) *Towards a skills revolution – a youth charter: report of the Vocational Education and Training Task Force*. CBI.

Education and Science, Department of (1989) *Post-16 education and training core skills*. DES.

Employment, Department of (1988) *Employment for the 1990s*. DoE.

Milton Keynes College (1988) Milton Keynes College annual programme 1988–1989 – A review (available on request from the college).

Milton Keynes College (1989) Milton Keynes College annual programme 1989–1990 Investing in people, developing skills (available on request from the college).

Milton Keynes College (1990) Milton Keynes College development plan 1990–1993 Moving into the nineties (available on request from the college).

Milton Keynes College (1990) Milton Keynes College corporate plan 1990–1994 From enterprise to achievement (available on request from the college).

Milton Keynes College (1990) Milton Keynes annual programme 1990–1991 From enterprise to achievement – an opportunity to affirm our learning culture (available on request from the college).

Milton Keynes College (1990) Milton Keynes annual programme 1991–1992 From enterprise to achievement – promoting a learning society (available on request from the college).

Peters, T. (1988) *Thriving on chaos: a handbook for management revolution*. Macmillan.

Trades Union Congress (1989) *Skills 2000*. TUC.

PART 4:

Working Together

12

HOW ARE DECISIONS MADE IN DEPARTMENTS AND SCHOOLS?

Peter Earley and Felicity Fletcher-Campbell

In this discussion on the importance of the sharing of decision-making [. . .] it is not the intention to adopt a systems approach whereby decision-making mechanisms are analysed – although structures existing in the phase two case study schools will be noted. Neither is it intended to engage solely in an exploration of the loci of power in schools and to describe micropolitical activity (what, and how, items get on the agenda; power relations between departments etc. – see, for example, Hoyle, 1982, 1986; Ball, 1987) – although reference will be made to this body of work in the course of the text. Rather, the chapter will look at the part played by middle managers as regards both their own involvement and their furthering of the involvement of others in decision-making within the department and within the school. It will also consider actual practices within schools as perceived by a range of staff.

Edwards (1985) considers that leadership and communication infuse all the activity engaged in by middle managers whatever the dimension of school life; the dimension of decision-making is no exception and it can, in fact, only be comprehended in the light of a concept of leadership. The NDC categorize management styles, team-building, decision-making and communication as 'leadership skills'. It could be argued that participative decision-making embraces a number of factors identified as contributing to school effectiveness (for example, collegiality, job satisfaction). Rutter *et al.* (1979) found that in effective schools there was clear leadership from the top but teachers felt that their views were represented. Similarly, openness of communication and collaboration were features of schools identified by Fullan (1982) as being good at managing change.

LEADERSHIP STYLES

A useful definition of leadership style is that given by Sergiovanni and Elliot (1975) who see it as the way an individual expresses leadership, uses power and authority, arrives at decisions and in general interacts with teachers and others. Various attempts have been made to draw up typologies of leadership styles (e.g. Lewin, 1944; McGregor, 1960; Likert, 1961; Blake and Mouton, 1964; Etzioni, 1964), some of which, it is argued (Nias, 1980), assume value connotations – for example, delineating the 'autocrat' as caring little for the feelings of others. One of the most useful models – reproduced in Figure 12.1 – is that of Tannenbaum and Schmidt (1958, 1973) which identifies six types of decision-making. Relating this to the contingency theory of Fiedler (1968) which takes account of situational variables, it can be argued that managers (especially school middle managers, who find themselves in such a myriad of situations) need to operate in all seven modes. Indeed, Hull and Adams (1981) contend that the styles of heads of department are usually hybrids. It is how each mode of decision-making is handled that determines its efficacy and the way in which it is perceived. For example, 'tell' and 'sell' decisions are quite acceptable provided that they are communicated in the right way, and the appropriate type of participation is as important as the basic concept of participation itself (Davies, 1983).

Whatever the style, it should be open and clear (Everard and Morris, 1985). Furthermore, Sutton (1985) contends that teachers must be secure in their knowledge of *how* different issues will be decided – that is, what mode will be utilized: 'What is most important here may not be so much the style itself as its consistency . . . Nothing is more confusing to staff than not to be able to foresee with reasonable certainty how a significant issue is likely to be resolved.' Other factors also need to be considered: the autocratic mode may be quickest at the point of decision-making but has a long implementation time; a decision will take longer to arrive at by a consultative process but will increase commitment and implementation is likely to be faster (Hull and Adams, 1981; Everard and Morris, 1985). Furthermore, there is a limit to the energy of staff (Buckley and Styan, 1988) and an expectation that discussion will not drag on interminably (Weindling and Earley, 1987).

[. . .] Routine activities may be differentiated from higher level ones, a distinction which would seem to parallel 'transactional leadership' – the 'fixing and dealing which are necessary in administration' – and 'transforming leadership' which involves 'leaders and followers raising one another to higher levels of motivation' (McGregor Burns, 1979). It could be argued that it is in transforming leadership that participative decision-making is crucial and this would explain why this seemed to be a feature of the more effective departments in the NFER study. A middle manager can be extremely *efficient* – as opposed to effective – by operating in the 'tell' and 'sell' modes, for these are perfectly acceptable – and, indeed, probably most appropriate – for administrative tasks. However, essential for *effectiveness*, are two basic leadership functions – task achievement and the fulfilment of colleagues'

Figure 12.1 Types of decision-making (from Tannenbaum and Schmidt, 1958)

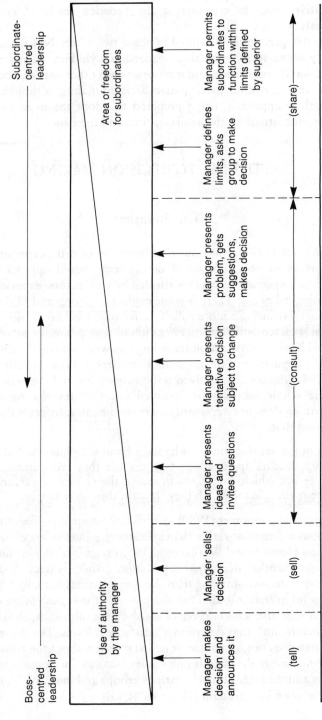

social needs (Hoyle, 1986) – and it has been suggested that the department head's role needs developing significantly away from focusing purely on administrative tasks to considering the broader needs of colleagues as professionals.

The effective practitioners studied in phase two of the NFER research were not directly asked to describe their leadership style but, on reflection, most considered – and observation and interviews with other parties would confirm this – that they favoured participative decision-making although they were flexible in their approach, being prepared to adopt the most suitable style according to the situation, the available time and the issue.

ATTITUDES TO DECISION-MAKING

The literature

Hull and Adams (1981) point out that members of a department may have expectations as to how a head of department should approach decision-making. These expectations may be affected by two factors: experience to date and psychological needs. There is some evidence (Knoop and O'Reilly, 1976) that, although favouring a more collaborative role, teachers do not want absolute control. Belasco and Alutto (1972) found that desire for increased participation and levels of satisfaction regarding this were not equally distributed in the teaching population. Primary school teachers in Nias' (1980) study condemned heads who totally devolved responsibility for making decisions which affected the whole school. Nias pointed out that the decentralization of decision-making does not *necessarily* increase the job satisfaction of all teachers. She found that:

> Maximum job satisfaction went hand-in-hand with humane but positive leadership, leadership to which teachers felt they were encouraged to contribute but which gave them in return the chance to perform effectively the main role for which they thought they were employed.

An investigation by Bloomer (1980) identified the desired profile of the head of department as a democrat rather than an autocrat, and evidence from a survey conducted by Howson and Woolnough (1982) suggested similar findings.

The measurement of 'decisional deprivation' (when individuals desire more participation in decision-making than they perceive they actually have) is difficult, but useful in that it underlines the point that it is *perception* of involvement, rather than the actual *degree* of involvement (although, clearly, the two may be concomitant), that determines satisfaction levels. The degree of participation alone does not, of course, reveal very much about the political reality of decision-making in the institution as other factors – for example, the content of decisions and the stage at which various groups and individuals are involved – have to be taken into account (Conway, 1985).

The NFER study

What both the middle managers and the teachers in the NFER study spoke of negatively as regards decision-making were 'rubber-stamping' meetings and 'cosmetic consultation'. Such behaviour was, in fact, more frequently referred to with regard to middle managers' involvement in whole-school decision-making than teachers' involvement within departments. Most department and faculty heads, in both phases, acknowledged the value of open discussion within departments and the following statement by a phase one head of department was atypical: 'I don't think it's the department's job to produce materials or that things are best done in consultation – I'm weary of verbal proceedings.' Generally, it was *outside* departments that discussion became problematic; within departments participative decision-making appeared to be the norm.

Especially in the phase two schools, teachers regarded the part they played in decision-making within the department very positively. They felt that their department head was accessible and that they were able to express their views freely. However, the degree to which they were involved and the quality of participation varied according to the way in which the department head operated and was affected by a number of factors such as the information made available and the 'health' of the team. The 'good' heads of department allowed staff 'to have access to their thinking': they discussed issues and deliberated openly. In the effective departments, it is probably true to say that staff were aware of their own ability to participate and their experience or lack of it. However, in the less effective ones, where staff were deprived of opportunities to widen their horizons, teachers could well perceive that they had a satisfactory degree of involvement but yet be unaware of their own shortcomings and that they were 'speaking in ignorance', opportunities to extend professional experience and expertise having been denied them.

Davies (1983) quotes research evidence which suggests that participation in decision-making can promote better decisions, although an NFER case study headteacher questioned whether the outcome of involvement in decision-making was reinforced emotional commitment to the institution or improved practice. Teachers' participation in decision-making may improve their sense of efficacy and thus enhance morale (Dembo and Gibson, 1985). Many middle managers were aware of the expertise that lay within their departments and wished to capitalize on this. A head of department said: 'If there were a staff disagreement, I would never say, "You'll do this anyway." All the staff in my department are older and more experienced than me.' And a faculty head observed: 'I've risen through the department and am not an imported HoF who can come in and pretend they've got all the answers . . . I'm learning as much as everyone else.' A head of department who had had industrial experience remarked: 'In education we do not make the most of people who are experienced. In industry they have moved towards corporate decision-making.' A deputy head, referring to one of the phase two nominees, said: 'He is prepared to listen even though at times he may appear not to do so. When we were changing from mixed ability to banding, he listened and acted on the department's advice.'

Generally, teachers in the NFER study felt that they had little say in whole-school policy-making; they were either not consulted or were asked for opinions *after* the SMT had decided upon a course of action – the latter situation gave rise to more acrimony than the former. Teachers did not mind decisions being made at a senior level, often saying 'Someone has to decide' or 'That's what they are paid to do', and realizing that a number of decisions were most appropriately made at this level; they were prepared to be 'told' or 'sold' decisions. However, they *did* object to being treated 'unprofessionally' and their time being wasted in pseudo-discussion and cosmetic consultation when decisions had already been made and were unlikely to be modified. Frustrations arising from situations such as these have been identified as causes of stress, which itself leads to underperformance (Dunham, 1984).

THE PROMOTION OF PARTICIPATIVE DECISION-MAKING WITHIN DEPARTMENTS

Hoyle (1986) identifies four reasons for the increase of pressure for participative decision-making: the change in the socio-political climate of the 1960s; the growing need for greater teacher collaboration for curriculum change; the increasing complexity of schools which undermines the single person kind of leadership; and the growth in management courses which emphasize particular approaches. In the NFER case study schools there was evidence of an assumption that the participative mode was desirable.

If expertise is found within a department, it is logical that a new young department head will wish, out of self-interest if nothing else, to tap it. However, if the expertise is undeveloped, what can the middle manager do to promote participative decision-making which, if it is not to be an 'exchange of ignorance', depends on informed discussion? It is not insignificant that, in the nominated departments, there were a number of related factors which went alongside participative decision-making and, rather than any one leading to another, it is arguable that they were interdependent and coexistent.

The involvement of staff in decision-making – with its perceived benefits in terms of staff development, commitment, willingness to change etc. – cannot just happen. Most of the effective practitioners had worked at it, even if indirectly, largely by generating a climate in which it could flourish. In those departments and faculties where staff had been accustomed to an autocratic leadership style, they had to learn *how* to participate when there was a change of leader. A department head whose own observed departmental meetings were an exemplar of participation, remarked, regarding the situation in the whole school:

I think that the new head is trying to consult staff now. It's difficult making staff feel some responsibility when they have not been accustomed to it – the previous head was a complete autocrat and never asked anyone about anything.

Another newly appointed faculty head remarked that his staff were longing to get involved in faculty matters but 'did not know how to as yet' as the previous head of faculty had done and decided everything. A phase two head of department similarly observed: 'The first few times we met as a department it was a bit uncomfortable but now everyone expects to express views and there's a very good spirit.'

It was the 'open' departments that practised participative decision-making – not merely because they had a philosophy that placed value on democratic processes *per se*, but because the staff were privy to everything that was going on and were kept fully informed. The teachers had both the necessary information and background knowledge on which to form opinions and make decisions, and the benefit of sharing others' views and experiences, thus broadening their own horizons. Participation was an on-going process and was not confined to organizational structures.

An aspect of the role of the head of department is to encourage and facilitate others to become leaders and, in the view of many senior staff, this was just as important as the middle managers themselves taking the initiative (although, undoubtedly, it is imperative to strike the right balance between devolution and accountability). Yeomans (1987), albeit discussing management in primary schools, wrote: 'The greatest demand on collegial leadership is that the leader as member is sufficiently secure to enable colleagues to lead effectively.' An NFER case study headteacher observed: 'The absolute key to departmental improvement is to involve everyone in everything that goes on. If you can get ideas flowing then you have a structure for making improvement. On the other hand, you have got to have ideas yourself and be seen as a leader.' Another, a newly appointed head, saw the ethos of the whole school affecting what went on within departments:

> There must be ownership of problems in teams and people must not see things in terms of the person above them solving problems . . . When I came here the SMT was not working as a team . . . I felt that there could be no progress until SMT was right. Then I could look at middle management and the process would go down through them for more democratic participation among the teachers.

COLLEGIALITY AND TEAM-BUILDING

Hoyle (1986) writes about 'collegial authority' – the 'pattern of authority which is held to be appropriate to organisations which are staffed by professionals' and which ensures that bureaucracy and hierarchy do not restrict latent expertise. He considers that, largely on account of salary differentials (other than increments for length of service), schools are not characterized by collegial authority and it is not inherent in the system. Those with higher status or salary have power thrust upon them to make decisions. In the NFER research, this feeling was evident: a phase two head of department remarked that he felt it his duty to represent staff at meetings to save their time and a number of teachers interviewed said that they thought that middle managers were paid to make the decisions even if they should consult staff first. The phase one fieldwork – and some phase two – was conducted during industrial action when many of the formal consultative structures had broken down. One department had learnt from the experience. The department head said:

> Before [industrial] action, I'd set up working parties . . . during action, I've written all the courses but now the staff are criticizing them – positively not negatively. It's made them aware of the value of coming together as a group to work things out.

Hoyle (1986) contends that participative decision-making is not a 'right' but something bestowed by a benevolent manager. (For a contrasting view see Watts, 1986.) The arrival of such a benevolent manager at whatever level was often commented upon:

> Decision-making at this school has changed a lot since the arrival of the new deputy. Also, the new HoD has been much keener than his predecessor in getting involved in the school. The same process of democratisation has happened in our department and in the school.

A recently appointed phase two headteacher wrote (in a school document):

> Good communication and participative decision-making is a necesary condition for staff commitment if the school is to move forward. I see the staff of a school broadly as a collegiate group of professionals . . . It is a matter of professional faith in one another.

Arguably, with GCSE syllabuses and the growth of course teams demanding greater interaction among teachers, collegiality within schools could be strengthened. Some of the activities engaged in in connection with GCSE are akin to those identified by Little (1982) as being crucial for the sort of collegiality which results in continuous professional development, namely: frequent, continuous and precise talk about teaching practice; observation and constructive criticism; joint planning, designing, researching, evaluating and preparing of teaching materials; and exchange of good practice.

Research has also been conducted in industry and commerce into the optimum composition of management teams and it has been found that they work best if various ideal types are represented (for example, Belbin, 1981, makes reference to the 'shaper', the 'monitor–evaluator', the 'resource-investigator', the 'completer–finisher'). Interesting though such evidence may be, it is only marginally transferable to schools – where the composition of teams is largely determined more by luck than good management. Appointments are made, primarily, on subject terms, both within the department and at middle management level. Some schools may find themselves in the fortunate position of having a large pool of suitable candidates for a post but others, particularly those in inner cities and those with vacancies in the shortage subject areas (for example, CDT, science, modern languages, mathematics) may find it difficult appointing someone to fulfil curricular needs, let alone having the required characteristics to fill any identified gaps in the team. The situation has often been exacerbated by redeployment and ring fence policies. Furthermore, each member of staff in a school is often a member of a number of teams (academic, pastoral, special issues working parties) in a way that is not comparable to the industrial or commercial situation. Thus, within the department, it is of considerable importance that middle managers have the skills necessary for building a team from the staff they have.

Many of the team-building strategies employed by the effective practitioners were closely related to the ways in which they promoted staff development. However, individuals can be professionally developed without being part of a team or participating in decision-making as a member of a group. Watts (1986) identified three important factors which facilitate a feeling of collectivity: the free flow of information, well-organized meetings and the sharing of responsibilities. These factors were features of the effective departments studied in the NFER research.

Free flow of information occurred when department heads willingly shared their own professional experience (lesson ideas, resources etc.), professional expertise from without the school (professional associations, courses) and information regarding broader curricular and professional matters affecting the whole school community. The effective practitioners were trying to widen the decision-making base, thereby increasing opportunities for alternatives to the curriculum already within the school and thus avoiding the constraints and parochialism to which school-centred innovation can fall victim (Hargreaves, 1987).

Such information can be conveyed both formally and informally. The danger of the latter is that only those who happen to be around at the right moment benefit and acquire the background for subsequent decision-making or involvement in relevant working parties. Thus, although effective departments were notable for their 'rich' conversations, they were very often also recognizable for the way in which formal meetings were conducted. Characteristics of meetings were the communication of information (for example, relaying the main points and the minutes of SMT meetings with middle management) as well as the encouragement of debate regarding issues affecting teachers in the school or the department. The latter issues are, possibly, the more contentious as they affect teachers' day-to-day life for it is, largely, subject-based decisions that impinge most obviously on the classroom practice with which teachers identify most closely. Participation, however, does not necessarily mean that teachers have any more *control* over the curriculum (Hargreaves, 1987).

At the time of the NFER fieldwork, schools were concerned with the implementation of GCSE. In some cases, the examining board to be used was determined by school policy, though in others, the decision rested with the department and department heads had circulated syllabuses among colleagues, selecting, in the main, the syllabus which was most in line with the type of work in which the department had already been engaged. In many cases, GCSE was spoken of as a facilitator of participation as teachers had to come together to discuss assessment and coursework.

When a head of department was very much in favour of a particular policy for the department or simply wanted participation in decisions regarding implementation, there was often conflict. The effective heads of department were sensitive to this and spent a lot of time in discussing proposals, giving reasons for decisions and trying to overcome feelings of threat by ensuring that staff received the necessary preparation, training and support for any changes in classroom practice. Where opposition was more ideological (for example, a strong feeling for teachers to retain a separate subject identity rather than move towards more integrated work), the problems were less easily resolvable and the department heads had to develop their powers of persuasion.

The effective heads of department tried to promote staff consensus about a proposed change – operating in the 'selling' mode. Middle managers were aware that, in their pivotal position, they had on occasions to 'sell' decisions made elsewhere (by, for example, the SMT, the LEA or the DES). There were limits, however, to the extent to which they would act according to the views of the majority and there was little evidence of totally democratic decision-making (i.e. decisions made according to a majority vote) or radical staff participation such as that earlier found at Countesthorpe (Watts, 1977). Nevertheless, a number of departments were, in fact, 'unanimous' on account of the good 'selling' job of the middle manager or the fact that appointments had been made on the basis of a shared educational philosophy. Generally, middle managers wanted to make the final decision should the occasion arise and the department was equally divided: 'In the department, if I feel someone is very against something I want, I'll drop it unless it's terribly important to me.' The words of one department head were typical of the feelings of many interviewed:

> Most people will accept a decision, though they may not agree with it, if you're open and honest with them. If you dictate to people and don't give reasons as to why you're acting in a certain way, there'll be friction and ill-feeling.

Certainly, there was dissatisfaction when reasons were not given or thought to have been inadequately explained.

Decision-making within departments has to be seen in the light of the fact that one of the functions of the head of department is to establish the department's aims and objectives: 'There is a need to establish priorities. There is an abundance of ideas in the department – it's a matter of choosing which to adopt.' Department heads who were prepared to take the lead, and set an example by doing what they had decided their staff had to do, were respected: 'The HoD is very stubborn but he has consulted us all. His attitude is "I'll try it and if it works you should try it too."'

Staff liked to see *outcomes* and what they reacted to negatively, both within the department and within the school, was lack of action after consultation. A head of department remarked: 'It's no good discussing ideas from probationers and scale 1s if they just get lost'; and a teacher observed: 'Whatever seems to be agreed, nothing seems to happen as a result.' A department head admitted to 'rationing' his attendance at meetings as 'there are endless meetings and nothing is resolved'. It must be made clear as to when the discussion has ended and a decision point reached. Teachers did not like uncertainty. In a phase one school a teacher remarked: 'We put things to our HoD but they just get lost so there's no point in taking them further. She sometimes makes an appointment to see the head but he just puts it off so she doesn't bother any more.' Equally, a head of department commented that decisions were apparently made by senior staff when teachers thought that they were in the middle of the consultative procedure.

The effective practitioners spoke of the importance of creating a feeling of belonging to the department: many organized social events – a weekly visit to the pub, a meal out together or joint sporting activities, for example. They felt that it was much easier to help colleagues, especially older ones, if they had created a social bond. It was not clear what was the key to the 'happiest departments', the ones where members worked as a team and where there was the greatest feeling of belonging. 'We're a keen department . . . Why? Because of the HoD's approach to the job . . . But all the staff are very nice people . . . It would be no good the HoD taking over the department at X (neighbouring school) because there are two very cynical teachers there.' This teacher implied that the head of department was lucky in having a naturally cooperative and amenable group to work with while, at the same time, acknowledging the part played by the leadership of the department head. Perceptions were often that the personality of individuals was 'given' and middle managers spoke of being fortunate with their staff in this regard. However, it is suggested that the behaviour of the middle manager played an important part, as evidence showed that teachers often fail under poor leadership, motivation declines when there is no professional development and there is a tendency to opt out when professional opinions are not taken seriously or are ignored.

The existence of department or faculty offices was considered to be a great help in creating a feeling of belonging to a team although, of course, there was the problem of 'isolationism' particularly in schools which had departments sited in separate blocks and when there was no central staffroom. A department head said: 'I've painted a room, put a kettle in it and claimed it as an office – there's more discussion now.' It was noticeable that of the faculties studied, those with offices were very often the ones which seemed to be most successful in creating a faculty identity (generally considered to be harder to achieve than a departmental identity) and most successful as regards the cross-fertilization of ideas and collaborative work; individual department rooms within a faculty tended to isolate teachers. As a further communication aid, some departments had a weekly bulletin. One, for example, besides giving administrative information (exam dates and deadlines, for example) announced jobs needing doing in the future so that staff could have time to think about them before the departmental meeting – this was appreciated by teachers in this department.

Problems as regards creating an identity and engendering a feeling of belonging to a team were caused by split sites – teachers were travelling in opposite directions and the valuable breaks and lunchtimes were spent commuting – and the existence of part-time staff. Heads of departments whose staff were likely to change from year to year (often in the 'new' areas like European Studies and PSE and subjects such as RE when there was only one specialist for the whole school) also spoke of the problem of creating identities: 'Social science is a hotch-potch. There are different teachers each year and a number of non-specialists.' In such circumstances, faculty arrangements were often helpful.

DEPARTMENT HEADS AND SCHOOL DECISION-MAKING

One of the criteria by which senior staff identified effective middle managers, and a quality which was highly valued, was the ability to take a wide perspective and see subject or area concerns in the context of the whole school. Middle managers who fought for their own corner regardless of the needs of colleagues in other departments and whole-school policies were regarded unfavourably. One phase two practitioner resolved this dilemma by trying to look at the pupils' total curriculum experience and considering the effect of a 'departmental stance'. Refusal to give up a period a week, for example, might mean that the pupils were denied something enriching, and was thus undesirable even if it meant that a department might have to revise its schemes of work if the period were relinquished. Issues involving compromise (which a number of middle managers regarded as inevitable 'once you see things in perspective') very often revolved round resource allocation.

It is with respect to interaction with senior management that the department head's pivotal position is, perhaps, hardest to come to terms with. A deputy head said:

> They would like to take a whole-school view but feel they would be betraying their departments. . . . They will talk with me privately but in meetings they find it uncomfortable to look at broad issues. Perhaps it's a 'them-and-us' situation – are they seen as siding with the head?

Often it was the case that there was conflict between the different perspectives as to what was judged to be of consequence:

> You have to persist if you want to take up something that is deemed low priority by SMT . . . It's best to go direct to the head. If you raise something under 'Any Other Business' at HoDs' meetings you can be seen as bolshie.

There was some evidence of what would appear to be poorly organized meetings. One practitioner spoke of the fact that although the agenda for heads of department meetings was apparently 'open', the discussion was poor and there was opting out because of apathy. This was because middle management were denied the background information with which they could make informed comment so 'you don't dare open your mouth because you'll look stupid'. At one school a middle manager claimed 'decision-making in this school depends on how "loud" you are and how well you get on with senior staff'.

Some practitioners realized the limited part that they could play in the light of the educational scene outside the school:

The HoFs' meetings have an agenda and papers in advance but both are set by the headteacher and there is no AOB [Any Other Business]. The head is trying to implement tremendous change from the LEA and the government and I think that's why he's taking control of the agenda.

Where agendas were not published in advance of middle management meetings, staff spoke of 'muddling along' and 'having to think on our feet'. The topics for discussion may partly be held responsible for lack of involvement:

The heads of department meetings are chaired by a DH (who rotate annually). They are negative and just turn into a moaning session . . . It was more positive last time . . . Why? Because the agenda was more positive, I think . . . There are no working parties generated from HoDs' meetings.

Where agendas included challenging issues rather than run-of-the-mill administration, commitment was stronger.

There were different committee structures and systems of consultation in the case study schools. In some, only heads of faculty or senior heads of department (usually the 'big' ones – English, science, maths, for example) met with the SMT; in others, all middle managers were included. The former arrangement was prone to accusations of elitism; the latter, of unwieldiness: 'Too large a meeting doesn't allow HoDs to be looked after and stunts growth.' At one school, over 50 per cent of the staff attended heads of department/teachers-in-charge of subject meetings. Department heads not included in meetings with senior staff felt frustrated, especially where they perceived that they were poorly represented by their head of faculty. Some department heads spoke warmly of the way in which their heads of faculty represented departmental concerns at heads of faculty meetings, but others were not so happy and there were instances of the heads of faculty 'blocking' a departmental initiative. A head of PE said: 'It's difficult having someone represent you when they don't care a hoot for PE.' Some schools attempted to overcome the problem by allowing heads of faculty to bring a head of department or faculty representative to meetings on a rota basis. This proved unsatisfactory for the heads of department, however, on account of the lack of continuity: they might become very involved in an issue at one meeting but then not be able to follow it through and, when they next attended, would find themselves in the middle of a new issue for which they had not the necessary background.

Heads of department were not always in the best position to judge how effectively their heads of faculty represented their interests but headteachers spoke of the varying communication skills of faculty heads. At one school there were violent reactions from department heads when new curriculum proposals were announced – an indication, the head thought, that they knew nothing about the lengthy discussion of the curriculum review that should have been passed on to them by their faculty heads. It was not just some faculty heads who seemed to have weaknesses here. A headteacher observed: 'I can think of an HoD who allows staff to discuss matters at meetings but the views he expresses at HoDs' meetings are seen as his own and not those of his department'; and another remarked: 'I always give reasons for my decisions but how far these get filtered down varies according to the HoD.' The effective practitioners were noted for the way in which they satisfied the communication needs of both those above them and those below them.

Furthermore, the 'power' of heads of department was perceived to be reduced by 'baronial' faculty heads: 'HoFs are very powerful people – for example, capitation is dealt with by them. In a sense, the HoD's role is reduced to that of ordering books.' A deputy head's comments are worth citing at length, illustrating as they do the shift in power that often results when middle management structures are modified:

> The faculty system developed because the HoDs/TiCs' meetings became too big and unwieldy. So the previous DH called the HoFs together as a think-tank. Up until that time the HoFs had not had any power. They did a curriculum review. We had presumed that the HoFs discussed various matters within their faculties but they hadn't, so when the review came out, it was a bit of a surprise to many people. Over this review, the HoFs had a lot more power but it's not really recognized. The HoDs and TiCs are quite happy to pass things over to HoFs – the little tasks – but don't like giving them power.

On the micropolitical front, several heads of faculty spoke of the additional power that they had when promoted (power 'won', doubtless, from the department heads who can be the losers when faculties are set up). One said: 'Things have happened which would never have got on the agenda if we had just had departments and not a faculty structure.' Another, a head of science and maths faculty observed: 'I get a more serious hearing from the head than if I'd just been head of science.'

The 'chair' of the faculty rotating between heads of department was something that was discussed and offered as a solution to 'baronial' faculty heads, but the practice was not encountered in any of the schools studied in the NFER project. However, the new incentive allowances could make this possible and give greater responsibility to individuals for a specified period. Clearly, much depended on the management skills of the faculty head. In those cases where heads of faculty took a different view when seeing the needs of the faculty and constituent departments in the context of the needs of the school as a whole, it was important that they gave adequate feedback and explanation to their staff.

Some headteachers were trying to develop the middle management level and this was particularly the case in the phase two schools. Whether or not this was symptomatic of the fact that there were, by happy chance, several very able practitioners at this level, or whether they had become effective on account of senior management support, can only be conjectured but a phase one head-teacher did say that he could not involve middle managers more as they were of such poor quality (though, clearly, what he and the deputies could have done to rectify this situation is an important consideration).

A phase two headteacher said:

> In the past, HoFs meetings have been just information giving and a communication channel. I want to give them things to grapple with – for example, capitation, staffing and rooming decisions. I was encouraged this morning. An HoD came to me and said: 'Perhaps you could discuss that at the next senior management meeting.' When she came to the school a year ago she would ask *me* for a decision – she saw me as an authority.

At another school, the headteacher said: 'Before, the situation was very much "We can't do anything without first asking the head." I wanted to try to build up cells of several people that would help with team-building.' Elsewhere, a faculty head said: 'In HoFs meetings we used to discuss little things like litter and truancy but we're now beginning to look at curricular issues. We all want a clear decision from each meeting.' A deputy at this school commented that heads of faculty meetings had got out of control because things were being deferred as there was so much to be discussed under matters arising from the previous meeting. So they decided to have one meeting chaired by the deputy and the next without him and with a rotating chair. 'Participation, excitement and involvement are in the blood of the meeting now.'

How did senior staff encourage the involvement of both middle managers and their staff – either as individuals or as departmental representatives – in issues concerning the whole school? At one school, the headteacher identified GRIDS as having helped to develop a team spirit and corporate identity and said that after the exercise, there had been less interdepartmental fighting. The self-review exercise had been well received but it was interesting to note what the head said in this respect: 'If we'd asked for a democratic decision, the staff might have rejected it. We wanted an opportunity to be involved and it was us, the SMT, who had most to lose as it would expose us the most.'

A phase two headteacher who, on taking up post, was concerned about the lack of coherence between committees, the fact that agendas were published at very short notice (if at all), the inertia at major meetings and the low degree of participation by middle managers and junior staff, published a discussion document on communication and decision-making at the school. It was planned to set up a number of working parties (on, for example, information technology, primary school liaison, curriculum development, multiculturalism, INSET). The headteacher hoped that 'all staff would participate in at least two groups according to their own professional interests and the skills and knowledge they have'. The paper continued:

> Each committee or working party would report regularly to the full staff through the committee chair. Debate, if appropriate, would take place,

followed by a full staff vote after which, if by voting the committee report had been accepted, it would become school policy.

Senior management, according to this headteacher:

> has the function of leading through exercise of its responsibility to initiate, to facilitate and to implement policy . . . Senior management executive decisions would be made in the light of policy decisions taken by the full staff and would seek the assent of staff and their willingness to act.

At another school, a deputy head went to all departmental meetings to provide the whole-school view and information regarding what other departments were doing. It was felt that it was very important to keep staff informed and enable them to 'be in control of the facts' to stop cliques forming. Another school, for similar reasons, started publishing minutes of SMT meetings because 'people felt that it had an aura of mystery although it has, in fact, always been very open'. A deputy head at a phase one school which strongly believed in participative decision-making attended departmental and faculty meetings and said: 'Sometimes I do not agree with decisions taken but I have to bite my tongue.'

PARTICIPATION IN CROSS-DEPARTMENTAL GROUPS

There was no overall pattern as regards the way in which general working parties were established. In those schools where the staff were divided into mixed groups (subject, sex, age, seniority, etc.) and the groups given a task to do, there was the advantage of ensuring that, theoretically, all staff participated – although, of course, there was the problem of 'passive involvement'. One headteacher felt that it was particularly important to move from the 'volunteer' model to a 'commitment' model – otherwise, as one senior teacher observed, 'the participation of scale 1 teachers in whole-school issues usually depends on the quality of the HoD as representative'. There was no evidence, in the effective departments, of staff being coerced into serving on working parties to try to influence outcomes in favour of the department or faculty, in the way that Bullock (1980) reports. Certainly, teachers' perceptions were that the experience was to their advantage. Sometimes, schools organized staff into groups to work on a task regularly or on a one-off basis (perhaps on an early closure day). One school had, before the industrial action, instituted timetabled curriculum area meetings so that all staff would be included.

There were, none the less, problems as regards staff involvement. The head of a phase two school said:

> I tried to resurrect a curriculum working party to debate issues, get ideas and involve staff, but no one wanted it. It is not that staff are too idle or busy or think that it is the SMT's job: it is just that they trust the SMT. They are very easy, pleasant and hard-working and will do absolutely anything that they are asked. Very few are ambitious as they want to stay

in this area and at this school . . . The bad side of this is the danger of stagnation.

In another phase two school a deputy commented:

> The staff don't like random groups for discussion . . . they like departmental or year groups . . . They are so predictable – you give up trying to rehearse arguments because you know how they'll react . . . The trouble is that staff don't take things seriously here. They either think that there's a Grand Plan – i.e. SMT have got everything worked out whether they like it or not – or they think 'Oh, they just want our opinions because they don't know what they're doing!'

Some schools were trying, structurally, to widen the decision-making base. In one – a community school – a finance committee was established to deal with capitation. This had previously been done by a deputy on a formula basis. The committee was formed by a representative from the staff association, the community department, heads of year and heads of faculty plus the registrar and an independent staff member.

Such structures should, in theory, break down departmental barriers. However, there was evidence that *some* practitioners were astute politicians and tried to manipulate senior staff, or school committees, to further their own departmental ends. One head of department said: 'I think that I have a disproportionate amount of influence on decision-making because I'm a member of so many committees.' The importance of 'the word in the corridor' was recognized and several department heads spoke of using the tactic at meetings of asking for twice as much capitation as was reasonable, in the belief that a satisfactory compromise would be reached.

The extent to which such political activity is controlled largely depends on the mangement skills of the headteacher and deputies. Left to run its own course, it can result in departments erecting further barriers and the development of rigid departmental hierarchies.

SUMMARY AND DISCUSSION

There is a growing body of knowledge showing that effective schools are those that are good at two-way communication, listen to their teachers and take their views into account before making decisions. Effective management of a complex organization like a school is less likely without real opportunities being created for teachers to participate in decision-making processes. Most teachers like to be consulted about major issues and to have the opportunity to put forward ideas and suggestions. In general, however, many felt they had little say in school decision-making and particularly objected to being consulted after a course of action had been decided on. Senior staff were seen as having the right to make decisions but 'pseudo-democracy' was something to be avoided and could contribute to low morale. But expectations did vary according to the significance of the matter being discussed.

Elaborate consultative procedures over matters deemed inconsequential or of minor importance were seen as time-consuming and irritating. Similarly, indecisiveness and slow decision-making were seen as undesirable qualities in school leaders, and teachers liked to see an outcome from the consultative process. There is a need, therefore, for those in leadership positions to create *genuine* opportunities for participation and yet be prepared, on occasions, to make decisions with little or no consultation. A lot will depend on the issue and the level of commitment that is required.

Although, both in the literature and from the NFER research, participative decision-making was generally regarded positively, there were, none the less, dangers associated with it. Having to make decisions on many aspects of school policy may place too much responsibility on class teachers. Indeed, excessive commitment by teachers *may* result in neglect of their lesson preparation (Bullock, 1980). Some teachers may choose to opt out of working parties or not attend meetings, seeing their first commitment, as teachers, as catering for the needs of pupils and thus giving other matters (e.g. extra-curricular activities) preference. It appeared that job satisfaction was enhanced when teachers were able to contribute at the level they desired yet still perform their main role effectively.

The notion of leadership styles was discussed and a typology of modes of decision-making presented. Effective middle managers, it was suggested, need to be able to operate in all modes – there is no single style that can be identified as the most appropriate for every person in every situation. However, whatever style is used, it should be open and clear and, perhaps above all, consistent. Teachers need to know how decisions, both in departments and schools, are likely to be made and matters of significance resolved. Effective leaders were also shown to have a major concern for achieving tasks and for fulfilling the social and professional needs of colleagues. Leaders had to be adaptable to match constantly changing situations and it was important for department and faculty heads to lead by example and to be a source of ideas. But it was also important for them to encourage and facilitate others to become leaders and take the initiative. For this to happen, middle managers had to feel secure and confident in themselves.

The importance of collegiality was stressed but it was noted that, despite being staffed by professionals, schools tended to be more hierarchical than collegial organizations. Given recent changes, such as the introduction of GCSE and the development of course teams, collegiality within schools may grow but, at present, it has to be worked at and the creation of a feeling of belonging to a departmental team is an important responsibility of its head. Participative decision-making – along with other factors – can help generate such feelings. Whether teachers' involvement in decision-making is seen as a professional entitlement or something given to them by a benevolent manager is a moot point. It could be argued that such an important matter should not be left to the predilections of individuals and that the former view needs to become the predominant one if all schools and departments are to function more effectively.

It was important for department and faculty heads to have the requisite skills in order to create a team from the staff they had. Matters were made more difficult because most teachers did not belong exclusively to one departmental team – they were often members of several teams – and schools were rarely able to appoint the appropriate staff member to enable the department to compensate for any obvious team weaknesses. The team-building strategies employed were similar to the ways in which staff development was promoted and three significant factors were identified: a willingness to share information, experience and expertise; well-organized meetings; and the sharing of department and faculty responsibilities. Also important in generating a sense of belonging were regular social events and the existence of department and faculty offices. The latter were particularly important for faculties – it was generally thought more difficult to create a faculty identity – as they encouraged collaborative work and the sharing of ideas. Team-building and identification with a departmental or faculty unit were not helped by the existence of part-time staff and by split-site schools.

The middle manager's pivotal role was, once again, raised and there was recognition of the difficulties experienced by individuals who wanted to adopt a whole-school perspective yet not be seen as letting down the department or faculty team. It was suggested that department heads' involvement in school decision-making would be greater if the meetings they participated in were better organized, and commitment enhanced if the agenda always included educational/curricular items and was not dominated by administrative concerns. Also, as has been noted elsewhere, there is a need for the teaching profession 'to accept more readily that decisions made at middle-management level are real decisions and not just the start of negotiations, leaving the head with a crisis later' (Brennan, 1987).

Formal consultative structures varied between the 21 case study schools although the differences usually centred on the size of the middle management meeting. In schools where only a few middle managers met with the SMT there were the dangers of elitism or a 'them and us' situation developing, whereas those schools which included all middle managers were likely to be faced with an unwieldy group too large to enable proper discussion and decision-making to take place. It seemed to be quite difficult to achieve the right balance between the two. Where department heads/teachers in charge of subjects were not present themselves in these meetings, the representative function of the head of faculty was seen as of crucial importance. Indeed, the effective faculty (and department) heads were able to satisfy the communication needs of both senior management *and* their more immediate colleagues.

Finally, mention was made of several attempts to develop both department heads and other staff and to involve them in whole-school issues. The establishment of working parties showed no overall pattern and, in some schools, the staff were divided into mixed groups and allocated particular tasks to undertake. Again, the attempts to widen the decision-making base and involve more staff were not always as successful as the heads had wished.

NOTE

This chapter is part of a report of a national study of a sample of faculty/ departmental heads in 21 English and Welsh secondary schools (1986–1988). Phase I consisted of about 10 days spent interviewing staff in each of 16 schools within representative LEAs, and Phase II looked at 'effective practice' in 11 other schools within 5 different but representative LEAs.

REFERENCES

Ball, S.J. (1987) *The Micro-Politics of the School*. London: Methuen.

Belasco, J.A. and Alutto, J.A. (1972) 'Decisional participation and teacher satisfaction', *Educational Administration Quarterly*, 8, 1, 44–58.

Belbin, R.M. (1981) *Management Teams: Why They Succeed or Fail*. London: Heinemann.

Blake, R. and Mouton, J. (1964) *The Managerial Grid*. Houston: Gulf.

Bloomer, R.G. (1980) 'The role of the head of department: some questions and answers', *Educational Research*, 22, 2, 83–96.

Brennan, J.A. (1987) 'The emotional aspects of sustaining secondary headship', *International Journal of Educational Management*, 1, 2, 3–5.

Buckley, J. and Styan, D. (1988) *Managing for Learning*. London: Macmillan.

Bullock, A. (1980) 'Teacher participation in school decision-making', *Cambridge Journal of Education*, 10, 1, 21–28.

Conway, J.A. (1985) 'A perspective on organisational cultures and organisational belief structures', *Educational Administration Quarterly*, 21, 4.

Davies, B. (1983) 'Head of department involvement in decisions', *Educational Management and Administration*, 11, 173–176.

Dembo, M.H. and Gibson, S. (1985) 'Teachers' sense of efficacy: an important factor in school improvement', *Elementary School Journal*, 86, 2, 173–184.

Dunham, J. (1984) *Stress in Teaching*. Beckenham: Croom Helm.

Edwards, R. (1985) 'Departmental organization and management.' In: Edwards, R. and Bennett, D. *Schools in Action*. Cardiff: Welsh Office.

Etzioni, A. (1964) *Modern Organizations*. Englewood Cliffs, NJ: Prentice-Hall.

Everard, B. and Morris, G. (1985) *Effective School Management*. London: Paul Chapman Publishing.

Fiedler, F. (1968) 'Personality and situational determinants of leadership effectiveness.' In: Cartwright, D. and Zander, A. (eds.) *Group Dynamics*. New York: Harper and Row.

Fullan, M. (1985) 'Change processes and strategies at the local level', *Elementary School Journal*, 85, 3, 371–421.

Hargreaves, A. (1987) 'The rhetoric of school-centred innovation.' In: Hewton, E. (1988) *School-Focused Staff Development: Guidelines for Policy Makers*. London: Falmer.

Howson, J. and Woolnough, B. (1982) 'Head of department – dictator or democrat?', *Educational Management and Administration*, 10, 1, 37–43.

Hoyle, E. (1982) 'Micropolitics of education organizations', *Educational Management and Administration*, 10, 2, 87–98.

Hoyle, E. (1986) *The Politics of School Management*. London: Hodder and Stoughton.

Hull, R. and Adams, A. (1981) *Decisions in the Science Department*. Hatfield: Schools Council/Association for Science Education.

Knoop, R. and O'Reilly, R. (1975) 'Participative decision making in the curriculum', *High School Journal*, 59, 4, 153–158.

Lewin, K. (1944) 'The dynamics of group action', *Educational Leadership*, 1, 195–200.

Likert, R. (1961) *New Patterns of Management*. New York: McGraw-Hill.

McGregor, D. (1960) *The Human Side of Enterprise*. New York: McGraw-Hill.

McGregor Burns, J. (1979) *Leadership*. London: Harper and Row.

Nias, J. (1980) 'Leadership styles and job-satisfaction in primary schools.' In: Bush, T. *et al.* (Eds.) *Approaches to School Management*. London: Harper and Row.

Rutter, M. *et al.* (1979) *15000 Hours: Secondary Schools and their Effects on Children*. London: Open Books.

Sergiovanni, T.J. and Elliot, D.L. (1975) *Educational and Organizational Leadership in Elementary Schools*. Englewood Cliffs, NJ: Prentice-Hall.

Sutton, J. (1985) 'Staff Management II.' In: Frith, D. (Ed.) *School Management in Practice*. Harlow: Longman.

Tannenbaum, R. and Schmidt, W.H. (1973) 'How to choose a leadership pattern', *Harvard Business Review*, 36, 2, 95–101.

Watts, M. (1986) 'Leading the English department.' In: Blatchford, R. (Ed.) *The English Teacher's Handbook*. London: Hutchinson.

Yeomans, R. (1987) 'Leading the team: belonging to the group?' In: Southworth, G. (Ed.) *Readings in Primary School Management*. Lewes: Falmer.

13

THE DYNAMICS OF INTENSE WORK GROUPS:
a Study of British String Quartets

J. Keith Murnighan and Donald E. Conlon

This material has been abridged

[. . .] Groups are elemental organizational units that are stimulating ever-increasing empirical and conceptual research (Bettenhausen, 1991). This paper presents a different perspective by reporting a study of British string quartets, an unusual example of particularly intense work groups. This study focuses on the relationship between the quartets' internal dynamics and their success as a group. Our research began inductively, using semi-structured interviews, archival analysis, and limited observation as methods. [. . .]

Quartets are a unique form of work group in at least two important respects: they are self-governing (Hackman, 1987), essentially constituting their own organization, and their task is extremely intense, being artistic, immediate, complete, and reciprocally interdependent (Thompson, 1967). We determined from the data that the string quartets we studied faced three important paradoxes: the leadership versus democracy paradox, the paradox of the second fiddle, and the conflict paradox of confrontation versus compromise. Smith and Berg's (1987) central notions – that groups face inherent, unresolvable paradoxes and that they must accept, confront, and manage them – provided an organizing framework for our analyses. Analysis reveals that, in this context, successful string quartets understand and implicitly manage their inherent group contradictions while less successful quartets do not.

THE STRING QUARTET

String quartets are particularly intense work groups. Members are reciprocally interdependent (Thompson, 1967), using each other's outputs as their own inputs, and vice versa. Their interdependence is also complete and immediate: their work is done only as a unit; they cannot perform a string-quartet composition without all of the members working together simultaneously. They are artists who collaborate; they must simultaneously devote their concentration to their own and to each other's playing. Many quartet players commented in the interviews that the ability to listen and respond to each other was the most important characteristic that differentiated quartet players from soloists.

A string quartet is composed of two violinists, a viola player, and a cellist; their collective task is to reach a high level of coordinated sound. [. . .]

Each group tries to achieve a unique interpretation and a forceful presentation each time it plays a piece. Any composition can be played an infinite number of ways, with varying speed, emphasis, rhythm, balance, and phrasing. Thus, a quartet tries to stamp each performance with its own character and style and, even after considerable rehearsal, members can surprise each other or their audience with spontaneous flourishes. Quartet players feed off each other, as one cellist put it, trying to achieve 'a spiritual experience, . . . which is the ultimate one can hope for.' These groups rehearse as many as six hours a day, seven days a week, in addition to individual practice. [. . .]

The different positions within the quartet have different musical responsibilities. The first violinist is the musical leader of the quartet. Much of the traditional quartet music asks him or her to play the tune, often referred to as the 'top.' The first violinists' parts are usually the most difficult. When they perform well, they give life to each different presentation of a piece. The first violin is most easily heard by the audience [. . .]. Among the four players, he or she gets the most attention and acclaim; many quartets, for example, are named after their first violinists.

While traditional string-quartet pieces demand that the first violin dominate the music, they also require a complementary but nevertheless engaging sound from the second violinist. For a quartet to do well, the second violinist cannot get lost in the background. The phrase, 'second fiddle', aptly describes the second violinist's role. Since seconds play the same instrument as the first fiddle and must often echo the first, playing an octave lower, their task is doubly difficult. A second violinist has few leads and is rarely the centre of the music. He or she must blend but must at the same time be more than a second fiddle.

The viola player teams with the second violinist to form the 'middle' of the quartet. [. . .] Viola players are dependent on quartets as the main outlet for their musical expression. Most viola players began by playing the violin. [. . .] Often it provides a player with more opportunities for advancement, since competition among violin players is typically fiercer.

The cellist is literally and figuratively the base of the group, laying the foundation above which the tonally higher strings can shine. The cellist follows the first violinist in the number of leads and forms the 'bottom' of the quartet with the viola player and second violinist.

Different personal and professional attributes also seem to be required of the different players. On the one hand, many quartet members feel that the second violinist should be a better player than the first, as playing the weaker parts of the music well requires strong technical skill. On the other hand, strong musicianship is required of the first violinist: he or she may not be the best player, but he or she must have 'audition,' musical vision. The cellist must be completely dependable: without a solid base, the quartet simply cannot function successfully. Viola players have the fewest requirements but require of themselves that they produce a lovely sound. The best quartets ask each player to have a soloist's skills but not a soloist's temperament.

Our interviews indicated that most string-quartet players view their work as more than a job: they identify with and are inspired by the music they play. They report never being able to achieve their ultimate goal – to produce transcendent, glorious sound – for an extended period. They do have short experiences of this state of performance, akin to Csikszentmihalyi's (1990) concept of flow, 'the state in which people are so involved in an activity that nothing else seems to matter.'

British string quartets

During the time of this study, at least 21 professional string quartets lived and worked in Great Britain. Quartet players ranged in age from their early 20s to their mid-70s. Of the 20 string quartets studied, one included the same four members for 34 years; two were going through a membership change at the time of the study. Talent was uniformly high. [. . .]

The burgeoning quartet population led to an increase in the variance of experience, pay, number of concerts played, and ability. A competitive atmosphere developed among the younger quartets as they recognized that not all of them could survive – an expectation that is borne out by our data, which show that over half of these quartets have folded. [. . .]

The younger quartets typically handled their own business affairs, dividing the duties of concert scheduling, accounting, travel planning, and rehearsal coordination amongst themselves. As they prospered, they often hired a manager or agent for booking and scheduling. Agents almost always handled overseas concerts.

GROUP PARADOXES

Smith and Berg (1987) presented the idea that groups face inherent paradoxes. A paradox was defined generally (Hughes and Brecht, 1975) as a contradictory, self-referential statement or statements that generate a vicious cycle. [. . .]

Smith and Berg (1987) hypothesized that since paradoxes are inherent to groups, attempts to untangle these contradictions will lead to unending logical conflicts and group paralysis. They also suggested that groups must manage and be open to the expression of opposing group members' reactions. [. . .] Smith and Berg suggested that immersion in the opposing forces of paradox will reveal the links between the contradictions and the essential release that is needed for effective group action. That is, they recommended that paradox be understood, accepted, and even embraced.

Smith and Berg (1987) identified, via observation and anecdote, a series of paradoxes with roots in psychotherapy and clinical psychology. Our use of the concept of paradox is more localized and task-oriented. Our interviews provided the information that led to the identification of three paradoxes that appeared both obvious and centrally important to the functioning or philosophy of string quartets: leadership versus democracy, the paradox of the second fiddle, and confrontation versus compromise. [. . .]

The leader versus democracy paradox

All string quartets face two conflicting facts: (1) Quartet music typically gives the lead (i.e., most of the good music) to the first violinist; and (2) the players reported that they joined the quartet to have a voice in how they play. Members of orchestras, for instance, are bound by the conductor's decisions. Each member of a string quartet, however, can theoretically have one-fourth of the input in musical and business decisions. Members share equally in their concert fees and expect to share equally in intragroup influence. At the same time, the first violinist has most of the musical opportunities and responsibilities in traditional compositions. This also extends to the group's everyday business interactions: since first violinists are the most well-known and recognized members of each quartet, they are often pressed to act as the group's primary speaker and public relations person.

The paradox of the second fiddle

As we have noted, second violinists have unique task and role problems: they must have consummate ability that rarely finds complete expression; they must always play the role of supporter during a performance, even if the first violin seems wrong; and they get little attention but nevertheless provide one of the most salient bases for evaluating the quartet as a whole. Second violinists are critical to their group's success – as many quartet players observed when they discussed how quartets were evaluated: 'They're only as good as their weakest link' – but they are rarely recognized. To date, however, the general issue of talented but subordinate professionals has received almost no study.

The second violinist must echo rather than lead the first violin in the melody of a piece. Second violinists must stand in the background, both musically and in the public eye. Some second violinists may be serving their time as a second (like an apprenticeship) until the opportunity arises to be a first. The classic research on role conflict (Kahn et al., 1964) predicts that role acceptance is more likely to covary with group success than with role conflict. This hypothesis directly contradicts Smith and Berg's (1987) prediction that groups need to be open to and confront their contradictions.

The conflict paradox: confrontation versus compromise

Conflict is inevitable in groups (Ury, Brett, and Goldberg, 1988). With limited time to prepare for concerts, determining how a quartet will present every minor nuance of a composition opens the door for considerable discussion, if not outright discord. Because the members are so interdependent, whether quartets deal with their conflicts through the extremes of confrontation or compromise should have a tremendous impact on their success and continued existence.

The paradox of conflict was ably summarized by Brickman (1974), who noted that, on the one hand, conflict disrupts, injures, and needs resolution while, on the other, it may be necessary for change, group solidarity, creativity, and individual freedom. Avoiding open disputes invites the side effects of repressed conflict (e.g., frustration, shorter tempers, etc.); relying on compromise, however, may only generate mediocrity.

If similar demographics (e.g., Tsui and O'Reilly, 1989), such as school background, contribute to similar musical perspectives among the group members, musical conflicts may be easily handled and the preparation of a piece for performance can proceed quickly (Bettenhausen and Murnighan, 1985). At the same time, diverse points of view – an antecedent of musical conflict – can contribute to richly textured, creative performances (Janis, 1972). Optimal group functioning would balance similarity and diversity, capitalizing efficiently on group members' similar attitudes while also taking advantage of diverse creative inputs.

Thus, models of conflict resolution (e.g., Pruitt and Rubin, 1986) suggest that groups should eschew both avoidance and compromise in favor of an active, collaborative approach that focuses, in this situation, on musical rather than interpersonal conflicts. Smith and Berg's (1987) prediction is quite different, advocating confrontation rather than resolution. Although diversity along a multitude of dimensions is important to individual and group interaction, our data focus most directly on the quartet members' musical goals and preferences and demographics during rehearsals. [. . .]

Temperament, conflict resolution strategies, decision-making styles, and basic interpersonal skills can vary tremendously within a four-person group. Effective groups achieve the best balance of diversity and similarity so that members are familiar and sympathetic with each other's points of view yet different enough to be fresh.

METHODS

Participants

We contacted quartets first by letter and then by telephone. All of the members of 20 of the 21 quartets participated. Eighty professional string-quartet musicians responded in semi-structured interviews lasting between 45 minutes and four hours. All were active members of one of the 20 professional string quartets. [. . .] The study was meant to be exhaustive; almost all of the professional string quartets in England and Scotland were contacted. [. . .]

The interviews

Each interview included a structured set of questions; additional questions depended on the respondent's interests and inclinations. [. . .]

Questions were also designed for each position within the quartet. First violinists were asked if they would ever play second violin and why there had been no switches in this quartet. Second violinists were asked if they would like to be a first violinist and how they handled the dilemmas of being second. Viola players were asked if they still played the violin and what they would do if the quartet folded. Cellists were asked whether they heard better than the other quartet members (since their instrument is not right next to their ear), what they listened for, and whether they drank more than the other quartet members (an in-group stereotype of cellists).

Measures

Six measures of success included (1) concert *fee* in pounds sterling, (2) the number of *albums* recorded and in print, (3) the number of *mentions*, in the interviews, by members of other quartets, (4) the number of *concerts* in the last year, (5) the number of newspaper and magazine reviews between January 1 and July 1, 1981, in certain specified publications, and (6) the mean ratings of the abstracted reviews. Fee and concerts were taken from the interview transcripts. A quartet's standard concert fee was the measure used, even though quartets occasionally cut their fee for benefits and other special performances.

Stability. Stability was the time in years that the current quartet members had been together, taken from the interviews at that time.

Turnover. Quartet turnover was the number of membership changes within the group in the 9 years following the interviews. During this time, none of the quartets had two changes in the same position. Thus, turnover could and did range from 0 to 4; quartets that folded (a more drastic change) were assigned a score of 5. Two of the respondents from 1981 who were well informed about professional string quartets in Britain supplied the turnover data in 1990.

Demographic characteristics. All respondents were asked their age, in years, and the schools they had attended. Gender was also noted in the interviews. [. . .]

FINDINGS AND OBSERVATIONS

[. . .] The correlations among the six measures of quartet success showed strong relationships among fee, albums, mentions, and reviews [. . .] The low correlations between concerts and the other variables reflect a natural reaction acknowledged by some members of the more successful quartets to reduce their performance schedules. The low correlations for performance ratings may be due to reviewers' prior expectations: they typically exerted more stringent criteria on the performances of well-known, successful quartets.

Age, stability, and general success were also highly correlated with each other [. . .]. Turnover, however, yielded considerably smaller correlations with these measures. All but one quartet had at least one member change since 1981. Seven quartets folded, three due to either death or retirement. The other four had been ranked among the least successful quartets in 1981. [. . .]

The leader-democracy paradox

Most quartet members used the words 'leader' and 'first violinist' almost interchangeably. All of the top groups recognized that their task demanded a leader and that that person was naturally the first violinist. Many first violinists explicitly recognized the leader-democracy paradox. Two quotes from a successful quartet's first fiddle illustrate: 'I shaped and molded this quartet. I make them play the way I want them to play.' Later, he said, 'In a quartet, everyone must be satisfied with what they are doing, because it's a life's work. You don't have majority decisions. A minority of one is enough to break up the whole thing. If he doesn't like it, he can just go. You must satisfy everybody.' Another first violinist expressed the two sides of this paradox, saying first, 'If there are any real problems in the quartet, I suppose I sort them out.' Almost immediately after, he said, 'It's very democratic.'

Other members of the top groups either acknowledged both sides of the paradox or viewed the situation as being very democratic. One second fiddle said, 'He does dominate; he's an extrovert anyway. He likes central attention. And obviously that's very good for a first fiddle.' A little later in the same interview he said, 'We're fairly equal as far as decisions.' A cellist described the paradox metaphorically, emphasizing democracy: 'I'm sometimes the father and sometimes the son. I think we all are.'

Another cellist denied any additional influence for the first fiddle: 'How is he a leader? He's one-fourth of a quartet. It's no more than that.' Yet observations of his quartet in several recording sessions showed that the first violin was clearly controlling the sessions: He stopped the group when he heard a wrong note or a wrong phrase; he was the one who had to be satisfied before they continued recording; he was totally in charge.

Only one successful group adopted a philosophy that the first violin was the group's singular leader. This was expressed most strongly (not surprisingly) by the first violinist, 'I'm a bit of a dictator. It just seems logical that I decide.' Later he added, 'I don't think a democratic quartet can work.' He also assumed that the group members (if not the entire quartet community) agreed with him: 'I think everybody recognizes that.' His cellist concurred: 'You must go with the first.' The second violin was less convinced. He recognized the first violinist's influence and its limits: 'The leader has a heavy responsibility. But we all have to turn up in the same place at the same time.' Finally, the viola player, who had decided to leave the group, was clearly unhappy with their approach: 'It's disturbing that people don't want equality.' But he also acknowledged the requirements of the task: 'Yes, firsts have to have more say in decisions.'

The first violins in the bottom group tended to emphasize democracy and avoided acknowledging the group's strong task demands, as shown in this quote from a first violinist: 'Just because I'm leader doesn't make any difference.' The other members of this quartet, however, wanted the first to take more authority and exercise stronger leadership. The second violinist said, 'It would be better if he was more forceful.' The viola player concurred: 'He should take control in rehearsals. We're trying to push him that way.'

The less successful quartets were concerned about both the ability and the personality of their first violinists. Some groups were uninspired by their leader's play, e.g., 'He isn't producing the goods.' Others thought that the first violinist did not have the personal power to lead them effectively: 'Enthusiasm, yes, but he doesn't lead.' Later the same person said, 'He's a weak leader, no flair, not extroverted enough.'

The first violinist of a less successful quartet that survived and is currently doing well responded as if the group was a democracy ('If you're going to get along . . . you have to recognize that you all have feelings about certain things') but was clearly in charge of rehearsals. Group members recognized either the fact or the need for his leadership but did not see how he dominated rehearsals. One encouraged it: 'We have to help him to do it exactly as he wants to.' Although he controlled almost all the starting and stopping in rehearsals, the second violinist said, 'I don't think he has any more influence than anyone else,' and 'We take turns leading in rehearsals.' The cellist agreed, 'He doesn't direct the rehearsals.'

Another less successful group combined democracy and leadership in the worst way. The first violin described the group as 'very democratic'. Yet he acknowledged taking control without their consent: 'In concert, I do what I want to anyway.' The others were looking for more, saying, 'I want a first who will challenge me,' or 'The first needs inspiration.' This group did not survive and, before they folded, went through the trauma of firing their first fiddle.

The paradox of the second fiddle

Everyone felt that a second violinist was the most likely member to leave a quartet. Players assumed that the seconds had less to do, and thus they were frequently burdened with business responsibilities. While seconds did not often suffer in comparisons with first violinists on technical ability, they did suffer in charismatic or inspirational comparisons (with some exceptions). First violinists were in the forefront in concert, at social gatherings, and during discussions of musical interpretation.

Most quartet players recognized and acknowledged the difficulties inherent in the second violinist's role. Among the more successful quartets, the first violinists attributed their position as first to personality and, less importantly, ability. As one first fiddle put it, 'There are born leaders and born followers. However good he is, our second fiddle would never be a first – whatever he tells you.'

More importantly, second violinists in successful quartets were either content or resigned to their position. One said, 'I'm naturally a second fiddle. I think it's a basic psychological difference.' Another acknowledged that 'six years ago you might have been able to persuade me' to play first. Many were proud of their position, e.g., 'I don't mind saying I'm a good second fiddle.'

The other members of successful quartets were often quite complimentary of their seconds: 'Our second fiddle has a beautiful way of phrasing. Beautiful style.' Only one – a member of the quartet that openly acknowledged that their first violin was their leader – attributed little value to the position, saying 'he doesn't matter that much.'

First violinists in less successful groups were generally less understanding. They recognized the personality differences between the two roles but were not often complimentary. One was almost insulting: 'You shouldn't get away with anything if you're playing second, but you can.'

In the less successful quartet that is now doing well, the second violinist was very content with his position: 'I always remember thinking I'd like to play second violin in a quartet – which must sound like a funny sort of ambition because most people think playing second isn't very ambitious, but somehow it appealed to me more than playing first.' He also took great pride in his work, saying, 'The actual depth of sound comes from the middle two parts and the cello.' This reflected a famous second violinist's metaphor for a string quartet. In a BBC interview, he said that a quartet is like a bottle of wine. The first violin, who sits out in front and gets everyone's attention, is the label. The cellist, who acts as the base for the group, is the bottle. The second violin and the viola are *the contents*.

Another second violinist in a less successful quartet expressed more role conflict than anyone else. He stated 'There are some quartets that swap the two fiddles quite regularly.' We never saw or heard of this in any quartet – only when they played trios would the first violinist sometimes sit out. He expressed ambivalent aspirations: 'Yes, I'd play first. I've never considered myself a very happy second . . . but I don't know if I'd be any good at playing first.' He later repeated, 'As an actual leader, I don't think I'd be very good.' He didn't appreciate his task, especially in the traditional pieces: 'When you get a subordinate part, you feel you could throttle the composer.' He also got the story about the bottle of wine wrong: 'the second fiddle is the wine.' Finally, he was unhappy about his lack of social recognition: 'It's a very important position but people never seem to know about it.'

Although second violinists in successful quartets tended to accept their role, they still expressed a desire to be a first violinist as frequently as seconds in unsuccessful quartets. Approximately half of the second violinists in both the more and the less successful quartets expressed an interest in being a first fiddle; they also expressed reservations about their ability to succeed as a first. In our study, having a second who wanted to be leader appears to be unrelated to their quartet's success.

Confrontation versus compromise

At first glance, most conflicts within quartets focused on how they would play a piece – their primary task. Quartet members repeatedly noted, however, that many of these conflicts were less substantive than they appeared. As one second violinist put it, 'Bad mood, trouble at home, and outside sources lead to arguments.' Rather than continuing to confront each other, quartets often decided to abandon discussion when they were mired in a troublesome dispute. They could return to it later – maybe. Another second violinist expressed it best: 'If it's important, you can always bring it up another day.' They used what Pruitt (1981) called a time-out (extended for several days) or what Ury, Brett, and Goldberg (1988) called a cooling-off period. This is a particularly effective strategy for resolving irrelevant, disruptive controversies: They simply disappear due to a lack of continuing import.

When differences of opinion about how to play a piece did not disappear, successful quartets often decided to play it one way in one concert and the other way in the next. Playing the second interpretation, however, was rarely necessary, as the players typically incorporated in their play enough of each other's concerns when they played it the first time to satisfy the members who had held conflicting opinions. They did not openly compromise, but they avoided continuous confrontation.

Another popular strategy to resolve musical disputes gave precedence to the person playing the tune. Ironically, this strategy reinforced the philosophy that first violinists were also the groups' leaders: as the primary tune-players, they then controlled most of the authority for musical decisions. Thus, groups handled conflict, as well as the leader-democracy paradox, with effective inconsistency, espousing democracy while giving the first fiddle, the player of most of the tunes, the authority to resolve their most important musical disputes.

Delay, playing a piece both ways, and giving control to the person with the lead managed conflict by preserving the integrity of group members' opposing positions. Successful quartets used five additional strategies that also preserved a conflict's contradictions: (1) Members did not concede when they felt strongly about an issue. As one first violinist put it, 'You must not compromise.' (2) They played much more than they talked during rehearsals and realized that this was functional: 'When you play, what is right and what is wrong emerges.' Not only that, playing helped avoid disfunctional conflict: 'We have a little saying in quartets – either we play or we fight.' (3) They had well-established, implicit rules concerning what could be said and what couldn't: 'There are things you just don't talk about.' They recognized that Pandora's box would open if they violated these unwritten rules: 'Obviously you know where the sore points are. If you press on them, if you invite them, it's a massacre.' (4) They also recognized that they each shared the same superordinate goal: 'No matter how many rows we have about the music, we know we're talking the same language. We know fundamentally we want the same things.' Finally, (5) they expressed the general feeling that conflict was good: 'Tension is important.' Another put it more directly: 'You can sometimes flare up and have an argument; that isn't a bad thing provided that arguments are not carried outside.' He also said, 'Whereas four years ago we would accept compromise, now we're digging in there a bit, which is good.' Only one member of a successful quartet, the second violinist in the only quartet that gave strong authority to the first violinist, disagreed: 'Arguments rarely flare up. One sits stewing most of the time.'

The less successful quartets used five strategies, although their strategies were much less effective: (1) Many simply avoided conflict. One experienced first violinist said, 'There's nothing like a quartet to build tension. Things can start as a discussion and turn into an argument that can only be saved by having a stiff whiskey or something.' (2) They realized that they should play more in rehearsals, but they ended up talking too much anyway. The viola player in one group said, 'Yes, I think we argue too much and we should play more.' This group's second fiddle went farther: 'When we disagree, we play it one way and then the other. We still fight later – I don't think it ever gets resolved. There are quite a few unresolved issues.' (3) They had different perceptions about the nature of their conflicts. One member of a married couple referred to the two of them as 'more compromising.' The viola player in the same group felt differently: 'He makes the best case anyway, because he's insistent.' (4) They acquiesced in arguments and only expressed their continuing disagreement in the worst possible place – in concert. More than one first violinist indicated that they complied with group decisions about musical interpretation, but they played the tune their own way in performance. (5) They often compromised. One second violinist was unhappy about it: 'People tend to give way. I don't know if we really satisfy anybody. I think we should have a walkout once in a while.' The viola player in the same quartet agreed: 'The atmosphere isn't terribly nice. We never really argue fiercely about a piece.' Important conflicts resurfaced (sometimes because of previous compromises), even after discussion had apparently resolved the issue.

One unsuccessful group experienced almost continuous open conflict, primarily between two of its members. One may have enjoyed it, saying, 'I think people should argue and discuss all the time.' When asked about the best thing about being in a quartet, he said, 'Being able to tell someone what you think and not be sacked.' The two less combative members recognized the extent of their group's conflict: 'We have as much trouble as we ever had. . . . Yes, we have quite a few differences to resolve.' The second combatant, the first violinist, had a strong self-focus: 'It's a stable group I think. Resolve conflict? We often don't. I've come home in an absolute fury.' He clearly identified how intense and frequent their conflicts were: 'Occasionally, we have a rehearsal without a row at all. It does happen.' They estimated that they had only one rehearsal in ten that did not include a serious argument. The first fiddle acknowledged how wearing this was, saying, 'Every rehearsal is like a lesson with three teachers who disagree with each other.' He coped by being forceful: 'If you continue screaming at every opportunity, you have a bloody good chance of persuading them.' The news of this group's breakup was not surprising.

Similarity and diversity

[. . .] The members of the more successful quartets independently and almost unanimously described their incredible enthusiasm for quartet music as an obsession. They were unanimous (with one exception) in their opinion that the quartet repertoire represented each composer's greatest work. They also saw each of their fellow group members as very similar 'in all the important ways,' i.e., with respect to the music. They frequently said that the reason they were together was to play this wonderful music and that everything else was secondary.

The members of successful groups also tended to be friends. As one viola player put it, 'We are friends. . . . To play chamber music with someone you don't like – I can't imagine that. How can I play with somebody I don't like? He can be a Paganini for all I care. I think we play more and more to each other.' Several described a string quartet as a marriage, not to one person but to three, with the exception that there is no sex (which, of course, is not always true).

The more successful quartets had a strong internal focus: Their primary audience was each other. They played to please themselves individually and collectively before they played to please an audience. Consideration of what an audience desired rarely, if ever, entered into their determination of how to interpret and present a composition.

Three of the members of one of the more successful quartets were all students of the same violin teacher. Not surprisingly, they claimed that their similar learning experiences contributed significantly to their ability to play together as a group. Three of the four members of another successful quartet revealed similar philosophies by independently (and accurately) explaining the metaphor of a quartet being like a bottle of wine.

The less successful groups were much more negative about each other, their style, and the music; they also focused more directly on audience reactions. The only less successful group in which members said that they were friends was the group that has since prospered and did not fold. Less successful groups often suggested that similarity was not beneficial: 'We all have completely different personalities. I think this helps in a way. . . . We come from different schools and we do sound different. I think it makes for an interesting sound to have four different styles. . . . I think we all like the independent style.' The European style, however, dominated the British music scene, making this statement sound like a convenient justification for unsuccessful attempts to coordinate their individual sounds.

They also reported feeling little inspiration. When the first violin of one quartet was asked about the best thing about being in a quartet, his answer was 'It's the least boring.' The viola player from the same group acknowledged that 'We'll never be one of the greats.'

Quantitative analyses

Successful versus unsuccessful quartets

[. . .] Successful quartets had been together longer than less successful groups. They reported fewer nerves before a concert and more positive feelings when a performance was going well; they spent more time playing than talking in rehearsals; they more often felt a piece could be overrehearsed than did the less successful groups; and they were more interested in duplicating the musical rather than the technical aspects of their rehearsals in concert. They described their conflict-resolution strategies as more democratic and they attended to their audiences for feedback less than the members of less successful quartets.

Demographics

Relatively few quartets included a mix of sexes or a mix of ages. Thus, these results should be interpreted cautiously. Quantitative analyses of gender, age, and school backgrounds, however, suggested that similarity was positively related to stability, success, or both. Simple analyses of variance indicated that same-sex groups, compared with mixed-sex groups, were more stable and expected more stability, didn't think a piece could be overrehearsed, played more than they talked in rehearsal, felt conflict was healthy, liked modern music and travel, lost their nervousness during a concert, and came from less musical families. They also indicated that their minds wandered less when they performed and that they would be friends with the other members of their quartet even if they didn't play together.

We arbitrarily divided quartets on the basis of a 10-year difference in the range of their members' ages. Groups whose members were similar in age were more successful, had less severe conflict and less agreement evaluating their concerts, and felt that the first violinist was more in control of the music.

Similar school backgrounds were less frequent but led to greater success, stability, and expectations that they would continue to be together, more positive feelings about quartet music, fewer surprises and more control of the music by the first violinist, and not wanting to continue playing after concerts.

DISCUSSION AND CONCLUSIONS

The more successful British string quartets provided clear evidence that they recognized and managed the inherent paradoxes they faced. All of the groups except one espoused democracy. First violinists in the successful groups, however, recognized the need for a directive leader more than first violinists in the less successful groups. They took active control of many of the group's activities and acknowledged this in their interviews. They did not advertise their leadership, however, within their group. Instead, they advocated democratic action and, it appears, did so sincerely. Thus, they preserved the leader-democracy paradox by acting as a leader while simultaneously advocating democracy.

Other members of more successful quartets attributed more influence to the first violin when they were asked directly about it; they also stressed that their group was democratic. Inconsistent perceptions were adaptive: by ignoring or distorting the objective reality of the first violinist's influence, they felt that they had an equal say. In the less successful groups, members felt that democracy ruled too much: everyone but the first violinist looked for more leadership and authoritative action.

Second violinists in successful string quartets accepted their secondary role more than their counterparts in less successful groups. At the same time, they were openly appreciated by their fellow group members, even if they were underappreciated by their audiences. Successful group members attributed their two violinists' positions to personality rather than ability. They seem to have acknowledged that (1) they were good enough to have done well and (2) their weakest link was critical to their success. Less successful quartets, who had more doubts about their own competence, gave much less credit to their second fiddle. Like leader-democracy, this paradox required constant managing, as the second violinists in the successful groups were just as likely to aspire to be first violinists as those in the less successful groups. The paradox, then, did not disappear: it was also managed but was not acknowledged within the group.

Successful groups handled conflict with a variety of strategies that allowed the conflict to continue without being disruptive. Members worked out their differences as they played the music: they absorbed the conflict rather than compromising. They viewed conflict as constructive but let emotions dissipate and unnecessary disruptions disappear by dropping things for a while. They pushed their points of view in their arguments, then dropped the issue, letting its substance either resurface or find its way into their play. Conflict management was consistent with their performance goal – to produce an integrated, unified sound. Less successful groups compromised, talked more, and evidenced all the characteristics of groups that were 'stuck,' in Smith and Berg's (1987) terms, by trying to resolve their basic conflicts.

The balance between similarity and diversity within successful groups tipped toward similarity. Being of like age, the same sex, and having the same school background were related to stability, general success, or both, along with a variety of attitudes (e.g., liking travel, expecting stability, etc.) that may have contributed to making interaction easier.

Management of the leader-democracy and conflict paradoxes also overlapped: many quartets adopted a rule that the person playing the tune would have ultimate control of that part of the composition. As this was most often the first violinist, the groups were essentially centralizing control. They acknowledged the influence this gave the first violinist but were uncomfortable about admitting it. They also added that the rule was necessary if they were going to play well and that each of them controlled the interpretation when the music gave them the lead.

The inherent presence of paradox seems obvious in string quartets, supporting Smith and Berg's (1987) predictions. Members of successful quartets recognized the paradoxes, but they consciously avoided discussing them. Direct confrontation of these unsolvable contradictions appeared infrequently among the successful groups, which does not support Smith and Berg. Instead, paradoxes were managed implicitly. Players enacted both aspects of the leader-democracy paradox, subjectively perceiving that they had input (espousing democracy and the right to voice) while objectively giving the first violinist more influence in the group. Their success at managing the paradox of the second fiddle depended on second violinists accepting their secondary status while their colleagues supported them in their difficult role. And conflict was appreciated – up to a limit. Potentially divisive confrontations were put on hold so that only the important issues would resurface. Successful quartets did not resolve the contradictions in these three paradoxes. Instead, they recognized and tolerated them, and handled them quietly, rarely raising paradoxical issues for discussion. This may be why superordinate goals (Bass, 1985) are effective: they neither specify particulars with which group members might disagree, nor do they constrain different means for implementing the group members' goals.

Generalizing to other work teams

The string quartets' task and its demands on the group differ in important ways from many work groups'. Surgical teams, R&D units, and almost any other work group have less interdependent, less immediate, or less complete interactions than string quartets. Other groups may not face a leader-democracy paradox; legitimate authority may clarify formal power differences. Nevertheless, the desire for democracy is not unusual, and its contradiction within a group is typical. Similarly, the paradox of the second fiddle, while not being played out to such an extreme, is an analog for people who feel that their talents are underappreciated. And finally, as noted, conflict and diversity are ubiquitous, inherent group phenomena. The collection of different individuals into a group ensures that its members are at least somewhat dissimilar. When diversity leads to conflict, groups often feel compelled to respond. Thus, the underlying processes exemplified by string quartets may simply be magnified versions of the same processes in other work groups.

Thus, generalizability to less intense groups may still be possible. If the paradox-management tactics of string quartets are applicable, they would include (1) Leading quietly. Espousing democracy may be the philosophical basis for participative decision making; at the same time, groups typically need leaders (Shaw, 1971). Having a member fulfil the leadership role while others simultaneously feel that they have an equal say in things effectively satisfies both sides of the leader-democracy paradox. (2) Realizing that a group's weakest member is its most critical contributor for conjunctive tasks (Steiner, 1972) may encourage appreciation of marginal contributions to the group effort. (3) When facing conflict, groups might (a) leave hot topics alone to give everyone a chance to cool off (Pruitt, 1981; Ury, Brett, and Goldberg, 1988); (b) never settle for majority rule which, at a minimum, engenders minority dissatisfaction; and (c) know each other well enough to know what can't be said, i.e., ignore unavoidable dissimilarities and let policies evolve without raising issues explicitly. Groups might also foster similarity amongst themselves. Any group of people may be different enough to contribute sufficient heterogeneity to ensure richness and life to their group. Similarity may lead to longer, more productive, and more successful group life.

[. . .] Rather than adapting to their external market, successful quartets have kept their focus internal, possibly because of the intensity of their task.

This intensity may also accentuate the consequences of paradoxes (and other intragroup events) for string quartets. As many people said in their interviews, the best part of being in a quartet, after the music, was being able to interact so closely with three other people. Many followed this, however, by saying that the worst part of being in a quartet was also having to interact so closely with three other people. Nevertheless, the interactions of string quartets, in extremis groups, provide a magnified picture of how their interactions may proceed.

This study presents a strong argument in favor of Smith and Berg's contention that paradoxes are inherent in groups and a strong argument against their hypothesis that groups should confront their paradoxes. In this population, paradoxes are understood and accepted and managed implicitly by the members of successful groups. The push by less successful quartet members for their leaders to take more authority suggests that groups realize that they must sit right on the fence, wavering between conflicting paradoxical forces. Living with, understanding, and absorbing group paradoxes, as evidenced particularly by successful second violinists, may be an essential element for group success.

REFERENCES

Bass, Bernard (1985) Leadership and Performance beyond Expectations. New York: Free Press.

Bettenhausen, Kenneth L. (1991) 'Five years of group research: What we've learned and what needs to be addressed.' Journal of Management, Vol. 17 (in press).

Bettenhausen, Kenneth L., and Murnighan, J. Keith (1985) 'The emergence of norms in competitive decision making groups.' Administrative Science Quarterly, 30: 350–372.

Brickman, Philip (1974) 'Preface.' In Philip Brickman, (ed.), Social Conflict. Lexington, MA: D.C. Heath.

Butterworth, Tory (1990) 'Detroit String Quartet.' In J. Richard Hackman (ed.), Groups That Work (And Those that Don't): 207–224. San Francisco: Jossey-Bass.

Byrne, Donn (1971) The Attraction Paradigm. New York: Academic Press.

Csikszentmihalyi, Mihaly (1990) Flow: The Psychology of Optimal Experience. New York: Harper and Row.

Hackman, J. Richard (1987) 'The design of work teams.' In J.W. Lorsch (ed.), Handbook of Organizational Behaviour: 314–342. Englewood Cliffs, NJ: Prentice-Hall.

Hughes, P., and Brecht, G. (1975) Vicious Circles and Infinity. New York: Penguin.

Janis, Irving L. (1972) Victims of Groupthink. Boston: Houghton Mifflin.

Kahn, William A. (1990) 'University athletic teams'. In J. Richard Hackman (ed.), Groups That Work (And Those That Don't): 250–264. San Francisco: Jossey-Bass.

Pruitt, Dean G. (1981) Negotiation Behavior. New York: Academic Press.

Pruitt, Dean G., and Rubin, Jeffrey A. (1986) Social Conflict: Escalation, Stalemate, and Settlement. New York: Random House.

Shaw, Marvin E. (1971) Group Dynamics: The Psychology of Small Group Behaviour. New York: McGraw-Hill.

Smith, Kenwyn, and Berg, David (1987) Paradoxes of Group Life. San Francisco: Jossey-Bass.

Steiner, Ivan D. (1972) Group Process and Productivity. New York: Academic Press.

Thompson, James D. (1967) Organizations in Action. New York: McGraw-Hill.

Tsui, Anne S., and O'Reilly, Charles A. III (1989) 'Beyond simple demographic effects: The importance of relational demography in superior-subordinate dyads.' Academy of Management Journal, 32: 402–423.

Ury, William, Brett, Jeanne and Goldberg, Stephen (1988) Getting Disputes Resolved. San Francisco: Jossey-Bass.

14

DEVELOPING COMMUNICATION SKILLS IN INTERVIEWING

Colin R. Riches

INTRODUCTION: WHAT IS COMMUNICATION?

Probably the most neglected aspect of interviewing is the need to establish good interactive relationships with interviewees. There is a danger that in interviews where the *evaluative* function is emphasized attention is focused away from *interpersonal feelings and needs* (which influence outcomes) in the interests of forming views or making judgements about others. However, one needs to consider the influence of the interactive *process* which takes place within the interview and through which information is gained. As it takes at least two to effect this interaction, the attitudes and needs of the *interviewee* are important too.

The meagre research evidence available on interviewee repsonses shows that successful interviews are associated with situations where attention has been paid to these individual needs as well as the organizational ones (Sutton and Careleton, 1962; Vroom, 1966). One could counter this by saying that the interviewer is not a psychotherapist or counsellor and in most cases has to consider organizational needs first in interviews; interviewers have to confront interviewees with difficult and sometimes stressful questions for the benefit of schools and colleges and even the people being questioned. Even so there is a paradox here in that information of the highest quality is usually obtained from people when they feel that interview encounters are fair, relevant, stimulating and supportive. The gaining of quality information in an interview depends upon establishing good relationships between the participants. This is not to suggest that interviews should always be geared to meet interviewee needs alone, but to favour the view that they should not be forgotten in the clamour to get data – some of which might be obtained elsewhere in any case – because in that very process the giving of information will be stifled.

Interviewees have their own agendas. Interviews often serve other purposes than just evaluation by the interviewer; for example interviewees may like to find out whether what they learn in the interview is to their liking, to gain guidance in personal decision-making, or even to receive counselling.

Lewis (1980) points out that many of the attributes of successful counselling – empathy, non-possessiveness, warmth and genuineness – may be applied to all interviewing. He quotes the Gilmore formula: effective counselling = understanding + acceptance + sincerity × communication skills, and states that these are the basic qualities needed in interview situations in general. 'Understanding' is the ability to grasp clearly what is being said. No interviewer can work on misunderstandings. 'Acceptance' is a recognition of individual differences and their value. The opposite of this is stereotyping when a fixed view is held about a person who in reality will have complex characteristics of thinking and feeling. 'Sincerity' is an attribute which implies that both parties will be themselves. An interviewer depends on effective communication for successful counselling. The importance of such skills is shown 'in the amount of time devoted in conventional interview training to such issues as questioning techniques, summaries, non-verbal behaviour and interviewee perceptual rankings, ratings and comparisons' (Lewis, 1980, p. 114). In fact not enough time is spent in educational circles on such training. Additional communication skills, claims Lewis, are the ability to establish agreement over the objectives of the interview from the point of view of the *interviewee* as well as the *interviewer*, and the skill of reflecting the feelings and thoughts of the person being interviewed. Some of these important characteristics are often missing when teachers or lecturers and middle and senior managers interview colleagues, potential colleagues, students and parents. Communication skills cannot be rated too highly because they are vital prerequisites to successful interviewing.

COMMUNICATION SKILLS: RECOGNIZING THE BARRIERS

Before discussing how communication skills may be developed in the interview we need to consider why people fail to communicate effectively. All of us will have been involved to some extent in unsatisfactory communications, either as senders or receivers. The message 'Send reinforcements, we are going to advance' which became, as it passed through several intermediaries, 'Send three and fourpence, we are going to a dance' has similar serious parallels in millions of other failures of communication. Communicators in education, although they are in the business of teaching and learning, are not always successful in getting their messages across or in understanding the messages of others. We do not necessarily say what we mean or mean what we say in verbal or non-verbal behaviour (VB and NVB), or understand what those communicating with us mean to say. An anonymous sender of a communication once said to a receiver 'I know you believe you understand what you think I said, but I am not sure that you realize that what you heard is not what I meant!'

In the context of the interview we may communicate *to inform*, that is to give facts, although these cannot be easily separated from feelings or the interpretation surrounding those facts. In *motivating* through an interview we will be engaged in persuading or encouraging. We will be *seeking information* through the asking of questions. Very often interview activity may involve a combination of two or more of these types of communication. Communication takes place when a message is transferred satisfactorily to another party so that it can be understood and acted upon if necessary. It involves the meeting of minds through the ebb and flow of actions, reactions, questions and answers. The interview should be a *planned* communication event as distinct from random pieces of communication. It involves *people*, the asking of *questions*, the receiving of *answers* and conforming to certain *rules*, guidelines or norms. All interviews involve a *sender*, variously the interviewer or interviewee and a *listener/receiver* (the interviewer or interviewee) who will interpret the meaning of the one who sent the message. Because two human beings are never exactly alike they will not convey exactly the same meaning. A number of variables are responsible for this.

Communication is really about the five W's: 'Who, says What, to Whom, in Which channel, with What effect' (Lasswell, 1948). A basic model of communication (Lopez, 1965) highlights these variables. Starting with the *information source* (the sender) the message, filtered by the sender, is *encoded* into words, gestures, and postures. These are *transmitted* along various *channels* by *signals* such as the voice, muscles, etc. via a *channel*, which can be blocked by *noise* (i.e. *distractors*). The receiver picks up these audio-visual stimuli, which are then *decoded* into understandable meanings or ideas. The communication *destination* is reached when there is a shared understanding between the sender of the message and the receiver. By means of *feedback* the sender will know that the receiver has interpreted the message correctly. The following example of a piece of social interaction contains all the elements of this model (except the non-verbal ones).

A disillusioned and angry teacher (information source) says to a surprised head (receiver) at a staff appraisal interview, 'I'm sick and tired of working in this school; there's no chance of promotion, the value of my work isn't recognized and the sooner I can get out of this situation the better!' (encoding: signals – verbal and non-verbal). The head responds (feedback), 'I'm sure that you don't really feel that way; in any case I do have promotion in mind for you' (decoding). A flustered school secretary (sender) interrupts the meeting (noise) to say that Mrs Ponsonsby, chair of governors, wants to see the head (receiver) and cannot wait. The head replies, 'Oh dear, excuse me for a moment while I have a word with her' (feedback/noise for the interviewee and interviewer).

This incident, besides being an example of unsatisfactory communication for the appraisee, highlights how sensitive the process of communication really can be. The characteristics of communication which we can also derive from this dialogue, and the circumstances surrounding it are that communication is *dynamic*, i.e. as it proceeds the activity involves ongoing changes in the behaviour of those taking part; it is *irreversible*, i.e. once begun it cannot be taken back completely; it is *proactive*, i.e. it involves the total personalities of the participants; and it is *interactive*, i.e. meaning is conveyed in a variety of ways between the three people.

From this brief discussion of communication variables we may infer that the communication process involves the presence of thousands of stimuli, all competing for the sender's and receiver's attention. Barriers at any stage in the communication process means that messages will be garbled or not received at all. The flow of relevant information may be impeded, knowingly or unknowingly, by any of the parties in any interaction. In the in-depth communication of an interview, where a certain amount of stress is usually present, the extent of these barriers will be intensified. Interviewees will tend to be guarded in their communication to avoid appearing in an unfavourable light and may well be on the defensive if the interviewer is in the least bit threatening. Once the defensiveness has started it tends to continue throughout the interview in relation to matters where there is no threat at all; resistances are built up and free communication is inhibited.

What are the specific barriers to communication in the interview? There are various classifications of these in the literature but basically they may be broken down into a number of *sources* of communication distortion:

(1) Language or semantic problems: words and symbols may mean different things to different people and jargon can be confusing. We each interpret messages in terms of our own backgrounds, needs and purposes and in relationship to the particular context or situation. For example, in teacher interviews with parents – and even between teachers – educational concepts such as 'vertical grouping' and 'evaluation' are not necessarily understood in the same way. Also disorganized ideas and the use of the wrong word or phrase may lead to poorly expressed messages which confuse rather than enlighten. The confused question is an illustration of this. For example, 'In your present post are you responsible for both history and geography or did you delegate this and which of these subjects do you prefer to teach?'

(2) Attitudinal problems: participants in communication can easily have different values, which may reflect deep emotions, beliefs and prejudices, and refuse to recognize and understand other people's viewpoints. This affects the way in which messages are represented and interpreted and can be a fundamental barrier to successful counselling and other types of interview.

(3) Different perceptions of the problem: for example, in an appraisal interview what the appraiser may identify as lack of initiative by the person being interviewed may be perceived by the appraisee as the former's unwillingness to delegate responsibility to him/her.

(4) Undue emphasis on status: we speak of people 'standing on their dignity' and remaining so aloof and superior that easy exchange becomes extremely difficult. If interviewees are naturally reserved, lack confidence, are inarticulate or nervous, they will tend to be silent or to give mono-

syllabic answers when they face a person who is sheltering behind status. This is the opposite to establishing *rapport*, which depends on natural regard and respect by each participant.

(5) The problem of lack of time: when this happens interviewers will not be able to ask all the questions they need to nor to listen intently.

(6) Excessive selective perception: hearing what we expect to hear, related to our experience and background and/or what we know or believe. For example, if a person is favoured the 'halo' effect operates and if the opposite is the case the 'cloven foot' perception takes over.

(7) Noise: not only in the literal sense but also in the shape of destructive or confused messages, e.g. when members of an interviewing panel make contradictory comments to candidates (as in the example above).

(8) Selective retention/rejection: a failure to hear (and see) what is being said (or shown) and forgetting what has been told. This can happen because of lack of interest and concentration – remember that the mind can operate faster than a speaker can talk. Perhaps there may be physical barriers, such as fatigue, discomfort, excessive comfort and a stuffy room or the barriers of indifference or prejudice.

(9) The withholding of information: because 'knowledge is power'. Appraisal interviewing is full of examples of this when interviewees are kept in suspense, for example about what the head is to do with the extra allowance available for distribution.

(10) Premature evaluation of what is being said: in the interview situation this means that decisions are made in the mind before all the information has been given. In interviewing there is a tendency to make up one's mind about a candidate early and then to 'switch off' for the rest of the interview.

(11) Failure to discuss the artificial walls of silence which prevent a proper exchange of views (this can be related to status issues).

(12) Lack of training: skills about information flow and the exchange of understanding are missing, e.g. listening and questioning may not have been taught or developed.

'It is not enough to minimize the blocks to communication in general, we must examine the factors that *facilitate* the type of communication we want' (Rich, 1968, p. 27, emphasis added). The last of the twelve barriers listed above points the way forward to improvement. Some factors in communication may be out of the control of the sender or receiver. Nevertheless improvement is possible within areas which *are* under the individual's control. Effective communication is learned through training and experience. We learn to communicate effectively by having the appropriate techniques or skills, having the opportunity to practise them and having our performance reviewed by experienced commentators in a non-threatening environment. We have to realize too that it takes two *willing* communicators to make full communication possible, and in interviewing this is never certain. While usually in the selection interview both parties want to pay close attention to one another, in other types of interview there may well be resistance by one of the parties.

Even when the conditions are favourable we have to realize that barriers are not broken down easily. 'Any interview is in a continually changing balance between the factors that encourage communication and those that oppose it' (ibid., p. 25) because communication is rapid and ongoing. Birdwhistell (1970, p. 16) is right in saying that 'you can never not communicate' but the difficulty is in promoting the favourable factors towards successful communication. The way effective communication may be promoted is a large and involved subject and I cannot attempt to cover all aspects so I have chosen to select two main topics which have an important influence on successful interviewing: listening, and non-verbal behaviour.

LISTENING SKILLS IN THE INTERVIEW

Listening is probably the most important type of behaviour to be engaged in by the interviewer. An old Chinese proverb says 'God gave you one mouth and two ears. Why do you not use them in that proportion?' – and that is why it comes first in our consideration of specialized interviewing skills. However, practitioners seem more concerned about what they will say in an interview than what they will hear. Too often we say 'Go ahead, I'm listening' when although a voice is heard the words are not listened to and the *mind* is not engaged. Of all the skills of interviewing this is perhaps the most difficult to learn because throughout our lives we develop improper listening habits and become expert at the art of not listening when appearing to listen; having an interested expression when all the time we may be thinking about something else! This may be less serious in normal conversation but at the interview it is crucial and we cannot afford to miss even a single comment. The competent interviewer will be trained to listen intently and to try to understand exactly what the speaker is saying, rather than thinking about the next question to ask.

Real listening is *active* in the sense that what is said is taken in, thoughtfully considered and, if relevant, shapes future exchanges. A good listener listens with understanding, looks for what is actually meant through inflexions and words that could be clues to hidden meanings and to double meanings. This may mean following up what has been said by other questions. Active listening requires getting inside the speaker's point of view. Interviewers should resist agreeing or disagreeing with what has been said by interviewees and responding immediately to demands for decisions, judgements and evaluations as this inhibits free expression. We, as interviewers, cannot both talk and listen. As the average untrained interviewer talks for nearly three-quarters of the time in an interview it is not surprising that effective listening is neglected.

However, we have to recognize from the outset that effective listening is never total; when we listen we engage in *selective perception*. Because we are all different and have different purposes in our listening we will listen to different stimuli, and although we have 'heard' the same communication we are likely to assign a different significance to it. When there are many senders and receivers the interpretation will be infinitely complex. In an interview, in a one-to-one situation, there will be only one sender (from the interviewer's point of view), but if there is a panel of interviewers there will be a number of receivers and for each of the panel the rest of the group will be senders too and the extent to which they are listened to will have an outcome on decisions made.

Listening involves the filtering of a variety of stimuli. For a two-person model of communication exchange, which is met frequently in interviewing, Hunt (1980, pp. 67–8) has identified seven basic factors which influence a receiver's power to listen:

(1) Auditory and visual: the ability to see and hear with acuity.
(2) Concentration: the ability to focus exclusively on the exchange taking place and not to be distracted easily by outside influences. These may range from physical discomforts to stressful personal problems such as finance or family crises. Our memory may also be poor or uncultivated or we may just be very bored!
(3) Situational constraints: external factors such as noise, e.g. from the telephone, screaming children or even, as I discovered when interviewing the head of a school, cackling geese! The physical environment too may be so uncomfortable or so over-relaxed to the point of drowsiness that concentration is destroyed.
(4) The history of the communication relationship which has developed between the sender and the receiver.
(5) The perceived purpose of the communication exchange: if this is clear then the receiver will have some basis on which to decide whether to listen or not and this will influence the outcome of the interview.
(6) Perceived degree of difficulty of the message: if we cannot understand as interviewers (or interviewees) our attention will slacken, to say the least.
(7) Perceived utility of the message: if the message has some relevance to us and the outcome of the exchange is important then we will be well motivated to receive the message.

These factors are summarized in Figure 14.1.

The *interviewee* may be a source of distraction to the listening of the interviewer in a variety of ways. The interviewee, as the sender of the message, may lack verbal clarity or even have a poor command of the common language. There may be a mismatch between bodily and verbal signals. Vocal problems, e.g. a difficult accent or a speech impediment, and bodily mannerisms may discourage listening, and there may also be evidence of shyness, anxiety, tension, hostility or anger. One of the skills of being a good listener is being able to first *recognize* and then to overcome these sources of interference in the interviewee.

As interviewers we need to examine the techniques for positive and better listening. Probably it is useful to think of listening as operating at various levels. At the superficial level it is hearing what a person says in the *literal* sense. Many interviewers fail to reach even this level of competence. Next time you listen to what someone is telling you ask yourself what your level of recall

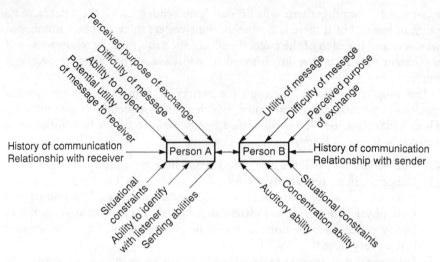

Figure 14.1 Model of a two-person speaker–listener relationship (Weaver, 1972, p. 68)

in fact is: you may get a surprise. Incidentally this is why it is so necessary in an interview to *record* what the interviewee is saying, as the research evidence so convincingly confirms. At this level the aim must be to listen to every word that is spoken and try to keep out every possible distraction. One problem related to listening is that we are sometimes thinking so much about what question to ask next – a sure sign of lack of preparation – that we only give a half response, i.e. we listen to what is said initially and ignore the rest. Research evidence shows that opening statements by respondents tend to be banal or non-committal and the real meat comes in the second half of the response. This does not mean that we should listen to the second half only; we should listen all the time! Of course there is a danger that we miss something when writing points down, but this does not mean that we should abandon recording but rather we should have pauses in the interview to do so, maybe reviewing with the interviewee what was said. This reviewing, reflecting back, or paraphrasing, puts what has been said into different words to see if what has been said is understood correctly.

As participant listeners at interviews we need to do more than literal listening, so to speak, and to engage in *in-depth* listening. We must go beyond the words to discern their real meaning. There is so much meaning about other people's attitudes to be read between the lines; in voice tone and projection, in word selection, e.g. emotionally laden words, and sentence structure and in the general mental set which word pictures convey. We can listen for areas of sensitivity revealed through responses; and for the significance of things which are not said. In a nutshell, we need to know what the other person feels and why they feel so. Total listening then involves nearly all the senses and a great deal of mental activity. We have to be aware also of the way in which our own biases and prejudices will influence our filtering of the responses.

Rae (1988) has provided a useful summary of guidance to listeners in interviews:

> Prepare for the interview and prepare to listen.
> Be interested in what is being said.
> Ignore one's own opposition to views being expressed.
> Do not try to forecast what the other is going to say.
> Ensure that all the physical factors have been considered – light, heat, ventilation, etc.
> Be aware of one's own value judgements and take these into account.
> Develop a receptive frame of mind.
> Try to put aside one's own problems or otherwise have somebody else to take the interview.
> Do not make assumptions early in the interview.
> Listen to what is being said and do not be distracted by delivery or mannerisms.
> Try not to form immediate impressions – but if you do, recognize them for what they are and take them into account.
> Listen for key issues.
> Take notes to avoid mind wander.
> Maintain eye contact.
> Do not interrupt.
>
> (Rae, 1988, pp. 59–60)

The importance of effective listening to the successful gathering of information and thus as a major step to effective interviewing, cannot be over-emphasized. We will be aided in our listening if we can appreciate fully the non-verbal communication signals that are sent out by people, either deliberately or involuntarily.

NON-VERBAL BEHAVIOUR (NVB) IN THE INTERVIEW

'Probably more feelings and intentions are communicated non-verbally than through all the verbal methods combined' (Tortoriello, Blatt and DeWine, 1978, p. 22), thus bearing out the old adage that 'actions speak louder than words'. However, we need to be aware of the problems of interpretation in seeking to understand the meaning of specific pieces of NVB. In the first place NVB is, to some extent, culturally conditioned. For example, as we move away from England the simple gesture of tapping the forefinger on the side of the nose indicates secrecy or conspiracy, 'Don't say anything about it', but as we move across Europe and into Italy the dominating meaning changes to become a helpful warning to 'Be careful, you are in danger, they are crafty' (Morris, 1977, p. 53). Secondly we can never be absolutely sure that we attach the same meaning to other people's bodily cues as they do themselves. We can test this by observing a friend's NVB and as we do so note down the gesture and what we think the other person is actually feeling at the time, e.g. 'Your arms were folded; I think you were being defiant'. We certainly cannot write a completely accurate dictionary of the meaning of each feature of bodily language. Another general point is that not all NVB is intentional; there is a fair amount of our NVB which is involuntary and 'leaks' through to the observer in spite of ourselves. For example, people usually lower their eyes away from direct contact with other people when they are lying or being deceitful. Most leaks happen through the legs and feet, fingers and hands and eyes – 'the window of the soul'. In interviewing we need to be perceptive and sensitive in recognizing such important signs. We are indeed interested here in understanding not only the NVB of interviewees but also our own NVB as interviewers. Although, for the purpose of discussion and analysis we draw a distinction between VB and NVB, in fact it is difficult to distinguish our words from our non-verbal cues. 'To leave the impression that you respond to someone's voice, appearance, facial expression, or the distance he stands from you, independently of one another, is to leave you with a distorted impression of the process' (Knapp, 1972, p. 1). The whole of this behaviour may be subsumed under the term 'body language'.

My list – by no means comprehensive – is as follows:

Elements of body language

Physical appearance

Gender, age, height, colour, weight, shape, build, muscularity, hairiness, grooming (e.g. neat, unkempt, tidy, clean, dirty), hair (style and length), smell/scent/perspiring, clothing and its many characteristics, other artefacts with which people decorate their bodies, e.g. glasses, make-up, jewellery.

Physical proximity

Distance, i.e. near or far, able to touch, depending on things like gender, status, activity and circumstance.

Physical posture (proxemics)

Slouched/straight, rigid/flexible, open/closed, turned towards/away, territorial command, e.g. in relation to space in a room.

Movements/gestures (kinesics)

Whole body, e.g. walking, running, swimming, relaxed/tense; part body, i.e. expression through arms, hands, legs, feet, toes, head, face, nose, cheeks, jaw, chin, mouth, tongue, eyebrows, eyes.

Necessary functions

Breathing, swallowing, blinking.

Paralanguage

Loudness, sharpness, softness, resonance, rhythm, rate of speech, intonation, accent, of the voice, vocalizations, such as those associated with the NVB of crying and sighing, sounds like 'ugh-ugh', 'um', 'ah', even silence!

Other activities

Looking, smiling, blushing, laughing, crying, fiddling, hand-shaking, touching, kissing, nail-biting, smoking, scratching, tapping, picking, stroking.

Bodily language – which is NVB in action for a purpose – involves the transmission of messages which are not coded in words, or organized in a language system. NVB plays the important role in interviews of reinforcing, contradicting or neutralizing the spoken word. The functions of NVB may be broken down into the following categories:

- *repeating*: the non-verbal cue (gesturing towards a person) repeats what the person has said ('This is Ms Jones, the Deputy');
- *contradicting*: if an interviewer fidgets and looks at her watch these gestures will contradict the response to the interviewee who has just had his tenth question answered and says 'I hope I have not asked too many questions', and receives the reply, 'Oh no, please go on';
- *substituting*: often a clear non-verbal message is a complete substitute for the use of words;
- *complementing*: when both the NVB and VB are the same the one complements the other;
- *relating and regulating*: non-verbal cues can signal to a person, e.g. to stop talking;
- *accenting*: this is non-verbal emphasis on a word or group of words which is equivalent to written underlining, italics, etc.

Each of these functions can help or hinder the communication flow between people. All may be in operation in the interview. There is a good deal of evidence that when verbal cues and non-verbal cues are contradictory the non-verbal ones win (e.g. McMahan, 1976; Keenan, 1976). The latter simulated two selection interviews with the verbal content the same but in one the non-verbal cues were approving and in the other they were disapproving. The candidates were found to be more comfortable and to create a better impression in the former situation than in the latter. Whenever there is an incongruity between words and actions people tend to believe the actions. That is why we especially need to articulate and be made conscious of NVB in interviewing. I will deal in turn with the major categories of NVB which have some bearing on activity in the interview.

Kinesics

As we have seen these refer to body behaviour and include body movements, gestures and postures. Bodily movements certainly indicate a number of conditions (Knapp, 1972):

(1) Attitudes – the extent of like or dislike which can be measured by general body orientation, such as when shoulders or legs are turned away to indicate disapproval.

(2) Status – people perceiving themselves to have higher status tend to face others directly, to put their hands on their hips, to have greater body relaxation and to keep the head erect (Mehrabian, 1971).

(3) Affective states or moods – when people display a large amount of body movement they may well be in a state of emotional arousal and the movements will vary according to the mood, e.g. head/face movements give information about anger and happiness and body movements about the intensity of the emotion, such as when a depressed person tends to have relatively few movements of the head and hands and many movements of the legs.

(4) Approval seeking – this is demonstrated by a high degree of gesturing.

(5) Inclusiveness – closed or open positions of the body.

(6) Interaction markers – specific body movements are associated with specific oral behaviours like a downward movement of head, eyelids and hands at the end of making a statement and an upward movement at the end of asking questions. Each communication exchange is unique.

Postures represent important cues in NVB because they demonstrate the attitude that one person has towards another. Dislike or uneasiness is usually indicated by rigid posture while, conversely, ease in the company of another is shown by leaning towards the subject of our liking.

Facial expressions

These have great communicative power; Mehrabian (1981) has suggested that facial cues have more force of meaning than either verbal or other non-verbal cues (7 per cent, 38 per cent and 55 per cent, respectively). This means that we rely a great deal on facial cues to indicate the meaning of a particular piece of communication and similarly others rely on those cues from us. But the messages they convey are complex, as researchers have discovered. Research by Ekman, Friesen and Ellsworth (1971) has indicated the areas of the face which best express particular emotions (although the evidence shows that at given moments our faces may show multiple emotions): happiness is shown in areas of the lower face and eyes, sadness in the eyes, surprise in the eyes and lower face, anger in the lower face and brows and forehead, disgust in the lower face, and fear in the eyes. Various studies of movements of the eyes have produced consistent evidence that we *avoid* eye contact with others when we want to avoid communicating, when physically close, when we dislike them, are deceiving them and when we anticipate a long and boring statement from them. We *seek* eye contact when we wish to indicate that channels for communication are open, when we are physically distant from the other person, when we like that person and when we are extremely hostile towards them. As interviewers it is important that we appreciate the non-verbal clues of facial expression as they are important communicators; they can encourage or discourage feedback, determine the intimacy of an encounter or even control the communication channel.

The use of *personal space* to communicate with one another is a fascinating subject. Human beings tend to have 'territories' like animals, which include the space surrounding our bodies, artefacts (purses, briefcase, books) which we carry around, objects in the *environment*, such as chairs, desks and tables, which we are using and larger territories like our offices and homes. People try to protect their territories and become disturbed when they are invaded. How close we are to one another, where we sit in a room and how we generally position ourselves in relation to others affects our own and our listener's level of conversational comfort. Personal space is that invisible area of physical/ psychological space which separates us from others. Burgoon (1976) carried out interviews between subjects of the experiment and interviewers to see the extent to which the interviewees' perceptions of the interviewers would change, depending on the amount of distance between them. This enquiry provided forceful evidence that if interviewers are to give negative feedback then they should keep their distance so as to avoid invading the interviewing space of interviewees, because this could cause defensive and hostile reactions. It is important for all communicators to pay attention to the use of space and to maintain the correct personal and social distance to give the ideal climate for social interaction to take place. Hall (1966) has identified four types of distances: the *intimate* (0–18 inches), reserved for close personal friends and intimates, *personal distance* (1½–4 feet), the normal distance for interpersonal conversations, *social distance* (4–12 feet), the norm for business transactions, and *public distance* (12–15 feet), i.e. outside the personal environment area. When someone invades the space of another she/he may be perceived as less credible.

There is evidence that an attractive *environment* produces responses indicating pleasure, comfort, importance, enjoyment, and a desire to continue the activity, and seems to determine the quality of the interaction which takes place there. The placing of furniture affects a variety of interpersonal variables. For example, interaction tends to be greater with individuals seated directly across a table from one another than with an individual seated at the end of the table from the rest of the group. Mehrabian (1981) has suggested that executives who interpose a desk between themselves and others may be perceived as less warm and personal than those who speak directly to each other with no barrier in between.

Perhaps it seems odd to think of *silence* and *time* as NVB characteristics, but insofar as they are not VB and do have an influence on human interactions they are relevant – and important. I have placed silence, somewhat misleadingly, in the category of paralanguage, although it goes there because it represents the spaces in between the voices surrounding the spoken word. Silence has important communicative functions: it provides a link between messages or to indicate that an interactive relationship has ended; it can heal or wound an emotional relationship; it can create tension and unease (that is, for example, interviewers tend to fill up embarrassing silences with ill-thought-out questions); and it can also be judgemental in the sense that it may indicate assent or dissent, favour or disfavour. Time tells us a lot about status; if you are allotted a short time for an interview this usually says something about the importance the interviewer attaches to it and to you.

CONCLUSION

I have dealt at some length with certain aspects of NVB because the interviewer should develop a sensitivity to non-verbal messages. By looking at posture, facial expressions, gestures, paralanguage and the use of environmental space, interviewers stand a much better chance of communicating effectively with others and reading the messages of those they are interviewing correctly. Interviewers may be oblivious to the non-verbal cues they are sending to the interviewee; the latter may be very much aware of them although they may not be able to put the feeling which they convey into their own words. Almost certainly if the interviewers convey the impression that they are bored or disapproving by their NVB this will be picked up and acted upon even though the verbal signals may be different.

Perhaps the most important NVB for the interviewer is establishing eye contact with the interviewee, who is more likely to communicate freely when this is done. However, this can be overdone when our looking is so intense that we stare and make the other person feel uncomfortable which, in turn, breaks the flow of communication. The *via media* is to look directly at the interviewee and to have a thoughtful and pleasant facial expression so as to convey real interest.

In applying our knowledge of body movements we learn that for an interviewer to sit erect throughout an interview communicates formality and makes the person he or she is trying to communicate with feel uncomfortable and inhibited. More informality without being sloppy encourages freer communication. We can also go too far in the other direction when we lean so far forward that we invade the candidate's personal space so much that he or she feels the encounter is threatening. Scowling and frowning, although they may only be signs of our own concentration, can give the impression that we are expressing disapproval. So again we should be very aware and sensitive to the various impressions our NVB may be creating. The interviewee will be sending out non-verbal cues too and these should be interpreted *alongside* the spoken word to give *information* about that person.

Exhibiting bodily language which encourages the interviewee to speak with confidence, or at least without feeling threatened, is an important part of the equipment to be used by the interviewer to establish *rapport*. Rapport describes a situation in which there is mutual recognition and reciprocation of the emotional state between people when they interact with one another. If you have any mannerisms which you know are disconcerting then seek to eliminate them if you wish to gain rapport with the interviewee. While awareness of the

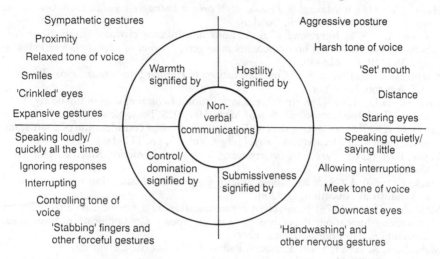

Figure 14.2 Zones of non-verbal behaviour for interviewers. Source: MacKay (1980)

individual elements of NVB which enhance or inhibit rapport is essential these may also be symptomatic of your attitude of mind, which lacks interest in the interview or is a demonstration of fatigue. Then you should do something about the underlying *causes*, of which the most unacceptable and off-putting mannerisms are but an expression. Therefore do not interview when you become fatigued and try to rekindle your interest in the interviewing process. The best way to achieve the latter is to take an interest in what happens in interviews – which you are doing now – and to practise the skills of interviewing which contribute to interest and success.

In Figure 14.2 MacKay (1980) has produced a chart setting out a model of zones of various types of NVB. Ideally one should work to be identified with the top left-hand quadrant; any behaviours which are in any of the other three quadrants are undesirable in successful interviewing, except in some very isolated examples of disciplinary interviews, but the strategy is always of doubtful value in ascertaining the facts of a case. Every interviewer's aim should be to cultivate rapport with the interviewee by non-verbal gestures, through attentive, perceptive and meaningful listening, as well as by what we ask and say.

REFERENCES

Birdwhistell, R. (1970) *Kinesics and Context*, University of Pennsylvania Press, Philadelphia.

Burgoon, J. (1976) Further explication and an initial test of the theory of violation of personal space expectations. Paper presented at the Speech Communication Association Convention, San Francisco, December.

Ekman, P., Friesen, W. and Ellsworth, P. (1971) *The Face and Emotion*, Pergamon, New York.

Hall, E.T. (1966) *The Hidden Dimension*, Doubleday, New York.

Hunt, J.W. (1980) *Managing People at Work: a manager's guide to behaviour in organizations*, McGraw Hill, London.

Keenan, A. (1976) Interviewers' evaluations of applicant characteristics: differences between personnel and non-personnel managers, *Journal of Occupational Psychology*, Vol. 49, pp. 223–30.

Knapp, M. (1972) *Nonverbal Communications in Human Interactions*, Holt, Rinehart and Winston, New York.

Lasswell, H.D. (1948) The structure and function of communication in society, in L. Bryson (Ed.) *The Communication of Ideas*, Harper & Bros, New York.

Lewis, C. (1980) Investigating the employment interview: a consideration of counselling skills, *Journal of Occupational Psychology*, Vol. 53, pp. 111–16.

Lopez, F.M. (1965) *Personnel Interviewing, Theory and Practice*, McGraw Hill, New York.

Mackay (1980) *A Guide to Asking Questions*, Business Association for Commercial and Industrial Education, London.

McMahan, E.M. (1976) Non-verbal communication as a function of attribution in impression formation. Paper presented at the Speech Communication Association Convention, San Francisco, December.

Mehrabian, A. (1981) *Silent Messages,* Belmont, Wadsworth, California.

Morris, D. (1977) *Manwatching*, Cape, London.

Rae, L. (1988) *The Skills of Interviewing: a Guide for Managers and Trainers*, Gower, London.

Rich, E.J. (1968) *Interviewing Children and Adolescents*, Macmillan, London.

Sutton, D.E. and Careleton, F.O. (1966) Students rate the college recruiters, *Journal of College Placement*, October.

Tortoriello, T.R., Blatt, S.J. and DeWine, S. (1978) *Communications in the Organization, An Applied Approach*, McGraw Hill, New York.

Vroom, V.H. (1966) Organizational choice: a study of pre-post decision processes, *Organizational Behaviour and Human Performance*, Vol. 1, pp. 212–15.

Weaver, C.H. (1972) *Human Listening, Process and Behaviour*, Bobbs-Merrill Co. Inc., New York.

15

STRATEGIES FOR MANAGEMENT DEVELOPMENT:
Towards Coherence?

Howard Green

This material has been abridged

INTRODUCTION

[At the outset it might be helpful to define our understanding of 'management' and I therefore refer the reader to two existing definitions of the word.] Both are task-focused and point to the central role of the people, the human resources, in an institution to achieve the tasks. So 'management' is 'the process of securing decisions about what activities the organisation (or unit of an organisation) will undertake, and mobilising the human and material resources to undertake them' (Hughes, 1985); or it is, 'achieving goals by, with and through people and managers and all those responsible for the work of other adults' (School Management Task Force, 1990). [. . .] In this context 'management development' can be defined as, 'the process whereby the management function of an organisation is performed with increasing effectiveness'.

There is clearly an imperative to improve strategies for management development at all levels in the education service. For example, Her Majesty's Inspectors (HMI, 1987) reporting on school and college inspections during the period 1982/86 wrote that, 'one of the most significant determinants of a good school was high-quality leadership and good management'. This was followed by a statement from the Senior Chief Inspector reporting on the state of England's education service and quoted in the *Times Educational Supplement* in 1990. He said, '. . . the management of schools leaves much to be desired. In only about a third of those inspected was senior management judged to be particularly effective'. [. . .] Therefore, the need for more coherent and effective strategies for school management development has never been more urgent. [. . .]

STRATEGIC PLANNING FOR MANAGEMENT DEVELOPMENT

The effective delivery of management development must begin with strategic planning at several levels in the education service.

Schools There is now much good practice available in terms of the effective planning and delivery of staff development, and within this broader context for management development, at school level. Such good practice must now become normal practice in all schools. The planning should have three main strands. The first is the drawing up of an institutional development plan (IDP) which is informed by an evaluation of the school. [. . .] The IDP, a relatively brief and readable document, will then be available as a basis for all other aspects of school planning such as curriculum development, staffing, budgeting and making decisions about the priorities for staff development.

The second is the establishment of a staff development committee which is broadly representative of all groups on the staff and has appropriate delegated authority to plan and deliver a school's programme of staff in-service education and training within the agreed framework of priorities set out in the IDP.

The third is a scheme of staff appraisal which is adequately resourced and provides information about individual development needs. Suitably anonymized, the outcomes of staff appraisal should be used as an additional source of background information by the staff development committee as they plan the use of the resources allocated to them.

Local network Local networks can help to prevent school-focused staff development from becoming too inward-looking by providing opportunities to work with colleagues from other schools in the area. [. . .]

Regional and national Effective planning for management development also requires a broader perspective at regional and national levels to help avoid too much 're-invention of wheels' and also to address strategic issues of more than local importance like the accreditation of programmes of management development and the preparation for headship. [. . .]

Other agencies Several other agencies will continue to make a significant contribution to management development at all levels.
(1) *Industry*: One of the most encouraging features of school management development over the past few years has been the increased involvement of personnel from industry working on the basis of a partnership with education. [. . .] A less regular feature of such co-operative arrangements is the movement of personnel *from* industry *into* schools or other aspects of the education service. [. . .]
(2) *Professional associations*: The teacher associations have also shown an increasing commitment to the professional development of their members and many now offer a wide range of courses and other forms of in-service education and training. [. . .]
(3) *Higher education and independent providers*: Higher education and a growing number of independent providers will continue to contribute to

school management development at all levels. In the future their success or failure in this role will depend much more on the pressures of the market-place. Schools, consortia and other networks of institutions or individuals will be shopping around for the best and most appropriate opportunities for management development at prices which they can afford. [. . .]

SUCCESSION PLANNING AND CAREER DEVELOPMENT

An overall strategy for management development should embrace the main-tenance and development of institutional management structures as well as the personal development of individual managers. From time to time key people will leave an institution for a variety of reasons and, although many individual resignations are unpredictable, local and regional patterns in vacancies are discernible. [. . .] Succession planning begins with this type of analysis and uses the results to consider the action required to increase the chances of filling vacancies with a minimum loss of overall management performance in an organization.

Large organizations are more able to implement in-house systems of succes-sion planning and can fill many vacancies through internal promotion. Schools on the other hand are representative of small and medium-sized organizations which can do much less to predict succession problems and must usually resort to external appointments to fill their vacancies. This means that they are more vulnerable to market forces over which they have little control. There is a danger that the move towards the local management of schools will compound the problem of fragmentation in the education service and put further limits on the possibility of succession planning at local level.

However, the education service as a whole has usually 'grown' its own managers. It is therefore quite possible to envisage an approach to succession planning which has a local perspective provided that overall data about teach-er supply and conditions is available at national level. Such data could then be supplemented by regional and local knowledge of staffing structures in schools, age structures, wastage rates and recruitment patterns which are potentially available to local education authorities (LEAs). Armed with this knowledge, LEAs and consortia of schools would then be in a position to adopt a more positive approach to succession planning. For example, they could take steps to increase the number of qualified applicants for particular types of vacancy in the locality by joint advertising, training and development programmes. [. . .] Both the development and the selection of staff could be informed, particularly at senior level, by the use of regional educational assess-ment centres which would provide a profile of managerial potential (*see* 'As-sessment for management development').

Individual career development is clearly an important concomitant of suc-cession planning. In-school staff development and the wider provision of in-service education and training must find the right balance between the require-ments of the present job, personal professional growth and preparation for promotion. Certainly careers advice and appropriate support in the planning of a personal development programme should be available to all teachers as should opportunities to gain experience of management responsibilities at a higher level.

Ideally such advice and support will be seen as essential features of staff appraisal schemes and staff development committees. Special attention is needed for those whose career patterns have been interrupted.

ASSESSMENT FOR MANAGEMENT DEVELOPMENT

Without some assessment of need, the time and money spent on the management development of an individual can be wasted or, at least, be of only limited value. Staff appraisal and self-analysis questionnaires may help to inform development needs but both are relatively limited and blunt instruments. There would be greater coherence at all levels of management development if we could approach the assessment of need, and then the provision of development, using a micro-surgeon's knife rather than the traditional blunderbuss, firing off development opportunities in the hope that a few will strike individual targets.

There is also much to be gained by raising the profile of personal and generic management competencies as a vital component of development programmes alongside the more traditional task-related and job-specific aspects of middle and senior management roles in schools.

For example, there are plenty of courses available to learn about curriculum planning, timetabling, budgeting and marketing the school but far fewer opportunities which focus on the development of generic competencies like judgement, decisiveness, leadership and written communication.

The Educational Assessment Centre (EAC) project, started in September 1990 and based in Oxford, worked with 28 clients from the maintained and independent school sectors in England, Wales and Scotland (including 22 LEAs). It is an important and ambitious attempt to meet both the requirements outlined above by providing senior staff with a detailed diagnostic profile for further professional development based on 12 generic management competencies. The initial aim of the EAC project is to improve the management competencies of future headteachers so that they will be effective managers as well as successful educators. [. . .] It should be emphasized that the project is applicable to management development in all aspects and phases of the education service.

Assessment centres have been used in both the public and private sectors of employment for over 50 years to inform the process of developing and selecting senior managers. Their use has been restricted to senior levels primarily because assessment centres that produce valid and reliable data are relatively expensive to establish and operate.

Establishing an assessment centre in a particular occupational setting is a complex and technical process which draws on the expertise of psychologists

Table 15.1   Education Assessment Centre: the twelve competencies

1. Problem analysis	Ability to seek out relevant data and analyse information to determine the important elements of a problem situation; searching for information with a purpose.
2. Judgement	Ability to reach logical conclusions and make high quality decisions based on available information; skill in identifying educational needs and setting priorities; ability to evaluate critically written communications.
3. Organizational ability	Ability to plan, schedule, and control the work of others; skill in using resources in an optimal fashion; ability to deal with a volume of paperwork and heavy demands on one's time.
4. Decisiveness	Ability to recognize when a decision is required (disregarding the quality of the decision) and to act quickly.
5. Leadership	Ability to get others involved in solving problems; ability to recognize when a group requires direction, to interact with a group effectively and to guide them to the accomplishment of the task.
6. Sensitivity	Ability to perceive the needs, concerns and personal problems of others; skill in resolving conflicts; tact in dealing with persons from different backgrounds; ability to deal effectively with people concerning emotional issues: knowing what information to communicate and to whom.
7. Stress tolerance	Ability to perform under pressure and during opposition; ability to think on one's feet.
8. Oral communication	Ability to make clear oral presentation of facts or ideas.
9. Written communication	Ability to express ideas clearly in writing; to write appropriately for different audiences – students, teachers, parents, *et al.*
10. Range of interest	Ability to discuss a variety of subjects – educational, political, current events, economic, etc; desire to actively participate in events.
11. Personal motivation	Need to achieve in all activities attempted; evidence that work is important to personal satisfaction; ability to be self evaluating.
12. Educational values	Possession of a well-reasoned educational philosophy; receptiveness to new ideas and change.

and professionals. The EAC model being adapted for use in the UK has been in operation for about 15 years in North America and Australia. It has been the subject of two large scale independent research studies and its high quality has now been proven.

There are four key stages in the establishment of any assessment centre and they have been followed in setting up the EAC project:

(1) Identifying the management competencies required for success

In the case of the EAC this would refer to success as a head. The list of 12 competencies is shown in Table 15.1. It will be reviewed and modified in the light of the experience gained from the pilot phase of the EAC project.

(2) Designing job-related exercises to test the competencies

Research suggests that the performance of participants on job-related exercises does provide good evidence of their likely behaviour on the actual job.

Table 15.2 shows the relationship between the 12 competencies and the job-related exercises that have been developed. At the heart of a high-quality assessment centre is the successful design of the job-related exercises to simulate a particular job and to tease out the management competencies. It can be seen from Table 15.2 that, in most cases, each competency is assessed in more than one exercise which provides several opportunities for a participant to demonstrate the competency.

(3) Training assessors to assess the performance of participants on the job-related exercises

Reflection over many years on the use of assessment centres suggests that they are most effective when the assessors are doing, or have done, the job for which the centre has been designed to assess potential. Therefore the assessors at the EAC are in most cases heads, those with headship experience or senior education officers/advisors who regularly work with senior teams in schools. The assessors undertake a rigorous and demanding training course and there is a small failure rate. Not all those in senior positions within the education service have the particular skills required to be an effective assessor.

(4) Producing a personal report about each EAC participant

It is important to stress that an EAC is a *process* not a place. However the participants and assessors will obviously assemble at a particular place, usually a hotel or management centre, to go through the process. It takes about one and a half days for the participants to complete the exercises observed by the

Table 15.2   Educational Assessment Centre: the relationship between the twelve competencies and the job-related exercises

Management competencies	Leaderless group discussions		Fact-finding	In-trays		Interview
	I	II		I	II	
1. Problem analysis	X	X	X	X	X	
2. Judgement	X	X	X	X	X	
3. Organizational ability			X	X	X	
4. Decisiveness			X	X	X	
5. Leadership	X	X				
6. Sensitivity	X	X		X	X	X
7. Stress tolerance			X			X
8. Oral communication	X	X	X			X
9. Written communication				X	X	
10. Range of interest						X
11. Personal motivation						X
12. Educational values	X	X		X	X	X

assessors. At this point the participants depart and the assessors then spend a further two to three days in 'consensus'. They go through every aspect of each participant's performance on the exercises in fine detail and agree the performance ratings. Each participant will have been directly observed by five of the assessor team during the completion of the exercises so that there is a broadly based, and therefore more objective, overview of performance. At the end of consensus each assessor will write a final report on one participant but will draw on the views of the whole assessor team. The report is structured according to the 12 management competencies with a section of strengths followed by a section of competencies which need improvement and finally some suggestions for further professional development. Within 15 working days of the end of an EAC each participant returns for a feedback interview with the director when they receive their personal copy of the report.

Early experience of the first EACs in the UK is confirming the fact that they have enormous potential to inform professional development by providing a diagnostic profile of strengths and weaknesses across 12 vital management competencies.

The initial focus for further development is always on the things that a participant can do 'on the job' supplemented by the opportunity to spend some time alongside another senior colleague in a nearby school. This can provide the opportunity to observe someone with a different style working in a less familiar context. For a deputy head wanting to prepare for headship, this might mean working more regularly with their own head (acting as a 'coach') and spending time alongside another experienced head (acting as a 'mentor'). To help with this developmental support, the EAC project is providing training for experienced heads in the process-skills of coaching and mentoring. [. . .]

A portfolio of further professional development opportunities [is also being prepared]. This will include a range of high quality and cost-effective opportunities currently available from providers of management development in both the private and public sectors. They have been analysed according to the 12 competencies so that if, for example, a participant is relatively weak in problem analysis, judgement, organizational ability and leadership then he can be directed to appropriate management development which focuses on that particular cluster of competencies. In so doing, we believe that the EAC process is getting us closer to the 'micro-surgeon's knife' of professional development referred to earlier in the section.

It is expected that EAC participants will also draw on other forms of support for their further development like the LEA, higher education, industrial placements and professional associations. Inevitably the EAC process will lead some participants away from headship as the next career move and towards alternatives which would better utilize their particular range of strengths. This outcome of the EAC process is just as important as the further development of those who will move on to headship in improving the quality of the next generation of heads. Being promoted to one's 'level of incompetence' is potentially disastrous for both the individual and the institution, particularly if that level is headship.

Although the main thrust of the EAC project is towards the *development* of future heads, the process can also be adapted to help inform the selection procedure for headship. A quite separate selection package has been trialled and will be made available to school governing bodies to use as part of the appointment procedure. It is hoped that this source of more objective data will be used widely by governing bodies in the future to guide their decisions when appointing a new head. The aim is certainly not to produce a clone of some ideal 'management-man' or 'woman' as heads of the future, but to acknowledge that heads do need a reasonably strong profile of management competencies (as well as other qualities) if they are to be really effective and run good schools.

Both the developmental and selection uses of the EAC process will enhance succession planning and career development at senior levels.

They should also help to achieve a much needed cultural shift to the way in which the teaching profession (and we are not alone in this) approaches the assessment of performance. We are too often stuck in the rut of seeing each other through rose-coloured glasses. For example, applicants for promotion are regarded as suspect if their references are not full of superlatives and yet, realizing that nobody can be that perfect, appointment panels are then reduced to frantically reading between the lines of a reference to search for the chinks in the shining armour or to making furtive phone-calls to current employers for an 'off the record' honest assessment.

Staff appraisal more often than not ends up with a general pat on the back with inadequate evidence about performance. Few line-managers get proper training in the skills of appraisal interviewing or how to give positive criticism to a colleague. Therefore who can blame them if they back off the more demanding aspects of an appraisal interview when it gets to the discussion about areas of relative weakness followed by the planning of a programme of further development?

The EAC process provides the detailed evidence on which judgements about an important aspect of performance (management competency) may be based. It is also much more open and honest than traditional methods for the assessment of performance. EAC participants are therefore at the cutting edge of an important cultural shift. Bearing this reality in mind, it is reassuring for the participants that the EAC process takes place on 'neutral territory' well away from their own school or employing authority.

Great care is taken to ensure that the assessors at a particular EAC are not known personally or professionally to any of the participants and that the security of the final report is carefully safeguarded.

The EAC assessors are also at the cutting edge of new attitudes to the assessment of performance. Remember that they are senior staff, usually heads, who agree to undertake assessor training, which they could fail, and also to put themselves in a learning situation alongside a group of their peers. The need [is] for heads to become 'head-learners', if they are to lead by example and encourage both staff and pupils in the view that education is a lifelong experience. [. . .]

Although the full EAC process may be too expensive for use outside the development and selection of heads, the principles and procedures on which it is based could be adapted for much wider use throughout education in assessment for management development.

PREPARATION FOR LEADERSHIP

Leadership now and in the future

At the Educational Assessment Centre 'leadership' [– which, because of its central importance, is discussed fully now –] is one of the 12 management competencies. It is quite narrowly defined as 'the ability to get others involved in solving problems; the ability to recognize when a group requires direction, to interact with a group effectively and to guide them to the accomplishment of a task'. A similar task-oriented definition is provided by Hughes *et al* (1985) although they expand it slightly to include an external aspect of the role: 'Professional leadership is concerned with task achievement, with group maintenance and development, and with the external, representative aspects of the role' (pp. 280–281).

Leadership skills at this level are not innate but can be acquired and developed. For example, Adair (1983) says, 'The traditional or "qualities" approach to leadership suggests that the person who emerges as a leader in a group does so because he possesses certain traits. This view has been rejected by academics'.

Both the above definitions of leadership make explicit the fact that leaders should not make all the decisions or carry out all the tasks in an organization themselves. Rather they should have the skill to empower and guide others in the accomplishment of tasks. The skills required to do this will focus on team-building. However such definitions mark a radical shift away from the [. . .] autocratic model of management. [. . .]

Hughes' (1985) description of the two main sub-roles of headship – leading professional and chief executive – presents a composite image (Figure 15.1) of institutional leadership. [. . .] Figure 15.1 illustrates the fact that school leaders must have developed both the leading professional (or educator) sub-role and the chief executive (or manager) sub-role effectively. The two sub-roles are, in practice, closely inter-related and must be maintained in a creative, not a destructive, tension. Hughes (1976) in an earlier publication puts it this way:

> The innovating head, it appears, relies partly on exerting influence on staff colleagues as a fellow professional: equally, however, he accepts his position as chief executive, and uses the organisational controls which are available to him to get things moving. Professional and executive considerations reinforce each other as complementary aspects of a coherent and unified strategy (p. 58).

The framework of qualities which holds these two sub-roles together in a 'coherent and unified strategy' and infuses all aspects of leadership is the individual's values, attitudes and vision. The Biblical adage, 'Without vision the people perish' (Proverbs 29 v. 18) has taken on a new meaning as a growing body of research has demonstrated that the most successful organizations have leaders with a strong personal commitment to a particular set of values plus a clear vision for the future. This is probably what commentators are referring to when they speak of the 'charismatic' aspects of leadership. Successful leaders will have a vision which inspires the commitment of other people.

It should be noted that all the boundaries in Figure 15.1 are dotted lines indicating that the two leadership sub-roles continually interact with each other, that both sub-roles are influenced by an individual's values, attitudes

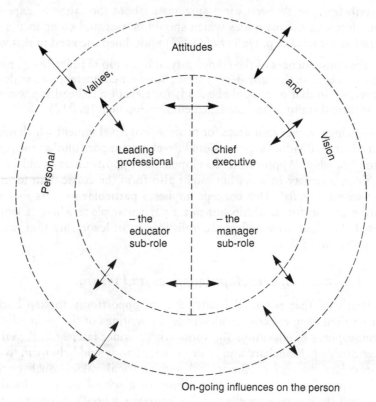

Figure 15.1   Aspects of the school leader

and vision and that effective leaders are willing to modify their position as a result of new demands and changing influences from outside. [. . .]

Coherence in the preparation for leadership

[. . .] The role of the head is rarely well-defined, certainly not in official documents. Hall *et al* (1986), having conducted research on headteachers at work, concluded:

> Our description and discussion of how secondary school headship is performed have recorded how different individual role interpretations can be. This degree of variance raises the question of whether government . . . should set out some guidelines for school management (p. 218).

However, it may be better that more detailed guidelines have not been set out centrally because they would almost inevitably become ossified and inhibit the redefinition that would be necessary as the context of schools changes. This is also one of the main arguments against a national staff college for training heads. [. . .]

Nevertheless, we *do* need some agreement about the range of experiences and development opportunities which should be essential components of the preparation for headship. Hall *et al* (1986) underlined the need in this way:

> . . . the consequences of the complexity of headship in practice . . . make it hard to believe that any deputy head, however competent and wide the experience in that post, could be ready for elevation to headship without prior formal training and management development (p. 217).

The following outlines four areas for professional development which might be required in an individual's 'professional development portfolio' as the preparation for headship. Appropriate developmental opportunities could be made available in a variety of ways but might also form the curriculum for a 'staff college *without walls*'. This concept implies a particular *process* that would prepare a person for headship but not a particular place where it would be delivered. The four areas reflect the holistic view of leadership that was illustrated in Figure 15.1. [. . .]

(i) Developing values and vision

[. . .] It is vital that potential heads have an opportunity to step back and reflect on their own experience alongside the writings of the great educators, the philosophers of education and those with a wider interest in the ethics of management, e.g. Blanchard and Peale (1988). This would help them to clarify and articulate their own educational and personal values. Such a process would prepare heads to share their vision for a school with the local community and, following consultation, to write the school's mission statement (also described as 'aims' or 'goals'!).

(ii) Developing the 'leading professional' – the educator sub-role

Future heads would also be expected to produce evidence of experience and professional development in the key area affecting schools and education. For example this might include: leading a team in successful planning and implementing a significant aspect of institutional change; training and/or experience in the following areas – classroom observation and staff appraisal; styles of teaching and learning; financial planning and resource management; staff recruitment and development; public relations and community education; work with governors; the law as it affects the education service; curriculum planning, staffing and timetabling; approaches to assessment and the evaluation of performance; student guidance; knowledge of the research on effective schools.

(iii) Developing the 'chief executive' – the manager sub-role

This aspect of preparation for headship would focus on the generic management competencies required by heads and would include participation in an assessment centre with subsequent management development. The relatively objective evidence about performance that is provided by assessment centres should, in particular, boost the chances for further promotion of groups currently under-represented in senior positions. Management development would also power an understanding of team-building, the role played by individuals as team members, and an analysis of personal preferences in terms of team roles. The latter insight should assist with building 'balanced' teams of staff wherever possible. During this aspect of their professional development, potential heads would also gain an understanding of situational leadership.

(iv) Developing a broader view – experience outside education

It might not be possible to make this a compulsory element in the preparation for headship, but all those with the ambition for headship should be strongly encouraged to gain some experience outside education. Ideally this would take the form of an extended project during a period of secondment [. . .] for senior staff before headship. More limited opportunities for experience outside education could be made available, for example by providing additional non-contact time for a local placement during term-time, a short (one or two week) placement during a school holiday or occasional work-shadowing [. . .]. It would also give potential heads a valuable opportunity to examine approaches to leadership and management in a different context and, in particular, important concepts like total quality management.

Preparation for leadership in all four of the areas outlined above would be supported by line-managers and, at senior level, by heads. Training should be provided for them in the skills of coaching and mentoring so that their support role for professional development and career planning is as effective as possible. It would also ensure that the main focus for development was 'on the job' experience.

A natural extension to this more coherent and comprehensive programme of professional development for headship would be the on-going in-service education and training of existing heads. Their own development would be enriched if they contributed to the preparation for headship by, for example, training as assessors at assessment centres, acting as coaches and mentors or helping with induction programmes for newly appointed heads. By helping in these ways they would also broaden and up-date their own skills and knowledge.

It is also assumed that the type of programme proposed as a preparation for headship would be undertaken, and the professional development portfolio assembled, over several years. The process would commence early in the career of a potential head. Ideally, appropriate elements would have been completed before promotion to a team leadership role at middle management level such as head of department or head of year.

SOME PRACTICAL CONSIDERATIONS

[. . .] The implementation of the strategies above and recommendations in these sections does, of course beg a number of important practical questions if we are to see a more coherent approach to school management development in the UK.

Where will the time be found?

All staff in schools are under immense pressure of work at the present time and it seems unlikely that this pressure will decrease, at least in the foreseeable future. There is also a legitimate and growing concern about staff taking time out of school for their own development and training with the result that classes are left to be covered. In this context it would not be surprising if personal professional development became a low priority and began to suffer from neglect. However caution is urged in drawing this conclusion and allowing such a scenario to become the reality. It is precisely when an organizational system is under most pressure that time must be found for professional development otherwise the system risks going into decline. [. . .]

In response to those who might respond by saying, 'But we have no time . . ', it is suggested that time might be found in the following ways. First, by making professional development a higher institutional and personal priority. Second, by making better use of the five in-service education and training ('Baker') days which are now part of the school year. Third, by giving up at least an equivalent amount of one's own time for personal professional development. Fourth, by proposing that a small proportion of the school budget is used to enhance staffing so that there can be an increase in non-contact time to be earmarked for professional development. [. . .]

It is most important that the senior team takes the lead in making professional development a high institutional priority. They must also find their own space. [. . .] The Secondary Heads Association (1989) publication, '*If it moves . . . a study of the role of the Deputy Head*', provided a clear indictment of the quite ludicrous, and often trivial, workload which was the daily grind of most deputy heads. How on earth can senior teams undertake their critical responsibilities for matters like strategic planning, evaluation and staff development if the deputies are worn out with the minutiae which should be done by other people? [. . .]

Where will the money come from?

Although central government should continue to make the funding of management development in the education service a high priority, there will never be enough money for all that is desirable. Following the introduction of local financial management more money is now getting directly into schools where senior teams and staff development committees can make the appropriate decisions about how it is spent. Hopefully they will be involved in local staff development networks so that resources are not wasted, for example, by 'reinventing wheels' or duplicating specialist forms of training. To allow sufficient development opportunities to be made available governors and heads will need to allocate a reasonable proportion of the school budget to staff (and their own) development. [. . .]

It is most important that some of the money for staff development is retained and ear-marked at local, regional and/or national levels for the wider needs of the service like senior staff development. There is a real danger that if all the money ends up in schools then little, if any, will be allocated to these wider needs. [. . .]

How will management development be delivered?

As much as the sources of funding for staff (and management) development are being fragmented within the education service, so is the means of delivery. Clearly, there is enormous potential for self-help from within a school. Too often people organizing development and training opportunities pay substantial sums of money to 'buy in' expertise when equivalent talent (or better) is there under their noses within the staff-room. So schools must keep an up-to-date inventory of the training and development skills available from within – another job for the staff development committee! [. . .] Staff should be paid an appropriate fee even if it is for preparing a programme or materials for the professional development of their own colleagues.

Beyond the school itself, one should look to the local area for suitable expertise. This might be another school, a local business, the LEA or an institute of higher education. Then there is the wider scene of regional and national providers like professional associations, industry, private companies (including the management colleges), consultants and, again, higher education.

To help make appropriate decisions about the right way to meet a particular professional development need, whether it is for a team or an individual, use should be made of local and regional networks. These can helpfully perform co-ordinating, quality control and information dissemination roles as direct outcomes of the type of strategic planning described [at the beginning] of this chapter.

Two final practical points should be considered when planning the delivery of management development. First, aim for the right balance between school-focused (and inevitably inward-looking) development and opportunities to get out of the institution to meet people with different experience who work in different contexts. [. . .] Second, although the number of management development providers, particularly commercial organizations and independent consultants, has been rapidly increasing, there has not been an equivalent improvement in quality.

How will professional development be accredited?

Management development opportunities range between the experience gained from reading a relevant book, going to an evening lecture, or doing something differently on the job, to completing a six-year doctoral degree. Across this range and between these extremes, there is a wide variety of existing accreditation including various certificates, diplomas, degrees and higher degrees. Despite attempts like the Management Charter Initiative to rationalize management development and its accreditation for all occupations and professions, it seems both likely and desirable that there will continue to be some diversity in future provision. [. . .]

If one accepts diversity as the likely reality, then one of the most sensible, and attractive ways ahead is to implement the idea of a 'professional development portfolio' (PDP) for all teachers. The PDP would be a similar document to the record of achievement for students. It would be issued at the start of a teacher's career, be recognized by both the profession and government (through the General Teaching Council and the Department of Education) and provide a flexible format for evidence of professional development within an agreed framework.

The framework might include the four areas described in 'Coherence in the preparation for leadership' plus two additional sections to cover a curriculum vitae and a personal log of important experiences and achievements.

The PDP would be the property of an individual but that person would be encouraged to keep it up-to-date, to use it for career planning and professional development and to make it available as a component of job applications. An important feature of the PDP would be items of accreditation like certificates, diplomas and degrees just as a component of a record of achievement might be public examination certificates. It would also provide opportunities for the teacher to record their own evidence about books read, short courses attended, training undertaken and experience gained.

However there does remain an urgent need to improve the structure and accreditation of formal management development courses and qualifications so that it will be possible in future to meet two requirements. First, to introduce sufficient modularity to courses so that transfer can be made between courses and levels without having to repeat components that have already been covered. Second, to acknowledge the relevance of prior learning and experience to decisions about the next appropriate step in an individual's professional development. Acceptable prior learning and experience should not be limited to formal courses and qualifications and should allow an individual to leap-frog lower level qualifications.

It almost goes without saying that applicants for senior posts, like deputy headships and headships, would be expected to have a very full and comprehensive PDP including both a wide range of experience and appropriate formal qualifications. But at the same time the PDP need not become a straight-jacket because the type of experience and qualifications that one would look for in the PDP of a potential deputy or head could change as the demands on senior staff in the future change. Equally, the availability and use of the PDP should provide a stimulus for personal and professional growth to teachers who did not necessarily want promotion to a more senior post.

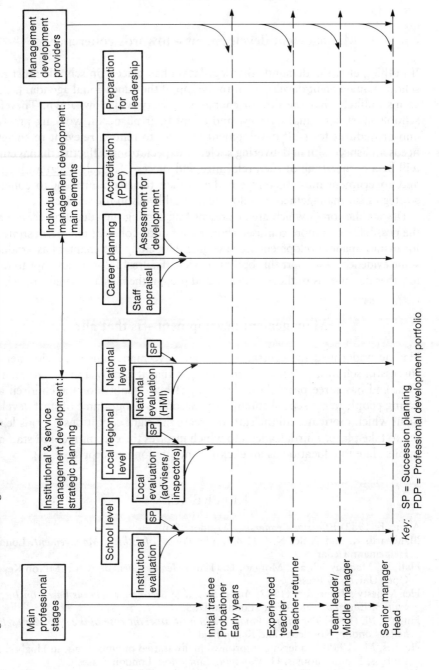

Figure 15.2 School management development – towards a coherent model?

Key: SP = Succession planning
PDP = Professional development portfolio

FINAL THOUGHTS

Management development – towards coherence?

If nothing else, the demands that legislation has placed on schools must raise school management development to the top of the educational agenda. [. . .] It seems unlikely that the rate of change in society will slow down. Therefore schools must continually review and adapt their purposes, working practices and procedures for staff development in order to remain relevant to society's needs and successful in delivering society's expectations. Effective management will be a cornerstone of such relevance and success. Schools, local authorities and government must therefore make explicit their commitment to coherent strategies for management development at all levels in the service.

Despite the forces which are at present fragmenting the education service and the possibility of a more confused short-term future, coherent long-term strategies for management development are emerging. Hopefully this chapter has produced some evidence to support this optimistic view. Figure 15.2 is an attempt to draw together the threads of these strategies and present them as a coherent model.

Management development – is that all?

Having underlined the central role of effective management development in successful schools, I close with the thought that it is only a means to an end. That end has three parts. First, learning of high quality for the children and young people in the school community. Second, a programme of staff development which motivates all the staff to create the right conditions for this learning to take place. Third, leadership which inspires the commitment of staff and pupils alike to education as an exciting and life-long enterprise. [. . .]

REFERENCES

Adair, J. (1983) *Effective Leadership*. London: Pan.

Blanchard, K. and Peale, N.V. (1988) *The Power of Ethical Management*. London: Heinemann Cedar.

Hall, V., MacKay, H. and Morgan, C. (1986) *Headteachers at Work*. Milton Keynes: Open University Press.

Her Majesty's Inspectors (1987) *An Appraisal of Secondary Schools based on Inspections in England. 1982–1986*. London: DES.

Hughes, M. (1976) *The Professional-as-administrator: the case of the secondary school head*. London: Routledge and Kegan Paul.

Hughes, M. (1985) Leadership in professionally staffed organisations, in Hughes, M., Ribbins, P. and Thomas, H. *Managing Education*. London: Cassell.

School Management Task Force (1990) *Developing School Management: The Way Forward*. London: HMSO.

Secondary Heads Association (1989) *If it moves . . . a study of the role of the Deputy Head*. Bristol: H.E. Iles Ltd.

PART 5:

Self-Management and Development

16

APPRAISAL AND EQUAL OPPORTUNITIES

Meryl Thompson

This material has been abridged

When women manage schools children's academic achievement is greater, teachers have higher morale and parents respond to the school more favourably. These conclusions from American research (Shakeshaft 1989) contrast tellingly with the evidence that in Britain women's promotion prospects for senior management posts have deteriorated in the last 20 years. This evidence of women's leadership abilities contrasts even more dramatically with the common assumption in Britain that qualities such as detachment and toughness, usually attributed to men, are essential leadership characteristics. The reason for these frequent contrasts between the empirical evidence and our personal assumptions, widely-held social generalizations and some theoretical hypotheses is that human beings largely act, not on the basis of objective facts or reasonable evidence, but on a series of unexamined assumptions and more or less sophisticated generalizations. Rather than make critical judgments, we pre-judge. We thoughtlessly and habitually use generalizations, including racial and sexual stereotypes, rather than examine each situation afresh. We tend to act emotionally rather than rationally. We condone behaviour in people we like, or who are like us, that we condemn in others. We make scapegoats. We project on to others behavioural characteristics we dislike in ourselves. Admittedly, some people show a greater degree of objectivity, more flexibility to modify their opinions and are less inclined to jump to conclusions than others, but the predisposition remains. Generalizations after all also help us to order and categorize our experience. In appraisal, where teachers are asked to make a series of wide-ranging professional judgments, this psychological and cognitive tendency will be the permanent backcloth.

Early in the debate about the introduction of appraisal for teachers it was argued that an open and formal appraisal scheme would be preferable to the present informal and covert way decisions concerning teachers' careers are made. Inherent in this argument is the assumption that appraisal, by providing a basis of objective criteria and a systematic procedure for professional development and career planning, would counter subjectivity and partiality and contribute to achieving equal opportunities in the widest sense. As the National Steering Group's Report (1989) stated, 'appraisal must operate and be seen to operate, fairly and equitably for all teachers' and 'should be used positively to promote equal opportunities by encouraging all teachers to fulfil their potential'. Equal opportunities issues are therefore central to implementing appraisal. Certainly, appraisal will lose credibility with sections of the profession if they perceive structural prejudices and discrimination unaddressed and unaltered.

[. . .] The undeveloped level of awareness of equal opportunities issues is one of the many deficiencies in educational management which appraisal tends to highlight. [. . .] Appraisers need to be aware of their legal responsibilities not to discriminate on grounds of sex, race or marital status and of the danger of stereotyped expectations which result in a biased approach when conducting appraisal. However, exactly how appraisal policies and procedures can address the existing inequalities in professional development and career opportunities for teachers arising from discrimination and stereotyping remains to be considered.

The legislation which outlaws discrimination on the grounds of race, ethnic origins, gender and marital status will apply to appraisal procedures because appraisal contributes to identifying staff development and training needs. Direct or indirect sex discrimination is unlawful under the Sex Discrimination Act 1975 in employment and includes discrimination in opportunities for promotion, transfer, training and education. Direct sex discrimination occurs when one person is treated less favourably on the grounds of sex than a person of the other sex is or would be treated. Indirect sex discrimination occurs when a requirement or condition is applied equally to men and women but has the practical effect of disadvantaging a considerably higher proportion of one sex than the other. The 1976 Race Relations Act makes direct or indirect discrimination on the grounds of a person's colour, race, nationality or ethnic origins similarly unlawful.

Therefore, as the NSG Report and the Equal Opportunities Commission recommend, each appraisal scheme should be monitored to assess how it works in practice. This will mean examining the outcomes of the professional targets for development and training identified by appraisal to see if there is an imbalance between sexes or ethnic groups which suggests that unlawful direct or indirect discrimination is occurring. If so, the cause must be identified to ensure that it is not discriminatory. However, the LEA's responsibility does not stop there, for if an employee unlawfully discriminates in the course of employment both employee and employer are responsible whether or not the employer knows or approves of the action, unless the employer has taken all reasonable steps to prevent discrimination. Therefore, LEAs must take positive action to prevent appraisers from practising discrimination by, for example, including unbiased managerial practice in the criteria for appraising appraisers and the provision of equal opportunities for all the staff in the criteria for appraising headteachers and by ensuring that any assessment criteria used in appraisal are not discriminatory. What is also clear is that LEAs must provide appropriate advice on equal opportunities directly to schools and in appraisal training. Knowledge of the legislation alone will not alter the existing management structures and structural prejudices which may cause discrimination and into which appraisal will be incorporated, and the introduction of appraisal requires that these are more fully understood.

Although women outnumber men in the teaching profession they are seriously under-represented in senior positions. In 1985, one in ten male teachers was a headteacher. For women the figure was one in 25. In the secondary sector women formed 55 per cent of the teaching force, but only 31 per cent of those on scale 3 or above, compared to 58 per cent of men. The latest DES returns for the primary sector in England show the same pattern with women disproportionately placed in posts of lower or no responsibility. Women formed 79.9 per cent of the full-time and 87 per cent of the part-time teaching force and of these, 76.7 per cent and 96.1 per cent respectively were on scales 1 and 2, compared to 35 per cent of male full-time teachers. Of the male full-time teachers only 9 per cent had no responsibility, compared to 32 per cent of the women. At the other end of the scale, 32 per cent of men were headteachers and 21 per cent deputy headteachers, compared with 7.5 per cent and 8.5 per cent respectively for women. Furthermore, even these statistics conceal the effect of including nursery and separate infant schools, where almost all teachers are women. In 1987 69.4 per cent of infant/junior headships and 79.6 per cent of junior headships were held by men, although they made up only 25 per cent and 34 per cent of the teachers in such schools.

Men's career chances are therefore substantially better than women's. As the EOC said, this is a wastage of skill and talent and a matter of concern to everyone involved with the teaching profession, because it may indicate a pattern of under-achievement by women in an area of employment in which there is a well-established tradition of female participation. The causal factors are difficult to identify. An AMMA survey found that although only slightly fewer women described themselves as interested in progressing through the career structure, 57 per cent of men compared to 34 per cent of women were heads, deputy heads or heads of departments. The reason seemed to be that 44 per cent of women teachers, compared with only 14 per cent of men teachers, had had a break in service lasting a year or more. Moreover, for men the breaks were usually for further study, training or research – activities which could improve promotion prospects. Women teachers were more likely to have made an enforced sideways move because of a change in the husband's job.

However, there is also extensive evidence that the present situation is in part due to a sex-differentiated management response to women's and men's development needs which determines what type of training and experience is offered to women and men teachers. [. . .] This is consistent with a survey of the insurance industry where a significant percentage of managers believed women were not interested in a career, while an overwhelming majority of the women considered career advancement a high priority for job satisfaction (Bargh, 1988). In the Civil Service women receive performance ratings as good as men, but lower promotability ratings. Women, it seems, are being excluded from promotion because of under-assessment by their line managers, who may act on unjustified assumptions quite subconsciously and attribute to all women attitudes and opinions which may not be held by the woman being appraised. The existence of such stereotyping is supported by research into women teachers' actual experience of discrimination. Women are commonly questioned in interviews, even by headteachers, on child care arrangements and domestic responsibilities. It is assumed that it is their work which will suffer because women must automatically undertake these responsibilities.

It is obvious that the standard pattern in teaching will be a male manager appraising a female. Even more frequently a white manager will be appraising a black teacher. The danger is that certain assumptions, attitudes and stereotypes which can shape the way an individual's potential is perceived could pervade the appraisal process. It is essential that appraisal training challenges rather than reinforces these attitudes. The common sex stereotypes can be categorized neatly. Prestigious qualities such as reason, objectivity, leadership, independence and authority have been attributed to men, while women have been allocated stigmatized qualities such as emotion, irrationality, passivity and dependence. [. . .] Al-Khalifa (1989) argues that recent developments in management theory, which stress school organizational problems as technical problems amenable to rational problem-solving, emphasize characteristics such as 'analytical detachment' and 'hard-nosed toughness' that are commonly seen as 'masculine'. Leadership characteristics are thus seen to correspond to the socially determined masculine sex-role.

Conversely, when women display just these characteristics their ambition and 'hardness' are seen as unnatural and unfeminine and result in pejorative comments. For there are also stereotyped perceptions of the appropriate and inappropriate behaviour and demeanours of each sex. The common conception of femininity involves modesty, deference (to the male), non-aggressiveness and being agreeable. As Spender (1989) says, 'In a society which assumes the politeness and deference of women towards men as the norm women who do not defer to men are often judged by men and women as socially unacceptable.' Men may prefer to promote women who are 'passive and non-threatening or at least capable of appearing so' (Shakeshaft, 1989). Cunnison (1989) argues that much male humour is designed to undermine women in authority by reminding women of their sexuality and by restating sexual and domestic stereotypes thus implicitly suggesting their administrative incompetence. Women can be deterred from ever assuming posts of responsibility over others and may still be discouraged from promotion by a widely-held assumption that their health and that of their families will suffer. There also remains a deeply-seated belief that men have more right to promotion because they are the main bread-winners.

Women's attitudes also contribute to the generalized supposition that management responsibilities at whatever level are more appropriately undertaken by men. Women are described and sometimes describe themselves as too diffident, poor at job interviews and playing safe in terms of the posts for which they apply. They lack confidence in their competence to teach science because it is perceived as 'masculine' and believe that their male colleagues can compensate for their own limited technical knowledge. Their stereotypes include the perception that male headteachers will inevitably be authoritarian, unbending and intolerant. Some women teachers also seem to credit men with higher standards and clearer vision, which may affect their ability to contribute professionally to their self-evaluation and to the professional dialogue of appraisal. Unexamined sexual stereotyping in the assumptions of appraisers and in the influence they have on the way women appraisees perceive and project themselves and their position can therefore influence appraisal. Appraisers and appraisees must be made aware of how sexual stereotyping can be part of our generally shared perceptions and that it can affect self-evaluation and self-presentation.

Male appraisers must be careful to estimate confident, autonomous and assertive (possibly young) women by the same standards as men. Men in general talk more and interrupt more in mixed-sex contexts. Women who consistently and successfully control verbal interaction are frequently criticized by men and are likely to be regarded as 'bitchy', domineering or aggressive. To allow a woman in an appraisal interview 80 per cent of the time to express her views and talk of her priorities may be very difficult for many men. [. . .] Women may need to learn to state clearly what they want from appraisal and discuss realistic timetables and programmes of action for achieving this because, 'too often women assume that if they have had a good performance review then the manager will automatically put them forward for promotion. In reality this is rarely the case' (Bargh, 1988). Women also tend to get less negative feedback, either through chivalry or a fear that women will burst into tears (and the man be discomfited in handling it). Thus they are frequently denied constructive criticism that could improve their performance. Therefore, both men and women need training in giving and receiving feedback constructively.

One stereotype which may particularly influence appraisal is the low status typically ascribed to infant and early years teaching, which is disparaged as an extension of mothering and child care. [. . .] Other stereotyped assumptions could influence the assessment of classroom management styles. Women teachers who establish discipline through developing relationships and reasoning with pupils rather than dictating to them are taken less seriously than 'hard teachers'.

It should be evident, therefore, that gender stereotypes do need to be considered in appraisal training if appraisal is to be fair and equitable and promote equal opportunities, but it may not be enough. For example, to make allowances for women's diffidence, male appraisers may press on women teachers managerial responsibilities and ambitions which women believe are genuinely inappropriate for them, considering their priorities and values. Men may be unable to appreciate this and misinterpret their reluctance to accept responsibility. This could reinforce the stereotype when what may be involved here are two differing value systems. This possibility is supported by evidence that male and female attitudes to work differ greatly. Comparative studies of men and women in 65 occupations found that most men work for money and career advancement. Men are always looking up the ladder for the main chance whereas women seek job satisfaction, a good working atmosphere and flexibility to fit family life into their careers. They emphasize doing a thorough job and doing the job well. Women work for self-fulfilment, for social relationships and like to feel they are making a contribution and are valued by colleagues. Research suggests that these attitudes are shared by teachers too. Women teachers value classroom teaching and put it as a priority. For them teaching and not management is 'real work'. They are more hesitant about career moves unless they have assessed their readiness. They weigh all the factors they feel impinge on their career and professional development, including their classroom strengths and weaknesses, their commitments outside work, and the obligations these present in maintaining relationships and meeting family needs. In comparison, men teachers show little interest in this kind of self-evaluation, do not mention their home situation and see their future essentially in terms of promotion moves. [. . .]

Many aspects of appraisal emphasize contributing to the development of others, whether colleagues or students, and this suggests that male values and modes of behaviour are not the most appropriate models. A value system of responsibilities and care seems more appropriate to appraisal than one of rights and individuality. Also, the American research already quoted indicates that women administrators spend more time with people, care more about individual differences, motivate more and their staff have more shared professional goals. Women administrators demonstrate a more democratic and participatory management style, exhibit greater knowledge of teaching methods and techniques and create a school climate more conducive to learning (Shakeshaft, 1989). Women are also considered 'better listeners' and listening skills are regarded as essential in appraisal. The skill is not only to let the appraisee contribute but to pick up nuances and to detect the underlying assumptions, attitudes and emotions that give the whole picture. It requires both empathy and a concern for others. Men may lack these skills because they are too used to dominating meetings and putting their own arguments. Certainly, women do not believe men are good listeners and often feel that men only take seriously ideas presented by men. In appraisal, listening is given a role as complex as talking, although in social life it is devalued in mixed-sex conversation and associated with passivity (Spender, 1985). Conventional male styles of verbal interaction will not dominate in appraisal and because this disturbs the balance of power between the sexes may add to the discomfort of interviews with the opposite sex.

In other ways, too, women teachers' values, their attitude to being a good teacher and their tendency to be more introspective and hesitant about their professional strengths and weaknesses may be a more appropriate starting point for appraisal. For appraisal is not directly and immediately about promotion, although the qualities and strengths it enhances and develops should not be irrelevant to the qualities and strengths required by teachers with managerial responsibilities. It is about continuous and systematic development as a professional. This makes appraisal relevant for all teachers at whatever stage of their careers. It relates appraisal to improving the quality of learning experiences for children and simultaneously promoting job satisfaction and professional pride and autonomy in teachers. Ironically, male weaknesses, in failing to evaluate the intrinsic quality of the job they are doing, in having too much uncritical confidence in their own worth and promotability and in valuing where they are going more than the fulfilment to be gained from making a contribution here and now, may make this essential formative and developmental element of appraisal less satisfying and less convincing for them. There are interesting parallels with boys' and girls' attitudes to records of achievement where there is evidence that girls understand the purpose of the formative processes better than boys. The National Steering Committee concluded that girls 'tend to be more forthcoming and skilled in discussion and value the opportunity for one to one contact with their teachers. On the other hand boys tend to have a keener sense of the external audience for the records of achievement rather than relationships.'

However, if by and large men are to be the appraisers then ensuring male commitment to formative appraisal and to the intrinsic and personal elements of professional development must be an essential part of appraisal training. Otherwise male appraisers may find women's attitudes to work deficient because they regard career-centred values as the measure of seriousness and interest in work. If commitment to appraisal for professional development remains superficial and only thinly conceals the expectation that appraisal is about promotion for those with the right qualities – masculine ones – women's likely expectations for appraisal will be severely disappointed. Men in managerial positions could even have their power reinforced. Formative appraisal requires openness and critical self-evaluation, but power, it is argued, often lies with those who do not disclose their vulnerabilities and who abstain from self-revelation and withhold personal information. Remaining aloof while someone else discloses personal information facilitates dominance. If formative appraisal were to reinforce this dominance and leave women more vulnerable, women would have to think carefully about its consequences.

Moreover, if the developmental purpose of appraisal is not fully understood and implemented, the consequences will be dysfunctional. Appraisal would not then contribute to improving professional dialogue or to a better understanding and appreciation of the skills of teaching or to sharing what we learn to improve the teaching and learning environment of the school. It would not help teachers fulfil their potential. Appraisal as conceived by the pilot projects and the NSG, however, will focus on reflection, self-evaluation, professional development and improving teaching and learning and not only on promotion. It is likely to change the focus of teaching to one that is more congenial to women. As managerial responsibilities begin to include responsibility for appraisal – and thus the responsibility to encourage the skills of teaching analysis and classroom observation and obligations to the development of professional colleagues – managerial roles will also be more in line with women's values. The role of headteacher as an educational leader will be more attractive to women than the role of headteacher as administrator.

[. . .] If we are to ensure fair and unbiased appraisals, sexual stereotypes and our common assumptions concerning women's place in society must be replaced by a more objective and more individualized assessment of their relative professional strengths and weaknesses. The same considerations apply in other areas of stereotyping and prejudice, such as the assessments made of teachers from ethnic minorities and in age discrimination.

The under-representation of teachers from ethnic minority groups is another major concern to all those in education and from January 1990 returns must be made on the ethnic origins of teachers. The aim is to provide data to support fair and equal employment opportunities and additional details of sex, age, phase, specialism and form of employment will be collected by the DES. However, in 1988 a survey of eight LEAs found that only two per cent of teachers was black and evidence showed that they were disproportionately on the lower salary scales. It concluded that teachers from ethnic minorities do not enjoy the same career progression as white teachers and headteachers do not encourage them to apply for vacancies within the school in the same way as white teachers. An ILEA survey in1987 found that 'black teachers were severely and negatively affected during reorganization and amalgamations of schools when demotions were more likely for black teachers than promotions or holding on to their substantive posts.'

In order to counteract structural prejudices and discrimination, appraisal training will similarly need to acknowledge the context in which ethnic minority teachers find themselves – a context which is rarely openly discussed. Teachers from ethnic minorities will be well aware of racial prejudice and stereotypes, of racial attacks on minority groups and of racist graffiti. [. . .] These teachers may even have experienced racist remarks from their own teachers and racist attitudes restricting their own educational achievement by an underestimate of their potential. Grievances on grounds of racial harassment are not unknown in teaching, although there is little firm evidence of their extent. There is also the 'insidious, unconscious racism of white teachers who fail to recognize that their black colleagues may feel ill at ease in a mainly white staff room or may need some support to cope with harassment they suffer outside school' (AMMA, 1988). However, this social context and the way it influences relationships with colleagues and their perceptions is not always understood in teaching.

Only now are black teachers' experiences and perspectives of schools and their management finding a wider audience. These experiences include having their identity, as black persons and members of minority groups, ignored, particularly as students, yet finding their working lives dominated by issues to do with race. Assumptions are made that black teachers can speak for all the local black community even if they personally know little about other ethnic groups and cultures. They are used as convenient intermediaries to pass on messages or discuss difficult issues with black colleagues and are expected to fill disciplinary and pastoral roles in delicate situations, often being asked to intervene on behalf of the school rather than in the interests of the black pupils and parents. As one black teacher said, 'A school can deflect allegations of racism by using its black staff to deal with situations of tension, and even by citing their existence as proof of its commitment to challenging racism' (Bangar and McDermott, 1989; McKellar, 1989).

It is frequently assumed that black teachers will work only or largely with ethnic minority children. A revealing example of this pervasive attitude occurs in a supposedly exemplary appraisal interview. A young teacher is asked, 'Have there been any disappointments during the year?' and responds with, 'Not really apart from the fact that I still don't have my own class. I think that people see me as some sort of superior classroom helper. I'm not. I'm a fully qualified teacher, but just because I can speak Panjabi I have to stay . . .' The explanatory comment acknowledges this is an important and valid point and a highly emotional issue which a teacher would quite legitimately want to make sure was raised during the appraisal interview. The advice to the appraiser is that one cannot allow the interview to be side-tracked from the agreed agenda because the headteacher has to deploy the staff to meet the children's needs (Rhodes, 1988). Thus the issues of equal opportunities, structural prejudice and personal identity are ignored.

Teachers from ethnic minorities have the same right to opportunities for complete professional development from appraisal and the same right to be regarded as individuals, which means that their specific needs and experience as a part of a minority group cannot be ignored. School management must become aware of how it may be involving these teachers unreasonably. Fair and equal treatment means varying and sensitive treatment. It requires understanding, confidence and maturity in the appraiser which may not be acquired unless the introductory materials and appraisal training emphasize the significance of these issues and help appraisers to develop the necessary understanding and skills.

It is perhaps only now being recognized that prejudices that limit equality of opportunity extend to stereotyped assumptions about what is appropriate and beneficial at varying ages. Potentially this is sexual discrimination and the EOC recommends that on these grounds age limits for access to training and promotion should be questioned. However, on all grounds for equality, appraisal training should ensure that it is not assumed that in-service training (with its related expenses) is inappropriate for those near retirement or that teachers over 50 will prefer premature retirement to challenges in the classroom and increased responsibilities. In fact, the AMMA survey found 70 per cent of the 40–49 age group and 48 per cent of the over-50s still interested in progressing in their career.

There are also important factors which are relevant to inter-personal skills training. Although individuals vary, it is generally more difficult to adapt one's teaching styles if these are the product of some 30 years' experience. All change brings with it a sense of becoming de-skilled and demoralized and a certain percentage of fear. Appraisers should be particularly careful not to damage the sense of self-worth and the lifetime achievement of those very near the end of their teaching career and to allow for the psychological process of adapting to retirement. Appraisal by younger teachers may threaten the sense of dignity of older teachers. Mores, courtesies and vocabularies do change but nothing in appraisal should precipitate the decision of an experienced but perhaps de-moralized professional to leave teaching. Many teachers, particularly men, who tend to have greater expectations of promotion, must come to terms with disappointment as they age. Sometimes male anger and resentment may be deflected on to women, especially those on their way up. As appraisers, women may have to learn to manage this and turn it into something positive. Certainly, to achieve the trust and confidence of these experienced classroom teachers will require considerable professional and personal skills.

It should now be obvious that issues of equal opportunities must be integrated at every stage of implementing appraisal. LEAs have been asked to set the climate for appraisal and to raise awareness. In particular, positive reassurances should be given at this stage that equal opportunities will be respected. Each LEA should make it clear that the existence of racial and sexual harassment is a legitimate area of concern. Sexual harassment is possibly the most difficult area of inter-personal relationships in appraisal. It has been defined by the NUT as 'any uninvited, unreciprocated and unwelcome physical contact, comment, suggestion, joke or attention which is offensive to the person involved and causes that person to feel threatened, humiliated, patronised or embarrassed.' It may create a threatening and intimidating working environment, adversely affect job performance and, in extreme cases, may cause a person to seek to leave the school. Sexual harassment is widespread with surveys all showing a high proportion of women reporting unwanted attentions from men.

In the only specific survey of women secondary teachers 65 per cent of the 246 respondents had experienced sexual harassment, predominantly from male colleagues (Addison and Al-Khalifa, 1988). The most common experience, of being eyed up and down or of suggestive looks at parts of the body, was recorded by two in five of the respondents. Regular sexual jokes and innuendo were reported almost as often. More than one in five of the women teachers had experienced 'touching, brushing against, patting, pinching or grabbing.' Even more seriously one in ten reported a direct sexual proposition and six reported forcible sexual aggression from male colleagues. For appraisal, the most serious aspect is likely to be the pervasiveness of suggestive looks and sexual innuendo. Classroom observation could become a degrading and humiliating experience for women teachers, resulting in considerable modifications to manner, behaviour and dress, and imposing a high degree of unnaturalness in order to avoid being the object of unwanted sexual attention in a professional teaching environment. Women will be unable to continue the avoidance tactics reported by a third of the respondents in the survey. Sexual remarks, jokes and innuendo can be part of 'staffroom banter' and to complain can be regarded as churlish. Like black people complaining of racism, women are often told that they are imagining that actions are suggestive or lascivious. Yet sexual jokes and generally making fun of women constantly draw attention back to a woman's sex and femininity. Subtly, this implies that women are less competent and less committed to their job and undermines their authority.

If appraisal is to be as positive and supportive for women as for men these issues will have to be confronted to end what one teacher in the survey described as 'fighting two battles – the things you want to achieve professionally and how to cope with men, because in their eyes you are a woman and not a teacher.' Women teachers must feel confident that they will not have to tolerate the danger of behaviour which may be bearable in the semi-social context of the staffroom but which impairs and diminishes the professional interaction essential in appraisal. It would also be unendurable for women teachers who have experienced 'touching up' were the appraiser the perpetrator. Close proximity in a private interviewing room would bring the fear of humiliation and negate a woman teacher's ability to evaluate her professional contribution. However, sexual harassment is often unreported because it causes high levels of anxiety and stress. Women find it difficult to talk about. In the Birmingham survey 74 per cent of the women did not complain at all, largely because they believed the reaction would be negative and that what had happened would not be regarded as serious enough; when they did complain 31 per cent reported that no action was taken and where action was taken 71 per cent was not satisfied with the outcome.

Appraisal requires an open recognition that sexual harassment is properly regarded as a disciplinary misdemeanour which will tangibly affect career prospects if a managerial position is exploited. LEAs must take particular care to deal effectively with all complaints of harrassment and, most importantly, not assume that they are made by women who are over sensitive. Awareness-raising materials, training courses for appraisers, and management courses should raise the issue so that before the introduction of appraisal each school examines whether its ethos and climate allows all its teachers the same personal respect. It should be widely acknowledged during awareness raising that the selection of an appraiser would be reconsidered sensitively if sexual or racial harassment was a factor.

Satisfactory appraisal should also include an assessment of the awareness of equal opportunities issues within the LEA. The legal basis for direct and indirect discrimination and the NSG recommendation on the dangers of stereotyping and bias should be widely disseminated and referred to in both the preliminary literature and the training programmes. The training programme should incorporate the factual information on the position of women and ethnic minority teachers in the profession and disseminate relevant research. Some authorities may wish to disseminate their own equal opportunities policies and some schools may consider integrating gender and race issues raised by appraisal with issues related to the curriculum and in line with their own school policies. The selection of trainers should also ensure the best possible balance of gender and ethnic groupings, especially where the LEA decides to train its own trainers. A balance here between age, sex, ethnic grouping and position in the teaching hierarchy can do a great deal to overcome the imbalance in a typical school's management structure and contribute to creating the right climate for emphasizing equal opportunities in appraisal.

The principle that appraisers must guard against anything that distorts reality, favourably or unfavourably, is embodied in all appraisal schemes and so sexual and racial stereotypes, and the unexamined prejudices and assumptions which are often part of our behaviour patterns must be considered and explained in appraisal training. For example, performance or behaviour which would be overlooked or condoned in one sex must not be noted as significant in the other. Appraisees, too, need to understand the significance of stereotyping in their inter-personal transactions and in self-evaluation and self-presentation. Undoubtedly this will be one of the more difficult areas of training since it requires not only attitudinal changes but the development of self-critical skills. The training must be experiential and allow teachers the chance to recognize when they are using unexamined assumptions and stereotypes. Video-taped situations and paired observation can help to alert teachers to what not to do. In skills such as handling potential conflict it is likely that repeated practice, coaching and remedial training will be appropriate. For some people this aspect of appraisal training will not be comfortable and schools and LEAs should give serious consideration to the need for counselling both during training and to protect those who feel unfairly treated because of intended or unintended stereotyping when appraisal is implemented.

Equal opportunities should also be part of the criteria for assessing the school and the educational system. The extent to which the LEA or the school is delivering equal opportunities can be measured by the nature of the staffing structure, the allocation of incentive allowances and the outcomes of appraisal. To be effective, this requires efficient monitoring of where both ethnic minority group teachers and women teachers are in the educational system relative to their experience and qualifications.

LEAs will also have to consider how well their own structures reflect a concern for equal opportunities issues. Men make up 75.5 per cent of the total advisers but women make up 40 per cent of the primary advisers and only 17.5 per cent of the secondary ones (Stillman and Grant, 1989). It is likely that similar sexual and racial stereotypes and similar prejudices are prevalent within LEA management. The need to update and enhance the skills of LEA advisers and officers is now widely recognized and should include equal opportunities issues, particularly in the light of the introduction of appraisal. Researchers, too, can contribute by always looking for possible differences in male and female teachers' experiences, skills and attitudes in teaching. Age and membership of an ethnic minority group should be regarded as possibly significant variables wherever relevant. In this way we can improve the evidential base, against which we can test our assumptions.

However, all this will be irrelevant if sensitive and practical steps are not taken genuinely to face gender and race issues in schools. Situations where graffiti is referred to in assembly because of the damage to property rather than for its racist nature and where sexual harassment by students is regarded as a disciplinary failure in the teacher rather than an issue for the school, cannot co-exist with a climate that ensures a fair appraisal for all teachers. Neither can we ignore the influence practical problems, such as lack of child-care facilities, have on women's ability to concentrate on their own professional development through INSET. The approach to equal opportunities must be consistent and unvarying or else the intent that appraisal should be used positively to promote equal opportunities will lose its credibility.

It is difficult to see how writers on appraisal can describe it as a fairer and more up-to-date basis for making professional judgments and yet, as so many do, ignore equal opportunities issues entirely. The NSG has quite properly placed fair and equitable treatment of all teachers at the centre of the appraisal process and has stated categorically that appraisal should be used positively *to promote equal opportunities* by encouraging all teachers to fulfil their potential. It has recognized that stereotyping and the bias that arises from both prejudice and partiality are barriers to fairness and equity. The stark fact is that we can make no attempt at an objective assessment without consciously and explicitly considering the effect our unexamined assumptions and our own value system have on the process and without testing our assumptions against behavioural and other evidence. This applies in every appraisal. The issues raised by gender, race and age are, however, deeply embedded in both our subconscious and our emotive ways of thinking. They must be faced directly and specifically. The introduction of appraisal moves equal opportunities issues to the pivotal point in awareness raising and training and makes this the greatest challenge and the greatest opportunity for radical change in the structure and the values of the teaching profession.

REFERENCES

Addison, B. and Al-Khalifa, E. (1988) *Sexual Harassment in Birmingham Schools and Colleges, Report of the Birmingham Teacher Survey*, 53–7, Teacher Research Group.

Al-Khalifa, E. (1989) 'Management by halves: women teachers and school management', in De Lyon, H. and Migniuolo, F.W. (eds), *Women Teachers: Issues and Experiences*, 83–96, Milton Keynes: Open University Press.

Al-Khalifa, E. (1987) 'Women's work', *Child Education*, October, 11–13.

AMMA (1988) *Striving for Equality; multi-cultural and anti-racist education today.*

Bangar, S. and McDermott, J. (1989) 'Black women speak' in De Lyon, H. and Migniuolo, F.W. (eds), *Women Teachers: issues and experiences*, 135–153, Milton Keynes: Open University Press.

Bargh, E. (1988) 'Equal opportunities and appraisal interviewing', *AUT Woman*, No. 15, Autumn.

Cunnison, S. (1989) 'Gender joking in the staffroom', in Acker, S. (ed.), *Teachers, Genders and Careers*, 151–70, London: Falmer Press.

DES (1989) *School teacher appraisal: a national framework,* Report of the National Steering Group on the School Teacher Appraisal Pilot Study, HMSO.

Gilligan, C. (1982) *In a Different Voice; psychological theory and women's development,* Cambridge, Mass.: Harvard University Press.

McKellar, B. (1989) 'Only the fittest will survive: black women and education' in Acker, S. (ed.), *Teachers, Genders and Careers,* 69–85, London: Falmer Press.

Rhodes, C.D.M. (1988) 'Practical appraisal in primary schools' in Bell, L. (ed.) *Appraising Teachers in Schools; a practical guide,* 44–57, Routledge.

Shakeshaft, C. (1989) Unpublished paper given to the American Educational Research Association, April.

Spender, D. (1985) *Man Made Language,* 2nd edition, 41–51 and 120–125, London: Routledge and Kegan Paul.

Spender, D. (1989) *Invisible Women: the schooling scandal,* 56–68, London: Women's Press.

Stillman, A. and Grant, M. (1989) *The LEA Adviser; a changing role,* 52–56, NFER/Nelson.

17

THE MANAGEMENT OF TIME

Cyril Wilkinson

While headteachers are not required to become experts in accountancy, marketing, law and so on, the range of their responsibilities, nevertheless, has widened. If senior staff are to continue to exercise academic leadership in addition to these new responsibilities then the management of time becomes a crucial issue on their agenda. The limitation of a finite amount of time is identified by many headteachers as one of the most serious constraints they face in attempting to meet the challenges presented by the changed managerial arena.

Images have been used to attempt to capture the nature of time. It has been presented as a commodity with a currency value which may vary in exchange rate according to social, geographic, or market forces. In some cultures one is made to feel guilty if time is 'wasted' while in others time is regarded more casually. Benjamin Franklin (1745) took the imagery a stage further when he counselled 'Remember that time is money': time is certainly now accounted in terms of sums of money per hour, per week, per month, and per year. The increasing use in education of techniques like cost-benefit analysis implies a hardheaded accounting of the cost elements in time. The delegation of financial management to school level will require those who have managerial responsibility to engage in this kind of accounting exercise. Managers in schools are often surprised to discover that a staff meeting of fifty members of staff for three hours at a nominal eight pounds per hour for each participant costs one thousand two hundred pounds. This puts a premium on the worthwhile utilization of time.

Time may also be seen as the composite total of that available to and utilized by all the staff in the school. The stipulation under the School Teachers' Pay and Conditions Order (DES 1987) of a minimum of 1,265 hours has made teachers particularly sensitive to the extent of their obligation in terms of time. Headteachers, therefore, have had to look at the total deployment of staff time and to agree with individual members of staff how their time is to be used. Clear job specifications for staff, negotiated through sympathetic and recipro- cal processes of appraisal which relate to the aims and objectives of the school and the priorities identified, can be useful instruments in achieving more effec- tive utilization of the total bank of time available. However, the dangers of teachers' contracts which are tightly defined may be seen in many American schools where principals find it impossible to hold meetings after school hours or to persuade staff to engage in extra-curricular activities. This chill wind is already being felt in the United Kingdom and can only be avoided by the establishment of sensitive relationships which allow flexibility.

In many of the devolved activities of LMS there will be a need for effective staff development if delegated tasks and functions are to be undertaken suc- cessfully. Such initiatives will demand valuable time and sympathetic provision by LEAs. For example, in many primary schools where curriculum develop- ment has been growing in volume and more closely associated with the new allowance structures, staff have been relating uneasily to unfamiliar roles. In such times of significant change and insecurity LEAs must be generous in providing opportunity for development and regeneration. It is important to build solid foundations for future evolution. Advisory and consultancy services working in partnership with institutions of higher education can offer invalu- able support and guidance. Schools can also look at different sources of provi- sion and buy appropriately, having made a searching diagnosis of needs and priorities. Educational institutions will have to learn, like many successful private sector organizations, that ongoing staff development is of key import- ance and costs money and time.

More responsibilities deriving from the [local management of] schools will demand more time. Local financial management is a key example. Decision- making structures will be required to determine financial priorities before arriving at the activities of budgeting and accounting. There has been a move- ment towards more participation in decision making at middle-management level and below but such democratic involvement consumes time. However, it need not be time taken up wholly in meetings. Staff can be encouraged to submit ideas and proposals in written form which may be considered by senior management and the problematic areas addressed specifically.

The other side of the coin is the removal of layers of intermediate admin- istration which inhibit the school's ability to act swiftly. In the past schools wishing to purchase items of equipment had to approach a purchasing officer in the LEA who followed a lengthy procedure of obtaining estimates and choosing an appropriate provider. While the headteacher is accountable to the school governors for good housekeeping and must spend wisely, it will now be possible to expedite purchase. Admission of pupils to schools, which is con- sidered in the second chapter of the 1988 Act, offers another example of time saving to hard-pressed management. [. . .] No longer do schools have to await the LEA decision on admission numbers arrived at (on occasion) in arbitrary fashion and often too late for effective decision making. Open enrolment may be threatening to many schools but it will certainly save time.

IDENTIFYING PRIORITIES

Approaches to more effective management of time have often taken as a starting point the compilation of a diary chronicling how time is utilized at present. This approach is predicated on a belief prevalent in management literature that it is important to know where you are now before determining where you want to go. The problem with this method of attack is the difficulty in designing an analytic instrument which makes sense of the myriad of data obtained. The result is that many investigations such as that undertaken by Hall, Mackay, and Morgan (1986) simply reflect what headteachers in schools already know – that their working day is hectic and fragmented and their activity characterized by brevity and variety. The approach proposed here is to identify priorities in the use of time as a first step so that the process of analysis and evaluation which follows is more clearly focused within an appropriate framework.

Establishment of priorities and goals is a key activity for the effective education manager otherwise s(he) is likely to be blown by whatever wind is strongest. In the nebulous world of education, where ends and means are questioned and disputed, the lack of clarity is often compounded by the manager who takes on everything that is asked of him or her and is unwilling to say 'No'. The setting of priorities is about deciding what is important and the following priorities profile is offered as an aid to such investigation.

Priorities profile

- *What are your long-term aspirations for the school?* A common problem claimed by staff in schools is that it is difficult to identify and sustain a clear sense of mission. The vision of the way forward becomes lost in the clinging mud of day-to-day problems and emergencies.
- *What do you identify as your role in pursuing these aspirations?* It is important that senior management takes a helicopter view so that the urgent and pressing but less important does not force out consideration of important objectives both in the short-term and long-term. The headteacher, in particular, has a central responsibility to keep the main objectives of the school in sight.
- *What do you see as your major management priorities?* Kotter (1982) maintains that it is crucial for the manager to have a clear 'agenda' with established priorities. He argues that, although the manager's world is frenetic, spasmodic, and often reactive, it is, nevertheless, purposive. For example, a deputy headteacher with responsibility for staff development may determine needs and exercise influence through the informal networks. The daily encounters with colleagues may provide opportunities to share and explore issues of concern both for the individual and the school.
- *What are the main management activities involved in pursuing these*

priorities? It is important for senior staff to identify the main management tasks and to decide which to retain and which to delegate. The head-teachers have considerable flexibility in determining what their major con-tributions are to be but must ensure that the various functions are clearly assigned. The headteacher retains ultimate accountability and the functions newly devolved to school level must be included among the priorities.

By a carefully planned and clearly articulated process of delegation senior staff can have a more certain picture of the specific activities each wishes or is required to be engaged in. For example, within the new framework of the national curriculum a senior teacher may have curriculum design as a high priority. It will be necessary to look beyond the 'global curriculum' and to identify key areas for attention. Such areas may be determined by the core and foundation subjects of the proposed national curriculum or it may be expedi-ent to respond to growing and newly developing areas like economic aware-ness, health education, and information technology. In both cases it is necessary to decide the nature of the support to be given, the action required and the demands on energy and time.

Primary schools will have particular difficulty in finding time for curricu-lum development and in addressing the many activities associated with LMS. As primary teachers tend to relate to one class or grouping for most of the working day it is not easy to find cover to release staff. This is also par-ticularly true of the teaching principal in smaller schools. Some schools have met this challenge by adopting pedagogical approaches like team teaching and resource-based learning. Other primary schools have formed cluster groups or consortia to allow exchange of staff and, in some cases, an extra member of staff has been negotiated with the LEA to manufacture free time and to obtain specialist curriculum expertise. The challenge is to look closely and critically at prevailing practice and to devise ways of making time available.

PRESENT USE OF TIME

The following questions should assist the manager to compile a more complete picture of present management activities and to compare these with the desired activities identified through the use of the priorities profile paying particular attention to the new demands imposed by the 1988 Act.

(1) What are the main management activities in which you engage at present?
(2) How are these activities determined? (job description, prescription from above, negotiation, established practice, self-determination.)
(3) Are these the activities identified as your priorities?
(4) How much time do you give to important and less important tasks as you see them?
(5) How much time do you spend on activities which you feel do not benefit pupils, staff, the school or yourself? On whom/what is this time spent?

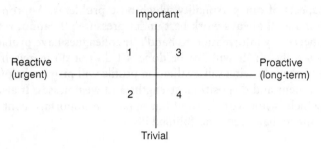

Figure 17.1 Classification framework

A searching, rigorous response to the above questions requires some kind of methodical investigation of present practice. The priorities identified and ordered earlier and the nature of the specific questions to which an answer is desired will determine the choice of approach used to ascertain how time is currently spent. It is desirable for the individual to design a specific instrument on the basis of the priorities identified. Too often instruments are designed without a clear perception of the exact information that is required and in what form it is wanted.

Figure 17.1 offers a simple four quadrant framework which may be used to locate and analyse the spectrum of management activity recorded in the time log. It is likely that most managers operate in quadrants 1 and 2 and are therefore working under constant stress and pressure. Often they may not be initiating events but are merely reacting to demands from others. Perhaps they are unwilling to say 'No' and therefore are doing many of the tasks which should be done by colleagues. There may be a lack of clarity about role and functions in the school so that unexpected problems are more likely to surface. Quadrant 2 is perhaps the most uncomfortable and least satisfying in which to reside although some managers may be happy to feel busy engaging in trivial pursuits. A manager in quadrant 3 is more likely to be undertaking important tasks and addressing key problems in circumstances over which s(he) has control and influence. Hopefully the message is clear – routine and trivial administrative tasks and crisis action are categories of activity that should be reduced and replaced as far as possible by the important, whether immediate or long-term. Perhaps one of the positive outcomes of the 1988 Act will be to encourage schools and their governing bodies to engage in more proactive long-term activities and in this context the issue of strategic planning addressed later in this chapter is of particular importance.

SELF-EVALUATION

The scrutiny of how time is utilized leads inevitably to scrutiny of self. It is only by knowing ourselves better that many of the difficulties and resolutions may be identified. Often we are inclined to step back and refuse to acknowledge certain aspects of our personality which pose problems. Appropriate excuses are often made: 'I always work best under pressure'; 'I cannot respond until I have the necessary information to hand'; 'If colleagues have problems I cannot refuse to see them'; 'It will not be done if I do not do it myself'. An honest response to the following self-evaluation profile will provide helpful indicators of temperament and disposition, strengths and weaknesses. It also asks about activity which is not work related but makes an important contribution to a more complete, balanced, and fulfilled life.

Self-evaluation profile

- Which management activities do you do best?
- Which management activities do you dislike doing?
- When and in what circumstances do you feel under time pressure?
- Do you feel that you succeed in balancing work-based activities and your private life? If not, which areas are neglected?
- Do you feel that generally you have energy and dynamism to spare?
- Do you manage to build free time into your working day?
- If you could remodel your job what changes would you make?
- If you could reorder your allocation of time what changes would you make?

The answers to the above questions should increase self-awareness and identify some of the time problems that managers typically encounter. Often managers will choose to do things which they like or which they can do well. Where there is lack of competence or tasks are disagreeable and difficult then these are likely to be left undone. This has implications for self-development and staff development in the school. The self-evaluation profile can be used to identify interests, strengths and weaknesses of senior members of staff. However, it is likely that areas will be identified in which no member of staff appears to have a particular interest or expertise. Nevertheless, these areas have to be attended to and competences have to be developed so that all aspects of the management task are accomplished. [. . .] As stated earlier the headteacher does not have to become an accountant but often expertise does reside at a senior level within the school. Ideally there is a case for an ancillary addition to establishment with expertise and seniority.

Research into educational institutions (Martin and Willower, 1981) has indicated that early morning is often the busiest time – telephone calls, correspondence, unresolved problems from the previous day are typical pressures on the manager. Schools are also characterized by cyclical activity. Budgeting, requisitioning, timetabling, and the preparing of reports and profiles are characteristic examples and may be alleviated by appropriate delegation and dispersion. It is likely that the reader can identify colleagues who are 'workaholics'. Typically they work long hours and bring reams of paper home. Family, friends and leisure suffer at the expense of work. Adair (1988) points out that the Pareto principle also applies to time – 80 per cent of the really productive, creative work will be done in 20 per cent of the time. Allocation of appropriate time to home, family, relaxation, and recreation will lead to a happier, more fulfilled, balanced life style and reduce the likelihood of stress-related illnesses. Research has indicated that managerial activity is often fragmented, unremitting, and spontaneous. Much of this piecemeal, disjointed behaviour may be positive and purposive but equally much may occur because of lack of organization and the assumption of an unthinking management style.

OBSTACLES TO EFFECTIVE TIME MANAGEMENT

The last two questions in the evaluation profile ask managers to look critically at their present activity and allocation of time and to devise ways in which both may be revised to increase effectiveness. Such diagnosis may be helped by the identification of recurring problems in managing time which may be tackled and overcome.

Procrastination

To defer or put off action until some future time without reasonable justification is a very human failing. Compelling reasons may be sought and produced: 'I'm too busy now to respond to that problem – I'll look at it again when I have more time' or 'Allow the dust to settle'. It may be on occasion that deferment is a sound course of action but if it happens habitually then its validity must be questioned. Often unpleasant or demanding tasks are put off which become more difficult with each succeeding day. In addition, work piles up and important information may be buried with it leading to missed deadlines. If it has become habitual to be dilatory then one must determine to break the pattern. Often it is a case of taking a simple, first step – that meeting with the awkward member of staff or breaking of unwelcome news – which often turns out to be less threatening than was imagined. It is perhaps more difficult to change behaviour which reflects a casual and easy-going personality. The setting of personal deadlines and adhering to them offers one way of establishing order and priority. It is salutary to remember that tomorrow never comes and the temptation to defer should be resisted.

Open door

'Open door' became a fashionable management maxim in the 1960s. It suggested management which was accessible, responsive and sympathetic but for many managers the other side of the coin was a plethora of often unwelcome interruptions. Clearly it is important to offer ready access to staff, parents, or other parties if the need arises and in such circumstances interruptions may be inevitable. However there are valid and invalid interruptions, and judgements have to be made to decide the validity of claims on time. There are a number of filters which may be employed. If structures and channels of communication are clearly delineated the caller may be referred to the pertinent member of staff. Very often headteachers and senior managers have a secretary or access to one who can defer callers, keep them at bay or pass them to the appropriate colleague. This has implications for effective delegation which will be considered later. When the enforced interruptions are inevitable there are strategies which may be employed to abbreviate them:

- Identify the purpose of the visit and stick to it.
- Set apart times of the day for open access.
- Limit the time for each caller and specify it.
- Body language is important: do not become comfortably seated and established.

Task jumping

Often the most frequent source of interruption is the manager him(her)self. If a task becomes difficult then one is tempted to turn to something else. Many find it difficult to concentrate for protracted periods of time. It is prudent to remember that more is likely to be achieved in one hour of continuous application than in several hours of interrupted work because a recovery period is necessary after each stoppage. It is expedient to discover if the task jumping is self-inflicted. Mintzberg (1973) found that five chief executives under investigation 'frequently interrupted their desk work to place telephone calls or to request that subordinates come by'. Martin and Willower (1981) in their investigation of the managerial behaviour of five high-school principals found that most (81.4 per cent) of the activities that the subjects entered into ranged from one to four minutes and the modal time duration for the 3,730 tasks observed over 25 days was one minute. Also 50 per cent of all observed activities were interrupted. They call this pattern of behaviour 'The busy person syndrome'. Perhaps the sheer volume of work may offer some explanation but it would also appear that the managers contributed in part to the problem. Effort is required to break the frenetic cycle of activity and to build in some more coherent pattern of work.

Administrivia

In management terminology a distinction is often made in the United Kingdom between management and administration. Administration is portrayed as the mechanical, routine support and maintenance of a system with administrators frequently lacking the authority to make judgements and decisions in key areas like policy making and the allocation of resources. On the other hand, management involves crucial processes like problem solving, planning, decision making, organizing, leading, and influencing. The term 'administrivia' has a further connotation implying engagement in trivialities and unimportant detail. Hall, MacKay, and Morgan (1986) in their study of fifteen headteachers demonstrated that some devoted considerable time to such activity and it is certainly a common complaint by headteachers that 'administrivia' so often takes over. There are clear implications for judicious delegation and the sharing out of routine matters to allow senior management to address important matters of policy and its implementation.

Meetings

Hall, Mackay, and Morgan (1986) also discovered that an overwhelming volume of headteachers' activity was interpersonal. While many of the interchanges were with individuals, a considerable amount of time was taken up with meetings. A meeting may be described as the organized or spontaneous coming together of people at a common time and place for specific purposes. These purposes may be predetermined or may arise from a chance encounter with a group of colleagues. Because meetings may take up and waste substantial amounts of time headteachers have to consider them critically. They may decide to carry out a review of meetings in the school and, in particular, those which they attend. Relevant questions may include:

- Are the meetings (series of meetings) necessary?
- If they are necessary what is their purpose?
- How often do they take place?
- How many meetings are required?
- Do I need to attend? If the answer is 'yes', do I need to attend all of them?

There is no doubt that meetings contribute vitally to the effective management of a school but it is to be suspected that many unnecessary meetings are held when the group has already fulfilled its function or when intervening activity or time for reflection is required. Meetings may serve a variety of purposes including the following:

- Information giving/exchange
- Direction
- Problem solving
- Discussion
- Negotiation
- Decision-making

It may well be that many of these activities occur in the course of a meeting but it is helpful for the manager to have a clear, predominant purpose in mind. [. . .] Because meetings are costly as illustrated earlier, the manager may decide to be ruthless in their review.

However, in a dynamic school, meetings are important instruments which encourage commitment and participation and if they are necessary then there are ways of saving time. It may be appropriate to delegate functions to smaller groups who report back either to senior management, larger groupings, or full staff meetings. It is worthwhile to prepare carefully and to provide preliminary documentation which may be digested before rather than during the meeting. If possible formal meetings should not be called at short notice. Agenda should be brief and adhered to.

The chairperson occupies a key position in acting both as leader and adjudicator. The chairperson can decide in advance what is the maximum time for each item and, if necessary, operate a guillotine. The tone of the meeting may be set by a clear exposition of the purpose of the meeting and by demonstrating conciseness and clarity throughout. It is sound practice not to allow decisions arrived at in previous meetings to be reconsidered and reversed unless there are serious reasons for so doing. The chairperson can discourage the discursive, dominant, and dilatory and be firm, fair and supportive without being dismissive. The momentum should be sustained without losing healthy, pertinent discussion and the generation of ideas.

STRATEGIES FOR MORE EFFECTIVE TIME MANAGEMENT

Having identified some of the problems which may contribute to time pressure for those who manage schools some strategies for recovery, if not total cure, emerge from the process of diagnosis.

Planning and the setting of goals

Many experts who have pronounced and written on management, stress the importance of setting goals or intentions for the organization and by implication for those who work within it (Bolman and Deal, 1984). This projection of targets, a looking and thinking forward in time, is central to the process of planning. While recognizing the political and transitory reality of schools it is nevertheless possible by careful, proactive planning to make more effective use of time. The term 'goal' clearly derives from sporting endeavours and is the declared intention of teams of players. There is the implication that all team members are or should be co-operating and contributing to that end. Such a claim should not be taken for granted in organizations like schools where territory and competition are central to the culture and value systems, and may stimulate behaviour which does not seek to pursue common aims. Equally status, reward, autonomy, professional interest and individual fulfilment are personal goals which may not be in harmony with the goals of those who manage and therefore seek the general good of the school. [. . .]

Figure 17.2 presents a model of planning which may be applied to schools and identifies key external and internal participants and sources of influence.

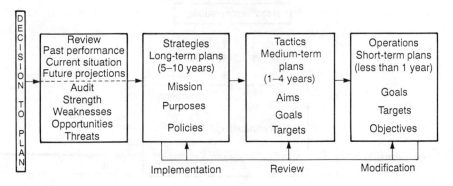

Figure 17.2   The planning process

The activities of review and audit seek to offer a more complete picture of the working environment. Review reminds us that knowing where we have been (the past) and where we are (the present) are vital contributions to determining where we want to go (the future). The activity of audit identifies what opportunities and threats are facing the school and what are strengths and weaknesses. This exercise reminds us that managing is the art of the possible and the process of audit is about deciding what is possible.

Mission has become a popular term in planning parlance and refers to the overall aspirations of the school. The mission statement may be regarded as the foundation stone of school purposes and policy. The terms 'aim' and 'goal' are often used interchangeably and express in general terms intentions which the school seeks to pursue. Targets and objectives are usually more specific declarations of intent often expressed in behavioural terms. It is sound practice to make aims, goals, and objectives as specific and realistic as possible and to ensure that they are attainable but demanding. It is also expedient to set reasonable deadlines which may be modified if circumstances change. By judicious management of time the headteacher can ensure that (s)he is properly engaged in the development of strategies and tactics rather than becoming totally enmeshed in short-term operations.

Delegation

There is, in a typical school, an often untapped bank of expertise and knowledge available from both staff and pupils. Frequently senior managers are tempted to undertake tasks which can be carried out very competently by others. The delegation of such tasks should free the manager to engage in higher order management activities like planning, policy making, and innovating. [The modern] management arena also indicates priorities which will be high on the agenda of schools in the near future. Banking offers the term 'audit' to management vocabulary to indicate that talent and competence can

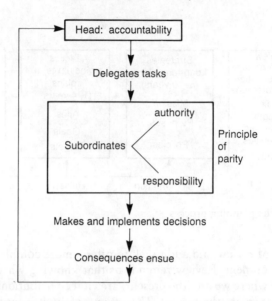

Figure 17.3   The process of delegation

be identified. Staff may be encouraged to specify their strengths by means of a sensitively administered questionnaire or through skilful appraisal techniques. The utilization of those strengths offers a rich source of fulfilment and motivation at a time when a lack of mobility both within and between schools is likely to lead to debilitation and declining morale. Delegation should also be an important tool of staff development and it should not be seen as an opportunity for passing the unpleasant, boring aspects of management to other staff. Joan Dean (1985) offers a useful questionnaire: if the manager responds affirmatively to statements about working long hours, concentrating on minutiae, carrying out jobs which could be done by others and believing that the manager can do most jobs better than colleagues then it is likely that there is not enough delegation.

The simple model in Figure 17.3 illustrates the delegation process. The principle of parity indicates that the process of delegation involves giving the subordinate sufficient authority to carry out a decision as well as responsibility for it. In the education system ultimate accountability resides with the headteacher although authority and responsibility may be delegated. However, it may be difficult for staff who are relatively junior in the school to exercise authority over senior management or, on occasion, middle management such as heads of department and year heads. This may necessitate political skills such as negotiation, bargaining, persuasion and compromise. One has also to remember that professional teachers are likely to resist bureaucratic control as typified in the terms 'boss' and 'subordinate'. It may be more acceptable for the superior to present themselves as a co-ordinator, facilitator or enabler managing a team of professional specialists.

Effective delegation may consist of the following activities:

- Find out the competences and experience of intended delegates.
- Introduce intention and ascertain willingness.
- Organize relevant staff development activity.
- Define parameters and outcomes of task and allocated resources.
- Check understanding and agreement.
- Determine procedures and structures which may be followed if problems arise: delegation is not abdication.
- Provide for contingencies.
- Grant and make public the necessary authority over staff and resources.
- Offer feedback and positive reinforcement where appropriate.
- Carry out regular review unobtrusively.

Peak time

There are differences between individuals in relation to when they work best. Some maintain that they work most effectively late at night while others prefer to rise early and use the first hours of the morning. Physiologists claim that the human metabolism is governed by biorhythms or cycles which are reinforced by the imposed periods of sleep and waking. This would suggest that people should be fresher and more energetic in the morning after a good night's rest. Given that the human body also burns energy through the course of a hard working day it is likely that teachers who have worked hard from early morning to the end of the school day may find it difficult to regenerate themselves to reasonable levels of efficiency in the evening. The argument to date supports the validity of testing one's capacity to work in the early morning if this has not been tried before or at least to use the morning hours in preference to afternoon or evening. Research also indicates that people work better if there are breaks to allow the system to revitalize itself. The number and timing of breaks may be determined by the nature of the task being undertaken. Creative work demands freshness and dynamism while routine administration may be less demanding. Nevertheless, repetitive work also demands concentration if mistakes are to be avoided.

Psychologists claim that the mind works even during sleep and in the process of sleeping on a problem the subconscious mind may offer a solution. Apart from the possibility of new insights it also makes sense to 'sleep' on an important decision to avoid arriving at unwarranted conclusions in the heat of the moment. Adair (1988) offers the concept of 'moonlighting' which he describes as waking naturally in the early hours of the morning with ideas tumbling in the mind. He suggests that those ideas should be recorded and captured. The danger of saturation and exhaustion through working too long supports the wisdom of suitably apportioning the school day if protracted concentration is required. Such endeavour can be punctuated by less demanding activities such as more informal conversations with staff or visitors.

Free time

Long working hours, excessive paper work, the pressure of deadlines, frequent interruptions, and the intrusion of the unexpected all contribute to a working environment which offers no opportunity to recharge batteries or to pause for reflection and critical review of what the school is doing and where it is going. Unremitting pressure of work is likely to lead to stress and the myriad of accompanying symptoms which are often recognized only at crisis point. Perhaps the increasing inclusion of consideration of stress in conference sessions and the growing volume of research into its causes and remedies are indications of a growing recognition of pressures in schools, not least the pressure of time. If the manager can set apart a period of time each day for quiet reflection and consideration of what tomorrow and the longer term future may bring, it is more probable that s(he) can remain in control of the management environment. The time log mentioned earlier offers an instrument to review critically what is being done. The manager can ask two questions: 'Is this activity necessary?', and 'What would happen if I did not do it?' Delegation and the reduction of time spent in attending meetings and routine administration may offer the opportunity to do less a little better and to make that small but vital oasis of free time for regeneration and relaxation. Colleagues and secretaries may be conditioned to respect and protect it and the location of the daily half an hour may alter from day to day to accommodate the changing pattern of management practice.

CONCLUSION

This chapter has concentrated on the identification and setting of priorities as a framework for effective management of time. It therefore would seem appropriate to distil what has gone before and to identify some guidelines to assist managers in educational institutions to use their time better.

- Identify long-term, middle-term, and short-term goals/targets for the school and yourself.
- Determine the important and less important tasks and allocate time accordingly.
- Engage in frank self-analysis to discover strengths and weaknesses.
- Increase proactivity and reduce reactivity where it is possible.
- Review utilization of time periodically (termly, six-monthly).
- Delegate effectively.
- Look critically at the management of meetings and individual encounters.
- Use peak time and build in periods of free time.
- Balance work and private life.
- Set reasonable deadlines and reduce procrastination.
- Learn to say 'No'.
- Plan your programme of activity daily, weekly, termly, and annually and try to stick to it without threatening responsiveness and flexibility.

It may be expedient to remember Murphy's Law which offers wise advice not merely about time but about the complex world of management:

> 'Nothing is as easy as it looks.
> Everything takes longer than you expect.
> And if anything can go wrong it will
> At the worst possible moment.'

REFERENCES

Adair, J. (1988) *Effective Time Management*, London: Pan.

Bolman, L.G. and Deal, T.E. (1984) *Modern Approaches to Understanding and Managing Organisations*, San Francisco: Jossey Bass.

Dean, J. (1985) *Managing the Secondary School*, London: Croom Helm.

DES (1987) *School Teachers' Pay and Conditions*, London: HMSO.

Franklin, B. (1745) *Advice to a Young Tradesman*, Philadelphia: Humphreys.

Hall, V., MacKay, H., and Morgan, C. (1986) *Head Teachers at Work*, Milton Keynes: Open University Press.

Kotter, J.P. (1982) *The General Manager*, London: Free Press.

Martin, W.J. and Willower, D.J. (1981) 'The managerial behavior of High School Principals', *Educational Administration Quarterly*, vol. 17, no. 1.

Mintzberg, H. (1973) *The Nature of Managerial Work*, London: Harper & Row.

Wilkinson, C. and Cave, E. (1987) *Teaching and Managing: Inseparable Activities in Schools*, London: Croom Helm.

18

TEACHERS' COPING RESOURCES

Jack Dunham

[. . .] My research has revealed considerable differences between teachers in their responses to similar experiences in school, for example, during reorganization and other major changes some teachers reported few signs of adverse reactions and gave several indications of positive responses such as an increased zest in their teaching. These results directed my attention to the strategies teachers use when they encounter heavy work pressures. I found that they were using a broad range of resources which I shall identify in this chapter as personal, interpersonal, organizational and community.

This view of coping resources is very similar to a number of approaches which have been made towards understanding how people cope with adversities without developing major stress reactions. Caplan (1964) identified the seven characteristics of coping behaviour as:

(1) Active search for information
(2) Free expression of both positive and negative feelings
(3) Asking for help from other people
(4) Breaking problems down into manageable bits and working through them one at a time
(5) Fatigue countered in pacing of one's efforts
(6) Active mastery of feelings where possible but acceptance of lack of control when it occurs
(7) Trust in oneself and optimism about outcome.

A study by Mechanic (1967) published three years later proposed that when people attempt to cope with heavy pressures they bring into operation skills, experience, knowledge and personality characteristics in addition to supportive relationships at work, at home and in the community. This perspective suggests that in attempting to understand stress reactions more attention should be given to problem-solving and coping behaviour. The writer argued:

> If we are to understand the stress situation of a man falling out of a boat, the main determinant of how much stress he experiences will be whether or not he can swim.

He argued that the extent to which individuals experience stress in any situation depends on the manner in which they assess both the demands and their competence in dealing with them, and in their preparations of the skills necessary for them to handle these demands with a greater sense of competence.

A third perspective on coping resources which is similar to the one I use in my work with teachers suggests that coping has two functions. First, coping is concerned with changing a situation which is stressful. This may be achieved either by altering the nature of the situation itself or by modifying a person's perception of the situation. The second function of coping is to deal with the thoughts, feelings and bodily reactions to stress rather than to attempt to change the stress situation or a person's perception of it. Both kinds of coping require the use of positive factors which Lazarus calls 'uplifts'. He suggests that the most frequently used are: relating well with a spouse or lover, relating well with friends, completing a task, feeling healthy, getting enough sleep, eating out, meeting responsibilities, visiting, telephoning or writing to someone, spending time with one's family, having pleasurable activities at home (Lazarus, 1981).

This list has interesting similarities with the coping actions identified by teachers in my research and in a study of staff stress in secondary schools in York reported by Kyriacou (1980). In his investigation three different types of resources were identified. The first consisted of talking about problems and feelings to others and seeking support from friends, colleagues and family. The second kind focused on different ways of dealing with the sources of stress. The third type of coping actions was mainly directed towards out-of-school activities and seemed to be aimed at distracting the teachers' attention away from stress at work to more pleasurable and relaxing interests. Kyriacou also asked the teachers which resources they often used to try and reduce stress. The twenty most frequently used coping actions were:

- Try to keep things in perspective
- Try to avoid confrontation
- Try to relax after work
- Try to take some immediate action on the basis of your present understanding of the situation
- Think objectively about the situation and keep your feelings under control
- Stand back and rationalize the situation
- Try to nip potential sources of stress in the bud
- Try to reassure yourself everything is going to work out right
- Do not let the problem go until you have solved it or reconciled it satisfactorily

- Make sure people are aware you are doing your best
- Try to forget work when the school day is finished
- Try to see the humour of the situation
- Consider a range of plans for handling the sources of stress – set priorities
- Make a concerted effort to enjoy yourself with some pleasurable activity after work
- Try not to worry or think about it
- Express your feelings and frustrations to others so that you can think rationally about the problems
- Throw yourself into work and work harder and longer
- Think of good things in the future
- Talk about the situation with someone at work
- Express your irritation to colleagues at work just to be able to let off steam.

A more recent research study using the 'Ways of coping' checklist developed by Lazarus has been presented by Parkes (1988). She investigated the coping strategies that students taking a one-year PGCE course used to deal with a stressful episode. Her findings showed that their stress levels were low when coping strategies were strong and vice versa. Social support was a very significant factor in effective stress management for these student teachers.

My attempts to identify the resources which staff use to reduce stress are based on two methods. I ask them, 'How do you try to reduce your work stress?' and I also invite them to identify their coping strategies on a checklist. Their answers to this question and the items that are ticked on their checklist suggest that they are using a wide range of skills, techniques, knowledge, experience, relationships, thoughts and activities which I have classified as personal, interpersonal, organizational and community resources.

Personal resources include work strategies, positive attitudes and positive pressures such as designing course or lesson material and a certain amount of variety, switching off, trying to come to terms with each stress situation, self-pacing, bringing feelings and opinions into the open, acceptance of the problem and learning the job in more detail. The out-of-school activities which teachers as individuals use to reduce feelings of tensions, anger and agitation include gardening, painting, walking, cooking, baking, cycling, driving their cars fast and praying.

The interpersonal resources which teachers use include talking over stressful incidents with their partner, meeting people who are unconnected with teaching and talking to a friend who has a similar job and using him or her as a sounding-board and 'a verbal punching bag'.

Organizational resources come from colleagues in school with whom they are able to discuss their problems, worries and feelings. They also include supportive departmental, pastoral and senior management teams, in-service training and induction courses and help from advisers and education officers.

Community activities reported by teachers include bell-ringing, squash, badminton, football, drama and choral singing.

The use of some of these resources in the process of coping with stress is very clearly expressed in the following three reports. The first is from a head of faculty:

How do I cope?
(1) Sometimes the very complexity and difficulty of my work makes it enjoyable. I also enjoy leading a team and exercising responsibility.
(2) I am a very active person, professionally and socially. I can compartmentalize things.
(3) I am a good organizer and within my faculty I have fairly efficient administrative and organizational systems.
(4) I keep many projects, at various stages of completion, on the go at once.
(5) Usually I can motivate others and lead charismatically.
(6) I am fairly lucky in the members of my departmental team who can shift some of the workload away from me.
(7) For eight years I practised Martial Arts at a fairly high level, eventually achieving a Black Belt. I occasionally exercise the technique of restraint and self-control to produce inner and outer calmness that I was taught and picked up in this situation. This is a great help and I tend to remain fairly calm and approachable even under stress.
(8) I am still a keen sportsman, playing soccer at weekends and occasionally training and running in the week. This is a great help in relaxing stored-up aggression.

The second analysis of the coping process was written by a head of sixth form:

My ways of relieving stress factors are varied, but within school the satisfactory completion of a major task in itself helps relieve pressure. Also, for myself, the peaceful interaction in teaching a sixth-form group in my room helps greatly in focusing one's mind and having a chance to enjoy more academic pursuits. At home, I can only fully relax by doing something different, not sitting and thinking about what I haven't done in the day. I need to be active and out enjoying a completely different set of circumstances (mostly away from the people with whom I work).

The third report was written by a MPG teacher:

This coping resource is only employed on days when I am at school. As soon as the bell rings for lunch I leave the school and run four or five miles in the surrounding countryside. I time my return and subsequent exit from the changing room to coincide with the bell for the end of lunch. This activity has now become a vital part of my day. I refuse to give up my lunchtime for any meeting in school and in the early days encountered much hostility from colleagues who felt I obviously had time to spare and that I should be engaged in school work. Explanations about relaxation and the appreciation of the changing seasons, open air and varieties of weather fell on deaf ears. However, I persisted and most staff now accept that I am simply not available for *anything* at lunchtime. This, I feel was the beginning of my discovery of the ultimate coping resource and that is simply that 'it doesn't really matter'. In other words, the root of my beliefs is that school is not my life, but is part of it. It is a job that enables me to feed myself, provide myself with shelter, keep warm and enjoy myself. That is not to say that I am not dedicated. I enjoy my job and take great care over the education of the pupils in my charge, but I have come to realize that, whatever demand is made upon me, is not so important that it has to dominate my life. I ensure that what needs to be done gets done, but without it controlling or affecting my private life. After the first few times of saying 'no' or apologizing to a class for a delay in marking work, or leaving a meeting early, it is surprising how much pleasanter life becomes, for the simple reason that I am in control of the demands made upon me, rather than the demands controlling me.

The strategy of personal control is a valuable uplift for this person [. . .] The other two traits are commitment, which this teacher's report also identifies, and the perception of work pressures as challenges rather than as threats or as acceptable and enjoyable rather than as sources of stress. My recent research has identified many positive aspects of teachers' work. These include:

- The general 'busyness' of the day and the variety of tasks to get through.
- Interaction with students in a teaching situation.
- Preparation and implementation of new teaching methods or topics not taught before.
- The opportunities to do one's own thing without anyone breathing down my neck.
- The challenge of a constantly changing environment.
- Reading and reflecting and acting on any conclusions.
- The unpredictability of the job – not knowing what might happen during the day.
- Working to deadlines (provided that there aren't too many things working for the same deadlines).
- Trying to find solutions to problems.
- Researching the subject.
- The pressures of preparing, organizing and presenting academic work to students and getting them to the point of peak performance exactly at the time of examinations.
- New challenges when relevant, sensible, etc.
- Lessons which go well.
- Working with others to achieve an outcome.
- Preparing lessons, teaching lessons and marking homework, but even these items are becoming less and less enjoyable because of other pressures.
- All the pressures produced by everyday classroom teaching including conflicts and difficulties are acceptable and produce little or no stress.

The coping methods used by teachers can be seen in the following brief statements, which are grouped into the four categories of personal, interpersonal, organizational and community resources. The personal action is sub-divided into four types: work strategies, positive attitudes, positive pressures and out-of-school activities.

PERSONAL RESOURCES OF TEACHERS

Work strategies

- By working harder – this certainly raises one's self-esteem and not infrequently removes the cause of a stressful situation.
- Making a positive effort to be more efficient and organized.
- By having at least half an hour lunch break daily. I used to work straight through.
- Having in my own mind a clear sense of priorities of what has to be done.
- Spreading the workload by listing essential jobs at the beginning of each week.

Positive attitudes

- Recognizing the dangers of allowing stress factors to combine in my mind so that I reach hyper self-critical conclusions: I'm under stress – I can't cope – I can't teach – I'm an inadequate person.
- Planning several events, including new and interesting activities for future weeks or weekends.
- Say to myself – I have coped before – I will cope now.

Positive attitudes

- I enjoy the variety of work.
- Pressure which has a clean finishing point.
- Pressure with a purpose.

Out-of-school activities

- Hard physical exercise. Meditation, relaxation techniques and yoga exercises.
- Cuddling the cats.

INTERPERSONAL RESOURCES OF TEACHERS

The importance of good relationships can be identified in a number of statements concerning the social life of staff, which is as important to them as their school life. The support teachers receive from wife or husband or friends is frequently named as a very positive factor in stress reduction. Three statements can be used to illustrate different aspects of these relationships:

- I reduce stress by talking things through with my husband who isn't in the profession.
- My supportive relationship with my wife is of enormous help, not just in providing overt and tacit reassurance but also because of the physical benefits of a loving and satisfying sexual life.
- I am not afraid of discussing my problems or relating my 'horrific' days with a friend outside school.

ORGANIZATIONAL RESOURCES OF TEACHERS

Information from staff which can be classified under organizational resources is considerably rarer than personal or interpersonal. Support from senior staff is reported, but the importance of good relationships with colleagues is much more frequently described as a positive factor in tackling stress, as the following brief comment illustrates:

> Where stress is produced through disagreement with the action of the head I find discussion with colleagues and then the head helps to reduce stress – openness helps!

Another organizational factor is the boost felt after attending a supportive course and the resource potential of this experience can be identified in the following comments. They were written as part of the evaluation by members of my course in staff management at Bristol University. They were responding to the open-ended questionnaire item, 'What were the strongest features of the course?'

- The detailed preparation leading to very searching and relevant questions, the pooling of ideas and original solutions.
- Having a taste of academic life again.
- Stretching one's mind, learning new concepts and writing an academic essay again.
- Meeting other teachers from a variety of schools and backgrounds.
- The opportunity to meet so many friendly and supportive people.
- Learning a great deal which has had a great influence on my own self-perception.
- Enabling me to accept and manage my feelings of stress more easily.
- Your quiet accepting manner, which is just what is needed after a long day at school.
- The confidence you gave me.
- The interesting Thursdays, which I really looked forward to.

COMMUNITY RESOURCES OF TEACHERS

The community activities which teachers report – for example, football, gliding and sailing – seem to have for some of them an importance beyond that of relaxation or pleasure. The activities seem to enable them to assume life-styles which are alternatives to those followed in their professional roles. Their importance was indicated by a head of a mathematics department who wrote:

> For coping with stress, sometimes I become a workaholic in other directions, since outside school I am a District Councillor and Chairman of a Planning and Development Committee! This involves contact with the public and is an area where I can take decisions and carry the can! I also find walking helps or swimming or playing loud music. I also find, living nineteen miles from school, I have a pleasant journey home through open country which can either help me think through problems or switch off!

The deputy head of a primary school was using a very different lifestyle to reduce his feelings of stress which were mostly caused by his headteacher's non-delegating leadership style:

> If things become too irritating I go bell-ringing or don my crash helmet and ride on my extra-curricular motor bike up the M4 at 80 mph. This helps!

These brief reports of personal, interpersonal, organizational and community resources can now be compared with my second method of enquiry, which is

Table 18.1 Percentage of staff in a secondary school identifying coping resources

Coping actions of teachers	%
Working evening and weekends	68
More sporting activities	26
Withdraw from staff to avoid their problems	12
Work harder	30
Deciding priorities and dropping unimportant jobs	54
Catching-up with family life in holidays	56
Dropping low-priority school tasks	26
Closed door strategy	2
Saying to oneself, 'I'll get organized next time'	22
Relaxed breathing	10
Muscle relaxation	10
Exercise	34
Hobby to get away from school mentally	32
Talking to others	54
Working 9–5 then forgetting about the job	6
Becoming philosophical – doing what you can but without worrying too much	40
Trying to pretend that a lot of things are not important	8
Planning well ahead	60
Developing different styles of teaching to enable me to cope with a continuous stretch of it	20
Application of Christian faith	18
Compromise	34
Stopping and settle for an unmarked set of books	24
Sod the school work – go out	30
Give up after a point	10
Refusal to do task	4
Backtracking	0
Preparing and marking less well than I would like	60

the use of a checklist of coping strategies. One of my current checklists was used by one of my students in her school and Table 18.1 indicates some of the coping actions of her colleagues.

The stress-reducing techniques of headteachers and deputy heads have also been investigated by asking them the question, 'How do you try to reduce or prevent your work stress?' The resources of deputies include a wide range of work strategies, coping attitudes and organizational support. These methods appear to have replaced to some extent the benefits which their less senior colleagues enjoy from family, friends and community activities. Some examples of these methods follow:

PERSONAL RESOURCES OF DEPUTY HEADS

Work strategies

- Arranging my office (e.g. putting a bolt on the door) so that I can relax undisturbed for a short while before evening functions.
- Coping with the demands means recognizing what they are, learning by experience . . . reading professional literature, visiting other schools, trying to keep an open mind and trying to be objective.
- Arriving at school early (8.00 a.m.) to be available before school begins and to plan my day and try and ensure a clear desk by 8.30 a.m.
- As I get to know the staff, I know the ones whom I can trust and delegate some of the jobs I used to do myself.
- Consider a range of plans for handling sources of stress.
- List priorities.
- Try to plan my day so that I am available at peak times.
- When stress and pressure is at its peak in school, I leave my office and walk round the school grounds on my own. This gets me away from my desk and gives me the opportunity to clear my head; it generally works very well.
- Coming into school when no staff are present to work out strategies.
- Have a target date for deeper issues.
- Make sure that problems are well defined when you take them to the head.
- Try to be available and to set up routine meetings while the pressure is off.
- Investigate problems as soon as possible.

Positive attitudes

- Accept that many pressures are inevitable and part of the job.
- Think positively – what an interesting and varied job I have!
- Accept that some things will not get done.

- Accept the situation.
- Decide on my own standards for the job rather than those of the head.
- Attempt to discipline myself to doing one thing at a time (not always succeeding).
- Constant self-reminders not to take self and day-to-day crises too seriously.

Out-of-school activities

- A night at home on the headphones and stereo usually works.
- The cat-nap is a technique I use when the work is approaching midnight.
- Keep Saturday totally apart from school whatever!
- Joining an evening class (yoga) to make a complete break from school once a week. Also making determined efforts to attend whatever else is happening however tired I feel.

INTERPERSONAL RESOURCES OF DEPUTY HEADS

- Making strenuous efforts not to work all the weekend but spend at least one complete day with my family.
- By trying to get more involved with my own children.

ORGANIZATIONAL RESOURCES OF DEPUTY HEADS

- I have a very good relationship with colleagues, especially with my immediate most senior colleagues, which facilitates and makes more effective our mutual support.
- By teamwork and reliance on other colleagues.
- Finding allies among the staff to try to disseminate my ideas.
- Have a good personal relationship with staff.
- Teaching is my haven.
- Have a few colleagues with whom (in different areas of work) it is possible to let off steam and explode in frustration.
- Talk in relaxed way to people even if (especially when!) uptight.
- I unload on the head and the other deputy.

COMMUNITY RESOURCES OF DEPUTY HEADS

- Find activities entirely different from school.
- Going away every holiday period and half-term.
- Every weekend to have a 'treat' built in – the greater the stress in the week, the greater the 'treat'.

The strategies of headteachers are similar to those identified by their deputies though heads appear to have a wider range of relationships available to them at the organizational level and they seem to be able to make greater use of community activities. The following reports illustrate their attempts to reduce stress:

PERSONAL RESOURCES OF HEADTEACHERS

Work strategies

My decision to be firm about boundaries has been particularly helpful to me in coping with stress. I made the decision never to take work home and to have a set limit to evening and holiday work at school. While this is sometimes more honoured in the letter than the spirit – i.e. I do take inner worries if not paperwork home – I think it has helped.

Positive attitudes

The importance of identifying the sources of stress has been clearly articulated by the head of a primary school:

In looking back and trying to decide what was particularly stressful in the past two years I find it difficult first of all to distinguish what was usually stressful and what was a normal strain of the work.

I think that stress can be distinguished through its effect of lack of sleep, anxious waking or waking very easily and feelings of depression about work. On the other hand it is not quite that easy because I might be awake thinking about an important decision without feeling any undue sense of strain or depression (maybe excitement) and at other times feelings of stress may seem to be due to an accumulation of minor things (especially at the end of term) – in fact the stress is perhaps worst where there is nothing to which it can be directly attributed – and it can be that once a source of stress is identified it immediately becomes less stressful.

Out-of-school activities

I practise meditation regularly, which produces effortless relaxation (morning and evening). The morning session makes me alert and ready for the day and is a preventive measure against stress building up during the day due to the inner relaxation it produces. In the evening after a hard day's work I am able to totally relax (twenty minutes) which neutralizes any accumulated tension, either muscular or mental that may be present.

INTERPERSONAL RESOURCES OF HEADTEACHERS

I have become aware of the need for support and supervision, of the value of someone outside the situation who can help one to see things which are blocked or difficult in a relationship and where I am reacting unconsciously or defensively. I have found some support through encounter groups, personal relationship courses and more recently through training as a marriage guidance counsellor. I think this has helped me to come to terms with my own stress and worry and to be more able to help others cope with theirs.

ORGANIZATIONAL RESOURCES OF HEADTEACHERS

Staff support

I feel my stress is greatly reduced by the good relationship between the staff and me. We discuss all problems extensively and very informally and although obviously the responsibility rests with me, the support of the staff is invaluable to me.

The deputy head

The deputy head has a special role as someone whom I see regularly and with whom I can talk openly, trying out alternatives, thinking through possibilities, sharing my doubts or fears and arriving at a decision that I feel is broader-based than if I tried to sort it out on my own.

Senior management team

My stress has been considerably reduced by the opportunity to discuss with the senior management team the problems in school. I find that unloading my stress upon them relieves me of my own stress.

The governors

There has been considerable support and active interest in the school by the governors. Also we are again fortunate in that there are no personality clashes.

Outside professional support

Other heads and the Advisory Service have provided valuable support in that they are prepared to take the time to listen while I talk out a problem with them. This is sometimes all it takes to solve the particular problem.

The pupils

The children have been a surprisingly supportive resource. I made an educational point of involving and informing them (the over-eights) with the developments of the school-closure crisis and the resulting comments, work and supportive feelings that have come back have been very encouraging.

COMMUNITY RESOURCES OF HEADTEACHERS

I reduce stress by ensuring that my life is not on a single track. I do this by pursuing other interests – mainly music and sport – so that on Monday mornings my body and spirit are refreshed.

I find that as a member of a motor racing club being at a race meeting blocks out all other thoughts.

As a Chief Observer in the Royal Observer Corps I have different responsibilities towards my crew and this helps to focus attention away from school.

Two heads sent me their clearly defined frameworks of the factors which sustain them as they tackle the pressures of being the head of a primary school and the head of a comprehensive school. I would like to use them as concluding summaries to this chapter. In the framework of the primary school head there are ten strategies:

  (1) Make full use of rubbish bin
  (2) Sort out the trivial from the important
  (3) Talk through any anxieties with another person
  (4) Sleep on a problem
  (5) Go and work with the children
  (6) Do not allow my working life to intrude into my private life
  (7) Have a large gin and tonic on Friday evening
  (8) Take the dog for a long walk
  (9) Try to keep lines of communication as open as possible
(10) Remember to laugh.

In the framework of the head of the comprehensive school there are five major areas:

  (1) *Family life* I am happy and secure with an understanding wife.
  (2) *Job satisfaction*
      (a) good pay and a high standard of living
      (b) challenge of the job
      (c) I enjoy being a headteacher.
  (3) Access to *supportive colleagues* at the same level of management and also I have the school management team to whom I can delegate responsibility.
  (4) *Leisure activities:* squash, cricket, music, mountaineering and special short term interests such as rewiring the house and photography.

(5) *Switching off from work*
  (a) by living away from the school community
  (b) by mixing with people whose interests are not educational
  (c) by having the pleasure of two children.

This head's self-analysis identified a rich store of renewable resources. If the reports from other heads and teachers are reliable sources of information, his coping potential is stronger than many of his colleagues who cannot find satisfying activities in their communities, nor do they have the support of caring teams in school. They may not be able to talk freely with their colleagues because they do not trust them and they may possess only a few of the resources identified in this chapter. It is therefore realistic to suggest that many teachers need to learn to use more coping strategies. A wide range of personal, interpersonal, organizational and community attitudes, actions and activities has been discussed in this chapter and this list provides a sound basis for anyone wanting to learn to deal with work pressure more effectively.

REFERENCES

Caplan, G. (1964) *Principles of Preventive Psychiatry*, Basic Books, New York.

Kyriacou, C. (1980) Coping action and organizational stress among school teachers, Research in Education. Vol. 24, pp. 57–61.

Lazarus, R. (1981) Little hassles can be hazardous to health, *Psychology Today*, July, pp. 56–62.

Mechanic, D. (1967) Invited commentary in K.H. Appleby and R. Trumbull (eds) *Psychological tress*, Hemisphere, New York.

Parkes, K.R. (1988) Stress, coping and the work environment, paper given at the British Psychological Society meeting, December, London.

INDEX

ability
    excellence vision 140–2
accreditation
    Calderdale/Qudos Project 25, 31–2
    diploma model 26–7
    external factors 175
    prior learning/experience 25–6
    professional development 249–50
action learning sets
    Calderdale/Qudos Project 20–1, 23–4,
        30, 32
administration
    contrived collegiality study 86
advisers
    Calderdale/Qudos Project 24–5
AMA see American Management
    Association
American Management Association
    34
AMMA survey
    equal opportunities 257, 262–3
appearance
    communication skills 228
    appraisal skills 258–62
assessment
    Calderdale/Qudos Project 26, 31–2
    teacher appraisals 358–62
attitudes
    coping resources 289, 292–4
    decision-making 184–6
    interviewing skills 222–3
    strategic management 167

authority
    democracy paradox study 205, 208–14
    headteacher role 70–1
    influence 134
    women representation 95–6, 257
autocratic leadership style 182
autonomy
    see also authority
    collegiality comparison 63
    model school 149–50

behaviour
    communication skills 227–34
    sexual discrimination 255–68
body language
    communication skills 228–32
British String Quartets 202–18
BS 5750
    accreditation 47–9
budgeting
    model school 144–8

Calderdale/Qudos Project 19–33
    background
        action learning set 23–4
        assessor's role 26
        management standards 22–3
        mentor/advisor role 24–5
        prior learning influence 25–6
    conclusion 33
    diploma model 26–7
    establishing stage 19–22

issues involved
  accreditation 25, 31–2
  competence, MCI constraints 28
  development focus, need for 29–30
  generic language 27–8
  MCI model/management practice
    28–9
  mentors question 32
  motivation 30–2
  workload 30–1
second phase 26–7
third phase 32
Cambridge Institute of Education 65
capabilities
  higher order capacities 39–40, 42–3
  knowledge element 39
  managerial capabilities project 34–45
  sensitive awareness 40
  skills element 39–40
careers
  development planning 237–8
  sexual inequalities 255–68
Center For Policy Research 133
change
  educational management
    background 1–3
    meanings 3–4
    values 3–15
  external factors 175
  implementation causes/processes
    characteristics of 111–15
    continuation factors 125–7
    external factors 118–19
    innovation sponsorship 119
    key themes 120–5
    large-scale 110
    local factors 115–18
    monitoring 123–4
    perspectives of 11–12, 127–9
    practicality factor 114–15
    quality factor 114–15
    small-scale 110
  internal factors 175
  planning/flexible model 15
  sustaining, college case study 166–78
  sustaining excellence
    background 132–5
    implementation 136–8
    model school 132–50
  women and school management 104–5
clarity
  change factor 112–13
collaboration 12–14
  collegiality cultures 84–6
  collegiality question 62–3

PSSR collegiality project 67–70
Collaborative School Management Cycle
  budgeting 138, 144–8
  evaluating 148
  goal-setting 138, 141–2
  guidelines 140–9
  implementing 136–8, 148
  model school 138–50
  planning 138, 143–4, 146–8
  policy-making 142–3
  summary 149–50
collegiality
  change implementation 117–18
  contrived collegiality 80–94
    background 80–1
    case study 86–91
    collaboration elements 84–6
    conclusions/implications 91–2
    definition features 86
    discussion 81–4
    preparation time use 87–9
    SERTS support 89–91
    working practices 87–91
  critiques of 81–4
  decision-making study 187–92
  democracy paradox study 202–17
  political perspective 9–10
  PSSR project 62, 65–71
    cultural values 67–70
    headteachers 70–1
  research projects study 61–79
    background 61–2
    conclusion 75–7
    definition/identity discussion 61–5
  sexual discrimination 96
  women and school management 95–
    105
    discrimination 96, 101–2, 104
  WSCD project 65, 71–6
    community, sense of 73–4
    getting on together 74
    individuality acknowledgement 74
    knowing what's going on 74–5
    leadership image 75
    purposing the same 72
    working together 73
communication
  appraisal behaviour 258–60
  interviewing skills 219–34
community resources 290–4, 296–7
competence
  assessment 238–43
  Calderdale/Qudos Project 20–2, 25–7,
    29, 32–3
  managerial capabilities project 34–5

MCI model constraints 28
standards, identifying 22–3
consultation
SERTS support 89–91
continuity
managing change 125–7
contracts of employment
flexibility question 38–9
contrived collegiality *see* collegiality
conventions
collegiality study 83
coping resources
background 284–8
deputy heads 292–4
headteachers 294–7
teachers 289–92
'correct procedures'
TQM 53
counselling
communication skills 220
cultures
contrived collegiality 81–3,
85–6
curriculum
collegiality effects 81, 92
decision-making study 189–90
IDP basis 236
managerial influence 100
managing change 113, 120
model school 138, 142–3
strategic planning case study
171
WSCD project effects 71–2
Customers and TQM 49–50
definition 47, 49

decision-making
attitudes to 184–6
background 181
collegiality 64, 187–92
departmental 186–7
group participation 196–7
leadership styles 182–4
management 192–6
managerial capabilities 38–40
model school 132–3, 137, 139–40
NFER schools study 185–6
participative 186–7
planning models 156–60
strategic planning case study 167
summary/discussion 197–9
time-management 269–83
TQM values 51
women and school management 104
WSCD project study 71–5

delegation
strategic planning case study 167,
169–70
time-management 279–81
democracy
leadership paradox 205, 208–14
demographics
role comparison study 214
Department of Education and Science
planning project advice 156–7
deputy heads
coping resources 292–4
development processes
Calderdale/Qudos Project 19–33
diplomacy
managerial requirement 41–2
directors
role of 169–71
discrimination
evidence on 255–68
Drumcree High School 37

Economic and Social Research Council
collegiality 65, 75–6
Education Act 1986 139
Education Acts
innovatory planning 152–4
Education for Mutual Understanding
exercise 37–8
Education Reform Act 1988 35, 38
collegiality 61, 63
innovatory planning 164
strategic planning case study 170, 177
TQM stimulus 46
Educational Assessment Centre (EAC)
project 238, 240–3
educational change *see* change
effectiveness
decision-making study 182, 184, 189
time-management 269–83
efficiency
collegiality 97–8
collegiality study 88, 92
EMU *see* Education for Mutual
Understanding
environment
communication skills 231
planning for 152–3
EOC *see* Equal Opportunities
Commisssion
equal opportunities
teacher appraisals 255–68
Equal Opportunities Commission 256
ESRC See Economic and Social Research
Council

excellence theme
  managing a school 122–50
external factors 118–19, 175

facial expressions and communication
  230–2
finance
  management development 248
  management role 23
flexible planning *see* planning
friendship element 213
further education college
  case study 166–78

generic competences
  utilization 27–8
geo-identification 63
gestures and communication 228
goal-setting
  model school 138–9, 141–2
goals
  time-management 278–9
GRIST
  in-service training 105
group participation
  collegiality implications 64–5, 89–91
  decision-making 187–92, 196–7
  managerial capabilities project 36–9
  model school 138–40, 144–5
  string quartets study 202–18

headteachers
  change role 116–17
  collegiality impact 63, 70–1
  coping resources 294–7
  decision-making study 181–201
  effectiveness 42
  statistics on 257–8
  women and management 97–8
hierarchical structures
  TQM comparison 54–5
human resources
  strategic planning case study 167–76

IDP *see* institutional development plan
implementation
  causes/processes of 109–31
    background 109–10
    change, perspectives of 127–9
    continuation factors 125–7
    factors affecting 110–11
    key factors 110–19
    key themes 120–5
  collegiality criticism 82
  decision-making study 182, 190–1

management development 247–3
model school 136–8, 148
strategic planning case study 171–2,
  174–6
improvement characteristics 118
  key themes 120–5
information
  management role 23
initiative
  implementation process 120, 122
  model school change 135
Inner London Education Authority 96,
  99
innovation and planning
  background 151–3
  conclusion 164
  decision-making models 156–60
  flexible planning model 160–2
  research evidence 153–5
  rolling plans strategy 162–4
institutional development plan 236
intense work groups 202–18
interdependence
  work groups study 202–6
internal factors 175
interpersonal skills
  coping resources 289–90, 293–5
interviewing skills 219–34
  background 219–20
  barriers, recognition of 220–4
  behaviour 227–33
  listening 224–7
  relationships 219–20, 224–7, 232–3

job satisfaction 184
judgement
  management function 33
  problem-solving process 40–1

kinesics
  as communication skill 229–30

language
  generic competences 27–8
  interviewing skills 222, 229
  meanings/implications 3–4
leadership
  collegiality environment 62–3, 70–1,
    75
  decision-making study 181
  democracy paradox 208–14
  equal opportunities 255–6, 258
  model school 135, 139–40, 144, 150
  preparation for 243–7
  racial influences 101–4

styles of 182–4
time-management 269
TQM component 50–2
women and school management
    95–106
work groups study 205, 208–17
learning
    Calderdale/Qudos Project 19–22
    school model 145, 150
listening
    appraisal practice 260
    interviewing skill 224–7
local education authorities
    decision-making study 190, 193, 200
    innovatory planning 151–9
    management development support
        237, 242, 249
    managing change 115–16, 118–19
    teacher appraisal 256–7, 265, 267
Local Government Act 1988
    innovatory planning 152

management
    see also managerial capabilities
        project
    application of analogy 208–13
    Calderdale/Qudos project 19–33
    change implentation 109–31
    competence roles 23
    coping resources 284–97
    decision-making study 181–201
    development strategies 235–52
        accreditation 249–50
        assessments 238–43
        background 235
        career planning 237–8
        conclusions 252
        implementation 247–51
        leadership 243–7
    model school 138–50
        background 138–40
        guidelines 140–9
        implementation factors 136–8
    standards 20–2, 28–9
    time 269–83
    TQM approach 46–57
    women teachers 95–106
    work groups study 205, 208–13,
        208–17
Management Charter Initiative 35
    Calderdale/Qudos Project 19–33
    competence constraints 28
    model standards 20–2, 28–9
Management Task Force
    research 35

managerial capabilities project 34–45
    background 34–6
    group deliberations 37–9
    phase one 34–42
    phase two 42–5
    research methodology 36–7
    summary and conclusions 39–42
marketing
    strategic planning case study 171
MCI *see* Management Charter Initiative
meetings
    decision-making study 189
    interviewing skills 219–34
    time-management 277–8
mentors
    Calderdale/Qudos Project 24–5, 32
    managerial capabilities debate
        44–5
middle-managers
    leadership styles 182–4
    role of 170–1
Milton Keynes College
    case study 166–78
mission statement
    strategic planning case study 167–70,
        176
monitoring
    change management 123–4
motivation
    equal opportunities 260–1
    work groups study 213
multiple innovations *see* innovation
musical groups study 208–13

National Development Centre
    leadership skills 105, 181
National Foundation for Educational
    Research 182–6, 194, 198
National Steering Group's Report (1989)
    256
National Union of Teachers
    women in 95
National Vocational Qualification
    scheme 22
need
    change factor 112
networking
    school management 104
NFER *see* National Foundation for
    Educational Research
NGS Report
    equal opportunities 256
non-verbal behaviour (NVB) 227–32
NVQ *see* National Vocational
    Qualification scheme

Ontario
  collegiality study 80–94
operations
  management role 23
orchestra
  work groups study 202–17
organization
  collegiality environment 66, 83
  coping resources 290, 295–6
  political perspective 8–10
  restructuring theme 124–5
  strategic planning case study 166–78
  string quartet study 202–18
  TQM structures 50, 54–5

PAL Project *see* Peer Assisted Learning
  Project
paralanguage and communication 229
participation
  collegiality role 63
  decision-making study 186–7
  work groups study 202–17
Peer Assisted Learning Project 36
people
  management role 23
perception skills 222
personality
  role comparisons study 208–17, 213
planning
  see also strategic planning
  career development 237–8, 255–68
  change features 111–15, 120–2
  flexible strategy
    background 151–3
    conclusion 164
    decision-making models 156–60
    innovation environment 152–3
    key factors 155–6
    model for change 160–2
    research evidence 153–5
    rolling plans 162–4
  managerial capabilities project
    36
  model school 142–4, 146–8
  teachers' preparation time 87–9
  time-management 278–9
policies
  Center For Policy Research 133
  contrived collegiality study 81
  model school 138, 142–3, 149
political perspectives
  collegiality 83–4
  organization, types of 8–10
posture
  communication skills 228

preparation time
  collegiality study 87–9
Primary School Staff Relations project
  62, 65–71, 75–6
principal *see* headteachers
priorities
  time use 271–2
problem-solving
  change theme 123–4
  judgement element 40–1
processes
  TQM component 50, 53–4
professional accreditation 249–50
Project on Improving Urban High
  Schools 133
promotion
  career inequalities 255–68
  discrimination issues 95–6, 101–2, 104
PSSR *see* Primary School Staff Relations
  project
pupil expectations
  model school 140–1, 145–8

quality
  see also Total Quality Management
  BS 5750 accreditation 47–9
  change factor 114–15
  measurement 49
  strategic planning case study 169, 172
quality circles 53

Race Relations Act 1976 256
racism
  appraisal evidence 256, 262–3
  stereotype features 101–2
  women and school management
    101–2, 104
relationships
  change implementation 134–40
  collegiality environment 65–71, 73–4
  contrived collegiality study 85–6
  interviewing 219–20, 224–7, 232–3
  model school 134–8
  strategic planning case study 169–73
  teaching staff 38–9
  work groups study 202–6
  working together 181–200
research and development (R&D)
  Calderdale/Qudos project 19–33
  contrived collegiality study 86–92
  decision-making study 181–201
  flexible planning 153–5, 160–4
  managerial capabilities project 36–7
  PSSR project 65–71
  work groups study 202–18

WSCD project 71–5
responsibility
  collegiality role 88–9
  equal opportunities 260
  strategic planning case study 167,
    169–70
  time-management 270

School Teachers Pay and Conditions
  Order 269
schools
  Calderdale/Qudos Project 26–7
  decision-making study 181–201
  effectiveness criteria 197–9
  flexible planning evidence 151–65
  improvement practices 118, 120–5
  preparation time 87–9
  sexual inequalities 255–68
  women in management 95–106
security
  collegiality 69–70
self-evaluation
  time-management 273–5
SERTS *see* special education resource
  teachers
Sex Discrimination Act 1975 256
sexual inequalities 95–106
  appraisals 255–68
SMT
  decision-making views 190, 192,
    195–7, 199
special education resource teachers
  89–91
sponsoring managing change 119
staff relationships
  appraisal/assessment 238–43
  career development 255–68
  development/change theme 122–3
  personal resources 284–97
  PSSR project 65–71
  WSCP project 73–4
standards
  MCI model 20–3
status
  communication skills 222
strategic planning
  career development 237–8
  college case study 166–78
  innovation management 151–4, 160
strategies
  definition 167
  management development 235–52
  personal resources 289, 292, 294
  spontaneity 167
  time-management 278–82

stress 14
  coping resources 285–8, 294
  decision-making causes 186
string quartets study 202–18
  background 202–4
  conclusions 214–17
  methods of 206–7
  observations on 207–14
  paradoxes 204–6
structures 50, 54–5
  change process 124–5
  headteacher role 70–1
  strategic planning case study 170–2
  TQM component 50, 54–5
success measures analogy study 207–8
succession planning
  management development 237–8
sustaining change *see* change
systems
  strategic management 168
  TQM application 53

teachers
  appraisal 255–68
  change role 117–18
  contrived collegiality study 87–92
  coping resources 289–92
  women and school management
    95–106
teams
  TQM component 50, 52–3
teamwork
  decision-making 187–92
  TQM requirement 49
Technical and Vocational Education
  Initiative 152
time
  contrived collegiality study 87–9
  management 269–83
    background 269–70
    conclusion 282–3
    effectiveness strategies 278–82
    identifying priorities 271–2
    obstacles 275–8
    self-evaluation 273–5
  management development 248
Total Quality Management
  background 46–8
  components of 49–55
    customer 49–50
    leadership 50–2
    processes 50, 53–4
    teams 50, 52–3
    values 50–1
  definition 46–8

education implications 55–7
nature of 48–9
objections to 56–7
TQM *see* Total Quality Management
training
appraisal skills 258, 262–3, 265–6
Calderdale/Qudos Project model 20–2
higher order capacities 44
standards, identifying 22–3
TQM requirement 49
women and school management 104–5
transforming leadership 182
TVEI *see* Technical and Vocational
Education Initiative

values 1–15
and educational change 11–12
leadership 181–2
management theory 4–8
meanings and assumptions 3–4
organizational 8–10
PSSR collegiality project 67–70
staff appraisal 260–1
strategic planning case study 169
TQM component 50–1

TQM criticism 56–7
and working together 12–14
vision-building
change theme 120–2
excellent school model 132–50
Milton Keynes college experience 169

Whole School Development project 65,
71–6
wisdom
managerial capability debate 43
women
appraisal treatment 255–68
and school management 95–106
work processes *see* processes
working practices
see also collaboration
appraisal techniques 284–97
women and school management
95–105
work groups study 202–18
workload
Calderdale/Qudos Project 30–1
WSCD See Whole School Development
Project

AUTHOR INDEX

Page numbers refer to authors mentioned in the text; bibliographical details are located at the end of appropriate chapters.

Abercrombie, J. 69
Adair, J. 6, 244, 274, 281
Adams, A. 182, 184
Addison, B. 95–106, 258, 264
Al-Khalifa, E. 6, 95–106, 258, 264
Alexander, R. 63
Alutto, J.A. 184
AMMA 257, 262, 263
Anderson, B. 121
Anderson, S. 124
Apple, M. 92

Baker, Kenneth 177
Ball, S.J. 83, 181
Bangar, S. 263
Bargh, E. 258, 259
Barth, R. 122
Bass, B. 217
Beare, H. 132–50
Belasco, J.A. 184
Belbin, R.M. 188
Bell, S. 77
Bennett, Nigel. 1
Bennis, W. 121
Berg, D. 202, 204–5, 206, 215, 216
Berman, P. 13, 114, 116–17, 125–6, 129
Bettenhausen, K.L. 202, 206
Bird, T. 80, 82
Birdwhistell, R. 224

Blake, R. 182
Blanchard, K. 246
Blase, J. 83
Blatt, S.J. 227
Bloomer, R.G. 184
Bolman, L.G. 278
Boudon, R. 158
Boydell, T. 2
Brecht, G. 204
Brennan, J.A. 199
Brett, J. 206, 211, 217
Brickman, P. 206
Buckley, J. 182
Bullock, A. 196, 198
Bullough, R., Jr. 82
Burgoon, J. 231
Burgoyne, J. 2
Burns, T. 151
Bush, T. 55, 63, 65
Byrne, E. 95

Caldwell, B.J. 11, 132–50, 151
Campbell, Penny 61–79
Campbell, R.J. 10, 12, 61, 62, 63, 64, 65, 81, 82
Caplan, G. 284
Carelton, F.O. 219
Cave, E. 8, 34–45
Chell, E. 64

Clwyd County Council 101
Cohen, D. 119, 129
Cohen, M. 122
Confederation of British Industry 178
Conlon, D.E. 13–14, 202–18
Conway, J.A. 184
Cooper, M. 82
Corbett, H.D. 115, 126
Corcoran, T. 120
Corwin, R. 116
Coulson, A.A. 63, 64, 70
Cowden, P. 119
Cox, P. 121
Crandall, D.P. 14, 119, 124, 126–7
Crane, B. 158
Crawford, Megan. 1
Crosby, P. 48
Csikszentmihalyi, M. 204
Cunnison, S. 258

David, J.L. 112, 124
Davies, B. 182, 185
Davies, L. 98
Davis, J. 83
Dawson, J. 126
De Bono, E. 41
Deal, T.E. 83, 278
Dean, J. 280
Dembo, M.H. 185
Deming, – 48
Department of Education and Science 61, 63, 151, 178, 268, 269
Derr, B. 151
DES *see* Department of Education
DeSanctis, J. 129
DeWine, S. 227
Doyle, W. 114
Dunham, J. 14, 186, 284–97

Earley, P. 12–13, 152, 181–201
Ecob, R. 80
Edwards, R. 181
Ekman, P. 230
Elliot, D.L. 182
Ellsworth, P. 230
Elmore, R.F. 124
Employment, Department of 178
Emrick, J. 112
Equal Opportunites Commission 95, 101
Etzioni, A. 182
Everard, K.B. 97, 182

Farrar, E. 129
Fiedler, F. 182
Firestone, W. 115

Fletcher-Campbell, F. 12–13, 181–201
Franklin, Benjamin 269
Friesen, W. 230
Fullan, M. 11, 56, 80, 85, 109–31, 122, 124, 128, 181

Gabarro, J. 151
Garratt, B. 2
Gibson, S. 185
Gilligan, C. 268
Gitlin, A. 82
Gold, B. 116
Goldberg, S. 206, 211, 217
Grant, M. 266
Grant, R. 95, 96
Gray, H.L. 97, 98, 102
Green, H. 13, 235–52
Greenfield, T.B. 132

Hackman, R. 202
Hall, G.E. 126–7, 231
Hall, V. 164, 245–6, 271, 277
Handy, C. 53, 65, 97, 102
Hargreaves, A. 10, 62, 80–94, 189
Hartley, D. 84
Harvey, G. 124
Hayes, J. 34–5
Henry, J. 41, 45
Her Majesty's Inspectors (HMI) 235
Herald, K. 114, 126
Herzberg, F. 6
Holly, P. 61, 64
Hopkins, D. 56, 61
House of Commons 61
Howson, J. 184
Hoyle, E. 83, 97, 98, 156, 158, 181, 184, 187, 188
Huberman, M. 80, 84, 112, 114, 123, 126
Hughes, M. 235, 244
Hughes, M.G. 97
Hughes, P. 204
Hull, R. 182, 184
Hunt, – 225

ILEA *see* Inner London Education Authority
Inner London Education Authority 61, 95, 96, 98, 101
Ishenberg, D. 41

Jacobs, R. 35
Jagger, J. 8, 19–33
Janis, I.L. 206
Jantzi, D. 83

Joyce, B. 123, 128
Juran, – 48

Kahn, W.A. 205
Kant, L. 95
Kanter, R.M. 121
Keenan, A. 229
Keith, P. 116
Kennedy, A. 83
Khalifa, Al- *see* Al-Khalifa, E.
Knapp, M. 228, 229–30
Knoop, R. 184
Kogan, M. 9
Kyriacou, C. 285

Lasswell, H.D. 221
Lazarus, R. 285
Leithwood, K. 83
Lewin, K. 182
Lewis, C. 220
Lewis, D. 80
Lieberman, A. 61, 62, 63, 64, 80
Likert, R. 182
Limb, A. 12, 166–78
Lindblom, C.E. 129, 156, 158–9
Little, J.W. 62, 64, 75, 80, 82, 117, 118, 127, 188
Long, C. 62
Lopez, F.M. 221
Lortie 64
Loucks, S. 126–7
Louis, K. 112, 119, 120, 121, 122, 123, 124
Louis, S.K. 159–60

McCune, S.D. 156
McDermott, J. 263
McGregor Burns, J. 182
McGregor, D. 182
McGregor, J. 177
MacKay, H. 233, 245–6, 271, 277
McKellar, B. 263
McLaughlin, M. 113, 116–17, 124, 125–6
McMahan, E.M. 229
Majone, G. 129
Mangham, I. 102
March, J. 156, 157
Marsh, D. 120, 121, 123, 124
Marshall, J. 98
Martin, W.J. 12, 274, 276
Maslow, A. 6
Maughan, B. 80
Mausner, B. 6
Mayo, E. 6

Mechanic, D. 284
Mehrabian, A. 230, 231
Merriam, S. 153
Meyerson, D. 12
Miles, M. 80, 112, 114, 116, 123, 126
Miles, M.B. 120, 121, 122, 123, 124, 133, 137, 139–40, 144, 149, 159–60
Miller, L. 63, 80
Millikan, R.H. 132–50
Milton Keynes College 178
Mintzberg, H. 6, 7, 8, 11, 41, 276
Morgan, C. 245–6, 271, 277
Morgan, D. 36
Morris, D. 227
Morris, G. 182
Mortimore, P. 61, 62, 80, 115, 124
Mouton, J. 182
Murnighan, J.K. 13–14, 202–18
Murphy, J. 112, 124
Musella, D. 83

Nannus, B. 121
National Steering Group's Report 256
National Union of Teachers 95
Newton, E. 124
Nias, D.J. 63, 64, 65–6, 67, 69, 72, 76, 82, 85, 102, 182, 184
Nicholson, B. 95

Odden, A. 124
Olsen, J. 157
Olson, M. 9
O'Reilly, C.A. 206
O'Reilly, R. 184
Ousten, J. 80

Packwood, T. 64
Parkes, K.R. 286
Peale, N.V. 246
Pedler, M. 2
Peters, T. 2, 12, 121–2, 123, 167
Peterson, S. 112
Pfeiffer, R.S. 124
Pollard, A. 65, 71
Ponder, G. 114
Poster, C. 14
Pruitt, G. 206, 211, 217
Purkey, S.C. 61, 80, 133, 149
Pye, A. 42

Quicke, J. 84

Rae, L. 227
Reid, K. 61
Renihan, F.I. 156

Renihan, P.J. 156
Reynolds, D. 80, 84
Rhodes, C.D.M. 263
Richards, C. 62
Riches, C. 1, 13–14, 219–34
Rosenblum, S. 119, 123
Rosenholtz, S. 61, 80, 83, 91, 117, 121, 122
Rubin, J.A. 206
Rudduck, J. 81, 84
Rutter, M. 80, 181

Sallis, E. 47
Sammons, P. 80
Samuels, G. 55
Schein, E.H. 70, 83
Schmidt, W.H. 182
Schon, D. 88
School Management Task Force 235
Schools Council 79
Secondary Heads Association 248
Sergiovanni, T.J. 70, 133, 149, 182
Shakeshaft, C. 255, 258, 260
Shaw, M.E. 217
Shipman, M. 47
Showers, B. 123, 128
Shulman, L. 81
Sieber, S. 112
Simon, H. 156
Skilbeck, M. 81
Smith, A. 80
Smith, K. 202, 204–5, 206, 215, 216
Smith, L. 116
Smith, M. 158
Smith, M.S. 61, 80, 133, 149
Snyderman, B.B. 6
Southworth, G. 10, 12, 61–79, 82, 85
Spender, D. 258, 260
Spinks, J.M. 11, 138, 142–4, 148, 150, 151
Stalker, G.M. 151
Stallings, J.A. 123
Staratt, R.J. 133, 149
Steering Group's Report 256
Steiner, G. 156
Steiner, I.D. 217
Stenhouse, L. 81

Stillman, A. 266
Stoll, L. 80
Styan, D. 36, 182
Sutton, D.E. 219
Sutton, J. 182

Tannenbaum, R. 182
Thomas, N. 62
Thompson, J.D. 6, 13, 202–3
Thompson, M 255–68
Tomlinson, J. 62
Torrington, D. 52
Tortoriello, T.R. 227
Trades Union Congress 178
Tsui, A.D. 206

Ury, W. 206, 217

Vaill, P.B. 132, 149
Vaughan, F.E. 41
Vogel, M. 114, 126
Vroom, V.H. 219

Wallace, M. 7, 11, 61, 62, 151–65, 164
Watts, M. 188, 189, 190
Weaver, C.H. 234
Weber, M. 9
Weightman, J. 52
Weindling, D. 152, 182
Weiner, S. 157
Welsh Office 61
West-Burnham, John 8, 10, 46
Wignall, R. 90
Wildavsky, A. 129
Wilkinson, C. 8, 34–45, 269–83
Willower, D.J. 274, 276
Wilson, A. 90
Wilson, B. 120
Wise, A. 124
Wolcott, – 63
Woods, P. 83
Woolnough, B. 184

Yeomans, R. 65–6, 67, 76, 85, 187
Yin, R. 114, 126
Young, K. 3